Clinical Integration of Neuropsychological Test Results

Editors

Charles J. Golden
College of Psychology
Nova Southeastern University
Fort Lauderdale, Florida
USA

Ryan Bennett
College of Psychology
Nova Southeastern University
Fort Lauderdale, Florida
USA

CRC Press
Taylor & Francis Group
Boca Raton London New York

CRC Press is an imprint of the
Taylor & Francis Group, an **informa** business
A SCIENCE PUBLISHERS BOOK

First edition published 2025
by CRC Press
2385 NW Executive Center Drive, Suite 320, Boca Raton FL 33431

and by CRC Press
4 Park Square, Milton Park, Abingdon, Oxon, OX14 4RN

CRC Press is an imprint of Taylor & Francis Group, LLC

Library of Congress Cataloging-in-Publication Data (applied for)

ISBN: 978-1-032-31409-9 (hbk)
ISBN: 978-1-032-31410-5 (pbk)
ISBN: 978-1-003-30960-4 (ebk)

DOI: 10.1201/9781003309604

Typeset in Times New Roman
by Prime Publishing Services

Preface

Interpretating neuropsychological tests is a challenge to both experienced and inexperienced test users. The major problem arises because tests are not unidimensional but rather multidimensional. Thus, we might say that the Block Design subtest of the Wechsler tests measures visual-spatial or visual-constructive skills; however, in reality, the test likely encompasses a broad spectrum of underlying abilities. These underlying dimensions include comprehension of instructions, vision, focus, memory, abstraction, problem-solving, flexibility, insight, construction skills, and fine motor speed.Emotional or personality characteristics like anxiety, perfectionism, impulsivity, depression, malaise, frustration, stress, and motivation may also reflect performance. Finally, non-neurological medical problems, cultural impact, and language may impact speed, understanding, attention, focus, memory, and other physical dimensions. Any deficits within these areas may disrupt performance, resulting in scores that are not easily interpreted. In normal individuals, this is a minor issue as all skills may be roughly at the same level of performance. However, individuals with neurological, neuropsychological, and mental health issues may exhibit wide variations in the underlying skills. As a result, performances generating the same score may reflect significantly different issues, which in turn will develop a wide range of possible neuropsychological interpretations.

Luria's theory of functional systems (1973) indicates that each test does not reflect a single skill but rather reflects a functional system: a pattern of interconnections among disparate brain areas working in tandem to produce a specific outcome. Additionally, the pattern of interaction within the brain may vary among individuals. This variability reinforces that most performances can be achieved through multiple methods, some more efficient and effective than others. These systems are, in turn, impacted by emotional and non-neurological medical disorders that further interfere with optimal performance.

Thus, a trial-and-error approach may attack Block Design, an analytic approach that seeks to break down the design gestalt into individual pieces, or an integrative approach based on the visual-spatial aspects of the test. Each approach will work, but the time frames and success rates on specific tasks may differ. The chosen approach may or may not reflect the method that would yield the best score or performance a client may achieve from a neuropsychological perspective. In turn, we must understand how these neuropsychologically extraneous emotional and medical factors impact these scores.It is not possible for any book to cover all possible causes of a given client's performance. The original goal of this volume was to classify all the tests into basic areas such as intelligence, visual skills, spatial skills, language,

Table 1. General Neuropsycholgical Areas Reflected in Each Test.

Test (Alphabetical)							**Functional Area**
	Intelligence	Visual Skills	Spatial Skills	Visual Construction	Verbal Skills	Instructions	Abstraction
Block Design	P	P	P	P	S	S	S
Boston Naming Test	S	S	N	N	P	S	N
Category Test	P	P	S	N	S	P	P
Coding	P	P	N	T	T	S	N
COWAT	P	N	N	N	P	S	N
CPT III	T	N	N	N	N	P	N
Digit Span	P	N	S	N	S	P	N
Feifer (Reading)	P	T	N	N	P	P	N
Finger Tapping	N	N	N	N	N	P	N
Logical Memory	P	N	N	N	P	P	S
Purdue Pegboard	N	N	S	S	N	S	N
Stroop	S	N	N	N	P	P	N
Symbol Digit Modalities Test	S	S	N	N	S	P	N
Trail Making Test	P	P	P	P	S	P	N
TOVA	T	T	N	N	N	P	N
Visual Puzzles	P	P	P	N	S	P	S
Visual Reproduction	P	P	P	P	N	P	N
Arithmetic (WAIS-IV)	S	N	N	N	S	S	N
WAIS Index Scores	P	P	P	P	P	P	N
Wisconsin Card Sort	P	S	N	N	S	P	S
Wide Range Achievement Test	T	N	N	N	P	S	N

P=PRIMARY; S=SECONDARY; T=TERTIARY; N=NOT SIGNIFICANT

Flexibility	Attention	Concentration	Achievement	Memory	Motor
S	S	S	N	T	S
N	T	N	S	N	N
P	P	P	N	P	N
N	P	P	N	S	P
P	P	P	P	N	N
P	P	P	N	N	T
N	P	P	N	P	N
N	S	T	P	T	N
N	P	S	N	N	P
N	P	P	S	P	N
N	P	P	N	N	P
P	P	P	T	N	N
S	P	P	N	N	N
P	P	P	T	T	P
N	P	P	N	N	T
S	P	P	N	N	N
N	P	P	N	P	S
N	S	N	P	T	N
N	S	N	T	T	T
P	P	P	N	P	T
N	N	N	P	N	N

and so on, but it became obvious that any such classification ultimately led to an oversimplification of the nature of many of these tests. Upon finishing the chapters, it became more useful that tests be classified initially into one of three areas: specific skills tests, tests of effort, screening tests, and computer batteries.

Traditional tests like Block Design fall into specific skill tests and can be found in Section I. Table 1 lists the tests covered in this area, along with a breakdown of what major factors influence each test. These factors include General Intelligence, Visual Skills, Spatial Skills, Visual Construction, Verbal Skills, Instructions (based on the complexity and importance of the instructions), Abstraction, Flexibility, Attention, Concentration (sustained attention), Achievement, Memory, and Motor skills. This list is by no means exhaustive as many other areas (e.g., specific achievement skills, aphasias, sensory abilities) could have been added but play only a small or negligible part in the tests covered here.

The second section of the book covers tests of effort, specifically the MSVT, SIRS, and TOMM, which appear to be the tests most used to evaluate effort. The third section includes screening tests, primarily for dementia. The last section covers computerized test batteries. While they have been used most often in research, their prevalence in clinical examinations has become more common despite limited information on their relationship to the more traditional tests in Section 1. These tests typically attempt to measure many, if not all, of the areas covered in Table 1 and represent a growing resource for clinicians. It is hoped that the background information and clinical suggestions offer insights into how these tests may be interpreted. It is ultimately up to the examiner to use this information to identify patterns that help specify the nature of the deficits and their etiology, whether that arises from neuropsychological or other conditions. Such final analyses represent the most sophisticated use of neuropsychological information but are based on a sophisticated understanding of these basic tests.

The editors wish to apologize for many tests not included here. Our goal was to cover the most frequently used tests in clinical settings, but the sheer volume of possible choices required difficult choices. These may hopefully be included in a future volume.

Contents

Section IV: Computer Batteries

Section I

Individual Tests

CHAPTER 1

Block Design

*Zachary Peart** and *Ryan Bennett*

Block Design has been part of the Wechsler intelligence tests since the original Wechsler-Bellevue and is itself an adaptation of tests that existed previous to the Wechler-Bellevue. The test has undergone item and scoring changes throughout the various versions of the WAIS, but this chapter focuses on the current version. Block design today is a widely used neuropsychological test that assesses visuospatial abilities and is a core subtest on the Perceptual Reasoning index of the WAIS-IV (Wechsler Adult Intelligence Scale, 4th ed.; Coalson et al. 2008) but is also used as a stand alone test in some settings. The task involves analyzing and synthesizing designs, which requires spatial perception, nonverbal reasoning, as well as motor coordination to organize the blocks into the correct orientation. The ability to complete the block design task is thought to involve broad visual and fluid intelligence and relies on the integrity of various cognitive processes, including attention, memory, visual perception, and motor planning and execution.

Previous research has suggested that performance on the block design task may indicate general intelligence and overall cognitive abilities. Royer et al. (1984) found that the block design task was highly correlated with other measures of intelligence, such as the Wechsler Adult Intelligence Scale Full Scale IQ, and suggested that it could be used as a screening tool for cognitive impairment. In clinical neuropsychological practice, block design is commonly used to assess visuospatial abilities in individuals with brain damage or neurodegenerative disorders. The test has been shown to be sensitive to dysfunction in various brain regions, including the parietal lobe, which is critical for spatial processing and constructional abilities (Behrmann and Shomstein 2009; Warrington et al. 1986). By using the block design task in conjunction with other neuropsychological measures, clinicians can comprehensively understand an individual's cognitive strengths and weaknesses and develop targeted treatment plans.

Nova Southeastern University, Fort Lauderdale, Florida, USA.
Email: rb1934@nova.edu
* Corresponding author: zp112@mynsu.nova.edu

History and Normative Sample

The block design task has a rich history of development and ongoing revisions. Originally, Samuel Kohs (1920) created the task as a measure of general intelligence that is nonverbal in nature. However, as the Kohs block design test was used in clinical settings, there was growing concern that the assessment may be better suited to measure a specific ability rather than mental capacity (Kent 1934). With the development of the Wechsler Adult Intelligence Scale (WAIS), Wechsler (1955) included an adapted version of the block design task as a subtest of the general intelligence assessment. The subtest has been retained over subsequent revisions of the WAIS and continues to be modified based on reviews of clinical experience and research findings.

For instance, the most recent version of the block design task on the WAIS-IV was modified to include four new items to improve the difficulty gradient. Additionally, the instructions have been made more concise to increase the ease of use while reducing testing time. Despite these modifications, there is growing controversy over the system of points awarded for speed, so the number of time bonus items has been reduced, and the BDN process score was included to quantify performance without the addition of time rewards on the WAIS-IV (Coalson et al. 2008).

The most recent revision of the Wechsler Adult Intelligence Scale (WAIS) aimed to improve its normative sample by including a population representative of recent and relevant demographic variables such as age, sex, ethnicity, education level, and geographic region (Wechsler 2008). The normative sample comprised 2,200 healthy, non-clinical, English-speaking individuals with no sensory or motor impairments. Individuals who were taking medication or had a diagnosis that might impact test performance were excluded from the sample.

In order to ensure the sample was representative, the proportion of ethnic groups included in the normative sample was based on the racial proportion of individuals within the corresponding age group of the US population. Standardized start points were set based on national tryout data to minimize the number of administered items while avoiding frustrating the examinee with overly easy or difficult items, and time bonuses were implemented to reduce ceiling effects (Wechsler 2008). Overall, the updated normative sample of the WAIS provides a comprehensive and representative sample of the population, which improves the accuracy and relevance of the test results in the clinical setting.

Test Procedure

In order to receive credit, the block design task requires the examinee to replicate designs using blocks with red, white, or half red-half white sides within time limits ranging from 30 seconds to 120 seconds as the item's progress. The last 6 items on the subtest award faster performance by providing speed bonus points depending on how quickly the examinee successfully completes the design.

Administration of the block design task begins with the sample item. The examiner provides the examinee with verbal instructions and a demonstration of the task. The examiner presents 2 blocks to the examinee, and they proceed to construct a two-block design while referencing the picture in the stimulus book. Once the examiner has completed the demonstration, the examinee is instructed to replicate the task. If the examinee makes an error on the sample item, feedback is given to correct the design. At this point, the examiner can administer the items that follow, given the appropriate start point. Items 1 through 4 allow the examinee to reference a picture and model of the design, while items 5 through 14 allow only the picture. The age-appropriate starting point for children or individuals suspected of intellectual deficit begins at item 1, while those aged 16 through 90 will begin with item 5 (Coalson et al. 2008).

Item Difficulty and Types of Errors

The block design subtest of the WAIS-IV requires examinees to replicate designs of increasing difficulty as the test progresses. The number of blocks increases from 2 to 4, and then 9, respectively, and 4 of the designs are depicted with 45-degree rotations in the stimulus book, requiring the examinee to replicate the designs with the same degree of rotation (Wechsler 2008). Designs become more complex and require a higher level of visuospatial ability, making mental segmentation of the designs more challenging (Schorr et al. 1982). While many of the two- and four-block designs at the beginning of the test allow the examinee to easily detect implicit "edge cues" about where each block begins and ends, these edge cues become less salient as the examinee progresses further into the test. An example of such a design that does not present conspicuous edge cues is item 11, which appears as a set of 3 diagonal lines that span across the 3x3 matrix of blocks and is commonly more challenging for examinees of all ages (Rozencwajg and Corroyer 2001).

The examinee may make a variety of errors in constructing the designs, such as placement errors, rotation errors, and broken configurations (Joy et al. 2001; Troyer et al. 1994). While the exact significance of each error type is not fully understood, attending to and investigating these errors can provide valuable qualitative information about the nature of the deficit and functional impairment (Lezak et al. 2012).

Placement errors occur when a block displays the incorrect color side, while rotation errors occur when the examinee places the correct side of a block that is rotated incorrectly (Sattler and Ryan 2009). Broken configurations refer to designs in which the 2x2 or 3x3 nature of the design is violated (Joy et al. 2001). While occasional placement and rotation errors may be expected in intact examinees, broken configurations appear less common and may occur more frequently in older populations (Joy et al. 2001; Troyer et al. 1994).

If the examinee fails to complete the design within the time limit, they will receive a score of 0. While allowing the examinee to finish the item to maintain rapport is recommended, the score will still be counted as 0 (Sattler and Ryan 2009). Older adults may earn lower scores than their younger counterparts, but providing more time can attenuate this effect (Troyer et al. 1994). The examiner may find value in allowing the examinee extra time to complete the design, returning to challenging designs, and asking them to try again while verbalizing their strategy or using a physical model to copy (Sattler and Ryan 2009).

In addition to qualitative information provided by errors, the examiner can instruct the examinee to select correct and incorrect reproductions to gauge perceptual accuracy alone (Lezak et al. 2012). Careful attention to and investigation of errors can provide valuable information to the clinician in understanding the nature of the deficit and functional impairment.

Task Demands and Strategies

The block design task assesses various processing abilities dependent on each item's difficulty and the strategies the examinee utilizes to solve them. While the block design task shares similarities with other visuospatial assessments, such as drawing tasks, it requires a different set of cognitive abilities due to its abstract nature. Specifically, mental segmentation and mental rotation are recognized as key abilities that are directly related to performance on the block design task, in contrast to their relative lack of significance for drawing tasks such as the Rey-Osterrieth Complex Figure (Zappullo et al. 2021).

The block design task is a measure of visuospatial organization that involves several other processing abilities, including mental segmentation and mental rotation, which are directly related to performance on the task (Zappullo et al. 2021). Previous studies have identified 3 common strategies used by examinees: synthetic, analytic, and global strategies (Rozencwajg and Corroyer 2001; Schorr et al. 1982). The synthetic strategy involves forming a Gestalt mental representation of the design and mentally segmenting it, while the analytic strategy involves working systematically to segment the design into units and accurately placing blocks without relying on a Gestalt representation. The global strategy involves using trial and error to match the design to the item stimulus without relying on mental segmentation, mental rotation, or a Gestalt conceptualization of the design.

As the designs increase in difficulty, examinees tend to shift between strategies based on their conceptual level. Examinees may use the synthetic strategy on easier items that allow them to quickly segment the most salient elements of the design based on a Gestalt mental representation. However, as designs become more complex, examinees may switch to the analytic strategy to systematically segment the design into units and accurately place blocks based on frequent reference to the item stimulus. On the most difficult items, such as those without clear edge cues, examinees may use the global strategy and rely on trial and error to match the design to the item stimulus.

While it is generally agreed that most cognitively intact examinees rely on analytic strategies, research on impaired populations is lacking (Lezak et al. 2012). However, it is expected that examinees with neurological impairments will make the global strategic transition earlier than intact examinees when mental segmentation is too difficult. This trend is also observed in research on age, where children and older adults tend to use the global strategy more frequently (Rozencwajg et al. 2005; Rozencwajg and Corroyer 2001), reflecting the sensitivity of the block design task to developmental stages and decreasing fluid intelligence in older adults.

Scoring

In the block design task, the examinee is given credit if they complete the design within the specified time limit (Wechsler 2008). Items 1 through 4 are scored based on the number of trials required to complete the design, with a score of 0 for incorrect, 1 for correct on trial 2, and 2 for correct on trial 1. These items are typically administered to examinees under 16 or those suspected of intellectual impairment. The remaining items are scored as 4 if completed correctly. Additionally, items 9 through 14 offer time bonus points, allowing the examinee to earn up to 3 additional points on a given item for a total score of 7. However, if the blocks are spaced greater than ¼ inch apart or if the design is rotated 30 degrees or more, the item is scored as 0.

In order to calculate the block design raw score, the item scores are summed (Wechsler 2011). Additionally, the block design no-time bonus (BDN) score may be calculated by omitting extra bonus points awarded for speed. The summed raw scores are then standardized according to age groups to derive a scaled score. The scaled score is then combined with other scaled scores to calculate the Perceptual Reasoning Index composite score (Lezak et al. 2012).

Reliability

According to the technical manual (Coalson et al. 2008), the latest block design subtest in the WAIS-IV was designed to improve its reliability. Measures of internal consistency revealed that the overall reliability coefficient for the subtest was .87 across all age groups. Furthermore, all age groups had reliability coefficients of .80 or higher, with some age groups exhibiting coefficients around .90. Reliability coefficients were also calculated for various special groups, including individuals with intellectual giftedness, learning disabilities, ADHD, TBI, depression, Alzheimer's, and MCI. The average reliability coefficient for these groups was .90 overall. The intellectually gifted group had the lowest estimated reliability coefficient of .80, while the TBI group had the highest reliability coefficient of .96. Test-retest reliability was estimated with a sample of n = 298, and the block design subtest had a stability coefficient of .80.

Validity

Measures of convergent validity have been employed to support the construct validity of the block design subtest in the WAIS-IV (Wechsler 2008). Correlations between block design and other subtests on the WAIS-IV indicate that block design has the strongest associations with Visual Puzzles (r = .64), Figure Weights (r = .56), and Matrix Reasoning (r = .54), potentially reflecting the shared visuospatial component across each of these tasks. The block design subtest in the WAIS-IV also exhibits a high level of stability over time, as demonstrated by a correlation of.77 with the WAIS-III version of the same subtest (Wechsler 2008).

While the technical manual does not provide specific correlations between block design and measures outside of the WAIS, research suggests that performance on the block design task may be indicative of everyday spatial ability as measured by the Road Map Test and Everyday Spatial Activities Test (Groth-Marnat and Teal 2000).

Clinical Applications in Research

The block design subtest is a widely used measure of visuospatial ability and has been shown to be useful in predicting and differentiating populations and disease states (Coalson et al. 2008). For example, research has suggested that the block design subtest can predict the development of Alzheimer's disease in its early stages (Arnáiz et al. 2001) and can distinguish Alzheimer's disease from other types of dementia, such as vascular dementia (Heyanka et al. 2010) and Lewy body dementia (Oda et al. 2009). It has also been shown to be useful in the differential diagnosis of other dementias, such as frontotemporal dementia (Rascovsky et al. 2002). The block design task may also be sensitive to substance use, with chronic alcohol use being associated with lower scores on the task (Sullivan et al. 2002) and smoking linked to lower scores in an ADHD sample (Kalil et al. 2008). In addition, the task may be sensitive to certain errors in patients with focal epilepsy, with one study finding that those with right-hemisphere epilepsy made more broken configuration errors (Zipf-Williams et al. 2000).

Interestingly, children with autism have been found to perform better on the block design task than neurotypical individuals (Muth et al. 2014; Shah and Frith 1993), and even in adults with normal intelligence, the endorsement of autistic traits is associated with better performances on the test (Stewart et al. 2009). This has been interpreted as support for the theory of weak central coherence, which suggests that individuals with autism have a style of processing that facilitates better scores on block design.

Moreover, the task has also been shown to differentiate patients with schizophrenia from healthy individuals by using short forms of the task (Velthorst et al. 2013) and may help to identify PTSD veterans who exhibit reduced activation of the left hemisphere and cerebral asymmetries (Vasterling et al. 2000). Therefore, the block design subtest has demonstrated utility in predicting and differentiating various populations and disease states.

Interpretation

Although the block design task effectively measures visuospatial constructional ability, the assessment should not be used in isolation to make assumptions about the examinee's true level of ability. The clinician should carefully interpret patterns of cognitive abilities that are involved in the block design task and consider other confounding domains, such as attention, executive functions, visual acuity, processing speed, motor skills, and temperament.

1. Visuospatial deficits and/or right posterior parietal lesions often cause patients to distort designs or lose sight of the design configuration. In these cases, examinees will often perform poorly on other tests such as Matrix Reasoning, Visual Puzzles, or other visual-motor assessments.

2. Lesions of the left parietal area may result in confusion, simplification, or concrete handling of the tasks. These examinees might take longer to complete the items, but they can often correctly solve the designs when given an adequate amount of time.
3. A variety of brain lesions may impact the scores of block design beyond the left and right parietal areas. The clinician should use information from other assessments and the clinical interview to hypothesize about the cognitive ability that is lowering the score on block design. Examinees with a localized brain lesion may have difficulty completing the side of the block configuration that is contralateral to the lesion.
4. Examinees may attempt to use verbal mediation strategies or trial and error to substitute the mental visuospatial abilities that the task intends to measure. If they have a true visuospatial impairment, then other assessments that do not involve a verbal mediation component or guessing will be lowered. The clinician should carefully consider the strategies and the associated cognitive abilities the examinee exhibits during task completion.
5. Executive dysfunction may impact strategy and performance on the block design. Excessive impulsivity may result in examinees taking a random approach to constructing the designs rather than a systematic one. They may be able to solve the task with enough time but will likely work inefficiently and sporadically. These examinees may have difficulty with abstract thinking and display concrete handling of the task, such as attempting to match the sides and bottom of the blocks to the design. As block design is more abstract than drawing tasks, these examinees may perform better on visuospatial drawing tasks such as the ROCF. Probable frontal lobe difficulties can be corroborated by referencing assessments of frontal lobe inhibition like the CPT-3 or the Stroop. Difficulty with abstract thinking may be substantiated by referencing other assessments of frontal lobe function like the WCST or Category test.
6. Poor visual ability will depress the scores of the block design task if they cannot perceive the design. The clinician should ensure that the examinee uses corrective lenses if appropriate, and the presence of hemispatial neglect should be ruled out. Scores on primarily visual assessments of visuospatial ability can be compared, such as visual puzzles or the VFDT, to tease apart whether low block design scores are a result of the visual aspect or other aspects like complex spatial analysis, motor functioning, or time constraints.
7. The block design requires a combination of gross and fine motor skills. Therefore, scores will be depressed if the examinee perceives the designs correctly but has poor motor execution or visual-motor integration. If the examinee scores poorly on purely motor tests such as the Finger Tapping, the results of the block design should be interpreted cautiously or invalidated. If motor impairment is the cause of low block design scores, the examinee will likely show higher scores on visual puzzles and matrix reasoning.
8. As the block design is a timed test, slower performances will score lower even when correct. The clinician may benefit from allowing the examinee extra time to complete the item while still scoring 0 so that more information can be gathered on the extent of their visuospatial deficit. Tests of motor function

should be referenced to consider whether slow performances are due to slowing of motor execution. If processing speed is the issue, the examinee will likely perform poorly on other similar tests, such as coding and symbol search.

9. Information from the clinical interview or medical record should be considered, as many aspects of temperament may impact the speed of performance, effort, carefulness, or strategies used. If anxiety is present, the examinee may be excessively checking their work. Psychomotor agitation or apathy associated with depression may lower the speed of performance or the level of effort that is expended.
10. Because many factors and strategies may impact block design, close observation of how the client performs each item is important. Qualitative observation should allow the examiner to see whether the client is just slow in completing the design or has no understanding of the visual-spatial demands. When possible, clients seen as just slow should be allowed to exceed time limits to see if they can actually complete items (but this should not affect scoring).
11. Finally, as block design is highly correlated with general intelligence, it is most useful when it deviates from general intelligence. Thus, a poor block design score of 1 standard deviation below the mean is more significant when intelligence itself is above average; if intelligence as a whole is also one standard deviation below average, interpretation should be more cautious.

References

Arnáiz, E., Jelic, V., Almkvist, O., Wahlund, L.-O., Winblad, B., Valind, S. et al. (2001). Impaired cerebral glucose metabolism and cognitive functioning predict deterioration in mild cognitive impairment. NeuroReport, 12(4): 851–855. Retrieved from https://journals.lww.com/neuroreport/Fulltext/2001/03260/Impaired_cerebral_glucose_metab olism_and_cognitive.45.aspx.

Behrmann, M. and Shomstein, S. (2009). Spatial cognition and executive function. *In:* Squire, L. R. (Ed.). Encyclopedia of Neuroscience. Elsevier.

Coalson, D. L., Wechsler, D. and Raiford, S. E. (2008). WAIS®-IV Wechsler Adult Intelligence Scale®: Technical and Interpretive Manual: Pearson.

Groth-Marnat, G. and Teal, M. (2000). Block Design as a Measure of Everyday Spatial Ability: A Study of Ecological Validity. Perceptual and Motor Skills, 90(2): 522–526. doi:10.2466/pms.2000.90.2.522.

Heyanka, D. J., Mackelprang, J. L., Golden, C. J. and Marke, C. D. (2010). Distinguishing Alzheimer's disease from vascular dementia: an exploration of five cognitive domains. Int J Neurosci, 120(6): 409–414. doi:10.3109/00207451003597177.

Joy, S., Fein, D., Kaplan, E. and Freedman, M. (2001). Quantifying qualitative features of Block Design performance among healthy older adults. Archives of Clinical Neuropsychology, 16(2): 157–170. doi:10.1093/arclin/16.2.157.

Kalil, K. L., Bau, C. H., Grevet, E. H., Sousa, N. O., Garcia, C. R., Victor, M. M. et al. (2008). Smoking is associated with lower performance in WAIS-R Block Design scores in adults with ADHD. Nicotine and Tobacco Research, 10(4): 683–688.

Kent, G. H. (1934). Modification of the Kohs block design test. Journal of Applied Psychology, 18(4): 578.

Kohs, S. C. (1920). The block-design tests. Journal of Experimental Psychology, 3(5): 357.

Lezak, M. D., Howieson, D. B., Bigler, E. D. and Tranel, D. (2012). Neuropsychological assessment, 5th ed. New York, NY, US: Oxford University Press.

Muth, A., Hönekopp, J. and Falter, C. M. (2014). Visuo-spatial performance in autism: a meta-analysis. J Autism Dev Disord, 44(12): 3245–3263. doi:10.1007/s10803-014-2188-5.

Oda, H., Yamamoto, Y. and Maeda, K. (2009). The neuropsychological profile in dementia with Lewy bodies and Alzheimer's disease. Int J Geriatr Psychiatry, 24(2): 125–131. doi:10.1002/gps.2078.

Rascovsky, K., Salmon, D. P., Ho, G. J., Galasko, D., Peavy, G. M., Hansen, L. A. et al. (2002). Cognitive profiles differ in autopsy-confirmed frontotemporal dementia and AD. Neurology, 58(12): 1801–1808. doi:10.1212/wnl.58.12.1801.

Royer, F. L., Gilmore, G. C. and Gruhn, J. J. (1984). Stimulus parameters that produce age differences in block design performance. Journal of Clinical Psychology, 40(6): 1474–1485.

Rascovsky, K., Salmon, D. P., Hansen, L. A., Thal, L. J., Galasko, D. and Katzman, R. (2002). Disparate letter and semantic category fluency deficits in autopsy-confirmed frontotemporal dementia and Alzheimer's disease. Neuropsychology, 16(2): 190–196.

Rozencwajg, P., Cherfi, M., Ferrandez, A. M., Lautrey, J., Lemoine, C. and Loarer, E. (2005). Age related differences in the strategies used by middle aged adults to solve a block design task. Int J Aging Hum Dev, 60(2): 159–182. doi:10.2190/h0ar-68hr-rrpe-lrbh.

Rozencwajg, P. and Corroyer, D. (2001). Strategy development in a block design task. Intelligence, 30(1): 1–25. doi:https://doi.org/10.1016/S0160-2896(01)00063-0.

Sattler, J. M. and Ryan, J. J. (2009). Assessment with the WAIS-IV. Jerome M Sattler Publisher.

Schorr, D., Bower, G. H. and Kiernan, R. J. (1982). Stimulus variables in the block design task. Journal of Consulting and Clinical Psychology, 50(4): 479.

Shah, A. and Frith, U. (1993). Why do autistic individuals show superior performance on the block design task? Journal of child Psychology and Psychiatry, 34(8): 1351–1364.

Stewart, M. E., Watson, J., Allcock, A. J. and Yaqoob, T. (2009). Autistic traits predict performance on the block design. Autism, 13(2): 133–142. doi:10.1177/1362361308098515.

Sullivan, E. V., Fama, R., Rosenbloom, M. J. and Pfefferbaum, A. (2002). A profile of neuropsychological deficits in alcoholic women. Neuropsychology, 16(1): 74–83. doi:10.1037//0894-4105.16.1.74.

Troyer, A. K., Cullum, C. M., Smernoff, E. N. and Kozora, E. (1994). Age effects on block design: Qualitative performance features and extended-time effects. Neuropsychology, 8(1): 95.

Vasterling, J. J., Rogers, C. and Kaplan, E. (2000). Qualitative block design analysis in posttraumatic stress disorder. Assessment, 7(3): 217–226. doi:https://doi.org/10.1177/107319110000700302.

Velthorst, E., Levine, S. Z., Henquet, C., De Haan, L., Van Os, J., Myin-Germeys, I. et al. (2013). To cut a short test even shorter: reliability and validity of a brief assessment of intellectual ability in schizophrenia—a control-case family study. Cognitive Neuropsychiatry, 18(6), 574–593.

Warrington, E. K., James, M. and Maciejewski, C. (1986). The WAIS as a lateralizing and localizing diagnostic instrument: a study of 656 patients with unilateral cerebral lesions. Neuropsychologia, 24(2): 223–239.

Wechsler, D. (1955). Manual for the Wechsler adult intelligence scale.

Wechsler, D. (2008). WAIS-IV: Technical and interpretive manual. Pearson.

Wechsler, D. (2008). WAIS-IV: Administration and scoring manual. Pearson.

Zappullo, I., Conson, M., Zoccolotti, P., Trojano, L. and Senese, V. P. (2021). Building blocks and drawing figures is not the same: Neuropsychological bases of block design and Rey figure drawing in typically developing children. Child Neuropsychology, 27(3): 371–389.

Zipf-Williams, E. M., Shear, P. K., Strongin, D., Winegarden, B. J. and Morrell, M. J. (2000). Qualitative block design performance in epilepsy patients. Archives of Clinical Neuropsychology, 15(2): 149–157.

CHAPTER 2

Boston Naming Test
Second Edition

Casey Morocho

The Boston Naming Test was developed in 1978 and has become one of the most common measures for assessing naming in the past several decades (Kaplan et al. 2001). It is a measure of confrontation naming, which allows the screening of naming difficulties indicative of brain injury or dysfunction (Kaplan et al. 2001). It can also be useful for screening dysnomia or difficulty recalling words that greatly impact daily life (Boston Naming Test, n.d.). The test includes line drawings of objects that are commonly or rarely used (Kaplan et al. 2001). The order of the items reflects the frequency of the object being used (Kaplan et al. 2001). For example, frequently used words (e.g., bed) are placed toward the beginning, and rare words (e.g., abacus) are placed near the end (Kaplan et al. 2001). The test was originally developed for use with adults, but it has also been found useful among younger populations (Yeates 1993).

The original version of the BNT consisted of 85 items, which was shortened to 60 as part of the standard version created in 1973. In addition to the standard version, there is a short form and a multiple-choice version (Kaplan et al. 2001). The short version, which consists of 15 items, was created in conjunction with the short form of the Boston Diagnostic Aphasia Examination (BDAE) (Kaplan et al. 2001). It is also a good option when testing time is limited (Kaplan et al. 2001). The short form is located at the beginning of the stimulus book (Kaplan et al. 2001). The multiple-choice version consists of the same 60 items as the standard version but includes four word options on the stimulus page. The multiple-choice stimulus cards are located on the backside of the original stimulus card. Other versions of the BNT are available, including a Spanish and French adaptation.

Nova Southeastern University, Fort Lauderdale, Florida, USA.
Email: cm3318@mynsu.nova.edu

Normed Population

The first study of the Boston Naming Test produced normative data on subjects up to the age of 59 with the original 85-item test (Nicholas et al. 1989). When the 60-item test was created, the subject's scores were reanalyzed to only count their responses to the 60 items in the revised version (Nicholas et al. 1989). Despite limited information on the original and reanalyzed normative data for the BNT, several research teams have worked toward developing other sets of normative data.

In 1986, Van Gorp and colleagues collected data from 78 adults between the ages of 59 and 95 with no brain injury (Nicholas et al. 1989). The mean score for the sample was 54.31 (Nicholas et al. 1989). Another study produced similar mean scores based on 60 healthy adults ranging from 40 to 78 years old (Nicholas et al. 1989). The mean average score for subjects was 54.50, with a standard deviation 3.52 (Nicholas et al. 1989).

Test Procedures and Scoring

The examiner will utilize the stimulus book and expose the original stimulus cards. Each stimulus card on the standard version includes one line drawing of an object (Kaplan et al. 2001). Starting points will vary based on the individual's history (Kaplan et al. 2001). For example, children under age 10, people with language disorders, and other conditions may begin with item 1 on the standard version (Kaplan et al. 2001). Children and adults who are not suspected of having language difficulty may begin with item 30 on the standard version (Kaplan et al. 2001). An examiner who plans to use the short form of the BNT will start at item 1 (Kaplan et al. 2001). Once the starting point is chosen, the stimulus cards are presented in order. If an examiner chooses to start at item 30, items 31 to 60 will be presented in order (Kaplan et al. 2001). In addition, the examiner will allow the individual up to 20 seconds to give a response after the initial exposure (Kaplan et al. 2001). Correct answers will receive a checkmark in the first column of the score sheet (Kaplan et al. 2001). The time for a response to be made, also known as latency, will be recorded in the second column of the BNT scoring booklet (Kaplan et al. 2001).

During the administration, the examiner will have the opportunity to use stimulus and phonemic cues. Stimulus cues are short phrases that the examiner can use to clear any misperceptions of the line drawings or aid the individual when they do not know the name of the picture (Kaplan et al. 2001). The stimulus cue is provided in the brackets under each correct response on the scoring booklet (Kaplan et al. 2001). For example, item 14 is a mushroom with the stimulus cue "something to eat" (Kaplan et al. 2001). After telling the individual the stimulus cue, allow 20 seconds for a response (Kaplan et al. 2001). The examiner will place a checkmark in the stimulus cue column if the individual responds correctly after exposure to the stimulus cue (Kaplan et al. 2001). If the individual is still not providing the correct response or does not recognize the image, a phonemic cue will be used, and the individual will have 20 seconds to answer (Kaplan et al. 2001). Phonemic cues are used to aid the examinee by providing the beginning sound of the word (Kaplan et al. 2001). Normally, this type of cue involves the first consonant and vowel of the word (Kaplan et al. 2001). On the scoring sheet, it is displayed by an underline (Kaplan et al. 2001). For example, the phonemic cue "Mu" is used for item 14 (e.g., mushroom) (Kaplan et al. 2001). An examinee who answers correctly after being exposed to the phonemic cue will receive a checkmark under the "phonemic cue" column (Kaplan et al. 2001). If an incorrect response is provided, the response will be recorded verbatim in the "phonemic cue" column (Kaplan et al. 2001).

Each correct spontaneous and stimulus cue response will be counted toward the total raw score (Kaplan et al. 2001). The total raw score of the standard form is 60, whereas the total raw score of the short form is 15 (Kaplan et al. 2001). Basal and ceiling rules are in effect for scoring (Kaplan et al. 2001). The basal rule is defined as the first eight correct responses in the BNT (Kaplan et al. 2001). If an individual provides correct responses for items 30 to 38, the preceding items (e.g., items 1–29) will be counted as correct (Kaplan et al. 2001). The ceiling effect, or discontinue rule, is defined as the last eight incorrect responses (Kaplan et al. 2001). Once the ceiling rule is met, the examiner will stop the administration, and any succeeding items will not be administered or scored (Kaplan et al. 2001). Any incorrect responses will be written verbatim and will not be counted toward the total score (Kaplan et al. 2001).

Task Demands

An individual's naming ability is often believed to be a unitary construct. However, the ability to name an object involves several cognitive processes. First, the individual must be able to perceive the line drawing on the stimulus card through visual analysis. Second, the individual must be able to recognize the image and take the information through their semantic system. Once the information is processed, a possible word forms through the phonological lexicon. The brain begins to use the phonological buffer, which plans the exact motor movements that will be used to articulate the chosen word.

Reliability

It is important to assess the reliability of the BNT as it is a commonly used measure. Overall, the test is a reliable measure. When assessing its test-retest reliability, the measure scored good reliability between 2 weeks and 11 months (Harry and Crowe 2014). Even among clinical populations such as Alzheimer's disease, the responses for both uncued and cued responses after 6 months were considered 80% consistent (Spreen and Risser 1998). There is also a strong agreement between scorers (Spreen and Risser 1998).

Validity

In order to show the effectiveness of the measure, correlations between the BNT and other measures were found. For example, the Judgment of Line Orientation Test was deemed to have a small correlation (.28) to the BNT when used among healthy controls, possibly due to the visuoperceptual nature of both tasks (Madore et al. 2020). It was also found that small correlations existed with the Verbal Naming Test (0.22), Brief Visuospatial Memory Test, revised (0.30), California Verbal Learning Test (Second Edition) (0.26), and Delis-Kaplan Executive Function System (0.29) (Madore et al. 2020). It was moderately correlated with the Wechsler Adult Intelligence Scale (Third Edition) (0.34) (Madore et al. 2020). When examining the performance validity of the test, research has found that it is characterized by high positive predictive power and low negative predictive power (Erdodi et al. 2018). This detection profile should show clinicians to be cautious of examining BNT scores (Erdodi et al. 2018).

Clinical Applications in Research

Despite a lack of investigation into its psychometric properties and normative data, the BNT is a very important measure to use as difficulty in naming objects is a common symptom in several neurodegenerative diseases like Alzheimer's disease and temporal lobe epilepsy (Harry and Crowe 2014). It is also seen in individuals who have suffered a stroke, had dementia, or had encephalitis (Harry and Crowe 2014). Researchers have found that the BNT discriminates well between Alzheimer's disease, dementia with Lewy bodies, and normal aging (Harry and Crowe 2014). It is also suggested that BNT scores are evaluated in addition to assessing an individual's vocabulary (Harry and Crowe 2014). The BNT cannot differentiate between failure of retrieval and failure of knowledge, leading to misdiagnoses if a clinician only has access to the person's BNT scores (Harry and Crowe 2014).

Interpretation

Although the Boston Naming Test was designed to measure word-retrieval performance, a clinician should be cautious about solely relying on the individual's overall score. The clinician should use other measures of language ability prior to making a diagnosis or implementing a treatment. The examiner should also assess other cognitive domains.

1. Educational level appeared to influence the number of correct responses. Individuals with higher levels of education normally use a wider range of words, which can lead to higher scores on the BNT (Henderson et al. 1998). This may be related to a common factor found in neuropsychological assessments with an insufficient ceiling (Boston Naming Test, n.d.).
2. An individual can give responses that are used to name the item on the stimulus card but be deemed incorrect because it is not the targeted word. This can result in low scores despite the individual not having naming difficulty or any other impairment.
3. The test is sensitive to subcortical diseases such as multiple sclerosis and Parkinson's, even when overall cognitive abilities are slightly affected (Boston Naming Test, n.d.).
4. Dysarthria is characterized by difficulty in controlling the muscles used in speech. It can be caused by several medical conditions or brain injuries, leading

to difficulty articulating a word, slurred speech, or a strained voice (Mayo Foundation 2022). Individuals with dysarthria who complete the test may time out and be presented with cues. Their responses may be marked incorrect, thus leading to low scores.

5. Some individuals with aphasia experience the "tip-of-the-tongue" phenomenon and "word production anomia." As a result, many aphasic individuals will rely on cues to name the object (Matison et al. 1982).
6. Impairment of naming ability among individuals with Parkinson's disease (PD) is correlated with the severity of the disease. This is especially true for individuals with PD who present with bradykinesia. It is common for most PD patients to use cues for naming items (Matison et al. 1982).
7. The BNT can be used as a good measure of recovery of naming ability among individuals who experienced small strokes in the left posterior superior temporal-inferior parietal and the insula-putamen areas (Selnes et al. 1984).
8. Semantic errors and circumlocutions in patients with Alzheimer's disease were associated with low left mesial and lateral temporal lobe metabolism, which was measured with positron-emission tomography (PET) and fluoro-d-glucose (FDG) emission techniques (Welsh et al. 1995).
9. Limited anterior right or left temporal lobectomy in patients with left-hemisphere language lateralization did not impact positively or negatively on BNT performance (Boston Naming Test, n.d.)
10. The visual–perceptual ability of the individual should be checked if failures occur. Patients with right frontal damage may engage in "fragmentation responses" (e.g., the mouthpiece on a harmonica is interpreted as a line of windows in a bus) (Kaplan et al. 1983).
11. Apperceptive agnosia may lead to a failure in an individual's ability to see an object. This could lead to difficulty in the visual analysis of the stimulus card (Harry and Crowe 2014).
12. Associative agnosia causes a failure in the recognition of an object. The individual will be able to perceive the line drawing on the stimulus card, but this can lead to naming difficulty (Harry and Crowe 2014).
13. The phonological output buffer is the component responsible for the phonological information of a word until it has been articulated (Haluts et al. 2020). However, this process becomes impacted if an individual has difficulty carrying out the movements of speech, known as apraxia of speech (Harry and Crowe 2014).
14. Analysis of cultural background is important as well. The test has not been well studied across different cultural groups and subgroups. As the BNT is predicated upon prior exposure to these objects, individuals whose background results in poor exposure will make the test more difficult, while backgrounds where exposure is more common will make the test easier. As evaluations become increasingly multicultural, these issues req==uire more research, but for the moment, they need to be taken into account when analyzing the meaning of results.

References

Boston Naming Test: An Overview (n.d.). https://www.sciencedirect.com/topics/medicine-and-dentistry/boston-naming-test.

Erdodi, L. A., Dunn, A. G., Seke, K. R., Charron, C., McDermott, A., Enache, A. et al. (2018). The Boston Naming Test as a measure of performance validity. Psychological Injury and Law, 11(1): 1–8.

Harry, A. and Crowe, S. F. (2014). Is the Boston Naming Test still fit for purpose? The Clinical Neuropsychologist, 28(3): 486–504.

Haluts, N., Trippa, M., Friedmann, N. and Treves, A. (2020). Professional or Amateur? The Phonological Output Buffer as a Working Memory Operator. Entropy (Basel, Switzerland), 22(6): 662. https://doi.org/10.3390/e22060662.

Henderson, L. W., Frank, E. M., Pigatt, T., Abramson, R. K. and Houston, M. (1998). Race, gender, and educational level effects on Boston Naming Test scores. Aphasiology, 12(10): 901–911.

Kaplan, E., Goodglass, H. and Weintraub, S. (2001). Boston Naming Test Second Edition.

Madore, M. R., Scott, T. M., Fairchild, J. K. and Yochim, B. P. (2020). Validity of the Verbal Naming Test and Boston Naming Test in a sample of older Veterans. The Clinical Neuropsychologist, 1–12.

Matison, R., Mayeux, R., Rosen, J. and Fahn, S. (1982). "Tip-of-the-tongue" phenomenon in Parkinson disease. Neurology, 32(5): 567–567.

Mayo Foundation for Medical Education and Research. (2022). Dysarthria. Mayo Clinic. https://www.mayoclinic.org/diseases-conditions/dysarthria/symptoms-causes/syc-20371994.

Nicholas, L. E., Brookshire, R. H., MacLennan, D. L., Schumacher, J. G. and Porrazzo, S. A. (1989). The Boston Naming Test: Revised Administration and Scoring Procedures and Normative Information for Non-Brain-Damaged Adults.

Selnes, O. A., Niccum, N. E., Knopman, D. S. and Rubens, A. B. (1984). Recovery of single word comprehension: CT-scan correlates. Brain and Language, 21(1): 72–84. https://doi.org/10.1016/0093-934X(84)90037-3.

Spreen, O. and Risser, A. H. (1998). Aquired Aphasia (3rd ed.). Elsevier.

Yeates, K. O. (1994). Comparison of developmental norms for the Boston Naming Test. The Clinical Neuropsychologist, 8(1): 91–98.

CHAPTER 3

Halstead Category Test

Nisha Kajani

The Halstead Category Test is one of the earliest and most widely used tests to assess brain dysfunction. While it has been shown to be a reliable test in assessing brain damage, it is also a useful tool for understanding various types of processing and memory. Since the test is part of the Halstead-Reitan Neuropsychology Battery, it is usually interpreted in conjunction with other tests, although it is currently more used as a stand-alone test. It has been normed to multiple populations, and contemporary research has shown it to have an impact in not only understanding brain dysfunction but also understanding brain function in normal subjects through a range of neuropsychological and medical problems.

Normed Population

The Category Test has been used and normed to diverse cultural, national, ethnic, and racial populations. Multiple studies collected and developed norms for both the regular and intermediate forms of the test in regard to race, age, gender, and education (Boll 1993; Choca et al. 1997; Heaton et al. 1991). In 2004, Heaton et al. updated the African-American and Caucasian normative data for the Halstead-Reitan battery, including the Category Test. These established norms have been geared toward the American population, although norms for other populations have also been developed.

A study by Paredes et al. (2021) aimed to develop Category Test norms for Spanish speakers living at the United States-Mexico border. The results of the study found that age was correlated with the number of errors on the test, as well as education and gender. The study found that applying norms from English-speaking non-Hispanic White and Black populations overestimated rates of impairment in the native-Spanish-speaking Hispanic population.

Nova Southeastern University, Fort Lauderdale, Florida, USA.
Email: nk390@mynsu.nova.edu

A study by Santos et al. (2014) sought to create Portuguese-based norms for the Category Test. Women were found to have lower performance on the test compared to men. Age was a factor in decreased performance for both men and women, although men showed less decline after age 51 compared to women. A study by Kanmogne et al. (2018) developed demographically corrected neuropsychological test norms for the population of Cameroon. The normative data of the Category Test was the first in the country for assessing executive function and verbal fluency in the adult Cameroonian population.

Reliability

Shaw (1966) conducted a study to determine the reliability of the Halstead Category Test using the split-half method. The split-half method of reliability measures the internal consistency of the test by splitting it into two groups and comparing the results achieved in each half of the test. Shaw's study included a sample of 674 participants. The split-half reliability coefficient was .98, indicating no significant difference in the two parts of the test, thus affirming the reliability of the assessment.

Nici and Hom (2013) analyzed the consistency of the computer-based Category Test with the original version. The study compared the computer-based test results from evaluations of 25 patients who were matched pairwise with 25 patients previously tested with the original version. Matching was based on age, education, and diagnosis. The results of the t-tests indicated that the correlation between the total scores of the two test versions was .66, which showed only a moderate relationship between the two versions.

Validity

A study by Johnstone et al. (1997) used a sample of 308 adults with cognitive dysfunction to conduct a factor analysis using measures of reasoning through the Category subtests, intelligence through the Wechsler Adult Intelligence Scale (WAIS) revised, memory through the Wechsler Memory Scale revised, and other problem-solving abilities using the Trail Making Test. The study found that each Category subtests could be broken down into three-factor structures that measure specific areas of cognition. Symbol recognition and counting can be measured in Subtests I and II. Spatial reasoning can be measured in Subtests III, IV, and VII. Proportional reasoning can be measured in Subtests V and VI.

Goette et al. (2019a) conducted a factor analysis on each subtest of the computer-based Category Test to determine if the subtest measures were similar to factor structures previously determined by Johnstone et al. (1997). A sample of 105 adults was used as part of the factor analysis. The total number of errors per subtest was calculated, and a factor analysis was conducted compared to the previously identified factor structures. The results indicated that the factor analysis between the sample scores and previously identified factor structures normally converged, demonstrating the construct validity of the computerized version to be unchanged from the original slide-projector version of the test.

Donders (1996) conducted a study based on Reeder and Boll's (1992) short-form intermediate versions of the Category Test to determine if the short forms were valid in assessing children with traumatic brain injuries (TBI). The sample consisted of 87 children diagnosed with TBI. The study found that out of the three short-form intermediate versions available at the time, the test that used the first 15 items of every subtest was the most accurate and valid alternative to the full-length Category Test.

Test Procedures

Aside from how the test is delivered (computer or booklet), the administration of the test differs based on age group. The adult version of the test consists of 208 figures over seven subtests. The first six subtests focus on a single principle, while Subtest VII presents items that require the test taker to remember correct responses for the stimulus presented in the prior six subtests. The examiner shows different geometric figures and designs to the test taker. Something about the pattern presented in the figures/designs will remind the examinee of a number between 1 and 4. The examinee will choose the response they feel is correct (1, 2, 3, or 4) and then move on to the next question. Subtest I has eight items, Subtest II has 20, Subtest III has 40, Subtest IV has 40, Subtest V has 40, Subtest VI has 40, and Subtest VII has 20, for a total of 208 items. The examinee must tailor their responses based on prior items and feedback from the examiner (Thomas 2002). The examiner informs the test taker that only one rule or principle applies for each subtest, except for the last subtest, which involves more than one of the principles introduced in prior subtests. Even though there is no time limit to take the test, the average time to complete administration is 40 to 60 minutes. Incorrect responses are recorded as the primary measure once the test has been completed.

Scoring

Scoring for the Halstead Category Test consists of adding all the errors committed on each subtest. If the computer-based test is given, the application will calculate the total errors and the corresponding t-score. If the booklet version of the test is given, the examiner records the number of errors for each subtest and then adds them to get the total number of errors on the test. The total error raw score is then converted to a t-score using Heaton t-score conversion tables.

Item Difficulty and Types of Errors

The first two subtests are generally used to introduce the examinee to the assessment. Both subtests are considered easier compared to the rest of the subtests. Subtest VII is used as an overall measure combining attributes of the prior six subtests, making it more difficult for the test taker. A study by Lopez et al. (2000) tested for the internal consistency of the Category Test using a sample of 398 normal adult patients, brain-damaged patients, and undiagnosed patients. The reliability coefficient from the study was .9716, indicating adequate internal consistency reliability for the test. A parallel item analysis conducted found subtests I and II were above the normal range (>.80), indicating the questions were too easy (Lopez et al. 2000). According to Laatsch and Choca (1991), the normal range (r) for item difficulty should fall within .20 and .80.

Goette et al. (2019b) conducted an updated item response analysis for the test. The analysis was conducted on a sample of 211 adults. The study used a two-parameter, hierarchal, logistic item response model on Subtests III–VII for the analysis since the general assumption for the Category Test is that Subtests I and II are used to help ease the test taker into the test. The results indicated the items demonstrate a wide range of difficulties, with only a few items being excessively difficult (which were located in Subtest VI). The findings support the consensus of the reliability of the item response for the test.

Dysfunction in the brain was the primary reason for the development of the Category Test. Numerous studies have been conducted to reinforce the notion that the test is a good measure in differentiating patients who have brain damage compared to those who do not (Bornstein 1986; Reitan and Wolfson 1992). Despite its use, an agreed-upon false positive appears from the use of the test. Up to 18% false positive has been reported, indicating that 18% of the people tested may indicate brain damage through the test when, in fact, they do not have any (DeFlippis et al. 1979). The false positive can be linked to the presence of other disorders or medical conditions that can also promote a high rate of error on the test.

Multiple studies have been conducted over the decades to determine the viability of a short-form version of the Category Test (Boyle 1975; Kilpatrick 1970). The necessity of the short form is due to the severity of possible brain damage of test takers, their age, and/or the inclusion of the administration of other tests from the Halstead-Reitan neuropsychological battery. A study by Boyle (1975) found that a short form of the test would only take 15 minutes to administer but may produce a significant difference in quantitative performance. In essence, fewer questions would increase the chance of error.

Two of the more common short-form test versions are the intermediate and young child versions. The intermediate version of the test is for children between the ages of 9–15 and consists of 83 items. The young child version is for children between the ages of 5–8 and consists of 80 items.

Task Demands and Strategies

The Halstead Category is a test that measures cognitive functioning, abstract thinking, concept formation, visuospatial functioning, and memory. While the test was originally developed to measure functioning and damage to the frontal lobe, over time, it has come to measure other forms of brain injury as well as being sensitive to various mental disorders. As mentioned earlier, the test can be broken down into three-factor structures that measure specific areas of cognition (Johnstone et al. 1997). Symbol recognition and counting can be measured in Subtests I and II. Spatial reasoning can be measured in Subtests III, IV, and VII. Proportional reasoning can be measured in Subtests V and VI. Subtest VII adds a memory measurement as items are repeated from prior subtests, and test takers would need to remember what principle was used on those items to get the correct response successfully. The primary strategy for Subtests I through VI is using the first few items in each subtest to determine the type of pattern the designs/numbers indicate and using that pattern to find the correct response for the remaining items in the subtest. It is generally agreed upon that test-takers will use a similar strategy to find the correct response for each of the subtests, but the length of time in completing them may differ based on age, education, and type of disorder or brain damage incurred. The average time for individuals to complete the test is 40 to 60 minutes, but that number increases with different types of disorders and brain damage. Different levels of brain damage and various disorders can determine the difficulty of each subtest. For example, in a study by Goldstein and Shemansky (1997), schizophrenic patients were shown to struggle with subtest VII compared to the control group but adapted better to Subtest VI compared to the brain-damaged group of patients.

Clinical Applications in Research

According to Halstead and Settlage (1943), the initial purpose of the Category Test was to identify patients with brain damage. The test does a good job indicating some brain dysfunction, but it does a poor job predicting that particular dysfunction. At its most basic, the Category Test will indicate if there is a problem but will not identify what the problem is. Each of the following problem areas can lead to a poor performance on the test, indicating some level of sensitivity to the measure.

One area which can also lead to poor scores on the Category Test is substance abuse. Numerous studies have been conducted to measure the link between substance abuse with alcohol and poor scores on the test (Choca et al. 1997). The number of years of drinking, as well as the number of drinks per session, can inversely impact the scores. In addition, the greater the years of alcohol consumption, the lower the score tends to be (Jones and Parsons 1971; Parker and Noble 1977). A more recent longitudinal study by Alhassoon et al. (2012) found that longer periods of abstinence from alcohol led to an improvement in scores on the Category Test. Recent research has also shown that children cognitively impaired due to prenatal alcohol exposure performed poorly on the Category Test due to executive functioning deficits (Sperbeck et al. 2021).

Another area that can lead to poor scores on the Category Test is psychiatric disorders such as schizophrenia or depression. The deterioration of problem-solving skills for individuals with schizophrenia has led to poor scores on the test. Many studies have been conducted that use Category as a measurement for schizophrenic problem-solving impairment (Choca et al. 1997; Matarazzo et al. 1974). It is difficult to distinguish poor scores on the test, differentiating between brain damage and schizophrenia. One assumption is that the poor scores could be related to deficits in attentional and mental control, which people with schizophrenia often have problems with (Choca et al. 1997). People with depression have also been shown to achieve poorer scores on the test (Choca et al. 1997; Donnelly et al. 1980; Kellner et al. 1986)). The poor scores related to depression can be attributed to a worse ventricular-brain ratio, which correlates to individuals diagnosed with depression (Choca et al. 1997; Kellner et al. 1986). Despite the findings of prior research, a more recent study found that depressive symptoms do not have an impact on the performance of some neuropsychological tests, including the Revised Category Test (Gass and Patten 2022).

Learning disorders in children have also led to poorer scores on the Category Test. Specifically, children with learning disabilities tended to make more errors on the intermediate Category Test (Coutts et al. 1987). This trend continues to early adulthood for individuals suffering from a learning disability during adolescence (Sarazin and Spreen 1986). Other studies have found that poor performance on the test is limited to adolescents with an arithmetic learning deficiency and not those who can read and write well (Choca et al. 1997; Strang and Rourke 1983). Poor performance can also be extended to children and adolescents who have a history of delinquency or a behavioral disorder (Choca et al. 1997).

While most clinical validity research had been conducted decades ago and reaffirmed through the years, recent research has indicated that medical issues such as disease can also negatively impact scores on the Category Test. A study by Spies et al. (2012) on a group of South African women with human immunodeficiency virus (HIV) infection found that they suffered from neurocognitive dysfunction in memory and executive functioning. The sample consisted of 130 women (83 HIV-positive) who were given multiple neurocognitive tests. The results indicated there was a significant difference ($p < .05$) between scores of HIV-positive women and HIV-negative women. Another HIV-related study on a population in Cameroon reaffirmed the prior results (Kanmogne et al. 2018). Adults with HIV performed significantly poorer on the Category Test compared to the HIV-negative group.

Current research with the Halstead Category Test spans the spectrum of the diagnostic industry. As discussed earlier, studies have looked to expand the normed populations globally into multi-cultural dimensions. Since the past four decades have shown the test to be sensitive to non-brain injury-related neuropsychological issues, many studies have used the test to help assess the severity of specific disorders. The study into alcohol abstinence by Alhassoon et al. (2012) uses the Category Test to assess the level of cognitive recovery after abstaining from alcohol for many years. Using the test to analyze children for non-brain damage issues has also been effective, such as the study by Sperbeck et al. (2021) that successfully identified a decline in executive functioning for children exposed to alcohol prenatally.

Current studies have also successfully used the Category Test to assess improvement in the treatment of brain injury. A study by Kim et al. (2013) used the Category Test to assess the viability of using biofeedback to modify heart rate variability in individuals with brain injury. Heart rate variability (HRV) stems from emotional regulation. The study successfully used the Category Test to affirm the use of biofeedback to regulate HRV and produce better results in individuals with brain injury.

Interpretation

Interpretation of the Halstead Category Test has evolved over the decades since its development. While it was initially created to specifically assess brain damage, using the test as a singular assessment method is unviable due to its high sensitivity but low specificity. The following is a list of interpretations for the test that have developed over the past decades.

1. Premorbid levels of functioning need to be assessed to properly interpret test results (Matarazzo 1990).
2. T-scores between 40 and 60 are considered in the average range of functioning compared to the normed population.
3. Good scores reflect an intact brain, reasonable intellectual abilities, mature cognitive development, and efficient thought and concentration (Choca et al. 1997).
4. Poor scores can indicate brain damage, low intellectual ability, emotional interference, lack of cognitive development, or other neuropsychological/medical issues (Choca et al. 1997; Kanmogne et al. 2018; Spies et al. 2012).
5. The test cannot distinguish between brain damage and other neuropsychological issues.
6. Interpretation of the test showing frontal disorders can be done only when all other causes have been ruled out (Thomas 2002).
7. The likelihood of frontal deficits due to poor Category scores can increase based on better performance on other tests such as block design, digit span, part A of the Trail Making Test, language comprehension tests, and Raven's matrixes (Thomas 2002).
8. Based on performance on Wechsler-based IQ tests, IQ and number of errors on the Category Test are inversely correlated, except when referring to verbal IQ. As IQ scores go up, Category errors tend to go down (Thomas 2002).
9. Age and performance on the test are positively correlated. As age increases, so does the number of errors on the test. Different normed populations display different ages of severe differentiation.
10. Error pattern is important to consider when interpreting. A higher number of errors in earlier subtests indicates a greater likelihood of brain damage or other dysfunctions (Thomas 2002).
11. Inconsistent response patterns or failing to maintain a set may indicate learning deficiencies (Thomas 2002).
12. A prevalence of perseverative responses may indicate frontal lobe issues (Thomas 2002).
13. The test cannot generally differentiate between the various types of brain damage that may be present.
14. Memory inferences can be made if errors are lower in the first six subtests but higher by 15% on the last (memory) subtest (Thomas 2002).
15. Behavioral observations during the test can assist in further identifying specific issues.
16. The test should be used with a normed population.
17. There is some indication that individuals with cortical dementia score in the severely impaired range, while those with subcortical dementia score in the mildly impaired range (Thomas 2002).

18. Excessive alcohol consumption can lead to poorer scores in adults, as well as prenatal alcohol exposure in children (Alhassoon et al. 2012; Parker and Noble 1977).
19. Individuals with schizophrenia have been shown to score extremely low to the point they mimic some major brain damage (Choca et al. 1997; Matarazzo et al. 1974).
20. A poor score obtained with a test-taking time of less than 30 minutes is indicative of either a lack of motivation or impulsivity (Thomas 2002).
21. Challenges in understanding the purpose of the test can be indicated when scores on the WCST are impaired, but scores on the Category, COWAT, Stroop, and Trails B are normal (Thomas 2002).
22. Visuospatial challenges can be indicated when Category and TPT are impaired, but WCST, COWAT, Trails B, and Stroop are normal (Thomas 2002).
23. Challenges with verbal executive skills, possibly due to anterior left (dominant) hemisphere damage, can be indicated when WCST, COWAT, Stroop, and Trials B are impaired, but Category and TPT are normal (Thomas 2002).
24. Challenges with visual executive skills, possibly as part of lesions in the anterior right (nondominant) hemisphere, can be indicated when Category, WCST, and TPT are impaired, but COWAT, Stroop, and Trails B are normal (Thomas 2002).
25. Challenges with verbal analysis can be indicated when Stroop, COWAT, and Trails B are impaired, but Category, WCST, and TPT are normal (Thomas 2002).
26. Challenges with sustained attention can be indicated in impaired performance in the Category and other tests that measure sustained attention (Thomas 2002).

References

Alhassoon, O. M., Sorg, S. F., Taylor, M. J., Stephan, R. A., Schweinsburg, B. C., Stricker, N. H. et al. (2012). Callosal white matter microstructural recovery in abstinent alcoholics: a longitudinal diffusion tensor imaging study. Alcoholism, Clinical and Experimental Research, 36(11): 1922–1931. https://doi.org/10.1111/j.1530-0277.2012.01808.x.

Birnbaum, I. M., Taylor, T. H. and Parker, E. S. (1983). Alcohol and sober mood state in female social drinkers. Alcoholism: Clinical and Experimental Research, 7: 362–368.

Boll, T. J. (1993). Children's Category Test, the Psychological Corporation, San Antonio, TX.

Bornstein, R. (1986). Contribution of various neuropsychological measures to detection of frontal lobe impairment. International Journal of Clinical Neuropsychology, 9: 18–22.

Boyle, G. J. (1975). Shortened Halstead Category Test. Australian Psychologist, 10: 81–84.

Boyle, G. J. (1988). What does the neuropsychological Category Test measure? Archives of Clinical Neuropsychology, 3: 69–76.

Byrd, P. B. and Warner, P. (1986). Development of a booklet version of the Halstead Category Test for children aged nine through fourteen years: Preliminary validation with normal and learning-disabled subjects. International Journal of Clinical Neuropsychology, 8: 80–82.

Choca, P., Laatsch, L., Wetzel, L. and Agresti, A. (1997). The Halstead Category Test: a fifty-year perspective. Neuropsychology Review, 7(2): 61–75. https://doi.org/10.1023/b:nerv.0000005944.98635.16.

Coutts, R. L., Lichstein, L., Bermudez, J. M., Daigle, M., Mann, D. P., Charbonnel, T. S. et al. (1987). Treatment assessment of learning-disabled children: Is there a role for frequently repeated neuropsychological testing? Archives of Clinical Neuropsychology, 2: 237–244.

DeFilippis, N. A., McCampbell, E. and Rogers, P. (1979). Development of a booklet form of the Category Test: Normative and validity data. Journal of Clinical Neuropsychology, 1: 339–342.

Donders J. (1996). Validity of short forms of the intermediate Halstead Category Test in children with traumatic brain injury. Archives of Clinical Neuropsychology: The Official Journal of the National Academy of Neuropsychologists, 11(2): 131–137.

Donnelly, E. F., Waldman, I. N., Murphy, D. L., Wyatt, R. J. and Goodwin, F. K. (1980). Primary affective disorder: Thought disorder in depression. Journal of Abnormal Psychology, 89: 315–319.

Gass, C. S. and Patten, B. (2022). Depressive symptoms as a factor in neuropsychological test performance: MMPI-2 and selected tests of the Halstead-Reitan/Halstead-Russell Battery. Applied neuropsychology. Adult, 29(1): 133–138. https://doi.org/10.1080/23279095.2020.1720687.

Goette, W., Schmitt, A. and Nici, J. (2019a). A-14 An Updated Item Response Analysis of the Halstead Category Test. Archives of Clinical Neuropsychology, 34(6): 873–873.

Goette, W., Schmitt, A. and Nici, J. (2019b). A-15 Examining the Construct Validity of the Halstead Category Test-Computer Version: A Confirmatory Factor Analysis. Archives of Clinical Neuropsychology, 34(6): 874–874.

Goldstein, G. and Shemansky, W.J. (1997). Patterns of performance by neuropsychiatric patients on the Halstead Category test: Evidence for conceptual learning in schizophrenic patients. Archives of Clinical Neuropsychology, 12(3): 251–255.

Gong Y.X. (1986). The Chinese revision of Halstead-Reitan Neuropsychological Test Battery for Adults. Aca Psychologica Sinica, 18(1): 433–442.

Halstead, W. and Settlage, P. (1943). Grouping behavior of normal persons and persons with lesions of the brain. Archives of Neurology and Psychiatry, 49: 489–506.

Heaton, R., Grant, I. and Matthews, C. (1991). Comprehensive Norms for an Expanded Halstead-Reitan Battery. Odessa, FL: Psychological Assessment Resources.

Johnstone, B., Holland, D. and Hewett, J.E. (1997). The Construct Validity of the Category Test: Is It a Measure of Reasoning or Intelligence? Psychological Assessment, 9: 28–33.

Jones, B., and Parsons, O. (1971). Impaired abstract ability in chronic alcoholics. Archives of General Psychiatry, 24: 71–75.

Kamat, R., Ghate, M., Gollan, T. H., Meyer, R., Vaida, F., Heaton, R. K. et al. (2012). HIV Neurobehavioral Research Program (HNRP) Group (2012). Effects of Marathi-Hindi bilingualism on neuropsychological performance. Journal of the International Neuropsychological Society: JINS, 18(2): 305–313. https://doi.org/10.1017/S1355617711001731.

Kanmogne, G. D., Fonsah, J. Y., Tang, B., Doh, R. F., Kengne, A. M., Umlauf, A. et al. (2018). Effects of HIV on executive function and verbal fluency in Cameroon. Scientific Reports, 8(1): 1–13.

Kellner, C. H., Rubinow, D. R. and Post, R. M. (1986). Cerebral ventricular size and cognitive impairment in depression. Journal of Affective Disorders, 10: 215–219.

Kilpatrick, D. G. (1970). The Halstead Category Test of brain dysfunction: Feasibility of a short form. Perceptual and Motor Skills, 30: 577–578.

Kim, S., Zemon, V., Cavallo, M. M., Rath, J. F., McCraty, R. and Foley, F. W. (2013). Heart rate variability biofeedback, executive functioning and chronic brain injury. Brain Injury, 27(2): 209–222.

Laatsch, L. and Choca, J. (1991). Understanding the Halstead Category Test by using item analysis. Psychological Assessment: A Journal of Consulting and Clinical Psychology, 3: 701–704.

Lansdell, H. and Donnelly, E. (1977). Factor analysis of the Wechsler Adult Intelligence Scale subtests and the Halstead-Reitan Category and Tapping tests. Journal of Consulting and Clinical Psychology, 45: 412–416.

Lezak, M.D. (1995). Neuropsychological Assessment (3rd ed.) New York: Oxford University Press

Lopez, M. N., Charter, R. A. and Newman, R. J. (2000). Psychometric properties of the Halstead Category Test. The Clinical Neuropsychologist, 14(2): 157–161. https://doi.org/10.1076/1385-4046(200005)14:2;1-Z;FT157.

Matarazzo, J. D., Weins, A. N., Matarazzo, R. G. and Goldstein, S. G. (1974). Psychometric and clinical test-retest reliability of the Halstead Impairment Index in a sample of healthy, young, normal men. Journal of Nervous and Mental Disease, 158: 37–49.

Nici, J. and Hom, J. (2013). Comparability of the computerized Halstead Category Test with the original version. Archives of Clinical Neuropsychology: the Official Journal of the National Academy of Neuropsychologists, 28(8): 824–828. https://doi.org/10.1093/arclin/act075.

Paredes, A., Carrasco, J., Kamalyan, L., Cherner, M., Umlauf, A., Rivera Mindt, M. et al. (2021). Demographically adjusted normative data for the Halstead category test in a Spanish-speaking adult population: Results from the Neuropsychological Norms for the U.S.-Mexico Border Region in Spanish (NP-NUMBRS). The Clinical Neuropsychologist, 35(2): 356–373. https://doi.org/10.1080/13854046.2019.1709660.

Parker, E. S. and Noble, E. P. (1977). Alcohol consumption and cognitive functioning in social drinkers. Journal of Studies on Alcohol, 38: 1224–1232.

Pendleton, M. G. and Heaton, R. K. (1982). A comparison of the Wisconsin Card Sorting Test and the Category Test, Journal of Clinical Psychology, 38: 392–396.

Reeder, K. P. and Boll, T. J. (1992). A shortened intermediate version of the Halstead Category Test. Archives of Clinical Neuropsychology: the Official Journal of the National Academy of Neuropsychologists, 7(1), 53–62.

Reitan, R. M. and Wolfson, D. (1992). Conventional intelligence measures and neuropsychological concepts of adaptive abilities. Journal of Clinical Psychology, 48: 521–529.

Santos, I., Rodrigues, P., Silva, C., Costa, J. and DeFilippis, N. (2014). A-55 Portuguese Norms of the Halstead Category Test: Preliminary Data. Archives of Clinical Neuropsychology, 29(6): 523–523.

Sarazin, F. F. A., and Spreen, O. (1986). Fifteen-year stability of some neuropsychological tests in learning disabled subjects with and without neurological impairment. Journal of Clinical and Experimental Neuropsychology, 8: 190–200.

Shaw, D. J. (1966). The reliability and validity of the Halstead Test. Journal of Clinical Psychology, 22: 176–180.

Sperbeck, D. J., Whitbourne, S. K., Zelig, M., Shaw, R. M. and Craig, P. L. (2021). Halstead Category Test sensitivity to neurocognitive deficits in prenatal alcohol exposed and cognitively impaired children. Child Neuropsychology : a Journal on Normal and Abnormal Development in Childhood and Adolescence, 27(7): 984–994. https://doi.org/10.1080/09297049.2021.1936474.

Spies, G., Fennema-Notestine, C., Archibald, S. L., Cherner, M. and Seedat, S. (2012). Neurocognitive deficits in HIV-infected women and victims of childhood trauma. *A*IDS Care, 24(9): 1126–1135. https://doi.org/10.1080/09540121.2012.687813.

Strang, J. D. and Rourke, B. P. (1983). Concept-formation/nonverbal reasoning abilities of children who exhibit specific academic problems with arithmetic. Journal of Clinical Child Psychology, 12, 33–39.

Thomas, R. (2002). Halstead category test. pp. 167–171. *In*: Golden, C., Espe-Pfeifer, P. and Wachsler-Felder, J. (Eds.). Neuropsychological Interpretation of Objective Psychological Tests. Springer: New York. https://doi.org/10.1007/b107998.

CHAPTER 4

Coding

Megan Arnold[*]

Coding is a widely used test of visual-motor speed and a core subtest on the Processing Speed Index scale (PSI) of the Wechsler Adult Intelligence Scale, Fourth Edition (WAIS-IV). While using a key, the task requires an examinee to copy symbols that are paired with numbers within a specified time limit. In addition to processing speed, coding measures short-term visual memory, learning ability, psychomotor speed, visual perception, visual-motor coordination, visual scanning ability, cognitive flexibility, attention, concentration, and motivation. Previous research has suggested that coding also involves visual sequential processing and fluid intelligence (Groth-Marnat 2003; Kaufman and Lichtenberger 1999; 2006; Sattler 2008b). Therefore, coding is a valuable tool for assessing multiple cognitive domains in individuals.

History and Normative Sample

The original coding subtest was created by psychologist David Wechsler in the first edition of the Wechsler Adult Intelligence Scale 1955. The subtest has undergone many iterations of empirical and clinical testing, consultation, and debate to meet the standard set and expected by Wechsler and now by the present psychological community of researchers and clinicians (Wechsler 2008a). The most recent iterations were made during the transition from the Wechsler Adult Intelligence Scale-Third Edition (WAIS-III) to the WAIS-IV. At a general level, the WAIS-IV revision goals aimed to provide comprehensive and contemporary norms, as well as improve the psychometric properties, clinical utility, and user-friendliness of the test (Wechsler 2008a). The first modification to the coding subtest was its name; this subtest was referred to as Digit-Symbol coding in the WAIS-III but is now referred to as simply coding in the WAIS-IV—the second modification made to the coding subtest involved using new symbols to correspond with the number key. Two symbols were retained

Nova Southeastern University, Fort Lauderdale, Florida, USA.
Email: 2877@mynsu.nova.edu

from the WAIS-III but were paired with different numbers on the key, and four new symbols were introduced to replace more complex symbols (Wechsler 2008a). Other modifications to the coding subtest involved increasing the total number of sample items, methodically designing how the test items appeared, and increasing the total number of test items. For example, the total number of sample items was increased from four to six to allow additional practice and ensure exposure to all nine number-symbol pairings prior to proceeding with test items (Wechsler 2008a). In order to enhance the equal item difficulty that is recommended for measures of processing speed, each number now appears twice within each row, and the total number of test items was increased from 133 to 135 to accommodate this equal distribution (Wechsler 2008a). Lastly, aesthetic modifications were made to the coding subtest such that the symbols and numbers were enlarged to reduce visual acuity demands, and the boxes used to record responses were slightly enlarged to reduce fine motor demands.

The most recent revision of the WAIS was the product of a 4-year research program and involved an iterative process, with each stage of development leading to further refinements of the scale; one of the many stages of development involved standardization and incorporating a sample representative of the current population by considering various demographic variables. Trained recruiters, market research firms, and independent examiners used various approaches to identify individuals who met the specified inclusion criteria. All examinee candidates were screened for issues that could affect cognitive test performance. Some examples of exclusionary criteria used to disqualify individuals from the normative sample were: 1) primary language is not English, 2) uncorrected visual or hearing impairments, 3) taking medication that might impact cognitive test performance, and 4) previously or currently diagnosed with any physical condition or illness that might depress test performance (e.g., stroke, traumatic brain injury, psychotic disorder, etc.). The final normative data consisted of 2,200 examinees aged 16:0–90:11 that was stratified on key demographic variables (e.g., age, sex, race/ethnicity, self or parent education level, and geographic region) to ensure representative proportions of individuals (Wechsler 2008b). Except for the five older age groups (65:0–90:11), the sample consisted of an equal number of female and male examinees in each age group, and the proportion of racial groups was based on individuals within the corresponding age group. The geographical region was divided into the four major regions specified by the census report, including northeast (NE), midwest (MW), south (S), and west (W).

Test Procedures

Administration of the coding subtest begins by presenting the examinee with response booklet #1. Then, the examiner gives the examinee verbal explanations of the key, where each number is assigned a special mark. The examiner also completes the demonstration items while providing instructions on identifying and drawing the special mark paired with a number. Once the examiner has completed the demonstration items, the examinee is instructed to replicate the task using sample items. If the examinee makes an error on the sample item, the examiner is instructed to provide the examinee feedback and then prompt them to practice identifying and drawing the special mark that is paired with that specific number. If a left-handed examinee partially blocks the key with their left hand while completing the sample items, the examiner is instructed to stop the administration and place an extra response booklet to the right of the examinee's response booklet. This ensures the extra key is aligned with the key the examinee's hand is blocking. If the examinee completes the sample items correctly and appears to understand how to complete the task, the examiner will proceed with providing verbal instructions for completing the test items as quickly as possible without making mistakes until told to stop. All ages, between 16–90, begin at the same start point and are allotted 120 seconds to complete as many test items as possible.

Item Difficulty and Types of Errors

The coding subtest is unique in that "errors" are not acknowledged or corrected while an examinee is filling out the response booklet. In fact, the administration manual instructs the examiner not to provide the examinee with an eraser to correct mistakes. Even in the absence of an eraser, the examiner is instructed to discourage examinees from making spontaneous or excessive corrections to ensure their performance remains steady. There are a few errors that examinees can make when completing this subtest that are noteworthy. For example, expanding the symbols beyond the corresponding box (i.e., copying them too big), micrographic reproductions (i.e., copying them too small), distortion of reproduced symbols (i.e., incorrectly copies the symbol), or simply copying the digits instead of the symbols. These types of errors have been well-researched and propose important implications for an examinee's performance.

Task Demands and Strategies

As previously mentioned, the coding subtest measures processing speed, but it involves several other processing abilities, such as short-term visual memory, visual perception, visual-motor coordination, and visual scanning. Therefore, completing this subtest requires speed of information processing, visual acuity, and motor coordination. Coding is designed in such a way to be sensitive to poor performance and can detect those with various neurological conditions such as epilepsy, attention-deficit/hyperactivity disorder, and brain injuries (Donders 1997). Individual and situational factors that have been identified as influencing test behavior include planning, distractibility, reflectivity/impulsivity, verbal elaboration, visual elaboration, and the ability to perform under time pressure (McGrew and Flannagan 1998).

Scoring

If the examinee completes all the test items before the 120-second time limit expires, the administration ceases, and the completion time in seconds is written on the record form. If the examinee does not complete all the test items within the time limit, the completion time is recorded as 120 seconds on the record form. To score the examinee's responses, the examiner uses the cardboard coding scoring template by aligning the template so that the correct responses are above the examinee's responses. The scoring guidelines allow for one point for each correctly drawn symbol completed within the time limit. If the examinee, after realizing a mistake, spontaneously draws the correct symbol next to or on top of the incorrect response, one point is allowed for this item. Demonstration and sample items are not included in the examinee's score, nor are any items the examinee did not attempt. The total raw score is calculated by summating correctly drawn symbols completed in 120 seconds. The maximum coding total raw score is 135 points.

Reliability

Measures of reliability provided in the WAIS-IV technical manual suggest that the revised version of the coding subtest is comparable or improved. Because coding is a processing speed subtest, test-retest stability coefficients were used as the reliability estimates. These stability coefficients were based on the scores of individuals who participated in the test-retest study, which is the correlation between the scores on the first and second testing sessions corrected for the normative sample's variability. Evidence of internal consistency indicated that the overall reliability coefficient across all age groups was .86. The reliability coefficient across the 55–64 and 65–69 age groups was the highest ($r = .89$). The reliability coefficients for the three processing speed subtests (symbol search, coding, and cancellation) were not available for special groups, as these groups did not participate in the test-retest study.

Validity

In order to provide evidence of convergent validity, correlations between coding and other subtests on the WAIS-IV were provided in the technical manual. The hypothesis has always been that processing speed subtests are generally highly related to other processing speed subtests. This hypothesis was supported because coding strongly correlated with symbol search (r = .65) and cancellation (r = .42), perhaps reflecting the shared task demands and required cognitive abilities. Moderate correlations with other subtests were also noted. Additionally, when comparing the WAIS-IV version of coding to the WAIS-III version, a strong correlation was produced (r = .85). Specific correlations between coding and other measures beyond the WAIS were also offered in the technical manual, such as the WISC-IV (r = .72), the total score for the RBANS (r = .47), and the number-letter switching completion time for the DKEFS-TMT (r = .63).

Clinical Applications in Research

In addition to its function as a subtest within the most widely used intelligence scale, research has suggested that coding is useful in differentiating populations and predicting cognitive ability and disease states. Historically, research has suggested that processing speed abilities are associated with age, specifically age-related declines in performance, and with other measures of cognitive ability (Lindenberger et al. 1993; Salthouse 1996; 2000; Salthouse and Ferrer-Caja 2003). Variability on any WAIS-IV subtest across age groupings remains a hot topic, and many studies have set out to characterize the patterns of score changes with increasing age (Wisdom et al. 2012). Research has also indicated a significant correlation between processing speed and cognitive ability, specifically how processing speed measures like coding are sensitive in detecting clinical conditions such as ADHD, learning disabilities, traumatic brain injury, and dementia. Carlozzi et al. (2015) studied the clinical utility of the WAIS-IV in individuals with complicated mild, moderate, and severe traumatic brain injury (TBI). Individuals with mild, moderate, and severe TBI performed more poorly than controls across multiple indexes, including processing speed subtests (i.e., symbol Search and coding). The authors asserted that the processing speed index showed good sensitivity and specificity for classifying severity levels in individuals with TBI. Michel et al. (2013) also studied the clinical utility of the WAIS-IV but with individuals diagnosed with schizophrenia in comparison to controls. Analyses revealed significant impairment on several tasks, with the most significant group differences emerging at the processing speed index, including symbol search and coding.

In more recent studies, diversity factors, such as gender and sexuality, have been explored when considering similarities and differences across processing speed measures. Consistent with the literature on younger people, Faris (2015) hypothesized that straight women would have higher coding scores than straight men, gay men would have higher scaled scores than straight men, and straight women and gay men would not differ significantly. It was found that these groups did not reveal significant performance differences, suggesting that any age-related changes in cognitive abilities, such as processing speed, are not impacted by gender or sexuality.

Interpretation

Although the coding subtest effectively measures processing speed, the task itself should never be interpreted in isolation. Item responses and scores provide qualitative and quantitative information that is best interpreted in conjunction with a thorough history and careful clinical observations of the individual (Wechsler 2008b). Recording pertinent behavioral observations is essential to subtest administration and often aids score interpretation. A trained examiner will look for signs of neurological impairment (e.g., scanning difficulties), psychological problems (e.g., compulsive tendencies), education-related deficits (e.g., holding the pencil correctly), and/or situational variables (e.g., poor motivation) that may invalidate the subtest score (Ryan and Kreiner 2006). Specifically, the examiner should carefully interpret cognitive ability patterns involved in the coding task and consider other confounding domains, such as short-term visual memory, learning ability, visual perception, visual-motor coordination, visual scanning ability, cognitive flexibility, attention, concentration, and motivation. Below is a list of possible implications depending on an examinee's performance:

1. Memory Problems: During completion of the task, if an individual refers to the key on every item (i.e., references the key to locate the appropriate number and symbol pairing prior to copying the symbol), this may be indicative of short-term visual memory problems (Kaufman and Lichtenberger 1999).
2. Visual Scanning Problems: If an individual requires excessive time to locate the correct place on the key or locate the correct place on the protocol, this may indicate deficits in visual scanning abilities (Kaplan et al. 1991).
3. Visual-Motor Problems: If an individual draws the symbol(s) outside of the range of the corresponding box, produces micrographic reproductions, or produces uneven/light strokes while copying, this may indicate visual-motor problems (Kaplan et al. 1991).
4. Visual-Motor Coordination Problems: If an individual is observed with an awkward grip on their writing utensil or creates pencil strokes that are not fluid, this may indicate visual-motor coordination issues (Kaufman and Lichtenberger 2002).
5. Visual-Perceptual Problems: During the copying task, if an individual distorts their reproduced symbols, this may indicate visual-perceptual issues (Kaufman and Lichtenberger 2002).
6. Thought Disorder, Learning Disability, or Response Bias: If an individual produces an excessive number of incorrect number-symbol matches, this may indicate thought disorganization or an inability to learn (Joy et al. 2000).
7. Impaired Executive Functioning: During completion of the task, if an individual loses "set," forgets the nature of the task, demonstrates difficulties in shifting back and forth from numbers to symbols, or simply copies the digits instead of the symbols, this may be indicative of impaired executive functioning (Joy et al. 2003a; Kaplan et al. 1991).
8. Attention: Inability to sustain attention for the two-minute administration is often very disruptive. Clients who need to verbalize unrelated thoughts or whose attention is disrupted by depression, anxiety, pain, or environmental distractions will yield lower scores.

References

Carlozzi, N. E., Kirsch, N. L., Kisala, P. A. and Tulsky, D. S. (2015). An examination of the Wechsler Adult Intelligence Scales, Fourth Edition (WAIS-IV) in individuals with complicated mild, moderate, and severe traumatic brain injury (TBI). The Clinical Neuropsychologist, 29(1): 21–37. https://doi.org/10.1080/13854046.2015.1005677.

Donders, J. (1997). A short form of the WISC-III for clinical use. Psychological Assessment, 9(1): 15–20. https://doi.org/10.1037/1040-3590.9.1.15.

Faris, A. (2015). The aging brain: Differences in WAIS-IV coding subtest performance of older gay and straight men and women. Archives of Clinical Neuropsychology, 30(6). https://doi.org/10.1093/arclin/acv046.04.

Groth-Marnat, G. (2003). Handbook of Psychological Assessment (4th ed.). New York: Wiley.

Jenkinson, J. C. (1983). Is speed of information processing related to fluid or crystallized intelligence? Intelligence, 7: 91–106.

Jenson, A. R. (1982). Level I/Level II: Factors or categories? Journal of Educational Psychology, 74: 868–873.

Joy, S., Fein, D., Kaplan, E. and Freedman, M. (2000). Speed and memory in WAIS-R-NI Digit Symbol performance among healthy older adults. Journal of the International Neuropsychological Society, 6(7): 770–780. https://doi.org/10.1017/S1355617700677044.

Kail, R. (2000). Speed of information processing: Developmental change and links to intelligence. Journal of School Psychology, 38: 51–61.

Kail, R. and Salthouse, T. A. (1994). Processing speed as a mental capacity. Acta Psychologica, 86: 199–225.

Kaplan, R. F., Verfaellie, M., Meadows, M., Caplan, L. R., Pessin, M. S. and DeWitt, D. (1991). Changing attentional demands in left hemispatial neglect. Arch Neurology, 48(12): 1263–1266. https://doi.org/10.1001.archneur.1991.00530240067023.

Kaufman, A. S. and Lichtenberger, E. O. (1999). Essentials of WAIS-III Assessment. New York: Wiley.

Kaufman, A. S. and Lichtenberger, E. O. (2002). Assessing Adolescent and Adult Intelligence (3rd ed.). Hoboken, NJ: Wiley.

Kaufman, A. S. and Lichtenberger, E. O. (2006). Assessing Adolescent and Adult Intelligence (3rd ed.). Hoboken, NJ: Wiley.

Lindenberger, U., Mayr, U. and Kliegl, R. (1993). Speed and intelligence in old age. Psychology and Aging, 8(2): 207–220.

McGrew, K. S. and Flannagan, D. P. (1998). The Intelligence Test Desk Reference (ITDR): Gf-Gc Cross-Battery Assessment. Allyn and Bacon.

Michel, N. M., Goldberg, J. O., Heinrichs, R. W., Miles, A. A., Ammari, N. and McDermid, S. (2013). WAIS-IV profile of cognition in schizophrenia. Assessment, 20(4): 462–473. https://doi.org/10.1177/1073191113478.

Ryan, J. J. and Kreiner, D. S. (2006). The Quantified Process Approach to Neuropsychological Assessment. New York, NY: Taylor and Francis Group.

Salthouse, T. A. (1996). The processing-speed theory of adult age differences in cognition. Psychological Review, 103(3): 403–428.

Salthouse, T. A. (2000). Aging and measures of processing speed. Biological Psychology, 54: 35–54.

Salthouse, T. A. and Ferrer-Caja, E. (2003). What needs to be explained to account for age-related effects on multiple cognitive variables? Psychology and Aging, 18(1): 91–110.

Sattler, J. M. (2008b). Resource Guide to Accompany Assessment of Children: Cognitive Foundations (5th ed.). San Diego, CA: Author.

Wechsler, D. (2008a). WAIS-IV Administration and Scoring Manual. San Antonio, TX: Pearson.

Wechsler, D. (2008b). WAIS-IV Technical and Interpretive Manual. San Antonio, TX: Pearson.

Wisdom, N. M., Mignogna, J. and Collins, R. L. (2012). Variability in Wechsler Adult Intelligence Scale-IV subtest performance across age. Archives of Clinical Neuropsychology, 27(4): 389–397.

CHAPTER 5

Controlled Oral Word Association Test

*Christina Nunez** and *Ryan Bennett*

The Controlled Oral Word Association Test, also known as COWAT, is a common neuropsychological assessment that gauges an individual's verbal fluency, which is a facet of executive function. Specifically, in the COWAT, individuals are asked to rapidly produce as many unique words as possible that start with a particular letter, typically "F," "A," or "S," which is why it is sometimes referred to as the FAS test. There is a one-minute time limit for completing this test. The performance on the COWAT serves as a sensitive indicator of executive functioning and can highlight dysfunctions in the frontal lobe, the brain region that is instrumental in tasks requiring executive function. Therefore, the test is widely employed in clinical and research settings, diagnosing and monitoring conditions such as dementia, brain injuries, and other cognitive impairments.

Normed Population

The Controlled Oral Word Association Test (COWAT) has several scoring systems, which have led to the establishment of multiple normative data sets. These norms cater to diverse populations and languages. Selecting an appropriate set of norms is vital for a fair and accurate interpretation of an individual's performance. Two commonly used normative data sets for the COWAT in English are the original norms for the Benton Controlled Word Association Test—a component of the Multilingual Aphasia Examination—and the Heaton norms (Benton et al. 1983; Heaton et al. 2004).

Nova Southeastern University, Fort Lauderdale, Florida, USA.
Email: rb1934@nova.edu
* Corresponding author: cn584@mynsu.nova.edu

The original Benton norms were collected from a sample of individuals primarily from a rural background with limited educational achievement. Ruff and his team (1996) gathered data from a larger, more diverse sample to update these norms and make them more inclusive. This updated sample consisted of 360 native English-speaking volunteers aged between 16 and 70 years, hailing from various educational backgrounds (ranging from 7 to 22 years of education) and different living environments (urban, suburban, and a minority from rural areas). This new sample was stratified according to age, education, and gender.

The Heaton norms, developed by Robert Heaton and his colleagues, were specifically designed to accommodate demographic adjustments for African-American and Caucasian adults (Heaton et al. 2004). The sample for these norms consisted of 1,148 native English-speaking individuals from rural and urban areas across the United States. Participants had no history of learning disabilities, neurological diseases, significant head trauma, severe psychiatric disorders, alcohol or drug use disorders, or any other conditions that could potentially affect brain function. The average age of the sample was 50 years, with an average educational attainment of 13.8 years and a male representation of 52.4%. However, for demographic adjustment, the sample was broken down into two primary groups: 670 African Americans, with a mean age of 46.7 years, 13.3 years of education, and 47.2% male representation; 478 Caucasians, with a mean age of 54.6 years, 14.4 years of education, and 59.6% male representation. These norms help ensure a more nuanced and culturally sensitive assessment of performance on the COWAT.

Reliability

Internal Consistency

The reliability of the COWAT depends largely on the norms used and how well the individual fits the normative data. Overall, the COWAT has been shown to be a reliable measure with an alpha coefficient of .83 and an average intercorrelation of .61 (Ruff et al. 1996). Other studies found a similar alpha coefficient of .83, specifically utilizing the FAS letter combinations (Tombaugh et al. 1999). These findings suggest despite the brevity of the test, the measure is reliable and homogenous.

Test-Retest Reliability

The test-retest reliability of the COWAT has shown to be stable for six months with a significant correlation of .74 (Ruff et al. 1996). Other studies have investigated the COWAT test-retest reliability across different intervals of time. These studies also found the COWAT to be a consistent measure of at least .70 (Dikmen et al. 1999; Tombough et al. 1999). Additionally, one study examined the practice effects associated with the COWAT and other neuropsychological measures and found from baseline to one year, the scores on the COWAT did not significantly increase, suggesting stability in test and lack of practice effects (Basso et al. 1999).

Validity

Construct Validity

Little research has been done in the way of construct validity of the COWAT. One study showed when compared to measures of verbal intelligence and phonemic fluency, the COWAT was found to have a correlation coefficient of .44 to .87 (Henry and Crawford 2004).

Diagnostic Validity

Studies have shown a significant difference between individuals who are cognitively normal and individuals with amnestic mild cognitive impairment in letter fluency as measured by the COWAT-FAS (Malek-Ahmadi et al. 2011). A comparative study of COWAT outcomes was conducted on individuals with Alzheimer's dementia, vascular dementia, and Parkinson's disease (Lim et al. 2019). The study found all individuals presenting with mild conative impairment scored significantly lower than the control group on both semantic and phonemic fluency tests. Individuals diagnosed with vascular dementia and Parkinson's disease scored significantly lower than the Alzheimer's dementia group. The study suggests the COWAT is a sensitive measure of executive function within a group of individuals with mild cognitive impairment.

In a study conducted by Rey and colleagues (2001), the Controlled Oral Word Association Test (COWAT) was administered as part of the Multilingual Aphasia Examination to a group of Spanish-speaking patients who had suffered from closed head trauma. This version of the test used the letters P, T, and M, selected due to their comparable frequencies in the Spanish language. The study's findings highlighted the COWAT as the most effective subtest in differentiating between the head trauma group and a control group.

Test Procedures

Individuals are given 60 seconds to rapidly generate unique words beginning with a certain letter of the alphabet. Three trials were performed using three different letters of the alphabet for a total time of three minutes. Examiners who test in English frequently use F-A-S, although C-F-L and M-D-H were found to be parallel alternatives to F-A-S (Lacy et al. 1996). The examiner is to record exact responses verbatim during each trial as well as time the individual for 60 seconds for each trial. Before the first trial, the examiner informs the individual to verbally produce unique words that are not proper nouns (such as names of people or places) or say the same word with a different ending (such as write and writing). The individual is then given a letter of the alphabet and prompted to produce responses. The individual is then stopped after 60 seconds. The examiner provides the next target letter, prompts the individual to begin, and stops the individual after 60 seconds for trials two and three.

Scoring

In order to score the COWAT, one point is awarded for each unique word generated for each trial, which correctly begins with the appropriate letter of the alphabet. Points are not given for words that are repeated, words that begin with a different letter of the alphabet than the specified letter for the trial, words that are proper nouns, and the same word with different endings. The examiner sums the number of points per trial. The examiner then creates a total sum score by summing across all three trials. Total scores are then converted into t-scores and scaled scores using an appropriate set of norms. Although not directly calculated into the score, many examiners sum the number of repetitions and intrusions to serve as behavioral observations.

Item Difficulty and Types of Errors

Ideally, the trials would be equally difficult as the goal is to measure spontaneous word production. Therefore, letter selection is critical. In the English language, F-A-S are commonly used as many common words begin with these letters in the English language. A common parallel in the English language is C-F-L, while a less common parallel is M-D-H. It would be inappropriate to select letters of various difficulty, such as A-C-Z. Specifically, the letter Z would penalize the individual as fewer common words begin with the letter Z in English. Letter selection should be based on the language of administration.

Types of errors an individual can make include failing to abide by the instructions. Individuals may list names of people, names of places, and multiple endings to the same word, trying to generate as many words as they can. They may generate words that do not begin with the designed letter for the trial. Individuals may also say the same word more than once. They may also not produce words as quickly as possible, which can lower their score. Individuals may also produce nonsense words that would not qualify as a word. An individual may produce a word in a different language; this would be up to examine discretion for scoring. Individuals may also produce words that are phonetically similar, such as F- and Ph-, but begin with the incorrect letter. This error may result from inappropriate testing language, for example, testing a native Spanish speaker in English.

The examiner is also susceptible to errors. The examiner may fail to ask for the individual's native language and administer the test in the incorrect language, which would artificially deflate scores. The examiner may mismanage the time due to the writing demands and allow the individual too much time to respond. The examiner may be caught off guard due to the speed at which the individual produces word and does not write the words verbatim and potentially miss words, thereby compromising the score.

Task Demands and Strategies

The task itself seems easy, but the demands placed on the individual are great. Although the demands are great, they are short in duration, as the test takes less than five minutes to complete. Individuals are asked to work under time pressure and rapidly produce unique responses within a set of rules. The task can be difficult and sometimes overwhelming for some individuals. The individual may feel too pressured and unable to produce any more responses or repeat the same response multiple times.

Individuals vary in how they approach the task. A common strategy used is using the phonological sounds. Individuals will make the phonetic sound of the designated letter and use that to develop words. For example, if the individual is given the letter A, then they will repeatedly make the "Ah-" sound to generate words. One mistake that is made using the phonological approach is using words that phonetically sound the same but begin with a different letter, like "Ph-" instead of "F." An example of this is the word "philosopher," the word begins with the letter P but phonetically sounds like "F." These mistakes are common for multilingual individuals not testing in their native language. Another common approach used is categorical. Individuals who use this strategy will focus on a category and search for words that begin with the designated letter. For example, an individual may begin by using food words, then animals, and then articles of clothes. For the examiner, this strategy is easier to identify. A common mistake in this strategy is focusing too much on a specific category, which can put the individual at a time disadvantage.

Clinical Application in Research

Within the clinical context, the COWAT has been evaluated across a wide variety of individuals as a measure of executive functioning and frontal dysfunction. Research has attempted to expand the use of the COWAT as well as draw on some concerns in certain populations. Within an urban sample from a veteran's affairs hospital, the COWAT, along with the animal's categorical fluency test, was shown to be a valid measure of effort and performance. This study found the COWAT to have 90% specificity and 44% sensitivity in measuring testing effort in this sample (Sugarman and Axelrod 2015). This suggests the COWAT may be a good measure of effort in the clinical setting.

Research has also highlighted some concerns with interpreting the COWAT as a measure of executive functioning. One study highlighted the impact of emotional factors on the COWAT. This study found depression decreased COWAT scores and increased the variability in scores (Veiel 1997). These findings suggest emotional factors such as depression may influence executive functioning and mental flexibility. Another study administered the COWAT to a sample of Spanish-speaking individuals. They found performance was linked to socioeconomic status in this sample (Fortuny et al. 1998). Another study found a significant difference in COWAT performance among Black, White, and Hispanic veterans. These findings were still significant even after controlling for income and education (Johnson-Selfrigde et al. 1998). These studies suggest performance on the COWAT may be influenced by demographic factors.

Interpretation

Interpretation of the COWAT is based on the set of comparative normative data. According to the set of normative data selected, the COWAT will be transformed into t-scores for interpretation.

1. Impairments in language comprehension or the motoric production of language can significantly influence the outcomes of this test regardless of possible impairment in abstraction or flexibility. Both expressive and receptive language skills are necessary before interpretations are made that an executive deficit is present.
2. The interpretation of results becomes constrained if there are any signs of fundamental issues with receptive or expressive language skills or broader problems related to verbal intelligence.
3. Repeating identical or near-identical responses will exhibit deficiencies in mental adaptability and perseveration. In severe cases, the same word or form of a word might be reiterated multiple times.
4. An individual with damage to the left temporal-parietal lobe might struggle to navigate complex speech association systems.
5. An individual with damage to the frontal lobe might struggle to focus on the task at hand, leading to the surfacing of irrelevant associations.
6. Another outcome of frontal lobe lesions is that the examinee may demonstrate perseveration on the task.
7. Language of origin also plays a role. Clients whose first language is not the language the test is given in will generally show significantly lower scores.
8. Other clients may be bilingual, but the language of origin and the new language are impaired in these tasks. It is important to identify what language is used predominantly and what language the client thinks in. Such individuals may struggle with this task compared to monolingual individuals of similar intelligence.
9. Examinees with lesions to the deep subcortical region are likely to demonstrate slowed performance on the COWAT.
10. Individuals with speech and language difficulties may struggle with the task. The task may also create anxiety for these individuals.
11. Given that the task is largely time-dependent, individuals with low processing speed may perform more poorly on the task, but their executive functioning may be intact.

References

Basso, M. R., Bornstein, R. A. and Lang, J. M. (1999). Practice effects on commonly used measures of executive function across twelve months. The Clinical Neuropsychologist, 13(3): 283–292.

Benton, A. L., Hamsher, de, S. K. and Sivan, A. B. (1983). Multilingual aplasia examination (2nd ed.). Iowa City, IA: AJA Associates.

Dikmen, S. S., Heaton, R. K., Grant, I. and Temkin, N. R. (1999). Test–retest reliability and practice effects of expanded Halstead–Reitan Neuropsychological Test Battery. Journal of the International Neuropsychological Society, 5(04): 346–356.

Henry, J. D. and Crawford, J. R. (2004). A meta-analytic review of verbal fluency performance in patients with traumatic brain injury. Neuropsychology, 18(4): 621.

Lacy, M. A., Gore, P. A., Pliskin, N. H., Henry, G. K., Heilbronner, R. L. and Hamer, D. P. (1996). Verbal fluency task equivalence. The Clinical Neuropsychologist, 10(3): 305–308. https://doi.org/10.1080/13854049608406692.

Lim, K. B., Kim, J., Lee, H. J., Yoo, J., Kim, H. S., Kim, C. et al. (2019). COWAT Performance of Persons with Alzheimer Dementia, Vascular Dementia, and Parkinson Disease Dementia According to Stage of Cognitive Impairment. PM & R: the journal of injury, function, and rehabilitation, 11(7): 737–744. https://doi.org/10.1002/pmrj.12125.

Malek-Ahmadi, M., Small, B. J. and Raj, A. (2011). The diagnostic value of controlled oral word association test-FAS and category fluency in single-domain amnestic mild cognitive impairment. Dementia and Geriatric Cognitive Disorders, 32: 235–240. https://doi.org/10.1159/000334525.

Rey, G. J., Feldman, E., Hernandez, D., Levin, B. E., Rivas-Vazquez, R., Medd, K. J. et al. (2001). Application of the multilingual aphasia examination-Spanish in the evaluation of Hispanic patients post closed-head trauma. The Clinical Psychologist, 15(1), 13–18. https://doi.org/10.1076/clin.15.1.13.1911.

Ruff, R. M., Light, R. H., Parker, S. B. and Levin, H. S. (1996). Benton Controlled Oral Word Association Test: Reliability and updated norms. Archives of Clinical Neuropsychology, 11(4): 329–338. https://doi.org/10.1016/0887-6177(95)00033-X.

Sugarman, M. A. and Axelrod, B. N. (2015). Embedded measures of performance validity using verbal fluency tests in a clinical sample. Applied neuropsychology. Adult, 22(2): 141–146. https://doi.org/10.1080/23279095.2013.873439.

Tombaugh, T. N., Kozak, J. and Rees, L. (1999). Normative data stratified by age and education for two measures of verbal fluency: FAS and animal naming. Archives of Clinical Neuropsychology, 14(2): 167–177.

Veiel, H. O. (1997). A preliminary profile of neuropsychological deficits associated with major depression. Journal of Clinical and Experimental Neuropsychology, 19(4): 587–603. https://doi.org/10.1080/01688639708403745.

CHAPTER 6

Connors Continuous Performance Test, Third Edition (CPT-3)

Jonathan Gellman

The Connors Continuous Performance Test, Third Edition (CPT-3), is designed to assess sustained attention, impulsivity, inattentiveness, and vigilance in children and adults. The test is administered via computer and consists of letters appearing on the screen for 250 milliseconds at 1-second, 2-second, and 4-second intervals. The examinee is instructed to press the space bar or click a wired mouse for every letter that appears other than "X" and to do so as quickly as possible without making mistakes. The CPT 3 includes 360 trials, with 80% target stimuli and 20% non-target stimuli. The test is divided into six blocks of 60 trials, each lasting roughly 2 minutes and 20 seconds. Each block comprises three sub-blocks of 20 trials, in which the stimulus is presented at a consistent interval. The test is 14 minutes long and preceded by a 1-minute practice session, ensuring the participant understands the instructions. While the previous version of this test could be administered to clients from 6 years of age, the CPT 3 is standardized for children over eight. The Conners Kiddie Continuous Performance Test can be administered to 6- and 7-year-old children.

Normed Population

The CPT 3 was standardized on a normative sample of 1,400 individuals representing the US population in terms of race, geographical region, and level of education. Of the 800 individuals ages 8–17, 442 (55.3%) were Caucasian, 175 (21.9%) were Hispanic, 112 (14%) were Black, and 71 (8.9%) belonged to another racial group.

Nova Southeastern University, Fort Lauderdale, Florida, USA.
Email: jg3570@mynsu.nova.edu

With regard to parental education, 356 (44.5%) had not received any education above high school, 240 (30%) had completed some college, and 204 (25.5%) had completed a bachelor's degree or higher. Geographically, 136 (17%) were from the Northeastern United States, 174 (21.8%) were from the Midwest, 298 (37.3%) were from the South, and 192 (24%) were from the West. Of the 600 individuals over the age of 18, 402 (67%) were Caucasian, 86 (14.3%) were Hispanic, 70 (11.7%) were Black, and 42 (7%) belonged to another racial group. With regard to education, 268 (44.7%) had received no education beyond high school, 180 (30%) had completed some college, and 152 (25.3%) had completed a college degree or higher. Geographically, 110 (18.3%) were from the Northeast, 130 (21.7%) were from the Midwest, 222 (37%) were from the South, and 138 (23%) were from the Midwest. Males and Females were equally represented across age groups.

Test Procedures

All other computer programs should be closed, and the work area should be cleared prior to administration. The test cannot be paused, so it is advisable for the examinee to use the bathroom and have a drink of water before the test begins. The examiner recites the instructions aloud when they appear on the screen. If the examinee completes the practice session with an omission rate that exceeds 25%, the program will recommend that the practice session be repeated. The practice session should not be repeated unless absolutely necessary, as this may fatigue the examinee. During the test, the examiner should not engage in any activities that might distract the examinee. If the examinee asks a question, the examiner should indicate they can answer when the test ends. If the examiner sees that the examinee is not engaging with the task, they may redirect their attention one time. Examiners should note if the examinee displays significant anxiety, any irregularities in administration, as well as any warning messages displayed by the program (Conners 2014).

Factors Relevant to Performance

The Connors CPT may not be equally sensitive to attention deficits in all populations. Stern and Shura (2019) assessed the sensitivity of CPT 3 to ADHD among veterans. They found that of the nine measures, only HRT Standard Deviation and HRT Inter-Stimulus Interval Change scores were significantly higher among veterans with ADHD. The test also failed to discriminate between inattentive, hyperactive, and combined presentations. The limitations of the normative sample should also be considered when using this test. Miranda et al. (2008) compared Brazilian scores to the normative sample in the United States and found that Brazilian children performed better on all measures other than the percentage of omission errors.

While emotional problems have been associated with poor performance on attention tasks, Fasmer et al. (2016) found that the CPT 2 was able to effectively discriminate between ADHD and emotional problems in a clinical sample. Some studies have found that intelligence is associated with improved performance (Munkvold et al. 2014; Celeste et al. 2019). Several studies have demonstrated that medication impacts performance on the Connors CPT. Results indicate that methylphenidate, dextroamphetamine, and atomoxetine can reduce errors and variability among individuals with ADHD (Epstein 2006; Ni et al. 2016). Amphetamine was also found to enhance Detectability and reduce variability throughout the test among adults without attention deficits (MacQueen et al. 2018).

Research has demonstrated performance differences across age and gender, prompting the use of norms adjusted for both variables (Connors 2014). In addition to gender effects, Burton et al. (2010) found relationships between personality traits and CPT variables. Vigilance was positively correlated with neuroticism and negatively correlated with extraversion and agreeableness. Conscientiousness was associated with a more conservative response bias. In men, higher vigilance was associated with lower conscientiousness, while in women, it was related to lower extraversion. A liberal response style was associated with extraversion in men and neuroticism, openness, and lower conscientiousness in women.

Reliability

Internal consistency was measured by split-half reliability. The CPT 3 was found to have strong split-half reliability, with an estimate of .92 for the normative sample and .94 for clinical samples. After outliers were removed, test-retest reliability was found to have a median correlation of .67 at 1 to 5 weeks in a sample of 120 individuals from the general population (Connors 2014). Specific scores such as Variability (.56), Perseverations (.48), and Hit Reaction Time (HRT) Block Change (.12) demonstrated lower correlations, raising questions about whether they are sufficiently stable for interpretation (Gischlar et al. 2017).

Validity

A comparison of 346 individuals who had been diagnosed with ADHD and a matched sample without a diagnosis revealed statistically significant differences at small to moderate effect sizes (d =.1–.49). The individuals with ADHD received higher scores (reflecting poorer performance) in Detectability, Omissions, Commissions, and Perseverations. Their responses were also more varied than those of the control group, as reflected by Variability, HRT Standard Deviation, HRT Block Change, and HRT Inter-Stimulus Interval Change scores.

Incremental validity was assessed by comparing the rate of accurate diagnoses when clinicians used the CPT 3 in addition to validated symptom report measures to the use of the report measures alone. In a sample of 112 individuals ages 8–17, using the CPT 3, in addition to parent reports on the Connors Third Edition, was found to increase correct classification by 4.5%, sensitivity by 3.5%, and specificity by 5.5% and in a sample of 137 adults, use of the CPT 3 in addition to the Connors Adult ADHD rating scales increased correct classification by 3.6%, specificity by 7.7%, and sensitivity by 2.7% (Connors 2014). Intercorrelation between the scores was not assessed, and exploratory and confirmatory factor analyses were not conducted (Gischlar et al. 2017).

Research on the discriminative validity and clinical utility of continuous performance tests (CPTs) has yielded conflicting results. A systematic review of 6

CPTs, including the Connors CPT, concluded that there are mixed reports on whether they enhance clinical diagnoses (Hall et al. 2016). Wang et al. (2021) studied the discriminative validity of the CPT 3 and the Conners Continuous Auditory Test of Attention (CATA) among Chinese youth. They found that individuals with ADHD performed more poorly than controls on all measures other than HRT and Response Style. Their analysis indicated a correct classification rate of 72.1% when the CPT 3 was used alone. The correct classification rate increased to 80.6% when the CPT 3 was used in tandem with the CATA. Wang et al. (2021) concluded that both tests effectively discriminate individuals with ADHD from controls and that discriminate validity is increased when data from both tests are considered.

In adult populations, Pettersson et al. (2016) assessed the discriminative validity of several neuropsychological tests, including the CPT 2. They found that Commission and Variability scores demonstrated high specificity (91.7% and 85.4%, respectively) but low sensitivity (33.3% and 26.7%), resulting in poor overall classification accuracy. However, a logistic regression analysis revealed that when combined with the Diagnostic Interview for ADHD in adults (DIVA 2.0), the CPT 2 increased diagnostic accuracy by 10%. Baggio et al. (2020) examined the CPT 3 as a tool for detecting ADHD and assessing symptom severity in 201 adults who had previously been diagnosed with the disorder. They found that the CPT 3 scores indicated that only 51.7% of the participants were likely to have ADHD, with a classification error of 80.3% for inattentive presentation and 22.5% for hyperactive presentation. The authors concluded that great caution should be exercised when interpreting CPT 3 data in adult populations.

The research comparing the Connors CPT to other measures is limited. Shaked et al. (2020) examined the relationship between the CPT 2 and the State-Trait Personality Inventory (STPI), Behavior Rating Inventory of Executive Function-Adult Version (BRIEF-A), and the Stroop Color and Word Test. They found that these measures were largely unrelated to performance on the CPT 2. There was a positive relationship between Commission errors and the BRIEF-A's Behavior Regulation Index. However, given that no such correlation was evident with the BRIEF-A's inhibit subscale, the authors cautioned that this association may be attributable to a Type-I error. Goulart et al. (2018) assessed the correlation between measures of impulsivity in the CPT 3 and the CATA. They found that commissions and hit reaction time were significantly correlated across the two measures, with Pearson coefficients of .283 and .342, respectively. The shared variance was found to be low for Commissions (8.01%) and Hit Reaction Time (11.70%). The correlation for perseveration did not meet statistical significance. One study found that the CPT 3 was less sensitive to deficits in individuals diagnosed with ADHD than some other CPTs, including the vigilance tests of the Vienna Test System, Test Battery for Attention Performance, Test of Variables of Attention, and the Integrated Visual and Auditory Continuous Performance Test 2. No test characteristics could be identified to account for these differences (Fuermaier et al. 2022). The sample was limited to individuals with an ADHD diagnosis, so it is unclear whether the lack of sensitivity would result in increased specificity relative to other CPTs.

Embedded Validity Indicators

Several studies have examined the utility of CPT 2 indices as embedded validity indicators (EVIs). Findings indicated that error indices and composite EVIs yielded adequate classification accuracy in civilian and veteran populations (Scimeca et al. 2021). Ord et al. (2020) examined EVIs in the CPT 3 by comparing individual and composite scores to performance on the Test of Memory Malingering (TOMM). They found that individuals who failed the TOMM performed more poorly on Detectability, Omissions, Commissions, HRT Standard Deviation, and HRT Inter-Stimulus Interval Change. The highest classification accuracy was derived from HRT Standard Deviation and HRT Inter-Stimulus Interval Change, and composite scores that included these two indices were the best predictors of invalid performance. They cautioned that due to the low sensitivity of these measures, they should not be used in isolation and are better suited to rule in invalid performance than to rule it out. Scimeca et al. (2021) compared database CPT 3 scores to the results of several performance validity tests and found that Omissions, Variability, and two composite scores reached the threshold of acceptable classification accuracy. They concluded, however, that EVIs in the CPT 3 lacked psychometric utility to serve as a useful measure of performance validity.

Clinical Application in Research

While the Connors CPT is primarily used to assess ADHD, research has indicated that the test is sensitive to variations in attention and impulsivity associated with a number of conditions. Individuals with schizophrenia were found to have clinically significant Variability scores and to perform more poorly than controls on all measures other than response style and HRT Inter-Stimulus Interval Change (López-Luengo et al. 2014). Children with depression generally have a more conservative response style, slower reaction time, and commit more errors on the Connors CPT. In individuals with comorbid depression and ADHD, reaction time variability was found to be greater than in those with ADHD alone (Estis 2009). Munkvold et al. (2014) found that the CPT 2 could not discriminate between children with ODD and controls or between children with comorbid ADHD and ODD and those with ADHD alone. They did find a score difference for the comorbid group, but a regression analysis implicated IQ rather than diagnostic status as a significant predictor of performance. In an effort to assess whether intellectual disability impacts the results of CPTs among individuals with ADHD, Celeste et al. (2019) compared scores between children with ADHD with IQs above and below 80. They found that those with IQs below 80 were twice as likely to have three measures with a T-score exceeding 65 and performed more poorly on Omissions, Detectability, Hit Reaction Time, and Variability.

A number of studies examined the use of the Connors CPT for individuals with neurological conditions. Zane et al. (2016) compared the performance of a Mild TBI (M-TBI) group, a Moderate-Severe TBI (MS-TBI group, and a control group. The M-TBI group performed more Commission errors than the control group, and the MS-TBI group had a poorer Detectability score than the M-TBI group. The greatest difference was seen between the MS-TBI and control groups, as the former achieved significantly poorer scores on Variability, Detectability, Omissions, and Commissions. Kljajić et al. (2020) found that individuals with sagittal and metopic craniosynostosis both performed poorly on the CPT 3 and that they deviated from the norms on different measures. Lee et al. (2020) examined how CPT 2 performances differed by type and severity of aphasia. They did not find a difference between fluent and non-fluent aphasia. Aphasia severity was associated with impaired performance on Omissions and HRT. Research has also indicated that the Connors CPT is sensitive to Alzheimer's Disease and epilepsy (Connors 2014).

Interpretation and Scoring

The test is scored automatically by the computer program. The program can generate an Assessment Report to provide results for a single administration or a Progress Report to compare the performance of up to four administrations. Raw scores are converted to T-scores using gender and age-specific norms. Higher scores indicate poorer performance on all scores except C and HRT. For all other measures, scores above 60 are considered atypical. For HRT, a score below 45 or above 60 is considered atypical. The report includes a summary that lists atypical scores and indicates the likelihood of attention deficits. Re-administration should be considered if some scores could not be computed due to insufficient responses,. In the event of an unusual response pattern, the examiner should assess potential explanations (e.g., fatigue, lack of understanding or motivation) and readminister if needed.

The following scores are included in the report:

1. C measures response style as it pertains to the trade-off between speed and accuracy. A conservative response style indicates a greater emphasis on accuracy, a liberal style indicates a greater emphasis on speed, and a balanced style reflects a response style that is not strongly biased in either direction. The report will indicate how this can be used to interpret other scores, such as Commissions and Hit Reaction Time.
2. D-prime measures Detectability or the ability to discriminate target stimuli from non-target stimuli. It also measures the differences between signal and noise distributions.
3. Omissions are a measure of missed targets. Missing targets may be caused by failure to focus, and a high omission rate indicates inattentiveness.
4. Commissions are a measure of responses to non-targets. The interpretation of this score is dependent on the examinee's Hit Reaction Time. Fast reaction times and high commission errors indicate impulsivity, while slow reaction times and high commission rates indicate inattentiveness.
5. Perseverations are rapid responses within 100 milliseconds of the stimuli being presented, which is faster than it can be perceived and responded to. This may reflect a slow attempt to respond to a prior stimulus, an attempt to anticipate the stimuli, a repeated response, or a random response. A high rate of perseveration may reflect impulsivity or a very libel response style.

6. HRT is the average time from stimulus presentation to response across all items. Perseverations are not included in the calculation of this score. A slow HRT may indicate an atypically conservative response style or may result from inattentiveness. A fast HRT may be attributable to impulsivity when combined with a high rate of Commission errors.
7. HRT Standard Deviation measures the consistency of the HRT throughout the test. A high score indicates inconsistency and may reflect a loss of attentiveness during some parts of the test.
8. Variability similarly measures speed consistency, but unlike HRT Standard Deviation, it assesses speed variations across the 18 sub-blocks. If the HRT Standard Deviation is poor and Variability is average, there was an overall speed inconsistency but no significant change across sub-blocks.
9. HRT Block Change measures the slope of HRT throughout the test. A positive slope, represented by a higher score, reflects a decrease in HRT speed as the test progressed, indicating a loss of sustained attention.
10. Omissions by Block and Commissions by Block are used to augment the HRT Block Change score as a measure of sustained attention, as increases in error rates at later blocks indicate a loss of sustained attention.
11. HRT Inter-Stimulus Interval Change measures changes in reaction times across 1-second, 2-second, and 4-second intervals, with a positive slope indicating an increased reaction time at longer intervals. A high score indicates that processing declined in longer intervals due to loss of vigilance. Changes across intervals can relate to the ability to adjust to task demands or the need for more stimulation to maintain arousal.
12. Omissions by ISI and Commissions by ISI are used to augment HRT Inter-Stimulus Interval Change as a measure of vigilance, as increases in error rates at longer intervals indicate a loss of vigilance.

References

Baggio, S., Hasler, R., Giacomini, V., El-Masri, H., Weibel, S., Perroud, N. et al. (2020). Does the continuous performance test predict ADHD symptoms severity and ADHD presentation in adults? Journal of Attention Disorders, 24(6): 840–848.

Burton, L., Pfaff, D., Bolt, N., Hadjikyriacou, D., Silton, N., Kilgallen, C. et al. (2010). Effects of gender and personality on the Conners Continuous Performance Test. Journal of Clinical & Experimental Neuropsychology, 32(1): 66–70. https://doi-org.ezproxylocal.library.nova.edu/10.1080/13803390902806568.

Celeste, P. M., Esteban, V. P., Mariana, L., María José, G. B., Florencia, B., Christy, E. et al. (2019). Continuous performance test in children with intellectual disability and attention deficit hyperactivity disorder. Applied Neuropsychology: Child, 8(3): 246–252. doi:https://doi.org/10.1080/21622965.2018.1434077.

Conners, K. (2014). Conners Continuous Performance Test 3rd Edition and Conners Continuous Auditory Test of Attention: Manual. Toronto, Ontario, Canada: Multi-Health Systems.

Epstein, J. N., Conners, C. K., Hervey, A. S., Tonev, S. T., Arnold, L. E., Abikoff, H. B. et al. (2006). MTA Cooperative Study Group. Assessing medication effects in the MTA study using neuropsychological outcomes. Journal of child psychology and psychiatry, and allied disciplines, 47(5): 446–456. https://doi.org/10.1111/j.1469-7610.2005.01469.x.

Estis, M. F. (2009). Effect of comorbidity on the performance of children with ADHD on the Conners' continuous performance test (Order No. 3471530). Available from Education Database; ProQuest Dissertations & Theses Global: Health & Medicine; ProQuest Dissertations & Theses Global: Social Sciences. (885866562).

Fasmer, O. B., Mjeldheim, K., Førland, W., Hansen, A. L., Syrstad, V. E. G., Oedegaard, K. J. et al. (2016). Linear and non-linear analyses of Conner's Continuous Performance Test-II discriminate adult patients with attention deficit hyperactivity disorder from patients with mood and anxiety disorders. BMC Psychiatry, 16: 1–10. https://doi-org.ezproxylocal.library.nova.edu/10.1186/s12888-016-0993-4.

Fuermaier, A., Tucha, L., Guo, N., Mette, C., Müller, B. W., Scherbaum, N. et al. (2022). It Takes Time: Vigilance and Sustained Attention Assessment in Adults with ADHD. International Journal of Environmental Research and Public Health, 19(9): 5216. https://doi.org/10.3390/ijerph19095216.

Gischlar, K. L., Dombrowski, S. and Mahdavi, J. N. (2017). Conners Continuous Performance Test 3rd Edition. The Twentieth Mental Measurements Yearbook.

Goulart, W., Harcourt, S., Horne, K. and Golden, C. (2018) Reliability between Conners CPT-3 and CATA. Archives of Clinical Neuropsychology, 33(6): 703–794. https://doi.org/10.1093/arclin/acy061.120.

Hall, C. L., Valentine, A. Z., Groom, M. J., Walker, G. M., Sayal, K., Daley, D. et al. (2016). The clinical utility of the continuous performance test and objective measures of activity for diagnosing and monitoring ADHD in children: a systematic review. European Child & Adolescent Psychiatry, 25(7): 677–699. https://doi.org/10.1007/s00787-015-0798-x.

Kljajić, M., Maltese, G., Tarnow, P., Sand, P. and Kölby, L. (2020). [Formula: see text] Sustained attention and vigilance of children treated for sagittal and metopic craniosynostosis. Child Neuropsychology: a Journal on Normal and Abnormal Development in Childhood and Adolescence, 26(4): 475–488. https://doi.org/10.1080/09297049.2019.1682130.

Lee, J. B., Kocherginsky, M. and Cherney, L. R. (2020). Attention in individuals with aphasia: Performance on the Conners' Continuous Performance Test - 2nd edition. Neuropsychological Rehabilitation, 30(2): 249–265.

López-Luengo, B., González-Andrade, A. and García-Cobo, M. (2016). Not all differences between patients with schizophrenia and healthy subjects are pathological: Performance on the conners' continuous performance test. Archives of Clinical Neuropsychology, 31(8): 983–995. Retrieved from https://ezproxylocal.library.nova.edu/login?url=https://www.proquest.com/scholarly-journals/not-all-differences-between-patients-with/docview/1909170958/se-2.

Lundervold, A. J. (2014). Conners' continuous performance test (CCPT-II) in children with ADHD/ODD, or a combined ADHD/ODD diagnosis. Child Neuropsychology, 20(1): 106–126. doi:https://doi.org/10.1080/09297049.2012.753997.

MacQueen, D.A., Minassian, A., Henry, B.L., Geyer, M.A., Young, J.W. and Perry, W. (2018). Amphetamine Modestly Improves Conners' Continuous Performance Test Performance in Healthy Adults. J Int Neuropsychol Soc. 2018 Mar; 24(3): 283–293. doi:10.1017/S135561771700090X. Epub 2017 Oct 16. PMID: 29032769; PMCID: PMC5820221.

Miranda, M. C., Sinnes, E. G., Pompéia, S. and Francisco Amodeo Bueno, O. (2008). A comparative study of performance in the Conners' Continuous Performance Test between Brazilian and North American children. Journal of Attention Disorders, 11(5): 588–598. https://doi.org/10.1177/1087054707299412.

Munkvold, L. H., Manger, T. and Lundervold, A. J. (2014). Conners' continuous performance test (CCPT-II) in children with ADHD/ODD, or a combined ADHD/ODD diagnosis. Child Neuropsychology, 20(1): 106–126. https://doi.org/10.1080/09297049.2012.753997.

Ni, H. C., Hwang Gu, S. L., Lin, H. Y., Lin, Y. J., Yang, L. K., Huang, H. C. et (2016). Atomoxetine could improve intra-individual variability in drug-naïve adults with attention-deficit/hyperactivity disorder comparably with methylphenidate: A head-to-head randomized clinical trial. Journal of Psychopharmacology (Oxford, England), 30(5): 459–467. https://doi.org/10.1177/0269881116632377.

Ord, A. S., Miskey, H. M., Lad, S., Richter, B., Nagy, K. and Shura, R. D. (2021). Examining embedded validity indicators in conners continuous performance test-3 (CPT-3). The Clinical Neuropsychologist, 35(8): 1426–1441. doi:https://doi.org/10.1080/13854046.2020.175130.

Pettersson, R., Söderström, S. and Nilsson, K. W. (2018). Diagnosing ADHD in Adults: An Examination of the Discriminative Validity of Neuropsychological Tests and Diagnostic Assessment Instruments. Journal of Attention Disorders, 22(11): 1019–1031. https://doi.org.ezproxylocal.library.nova.edu/10.1177/1087054715618788.

Scimeca, L. M., Holbrook, L., Rhoads, T., Cerny, B. M., Jennette, K. J., Resch, Z. J. et al. (2021). Examining conners continuous performance test-3 (CPT-3) embedded performance validity indicators in an adult clinical sample referred for ADHD evaluation. Developmental Neuropsychology, 46(5): 347–359. doi:https://doi.org/10.1080/87565641.2021.1951270.

Shaked, D., Faulkner, L. M. D., Tolle, K., Wendell, C. R., Waldstein, S. R. and Spencer, R. J. (2020). Reliability and validity of the conners' continuous performance test. Applied Neuropsychology: Adult, 27(5): 478–487. doi:https://doi.org/10.1080/23279095.2019.1570199.

Stern, M. and Shura, R. (2019). A-10 Conners Continuous Performance Test-3 in the Evaluation of ADHD Among Veterans. Archives of Clinical Neuropsychology, 34(6): 869–869.

Wang, L.-J., Lee, S.-Y., Tsai, C.-S., Lee, M.-J., Chou, M.-C., Kuo, H.-C. et al. (2021). Validity of Visual and Auditory Attention Tests for Detecting ADHD. Journal of Attention Disorders, 25(8): 1160–1169. https://doi.org/10.1177/1087054719887433.

Zane, K. L., Gfeller, J. D., Roskos, P. T. and Bucholz, R. D. (2016). The clinical utility of the conners' continuous performance test-II in traumatic brain injury. Archives of Clinical Neuropsychology, 31(8): 996–1005.

CHAPTER 7

Digit Span

*Claire Stafford** and *Ryan Bennett*

The Digit Span Subtest is a cognitive assessment tool that is part of the Weschler Adult Intelligence Test (WAIS) and Weschler Intelligence Scale for Children (WISC). It is designed to measure a person's working memory, which is the ability to hold and manipulate information in the mind for a brief period. In the Digit Span Subtest, a series of numbers are orally presented to the patient at one-second intervals. Depending on the Digit Span subtype, the patient is then asked to recall as many digits as possible in a specified order. The Digit Span Forward (DSF) subtype asks the patient to recall the numbers in the same order as presented.

In contrast, the Digit Span Backward (DSB) subtype requires the patient to recall the numbers in reverse order. The Digit Span Sequencing (DSS) subtype, added in the WAIS-IV and WISC-V, asks the patient to recall the numbers in ascending order (from lowest to highest). The Digit Span Subtest is useful in assessing a person's cognitive abilities and can provide insights into working memory capacity and deficits. It can be used to identify learning disabilities, attention deficit hyperactivity disorder (ADHD), and other neurological disorders.

History and Normed Population

The Digit Span Subtest has a long history and has been an essential component of the Weschler Intelligence Scales since its inception. The first version of the test, known as the Wechsler-Bellevue Intelligence Scale, was published in 1939 by David Wechsler. The original Digit Span test included only the Forward and Backward subtypes. Over the years, the test has undergone several revisions and updates. Most recently, the Digit Span Subtest underwent several changes when the WAIS-IV was released 2008. One significant change was the addition of the Digit Span Sequencing (DSS) subtype, which asks the patient to recall the numbers in ascending order.

Nova Southeastern University, Fort Lauderdale, Florida, USA.
Email: rb1934@mynsu.nova.edu
* Corresponding author: cs3374@mynsu.nova.edu

Additionally, rhyming between sequential digits was eliminated, and the Backward subtest no longer included three-digit sample trials. Instead, all sample trials consisted of two digits. In order to create a better floor, the Backward subtest was modified to include two sample trials and six trials, each two digits in length. It was also emphasized that all trials should be administered to assess the varying difficulty levels. The Weschler Intelligence Scale for Children (WISC) also underwent changes following the release of the WISC-V in 2014. Similar to the WAIS-IV, changes were made to the Digit Span Subtest, including the addition of the DSS subtype, trials to DSF ceiling items, and gradient items. These changes were designed to improve the accuracy and reliability of the test.

Overall, the Digit Span Subtest has been an essential tool in measuring cognitive abilities for many years. Its various subtypes provide valuable information about a person's working memory and can help identify cognitive deficits in clinical and research settings. The changes made over the years have been aimed at improving the test's accuracy and ensuring that it remains a reliable and valid tool for assessing cognitive abilities.

The normative information for WISC-V Digit Span scores is based on a national sample (N = 2,200) collected from April 2013 to March 2014 (Wechsler 2014). The sample was said to represent U.S. English-speaking children ages 6 to 16 years and 11 months (6:0 to 6:11) based on 2012 data collected by the U.S. Bureau of the Census. The sample was divided into 11 age groups, with 200 children in each group. In order to ensure that the sample was representative, an equal number of male and female participants were placed in each age group. Additionally, the proportions of racial groups in the sample were based on the English-speaking racial proportions of children within the corresponding age group of the U.S. population. This helped ensure that the sample reflected the racial diversity of children in the U.S. within each age group. The normative sample was further stratified according to five education levels based on the years of school completed by the parent(s) and geographic location.

The normative information for the WAIS-IV Digit Span Subtest is based on a national sample (N = 2,200) representative of the U.S. English-speaking population of individuals ages 16 to 90 and 11 months (Wechsler 2008). The normative data was divided into 13 age groups with an equal number of males and females in each group (except for the five older age groups, 65:0 to 90:11). The proportions of racial groups within each age group were based on the English-speaking racial proportions of adults in the United States, ensuring that the sample was representative of the broader population. In addition, the normative sample was stratified according to five education levels based on the number of years completed.

Test Procedures

Digit Span consists of three components: Digit Span Forward, Digit Span Backward, and Digit Span Sequencing. During the administration of Digit Span Forward, participants are given a string of numbers (i.e., "5, 9, 4") that they are asked to repeat back in the same order that the examiner presented them ("5, 9, 4"). During the administration of Digit Span Backward and Sequencing, a string of numbers is read aloud to the examinee similarly ("5, 9, 4"), but the examinee is asked to respond differently. In Digit Span Backward, the examinee is asked to repeat the numbers in the reverse order of that presented by the examiner ("4, 9, 5"). In Digit Span Sequencing, the examinee is asked to order the numbers sequentially and say them back to the examiner ("4, 5, 9").

Task Demands and Strategies

The Digit Span Subtest evaluates various cognitive processes, including auditory processing, auditory discrimination, attention, and sustained effort. As previously mentioned, the subtest includes three subtypes: Digit Span Forward (DSF), Digit Span Backward (DSB), and Digit Span Sequencing (DSS). DSF measures the individual's ability to hold a sequence of digits in their working memory. DSB assesses the ability to manipulate information within working memory, which can be affected by procedural learning. DSS evaluates the mental manipulation of digits in ascending order. Examinees may use various strategies to complete the Digit Span tasks. Chunking, or memory re-coding, allows patients to remember shorter segments of a sequence to maximize their working memory. However, the examiner can negate chunking strategies by presenting the numbers with a constant pitch. Patients may also use articulatory rehearsal or finger movements, which involve repetitive sequencing of information until it is stored in their working memory. Research has found no significant differences in performance on working memory tasks between verbalization and visualization strategies. However, studies have shown that inhibiting articulation or finger movement can decrease Digit Span Subtest performance.

Item Difficulty

As the subtests progress, the length of the strings of numbers increases, subsequentially increasing test difficulty. Some studies have suggested that DSF and DSB scores should be interpreted differently. This research did not support this, as measurement invariance was reported in 127 heterogeneous neuroscience patients (Bowden et al. 2012). Current literature suggests DSB is more difficult than DSF, as supported by lower average raw scores (Wells et al. 2018). Strong associations were found between easy and harder items and Forward and Backward items on the subtest (Bowden et al. 2012). These findings suggest that clinicians should not interpret DSF and DSB differently. Other studies have suggested that DSB, independently, is a better indicator of attention processes (Hale et al. 2002). Overall, the findings suggest that the Digit Span Subtest is useful for assessing working memory and attention processes, and clinicians should interpret DSF and DSB scores together.

Scoring

The Digit Span Subtest includes items that can be scored as either "0" or "1." A score of "0" indicates an incorrect response, while a score of "1" indicates a correct response. If a participant scores "0" on both trials of an item, the test is discontinued. In order to evaluate the overall performance, process scores are calculated for each Digit Span subtype, including Digit Span Forward, Digit Span Backward, and Digit Span Sequencing. Process scores are obtained by summing the scores for all the items within a subtype. Additionally, discrepancy comparison scores are determined by the longest successfully recalled string of numbers (score of 1). Overall process scores and discrepancy comparison scores are calculated to evaluate the participant's performance, and all three parts of the subtest are necessary to calculate the WMI and FSIQ scores.

Reliability

The WAIS-IV technical manual reported a mean internal consistency reliability of 0.93 for the Digit Span subscale scores based on a normative sample (N = 2,200). These tasks measure what they are supposed to measure with 93% accuracy. Test-retest reliability has been found to be consistent over time for adults (approximately 0.70 to 0.080) while less reliable for children (approximately 0.56) (Turley-Ames and Whitfield 2003; Hitch et al. 2001). However, the reported reliability is based on a stratified coefficient known as Mosier's reliability (Mosier 1943). Mosier's reliability is a way of determining internal consistency reliability that combines multiple sources of true score variance. In this case, these sources are based on the sum of the three-digit Span scores.

As a result, Wechsler's reported reliability may not be equal to the actual reliability of the three independent Digit Span subtests, ultimately threatening score interpretations. Alternatively, when using an omega hierarchical coefficient, the internal consistency validity was estimated to be 0.74 (Gignac et al. 2017). This number is considerably lower than that reported by Wechsler (0.93). When excluding Digit Span Sequencing, the internal consistency reliability is reduced (0.64), suggesting that the addition of Digit Span Sequencing in WAIS-IV increased the internal consistency reliability of the measure (Gignac et al. 2017). Reduced reliability also results from the all-or-nothing scoring technique unique to Digit Span. Partial scoring, or credit for the total number of stimuli correct, could increase test reliability by providing a greater variety of scores and identifying more specific individual differences (Conway et al. 2005).

Several demographic variables are associated with Digit Span. Age, years of education, and, more variably, gender are among these variables. There is an established relationship between older age and poorer performance on tests involving working memory (GrÉgoire and van der Linden 1997). This relationship is most starkly observed in patients following age 65. There are mixed findings regarding the interaction between age and type of Digit Span (e.g., Forward or Backward) (Babcock and Salthouse 1990; GrÉgoire and van der Linden 1997). Literature suggests that, unlike DSF metrics, DSB metrics are significantly negatively correlated with age (Woods et al. 2010). Both DSF and DSB yielded significant positive correlations with education (Woods et al., 2010). In an educationally diverse older adult population (n = 784), older age, lower education levels, and female gender were found to be significantly associated with poorer performance on Digit Span (Choi et al., 2014). Along with these associations, significant interactions between the female gender and lower education levels via fewer opportunities should be noted.

Validity

Reliable Digit Span (RDS) is an embedded PVT component of the Digit Span Subtest. RDS is determined by the sum of the longest string of digits accomplished in which both trials were passed in DSF and DSB. This PVT is designed to evaluate effort and possible malingering.

Overall, Digit Span has been found to be a relatively weak indicator of attention compared to other similar tests. Tests, such as Picture Completion, have been found to account for more of the variance in performance on tests of attention (e.g., the Test of Everyday Attention) (Groth-Marnat and Baker 2003).

Clinical Applications in Research

Studies have found that children with ADHD do not perform significantly worse on DSB versus DSF, suggesting that DSB has poor diagnostic validity regarding identifying deficits in working memory tasks with high executive processing demands (Wells et al. 2017). Researchers have proposed that this shortfall may be due to the inability of children with ADHD to reach Digit Span list lengths that surpass those testing short-term memory. Remedies may include the use of partial scoring and the administration of higher list lengths (Wells et al. 2017).

Interpretations

Interpreting the results of the Digit Span Subtest involves considering the participant's performance on each subtype, as well as their overall performance on the subtest. The results can be used to assess the participant' working memory capacity and cognitive abilities. Low scores may suggest deficits in attention, concentration, or working memory, while high scores may indicate strong cognitive abilities in these areas. The scores can also be compared to age- and gender-matched norms to determine if the participant's performance is within the expected range. Additionally, the Digit Span Subtest calculates the working memory index (WMI) score and the full-scale intelligence quotient (FSIQ). These scores provide a broader assessment of cognitive abilities and can be used to identify potential learning disabilities, intellectual strengths or weaknesses, or other neurological disorders. Possible interpretations of scores include:

1. The overall performance on the Digit Span Subtest can be reduced by disruptions of working memory, attention, emotional disorders, and other psychological diagnoses such as anxiety and/or depression. Therefore, one's performance must be compared against measures or observations of current emotional and behavioral functioning prior to making a neuropsychological interpretation.

2. Injury or lesions to the left frontal, temporal, and/or parietal lobes that result in aphasia may drastically affect one's performance and ability to complete the Digit Span Subtest.
3. If an examinee scores higher on DSF than on DSB or DSS, it may suggest that they have sufficient working memory capacity but have not yet acquired the skill of mentally reversing numbers. Alternatively, it could indicate that they have difficulty with mental manipulation or organization of newly learned information.
4. A difference between DSF and DSB that is zero or negative (DSB > DSF) may indicate poor motivation or malingering.
5. Learning effects are evident in both DSF and DSB (Woods et al. 2010). These effects should be considered when cognitive abilities are retested using Digit Span.
6. If Digit Span Forward and Backward are performed in a normal fashion, deficits on the Sequencing Task may indicate frontal lobe disruption.

References

Babcock, R. L. and Salthouse, T. A. (1990). Effects of increased processing demands on age differences in working memory. Psychology and Aging, 5: 421–428.

Bowden, S. C., Petrauskas, V. M., Bardenhagen, F. J., Meade, C. E. and Simpson, L. C. (2013). Exploring the dimensionality of digit span. Assessment, 20(2): 188–198.

Choi, H. J., Lee, D. Y., Seo, E. H., Jo, M. K., Sohn, B. K., Choe, Y. M. et al. (2014). A normative study of the digit span in an educationally diverse elderly population. Psychiatry investigation, 11(1): 39.

de Paula, J. J., Malloy-Diniz, L. F. and Romano-Silva, M. A. (2016). Reliability of working memory assessment in neurocognitive disorders: a study of the Digit Span and Corsi Block-Tapping tasks. Brazilian Journal of Psychiatry, 38: 262–263.

Egner, L. E., Sütterlin, S. and Lugo, R. G. (2016). Prevalence of two-syllable digits affecting forward digit span test score: A potential reliability factor in digit span tests and new light to the word length effect. SAGE Open, 6(4): 2158244016681825.

Gignac, G. E., Reynolds, M. R. and Kovacs, K. (2019). Digit Span subscale scores may be insufficiently reliable for clinical interpretation: distinguishing between stratified coefficient alpha and omega hierarchical. Assessment, 26(8): 1554–1563.

Groth-Marnat, G. and Baker, S. (2003). Digit span as a measure of everyday attention: a study of ecological validity. Perceptual and Motor Skills, 97(3_suppl): 1209–1218.

Hale, J. B., Hoeppner, J. A. B. and Fiorello, C. A. (2002). Analyzing digit span components for assessment of attention processes. Journal of Psychoeducational Assessment, 20(2): 128–143.

Hilbert, S., Nakagawa, T. T., Puci, P., Zech, A. and Bühner, M. (2014). The digit span backwards task. European Journal of Psychological Assessment.

Hitch, G. J., Towse, J. N. and Hutton, U. (2001). What limits children's working memory span? theoretical accounts and applications for scholastic development. Journal of Experimental Psychology: General, 130(2): 184–198. https://doi.org/10.1037/0096-3445.130.2.184.

Hull, T. and Mason, H. (1995). Performance of blind children on digit-span tests. Journal of Visual Impairment & Blindness, 89(2): 166–169.

Mosier, C. I. (1943). On the reliability of a weighted composite. Psychometrika, 8(3): 161–168.

Reisberg, D., Rappaport, I. and O'Shaughnessy, M. (1984). Limits of working memory: The digit digit-span. Journal of Experimental Psychology: Learning, Memory, and Cognition, 10(2): 203.

Thursina, C. C. (2017). Reliability and validity of backward digit span for elementary school students attention deficit screening at Yogyakarta. Journal of the Neurological Sciences, 381: 189.

Turley-Ames, K. J., & Whitfield, M. M. (2003). Strategy training and working memory task performance. Journal of memory and language, 49(4): 446–468.

Wells, E. L., Kofler, M. J., Soto, E. F., Schaefer, H. S. and Sarver, D. E. (2018). Assessing working memory in children with ADHD: Minor administration and scoring changes may improve digit span backward's construct validity. Research in Developmental Disabilities, 72: 166–178.

Wechsler, D. (2008). Wechsler Adult Intelligence Scale Wais-Iv; Technical and Interpretive Manual. Pearson.

Wechsler, D. (2014). Wisc-V: Technical and Interpretive Manual. NCS Pearson, Inc.

Woods, D. L., Kishiyama, M. M., Yund, E. W., Herron, T. J., Edwards, B., Poliva, O. et al. (2011). Improving digit span assessment of short-term verbal memory. Journal of Clinical and Experimental Neuropsychology, 33(1): 101–111.

CHAPTER 8

Feifer Assessment of Reading

Claire Stafford

The Feifer Assessment of Reading (FAR) assesses a variety of mental processes underlying reading skills. The purpose of this assessment is to evaluate an individual's academic achievement in reading. The full FAR battery includes 15 subtests. The 15 subtests are as follows: Phonemic Awareness, Nonsense Word Decoding, Isolated Word Reading Fluency, Oral Reading Fluency, Positioning Sounds, Rapid Automatic Naming, Verbal Fluency, Visual Perception, Irregular Word Reading Fluency, Orthographical Processing Semantic Concepts, Word Recall, Print Knowledge, Morphological Processing, and Silent Reading Fluency.

Normed Population

The FAR is normed for ages 4 through 21. The battery was standardized on a nationally representative sample from the 2012 U.S. Census, consisting of 1,074 examinees from Pre-K to college, collected from more than 30 states (Feifer and Nader 2015). Grade-based norms are provided to allow clinicians to compare examinees to same-grade peers or grade-level curricula.

Reliability

Regarding internal consistency, all subtest median alpha coefficients were greater than 0.80, apart from Word Recall and Silent Reading Fluency: Comprehension (Feifer and Nader 2015). Alpha coefficients for the indices varied from 0.88 to 0.98. Test-retest reliability correlations ranged from 0.66 to 0.80 (Feifer and Nader 2015). Word recall (r = 0.66) was at the lower end of this range.

Nova Southeastern University, Fort Lauderdale, Florida, USA.
Email: cs3374@mynsu.nova.edu

Validity

In a comparison between the FAR and similar tests, such as the Process Assessment of the Learner – Second Edition: Diagnostic Assessment for Reading and Writing (PAL-II RW), Gray Silent Reading Tests (GSRT), and the Gray Oral Reading Tests, Fifth Edition (GORT-5), strong correlations were found between the FAR and the Phonological Coding Composite with Isolated Word Reading (r = 0.82), Orthographical Coding Composite with Isolated Word Reading (r = 0.70), and Irregular Word Reading (r = 0.76) and Semantic Concepts (r = 0.76) (Mulchay et al. 2022).

Test Procedures

The FAR can be administered as a paper and pencil measure or electronic tablet. While the full FAR battery includes 15 subtests, these subtests are not necessarily administered to every examinee. Phonemic Awareness includes sections labeled "Rhyming," "Blending," "Segmenting," and "Manipulation." In the Rhyming section, the examiner asks the examinee whether two words sound different (e.g., "apple and table") or the same ("nose and rose"). In the Blending section, the examiner asks the examinee to put parts of words together to make a full word (e.g., "cup and cake," to which the correct response would be "cupcake"). In the Segmenting section, the examiner says a word to the examinee and asks the examinee to tap the table for each part they hear (e.g., "railroad" would constitute two taps). In the Manipulation section, a word is presented to the examinee. They are asked to manipulate the word in some way and produce the new word (e.g., "Say spin without the /s/ sound," to which the examinee should say "pin"). In the Rapid Automatic Naming subtest, the examinee is asked to name a collection of pictures as quickly as possible.

The Semantic Concepts subtest is made up of two parts: Synonyms and Antonyms. In Synonyms, the examiner gives the examinee a word and asks them to provide a word with the same meaning. In Antonyms, the examiner gives the examinee a word and asks them to provide a word with a different meaning. In the Word Recall subtest, the examiner orally presents a list of words to the examinee and asks the examinee to recall as many words as they can in any given order. In the Verbal Fluency subtest, the examiner asks the examinee to tell them as many items that fit in a certain category (e.g., types of animals) as possible. In the Nonsense Word Decoding subtest, the examiner asks the examinee to pronounce words that are not real words. In the Isolated Word Reading subtest, the examinee is presented with a word list and asked to read the words aloud as quickly as possible. Sixty seconds are allotted for this task. During the Oral Reading Fluency subtest, the examinee is asked to read a given story out loud as quickly as they can. Sixty seconds are allotted for this task.

The Print Knowledge subtest is only administered to prekindergarten through first-grade examinees. During this subtest, the examiner reads item-specific prompts within a storybook. In the Visual Perception subtest, the examiner asks the examinee to draw a line through any letters that are written backward. The examinee is given an assortment of letters and asked to do as many as they can within the 30-second time constraint. Irregular Fluency is only administered to examinees in second grade or above. During this subtest, the examinee is asked to read a collection of words out loud as quickly as possible. The examiner stops the subtest after 60 seconds. During the Orthographical Processing subtest, the examiner uses a stimulus book to show the examinee a word. The examiner asks the examinee to remember the word. After one second, the examiner flips the page and exposes an assortment of letters. The examinee is asked to identify which letter was in the word they saw on the previous page.

During the Positioning Sounds subtest, the examiner uses a stimulus book and says a word (e.g., doll). Then, the examiner points to two phonemes (e.g., "/d/" and "/ll/"). The examinee is asked what sound is missing from the initial word that was given (e.g., "/o/"). In the Morphological Processing subtest, the examiner uses a stimulus book to present the examinee with an incomplete word. Then, the examinee is asked to choose the group of letters that best completes the word. During the Silent Reading Fluency subtest, the examiner exposes the stimulus book to the examinee and asks them to read the first story to themselves. After 60 seconds, the examiner asks the examinee to stop reading and circle the last word they read. Then, the examiner flips the page to expose questions about the story. The examiner asks the examinee to read these stories to themselves and verbally answer them. The process is repeated for the second story as well.

Variations within the test administration are subject to the clinician's discretion. Eight subtests are administered to students prior to kindergarten (Pre-K), 11 subtests to examinees in kindergarten and first grade, and 14 subtests to students in second grade and above. Test administration takes about 35 minutes for examinees below kindergarten, 60 minutes for kindergarten and first grade, and 75 minutes for second grade and above.

Scoring

Computerized scoring can be done via PARiConnect, the FAR's online assessment platform. The Phonemic Awareness Rhyming subtest score is the sum of the number of correct responses. Within the subtest, correct responses are scored 1 point, and incorrect responses are scored 0 points. All pre-basal items should be marked correctly. The Phonemic Awareness Blending subtest score is the sum of the number of correct responses. Within the subtest, correct responses are scored 1 point, and incorrect responses are scored 0 points. In the number of syllables column, the number should reflect the greatest number of syllables corresponding to a correct word. All self-corrections should be scored as correct. The Phonemic Awareness Segmenting subtest score is the sum of the number of correct responses. Within the subtest, correct responses are scored 1 point, and incorrect responses are scored 0 points. Correct responses should include the correct number of taps associated with the correct syllable. If the tap does not occur simultaneously with the verbal response, the response should be marked as incorrect. All self-corrections and pre-basal items should be scored as correct. The number of correct taps is determined using the greatest number of taps associated with a correct response. The Phonemic Awareness Manipulation subtest score is the sum of the number of correct responses.

Within the subtest, correct responses are scored 1 point, and incorrect responses are scored 0 points. All self-corrections and pre-basal items should be scored as correct.

The Rapid Automatic Naming subtest total score is the sum of the Trial 1 and 2 subtotals. The subtotals are the sum of the examinee's correct and incorrect responses. Any items incorrectly named or skipped should be counted as incorrect. Self-corrections should be counted as correct. The Semantic Concepts Synonyms and Antonym subtest scores are the sum of each subtest's correct responses. Correct responses are scored 1 point within the subtests, and incorrect responses are scored 0 points. All self-corrections and pre-basal items should be scored as correct. The item should be counted as incorrect if the examinee does not respond within 10 seconds. The Semantic Concepts subtest score is calculated by adding the Synonym and Antonym sub-scores.

The Word Recall sub-score is the sum of words correctly recalled. The number of repetitions and intrusions should be recorded as well. The Word Recall total score is the sum of the Trial 1 and 2 sub-scores. For the Verbal Fluency subtest, the number of correct and incorrect responses for each trial should be recorded. Correct responses are scored either 0, 1, 2, or 3 in accordance with the Verbal Fluency Scoring Guidelines. Scores of 0 are assigned for incorrect responses. Trials 1 and 2 of the subtest should be added together to calculate the Verbal Fluency subtotal. The Nonsense Word Decoding subtest score is the sum of the number of correct responses. Within the subtest, correct responses are scored 1 point, and incorrect responses are scored 0 points. All self-corrected items should be marked as correct. Responses must be stated fluently to be scored as correct. The number of words read correctly and the total time should be recorded for the Oral Reading Fluency subtest. To calculate the Oral Reading Fluency subtest score, divide the total number of words read correctly by the total time.

The Print Knowledge subtest score can be calculated by adding the number of correct responses. Correct responses are scored as 1 point, and incorrect responses are scored as 0 points in accordance with the provided item-specific scoring criteria. Self-corrections should be marked as correct. Correct targets and non-target errors should be recorded for the Visual Perception subtest. If the Words task was administered, add the correct number of targets for pages B and C and record this as the Visual Perception subtotal. The Irregular Word Reading Fluency subtest score can be calculated by adding the number of correct responses. Correct responses are scored as 1 point, and incorrect responses are scored as 0 points. Self-corrections should be marked as correct. The Orthographical Processing subtest score can be calculated by adding the number of correct responses. Correct responses are scored as 1 point, and incorrect responses are scored as 0 points. Self-corrections and pre-basal items should be marked as correct. The Positioning Sounds subtest score can be calculated by adding the number of correct responses. Correct responses are scored as 1 point, and incorrect responses are scored as 0 points. If the examinee provides the missing letters instead of the missing sounds, their response should be marked incorrect. Self-corrections and pre-basal items should be marked as correct. The Morphological Processing subtest score can be calculated by adding the number of correct responses. Correct responses are scored as 1 point, and incorrect responses are scored as 0 points. If the examinee provides the missing letters instead of the missing sounds, their response should be marked incorrect. Self-corrections and pre-basal items should be marked as correct.

For the Silent Reading Fluency subtest, the number of words read in 60 seconds for each story should be individually recorded. The comprehension scores can be calculated by adding the 0, 1, or 2-point responses for each story. These point totals should be determined using the corresponding table in the FAR manual. These individual subtotals are added together to calculate the Silent Reading Fluency Comprehension score. Silent Reading Fluency Rate can be calculated by dividing the total number of words read correctly by the total time.

The FAR yields five index measures: Phonological Index, Fluency Index, Comprehension Index, Mixed Index, and FAR Total Index. The results of certain groupings of subtests are used to calculate these indices. The Phonological Index is the sum of Phonemic Awareness, Nonsense Word Decoding, Isolated Word Reading Fluency, Oral Reading Fluency, and Positioning Sounds. The Fluency Index is the sum of Rapid Automatic Naming, Verbal Fluency, Visual Perception, Irregular Word Reading Fluency, and Orthographical Processing. The Comprehension Index is the sum of Semantic Concepts, Word Recall, Print Knowledge, Morphological Processing, and Silent Reading Fluency. The Mixed Index is comprised of the Phonological Index and Fluency Index scores. The FAR Total Index is made up of all scores. It should be noted that the Silent Reading Fluency subtest is not a part of scoring for any of the indices. Corresponding grade-based norms, grade equivalents for subtest scores, confidence intervals, percentile ranks, z-scores, and normal curve equivalents are provided for index scores.

Item Difficulty and Types of Errors

During the Isolated Word Reading Fluency subtest, items increase in difficulty.

Task Demands and Strategies

Phonemic Awareness assesses the examinee's ability to focus on and manipulate individual sounds, or phonemes, in spoken words. Nonsense Word Decoding assesses whether the examinee can use their knowledge of phonetic principles to sound out and read words aloud. Isolated Word Reading Fluency evaluates how quickly and easily the examinee can blend sounds. Oral Reading Fluency assesses how well the examinee can decode words embedded within the context of a story. Positioning Sounds requires the examinee to utilize phonemic localization skills. Rapid Automatic Naming requires attention, retrieval, visual tracking, and information processing skills. Verbal Fluency measures the ability of the examinee to retrieve words when given specific categories. Visual Perception evaluates the examinee's orthographic perception. Irregular Word Reading Fluency assesses how well the examinee can recognize text to identify words. Orthographical Processing Semantic Concepts task measures the ability of the examinee to hold and retain a visual-spatial image of the printed word form. Word Recall examines how well the examinee can organize verbal information to facilitate retrieval. Print Knowledge assesses the examinee's preliteracy skills. Morphological Processing evaluates the examinee's understanding of word meaning as well as vocabulary development. Silent Reading Fluency assesses attention and working memory.

Clinical Applications in Research

The FAR seeks to identify and evaluate four subtypes of dyslexia, including dysphonetic dyslexia, surface dyslexia, mixed dyslexia, and reading comprehension deficits. Dysphonetic dyslexia results in the examinee's inability to grasp the connection between letters and sounds (Feifer and Nader 2015). In contrast, examinees with surface dyslexia may have difficulty sounding out and recognizing words (Feifer and Nader 2015). When deficits in all these skills are present, this is referred to as mixed dyslexia (Feifer and Nader 2015). Additionally, reading comprehension deficits can be described as examinees who can read but have difficulty understanding the content of what they are reading.

Interpretation

1. Low scores on the Phonological Index may suggest phonological dyslexia. Phonological dyslexia is characterized by difficulty remembering, understanding, and piecing word sounds together.
2. Low scores on the Fluency Index may suggest surface dyslexia. Surface dyslexia is characterized by the inability to read words with letters that do not correspond with their typical associated sounds (e.g., an individual with surface dyslexia would have difficulties reading the word "out").
3. Low scores on the Comprehension Index may suggest reading comprehension deficits.
4. Low scores on the Mixed Index (a combination of phonological and surface dyslexia [as described above]) may suggest mixed dyslexia.
5. Low Phonological Awareness scores may suggest inefficient neural mapping between letters and sounds (Noble and McCandliss 2005).
6. Low Phonological Awareness Rhyming scores may suggest a hearing acuity issue or a hearing system that is particularly sensitive to sound (Giella 2019).
7. Poor performance on the Rapid Automatic Naming subtest may suggest difficulty recognizing text orthography or the norms of the writing system (e.g., spelling and punctuation) (Frijters et al. 2001).
8. Poor performance on the Rapid Automatic Naming subtest may suggest deficits in attention (Giella 2019).
9. Poor performance in the first section of Visual Fluency but not the second section suggests that the examinee may not respond as well to semantic cues (i.e., cues that take into account the meaning of words surrounding the target word) as letter cues (Giella 2019). In contrast, poor performance in the second section of Visual Fluency but not the first section suggests that the examinee may not respond as well to letter cues as semantic cues (Giella 2019).
10. Higher scores on Isolated Word Reading compared to Oral Reading Fluency could suggest that reading the words in stories may make pronunciation difficult for the examinee. Higher scores on Oral Reading Fluency in comparison to

Isolated Word Reading could suggest that the examinee relies on the context provided by the stories to identify words (Giella 2019).

11. If the Isolated Reading Fluency Rate is much higher than that of Irregular Word Reading Fluency, the examinee likely can phonetically put together familiar words; however, if the Irregular Word Reading Fluency Rate is much higher than that of Isolated Reading Fluency, the examinee may rely more on the visual representation of the letters to identify them (Giella 2019).
12. Difficulty with Silent Reading Fluency Comprehension questions may indicate that the examinee has underdeveloped attentional skills or low executive function (Giella 2019).
13. Low scores on Semantic Concepts may indicate poor vocabulary development (Giella 2019).
14. Low scores on Word Recall may suggest lower executive functioning (Giella 2019).

References

Feifer, S. G. and Nader, R. G. (2015). Feifer Assessment of Reading. Lutz, FL: Psychological Assessment Resources.

Frijters, J. C., Lovett, M. W., Steinbach, K. A., Wolf, M., Sevcik, R. A. and Morris, R. D. (2011). Neurocognitive predictors of reading outcomes for children with reading disabilities. Journal of Learning Disabilities, 44: 150–166.

Giella, A. K. (2019). Utilizing skills, error, and behavior analyses with the Feifer Assessment of Reading (FAR) and the Feifer Assessment of Math (FAM): Hidden gems that bring detailed strengths and weaknesses to light (white paper). Lutz, FL: PAR.

Mulchay, C., Wolff, M., Ward, J. et al. (2022). Test Review of the Feifer Assessment of Reading (FAR). J Pediatr Neuropsychol. https://doi.org/10.1007/s40817-022-00125-1.

Noble, K. G., & McCandliss, B. D. (2005). Reading development and impairment: behavioral, social, and neurobiological factors. Journal of Developmental & Behavioral Pediatrics, 26(5): 370–378.

CHAPTER 9

Finger Tapping Test (FTT)

Kriselli Castro

The Halstead-Reitan Finger Tapping Test, also known as the Finger Oscillation Test, is an assessment that measures psychomotor speed and motor function. Part of the Halstead-Reitan Neuropsychological Test Battery, it is considered a good tool for detecting motor and cognitive impairments, cerebral lesions, and cerebral lateralization (Strauss et al. 2006). It can be used as a standalone test to assess for manual dexterity or as part of a bigger comprehensive test to evaluate patients with Parkinson's disease, Alzheimer's disease, and Korsakoff syndrome, among others. While the Finger Tapping Test is a relatively simple measure, it can provide useful information in a range of clinical contexts. However, like any test, it should be used with other assessments and information to form a comprehensive understanding of an individual's cognitive and motor functioning.

Normed Population

The original normative data for the FTT was provided by Halstead, derived from a small sample of 29 subjects. However, given the small size of this sample, later researchers provided more extensive normative data based on larger and more representative samples. Heaton, Grant, and Matthews (1991) provided one of the most influential sets of norms. Their normative data, also known as Heaton Norms, were based on a more robust sample of 500 healthy adults. Developing these norms involved several steps to adjust for demographic variables. Raw scores from the sample were turned into scaled scores with a mean of 10 and a standard deviation of 3. Then, demographically corrected T-scores were predicted from the scaled scores, which were turned into residual scores by subtracting a participant's actual score from the predicted score. The residual scores were divided by the standard error of estimate and converted to T-scores. The Heaton Norms take into consideration age,

Nova Southeastern University, Fort Lauderdale, Florida, USA.
Email: kc2322@mynsu.nova.edu

education, and sex, allowing a more individualized interpretation of the test results. However, like any normative data, they should be used judiciously, considering the specific characteristics and context of the individual being tested.

Reliability

Reliability coefficients range from .58 to .93 for both normal and patient samples (Strauss et al. 2006). However, Matarazzo et al. (1974) found values as low as <.50 in both normal patients and patients with cerebrovascular disease who were retested after 3–5 months. This suggests that for some individuals, the FTT results may vary significantly over time, even when their neurological status is stable. In terms of consistency between hands, some research found consistent results, r = >.70, while others found the differences as unreliable, r = .50. Practice effect is minimal in both healthy and impaired populations (Strauss et al. 2006).

Validity

When considering between-hand asymmetry, finger tapping correlates highly in normal adults with Purdue peg placement (.78). This suggests both tasks depend on a common neural substrate, likely asymmetry in the corticospinal system. However, the correlation is lower between finger tapping and grip strength asymmetry (.41) (Strauss et al. 2006). Finger tapping moderately correlates (r = .46 to .51) with the Perceptual Organization factor of the WAIS-R, suggesting visual processing is important (Strauss et al. 2006). A small correlation (.25) was found with the Processing Speed Index in the WAIS-III, suggesting finger tapping involves a small amount of the same resources required in more complex measures in perceptual processing speed tasks. Although FTT's performance validity is often set on a binary validity cutoff of Pass/Fail, calibrated validity cutoffs for acceptable threshold are between .84–.90 (Erdodi et al. 2019).

Test Procedure

The examinee is presented with a Finger Tapper apparatus, a board with a tapping lever attached to a counter that records the number of taps completed. Administration should begin by demonstrating how the hand will be laid flat on the board with the index finger extended and placed over the tapping lever. The examinee should position their hand on the board so that the heel of the hand lays firmly on the board and the fingers lay flat on the board. The wrist and forearm should rest comfortably on the table. The examinee is shown what the tapping motion will consist of, i.e., only the index finger should move. The examinee may hold down their thumb with their free hand, or the examiner may hold the examinee's other fingers steady. The examinee should note that for a tap to be counted by the counter, the bottom of the tapping lever must hit the board and come all the way up.

After the demonstration, a practice trial should be administered. The examinee is instructed to place their dominant hand on the board. Their extended index finger is placed on the tapping lever, and all other extended fingers and the heel of the hand are to be unmoving on the board. The examinee is tasked with tapping the lever as quickly as possible within a 10-second practice trial. Timing should begin with the first "click" of the counter rather than with the instruction to start. The taps from the practice trial should be recorded in the record form before the counter is reset. After the practice trial, a 15-second rest period should be given before starting the first trial.

The counter should be reset after every trial. If the examinee does not stop after being instructed, the examiner should subtract the taps completed after the 'Stop' instruction from the counter and record that on the record form. A 15-second rest period should be given after every trial, and a 1–2-minute rest period should be given after every third trial. Additional rest periods may be provided if needed. If there is greater than a 5-tap discrepancy within the first five trials, another five trials should be administered. The examinee should not switch to the nondominant hand until all trials for the dominant hand have been completed. Once all trials for the dominant hand have been administered, the same instructions should be given for the nondominant hand, including a practice trial.

Scoring

In the Finger Tapping Test (FTT), the performance of each hand is assessed independently to identify potential differences in motor function between the left and right hand. The scoring process involves the following steps:

1. The client performs several trials, typically 5 or 10, of rapid finger tapping with each hand separately.
2. The number of successfully completed taps made in each trial is recorded.
3. All completed taps from the trials for each hand are then summed together.
4. The total number of taps is divided by the number of trials conducted. This yields the average or mean number of taps for each hand.

Task Difficulty and Types of Errors

FTT's biggest challenge is fatigue. It is recommended for the examinee to receive 15-second breaks in between each trial and a forced 1–2-minute break after every third trial if the participant chooses to skip the other breaks. Encouragement should be given if the examinee is observed slowing down toward the later trials. A trial should be discontinued if the examinee is not tapping correctly. The 15-second breaks may be extended if needed.

A common error during the FTT task is the examinee's inability to complete a full tap by having the bottom of the tapping lever hit the board. A practice trial focusing on the movement rather than speed can allow the examinee to understand how thorough tapping needs to be for the counter to count the tap.

Task Demands

The FTT measures psychomotor speed and motor function. Psychomotor speed is an important predictor of cognitive and physical function as it indicates the time it takes to process a cognitive operation. Previous research has indicated that tapping speed has been shown to be connected to multiple conditions, such as chronic alcoholism, multiple sclerosis, and chronic pain. The task requires speed, coordination, and pacing; these abilities can be impacted by alertness, focus, sustained attention, executive function, and processing speed. Thus, while FTT is a measure of psychomotor speed and function, other abilities are needed to complete the task (Strauss et al. 2006; Dodrill 1978; Wang et al. 2020).

Clinical Applications in Research

Psychomotor function is an important predictor of cognitive and physical function, with research indicating motor performance can predict cognitive impairments, cognitive function, and risk of future disability (Austin et al. 2015). In distinguishing between normal aging and dementia, the FTT can be a useful tool. Performance in this test, particularly the pace of finger tapping, is shown to be slower in both aging and dementia cases. However, the delay is usually more pronounced in dementia patients, helping to differentiate them from healthy aging individuals (Kluger et al. 1997). The FTT has also been used in assessing cases of spastic diplegia, a form of cerebral palsy, where similar delays in finger tapping are observed (Gao et al. 2015).

The FTT demonstrates sensitivity toward the lateralization of brain lesions. If a lesion is present in one hemisphere of the brain, performance tends to deteriorate in the hand opposite (contralateral) to that lesion (Strauss et al. 2006). Moreover, the FTT can assist in diagnosing brain dysfunctions, such as Parkinson's and Alzheimer's diseases. Signs of bradykinesia, a common symptom in these diseases, are detectable through slower tapping speed, loss of amplitude in tapping, and noticeable pauses between taps (Barut et al. 2013). In the context of Korsakoff's syndrome, a chronic memory disorder often linked to alcohol abuse, affected individuals tend to perform slower on the FTT than both alcoholics without the syndrome and healthy adults (Welch et al. 1997). In the case of traumatic brain injuries, patients with mild forms of such injuries have been found to complete fewer correct taps than patients with orthopedic injuries (De Monte et al. 2005). Furthermore, the speed of finger tapping, in both the dominant and nondominant hands, has been associated with the severity of the traumatic brain injury (Dikmen et al. 1995).

Interpretation

1. Impairment is noted when the dominant hand falls below 50 taps and the nondominant hand falls below 45 taps in the original system. When using the Heaton Norms, scores below 40 are considered impaired.
2. Problems on the dominant side are indicated if the nondominant score equals or exceeds the raw dominant finger tapping score. This suggests motor problems

arise from the dominant hemisphere or peripheral problems in the dominant hand.

3. Problems on the nondominant side are indicated if the nondominant hand's score is less than 80% of the dominant hand's score. This suggests motor problems arising from the nondominant hemisphere or peripheral problems in the nondominant hand.
4. Inconsistency in lateralization on FTT, Tactual Performance Test (TPT), and sensory tests suggests attentional and/or subcortical processes. This may be evident in disorders such as multiple sclerosis, depressive disorders, or after diffuse head trauma.
5. Poorer performance on finger tapping compared to the Purdue Pegboard indicates speed problems without fine motor coordination problems.
6. Poorer performance on the Purdue Pegboard compared to finger tapping suggests less speed impairment and greater problems in fine motor control. Poorer performance is defined by T-scores for one test that are one standard deviation or more below the T-scores for the other test.
7. Poorer performance on finger tapping compared to grip strength indicates speed problems with less strength or larger muscle problems. Overall, poorer performance on grip strength compared to finger tapping suggests less speed impairment and greater problems in gross motor strength.
8. When comparing T-scores for the Left and Right hands, a difference of more than 5 T score points (one half of a standard deviation) suggests slowness in the hand with the lower scores. Differences of more than 10 points indicate clear weaknesses,
9. Note that performance may be impaired by peripheral injuries to the hand and spinal cord that may arise from physical accidents. As such, weaknesses may not be attributable to brain injuries but may include spinal cord injuries or peripheral motor disorders.

References

Austin, A., McNames, J., Klein, K., Jimison, H. and Pavel, M. (2015). A statistical characterization of the finger tapping test: Modeling, estimation, and applications. IEEE Journal of Biomedical and Health Informatics, 19(2): 501–507, doi:10.1109/JBHI.2014.2384911.

Barut, C., Kızıltan, E., Gelir, E. and Köktürk, F. (2013). Advanced analysis of finger-tapping performance: a preliminary study. Balkan Medical Journal, 2: 167–71. doi:10.5152/balkanmedj.2012.105.

Bornstein, R. A. (1986). Classification rates obtained with "standard" cut-off scores on selected neuropsychological measures. Journal of Clinical and Experimental Neuropsychology, 8(4): 413–420.

Levine, C. B., Fahrbach, K. R., Siderowf, S.D., Estok, R. P., Ludensky, V. M. and Ross, S. D. (2003). Diagnosis and treatment of Parkinson's disease: a systematic review of the literature. Evidence Report/Technology Assessment, (57): 1–4.

De Monte, V. E., Geffen, G. M., May, C. R., McFarland, K., Heath, P. and Neralic, M. (2005). The acute effects of mild traumatic brain injury on finger tapping with and without word repetition. Journal of Clinical and Experimental Neuropsychology, 27(2): 224–39. doi:10.1080/13803390490515766.

Dikmen, S., Machamer, J. E., Winn, H. R. and Temkin, N. R. (1995). Neuropsychological outcome at 1-year post head injury. Neuropsychology, 9(1): 80–90.

Dodrill, C. B. (1978). A neuropsychological battery for epilepsy. Epilepsia, 19(6): 611–623.

Erdodi, L. A., Taylor, B., Sabelli, A. G., Malayna, M., Kirsch, N. L. and Abeare, C. A. (2019). Demographically adjusted validity cutoffs on the finger tapping test are superior to raw score cutoffs in adults with TBI. Psychological Injury and Law 12: 113–126. https://doi.org/10.1007/s12207-019-09352-y.

Gao, F., Mei, X. and Chen, A. C. (2015). Delayed finger tapping and cognitive responses in preterm-born male teenagers with mild spastic diplegia. Pediatric Neurology, 52(2): 206–13. doi:10.1016/j.pediatrneurol.2014.04.012.

Golden, C. J., Espe-Pfifer, P. and Wachsler-Felder, J. (2002). Neuropsychological Interpretation of Objective Psychological Tests. Kluwer Academic Publishers.

Heaton, R. K., Grant, I. and Matthews, C. G. (1991). Comprehensive Norms for an Expanded Halstead-Reitan Battery: Demographic Corrections, Research Findings, and Clinical Applications. Psychological Assessment Resources.

Heaton, R. K., Grant, I., Matthews, C. G., Fastenau, P. S. and Adams, K. M. (1996) Heaton, Grant, and Matthews' Comprehensive Norms: An Overzealous Attempt. Journal of Clinical and Experimental Neuropsychology, 18(3): 444–448, DOI:10.1080/01688639608409000.

Kluger, A., Gianutsos, J. G., Golomb, J., Ferris, S. H. and Reisberg, B. (1997). Motor/psychomotor dysfunction in normal aging, mild cognitive decline, and early Alzheimer's disease: Diagnostic and differential diagnostic features. International Psychogeriatrics, 9: 307–316.

Massman, P. J. and Doody, R. S.(1996). Hemispheric asymmetry in Alzheimer's disease is apparent in motor functioning. Journal of Clinical and Experimental Neuropsychology, 18: 110–121.

Matarazzo, J. D., Wiens, A. N., Matarazzo, R. G. and Goldstein, S. G. (1974). Psychometric and clinical test-retest reliability of the Halstead Impairment Index in a sample of healthy, young, normal men. Journal of Nervous and Mental Disease, 158: 37–49.

Morrison, M. W., Gregory, R. J. and Paul, J. J. (1979). Reliability of the Finger Tapping Test and a note on sex differences. Perceptual and Motor Skills, 1: 139–42. doi:10.2466/pms.1979.48.1.139.

Psychological Assessment Resources (PAR). (1992). Finger Tapper User's Guide. PAR.

Reitan R. M. (1979). Manual for Administration of Neuropsychological Test Batteries for Adults and Children. Neuropsychology Laboratory.

Schmitt, L. (2013). Finger-Tapping Test. In: Volkmar, F.R. (Ed.). Encyclopedia of Autism Spectrum Disorders. Springer. https://doi.org/10.1007/978-1-4419-1698-3_343.

Strauss, E., Sherman, E. M. S. and Spreen, O. (2006). A Compendium of Neuropsychological Tests: Administration, Norms, and Commentary, 3rd ed. Oxford University Press.

Wang, S., Jiaerken, Y., Yu, X., Shen, Z., Luo, X., Hong, H. et al. (2020). Understanding the association between psychomotor processing speed and white matter hyperintensity: A comprehensive multi-modality MR imaging study. Human Brain Mapping, 41(3): 605–616. doi:10.1002/hbm.24826.

Welch, L. W., Cunningham, A. T., Eckardt, M. J. and Martin, P. R. (1997). Fine motor speed deficits in alcoholic Korsakoff's syndrome. Alcoholism: Clinical and Experimental Research, 21: 134–139.

CHAPTER 10

Logical Memory

*Ines Tchienga** and *Karla Molina*

Logical Memory (LM) is among the original subtests included in the Weschler Memory Scale-I (WMS-I) published in 1945, which aimed to measure immediate and delayed verbal memory. The LM subtest consists of LM I (immediate recall), LM II (delayed recall), and LM III (delayed recognition). Unlike in previous versions, in the WMS-IV (Wechsler 2009), story two is not repeated for the Adult Battery. Moreover, the older adult battery includes a shorter story and offers repetition. For LM I, participants must immediately recall details of two short passages. Following a 20–30 minute delay, examinees are asked to recall details from the two original stories (i.e., LM II). Finally, in LM III, participants are asked yes/no questions about the stories. LM is frequently used in clinical and research settings due to its feasibility.

Use with Diverse Groups

The LM subtest effectively measures episodic memory, while addressing processes involved in memory encoding, storage, and recall (Li et al. 2006). For example, the LM subtest has been included in cognitive batteries for studies that investigated verbal memory ability among individuals with the following neurological conditions: temporal lobe epilepsy (TLE), Alzheimer's (AD) and vascular dementia (VD), cognitive impairment disorder (mild, moderate, and severe), and traumatic brain injury (TBI) (Ahn et al. 2019; Bouman et al. 2016a; Chapman et al. 2016; Gonçalves et al. 2017; Soble et al. 2014). Moreover, researchers and clinicians have employed the LM subtest to discriminate between suboptimal effort and malingering (Bouman et al. 2016b; Pliskin et al. 2021).

While the stories included in the LM subtest are Western-bound, they have been modified and adapted to non-Western cultures to ensure cultural appropriateness. For instance, the Korean version of the WMS-IV (K-WMS-IV) was developed and standardized in 2012 (Chey et al. 2012). Unlike the original WSM-IV, which

Nova Southeastern University, Fort Lauderdale, Florida, USA.
Email: km3303@mynsu.nova.edu
* Corresponding author: it212@mynsu.nova.edu

consisted of an adult version with two full stories (A and B) and an older adult version with a shortened story A and the original story B, the K-WMS-IV only includes the adult version with the full stories (Ahn et al. 2019). Similarly, the Japanese edition of the WSM-R was standardized on 316 subjects and only included LM I and II (Sugishita 2001). Although other subtests were adapted for cultural relevance, the LM original passages (A and B) were only translated into Japanese. Further, the scoring criteria for LM I and II in the Japanese edition were identical to the original American edition (Sugishita 2001).

Conversely, in another Japanese study, Takuya and colleagues (2016) constructed a neuropsychological battery and only used story A for both LM I and II. Also, the authors translated the original passage into Japanese and used the same scoring criteria. Similarly, O'Bryant and colleagues (2018) included the LM I and LM II in their neuropsychological battery to acquire normative data on monolingual and bilingual Texas Mexican-American adults. The authors used the original versions of both stories but provided translated versions for Spanish speakers. Lastly, Gross et al. (2020) developed a diagnostic assessment for older adults diagnosed with dementia in India, including all subtests of LM (WMS-IV). However, the names of persons and places were modified to make it more culturally appropriate for the Indian population.

Reliability and Validity

Test reliability refers to the accuracy, consistency, and stability of test scores across situations (Anastasi and Urbina 1997). Research on the WMS-IV reliability indicates that most primary subtests' (i.e., LM I and II) scores have moderate to high internal consistency. The average reliability coefficient was .82 and .85 for all ages for LM I and LM II, respectively. Regarding clinical populations, a study recruited 555 participants and found that the average reliability coefficient was .86 and .92 for LM I and LM II, respectively. Specifically, the AD, Autism Spectrum Disorder, TBI, Intellectual Disability (ID), MCI, and Learning Disability (LD) groups had the highest reliability coefficients for LM I and II. Test-retest reliability scores demonstrated consistency in scores after a 14–84 day delay for LM I and II (Weschler 2009).

LM and Verbal Paired Associates (VPA) are measured for the WMS-IV Auditory Memory Index, which examines immediate and delayed recall of auditory information. However, while LM assesses the ability to encode and retrieve information presented within a logical framework, the VPA does so for semantically related information. These subtests are highly correlated, with correlation coefficients of .44 and .48 for the immediate domain (LM I and VPA I) and .42 and .54 for the delayed condition (LM II and VPA II) in the adult and older adult sample, respectively (Weschler 2009).

Assets and Limitations

Clinical Utility

LM is one of several subtests used by clinicians for diagnostic purposes. Helmstaedter et al. (2009) and Gonzalez et al. (2007) have argued that memory deficits are often more prominent in patients with mesial TLE than those with lateral TLE. In support of this view, those in the mesial group showed pronounced deficits in verbal and nonverbal memory tasks with an associative component (Cohen and Eichebbaum 1993). Similarly, findings by Gonzalez et al. (2007) suggest no differences in lateralization between the TLE groups on verbal or nonverbal memory tasks, except on facial recognition, which was more pronounced over the right hemisphere. The authors have suggested that these null findings are due to the limitations of assessment tasks (low sensitivity), underpowered studies, individual differences in impairment, etiology in patient groups, etc. (Cohen and Eichebaum 1993; Gonzalez et al. 2007; Nolan et al. 2004; Wood et al. 2000).

Contrary to the pediatric literature, whose findings are less established on differences in memory impairment between mesial and lateral or right and left TLE, adult studies seem to suggest that null findings are partly due to the lack of measures sensitive to the effects of laterality. For example, Bouman et al. (2016a) examined the clinical utility of the WMS-IV to distinguish between mesial and lateral TLE in adult patients. Their sample consisted of 77 healthy controls and 75 patients (N mesial TLE = 31, N lateral TLE = 26, N left TLE = 11, N right TLE = 7). They found that patients with mesial TLE performed significantly worse than those with lateral TLE on LM I and Designs II. However, statistically significant differences were not observed between the groups on similar verbal memory subtests (i.e., LM II, DE I, VPA I and II). Further, there were no significant differences in performance in the WMS-IV subtests between individuals with right and left TLE. These results are in line with those reported by Jones-Gotman et al. (2010), Raspall et al. (2005), and Soble et al. (2014), suggesting that the WMS-IV lacks sensitivity to detect lateralized deficits. Nevertheless, the WMS-IV was appropriate in discriminating performance between clinical and non-clinical samples in visual and verbal memory tasks.

The psychometric properties and diagnostic utility of LM are inconsistent when detecting AD or MCI. Chapman and colleagues (2016) conducted a meta-analysis to examine how much LM and the Mini-Mental State Examination (MMSE) scores are used as eligibility criteria in AD clinical trials. They also assessed the validity of the cut-off scores of each measure. Their analysis suggests that LM II cut-off scores were clinically inadequate for distinguishing between normal cognition and MCI. Notably, LM II and the MMSE also lacked diagnostic accuracy when discriminating between MCI and mild AD dementia, which has been associated with factors such as age, education, large ceiling and floor effects, and learning biases. Similarly, Gonçalves and colleagues (2017) examined the utility of the Portuguese version of the WMS-III in discriminating between AD and subcortical vascular dementia (SVD) in the early stages. Their results showed that patients with AD performed significantly better than those with SVD on LM II. However, both groups performed similarly in the LM I. Nonetheless, from their results, SVD patients performed relatively better in delayed recall and preservation of recognition memory than AD patients, which is in line with previous work (Baillon et al. 2003; Graham et al. 2004; Loori and Sachdev 1999). Further, Gonçalves et al. (2007) postulated that the LM subtest showed good diagnostic accuracy for AD and correctly classified 89% of the patients, compared to 63% of the SVD patients. Conversely, others asserted that the LM and recognition memory subtests are two of the best neuropsychological measures for discriminating between AD and SVD (Kertesz and Clydesdale 1994; Tierney et al. 2001). Further, Lo et al. (2012) stated that LM has the highest test-retest reliability across different age cohorts.

On the other hand, Mathias and Burke (2009) and Matioli and Caramelli (2010) suggested that LM was inefficient at discerning between different types of dementias. While findings by Gonçalves et al. (2007) are compelling, it is worth noting that their sample size was small (control: N = 40, SVD patients: N = 16, AD patients: N = 36), and their overall sample had low formal education (control = 5.60 ± 2.73, AD = 4.64 ± 3.16, SVD = 3.19 ± 1.83), which is representative of the general elderly Portuguese population (Sá et al. 2012). In sum, there is mixed evidence on the clinical utility of the LM subtest in differentiating between diagnoses.

Aside from diagnostic purposes, LM III is an embedded Performance Validity Test (ePVT) used to detect malingering or lack of suboptimal effort. Additionally, Golden and colleagues (2000) reported that the recognition trial is useful, for it provides information regarding delayed memory and is far less incumbent upon the ability to produce complex speech. The manual does not provide specific cut-off scores but rather base rates of performance based on the total recognition scores (< 2%, < 5%, < 10%, < 15%, < 25%, or > 25%) (Wechsler 2009a). In a study by Bouman et al. (2016b), they compared the performance of the LM III among experimental malingerers, mixed-etiology patients, and healthy controls. They found that malingerers performed significantly worse than the other groups. In contrast, Soble and colleagues (2018) suggest that LM III demonstrated poor concordance with other PVTs and unacceptable psychometric properties using ACS validity-based rates (42% sensitivity/79% specificity). The authors evaluated the accuracy of the LM III as an ePVT on 97 participants with mixed etiologies (71 had a neurological condition and 21 had a psychiatric disorder) and found that 21% of those determined to be valid by the PVTs (i.e., WMT, WCT, and TOMM T1) were classified as invalid by the LM embedded validity measure, whereas 58% of those determined to be invalid based on the PVTs passed the LM embedded validity measure. Similarly, Pliskin et al. (2020) argued that LM III has relatively poor utility as an ePVT, particularly in cases of mild neurocognitive disorders, in which it was unable to differentiate valid from invalid performance accurately.

Clinical Interpretations

1. LM primarily assesses immediate and delayed verbal memory, in addition to auditory and working memory. Further, it examines the relationship between memory abilities and verbal learning.
2. Importantly, performance in this subtest can be affected by language proficiency, verbal comprehension ability, educational attainment, sensory deficits (e.g., poor auditory acuity), physical symptoms (e.g., fatigue), behavioral issues (e.g., impulsivity), medication effects, among others (Wechsler et al. 2009b).
3. Language proficiency and verbal comprehension ability are especially important when interpreting performance in LM because this subtest is presented using oral language. Therefore, when evaluating an individual's performance in LM, one should be cautious about making hypotheses about the etiology of poor

performance in this subtest, as the memory deficits might be explained by the aforementioned factors or by impairment in other cognitive processes (e.g., attention) rather than deficits in memory per se.

4. This subtest is designed to detect deficits in memory functioning rather than to diagnose specific conditions or etiologies. The WMS-IV provides contrast scores that allow the examiner to explore different hypotheses about what is contributing to the memory deficits, but it is not recommended to give a diagnosis based on performance in this subtest or the WMS-IV overall (Wechsler et al. 2009b).
5. In general, low scores in LM suggest difficulties recalling verbal information organized logically around a concept and presented sequentially. Poor performance is also indicative of deficits in the ability to recall major and/or minor details about a story after one (adult form) or two exposures (older adult form) and with (LM II) or without prompting (LM I).
6. At the subtest level, one should be cautious not to overinterpret a single low score since, due to intraindividual variability, obtaining one or two low scores is not atypical when clients complete a neuropsychological battery (Brooks et al. 2011). Thus, performance in LM subtests should always be interpreted in the context of a comprehensive neuropsychological evaluation to avoid inaccurate conclusions.
7. LM I measures the individual's ability to recall details about a story in a logical framework immediately after the information is presented. This subtest measures an individual's ability to encode information given verbally and keep that information in mind for a short period (i.e., working memory). Low scores in this subtest suggest difficulties in encoding and/or retrieving information immediately after it is presented.
8. LM II measures the individual's ability to recall details about a story presented in a logical framework 20 to 30 minutes after the information is acquired. Rather than measuring forgetting, this subtest indicates how much information is recalled after a delay, which depends on how much information was acquired initially. In that sense, poor performance in this subtest could suggest deficits in encoding, consolidating, and/or recalling information associated with long-term memory (Wechsler et al. 2009b).
9. In LM III, low scores suggest difficulties in answering yes/no questions about previously learned information. Generally, performance in recognition tasks tends to be superior to free recall tasks; thus, individuals tend to score higher in this subtest.
10. Poor performance in this test can also suggest malingering, although the evidence is mixed on the efficacy of this test as an embedded performance validity measure, as previously discussed.
11. To explore hypotheses about differences in recognition vs recall memory, contrasting scores in LM I, II, and III can be useful (Wechsler et al. 2009b).
12. The contrast between LM I and II can be considered a measure of forgetting previously acquired information. Low scores, in this contrast, indicate poor delayed recall specific to the person's immediate recall ability, suggesting higher than expected rates of forgetting (Wechsler et al. 2009b).

13. Inconsistency in performance between LM I and II should be carefully examined. Low scores on LM I can be associated with inattention, incomprehension of instruction, or anxiety.
14. Conversely, high performance in LM II can be related to learning biases and excellent retention. However, while memory performance improves over repeated trials, there is only one trial of each story in LM. Improvement from Story 1 to Story 2 may be related to learning how to take the test.
15. Scores substantially higher on LM II versus LM I may suggest that the client did not respond fully in LM I due to anxiety, motivation, or other non-memory factors. In such cases, LM II should be regarded as more accurate.
16. Low scores on both LM I and II may suggest genuine memory problems that can be affected by psychiatric, emotional, or physical distress.
17. When interpreting LM scores, clinicians should consider factors such as the reason for referral, testing attitudes, and cultural background. More importantly, performance on similar subtests (i.e., Verbal Paired Association, Verbal Fluency, Information (WAIS-IV), Rey Auditory Verbal Learning Test, etc.) will provide a comprehensive understanding of the client's presenting problem.
18. In summary, studies have shown that memory function is affected by emotional, physical, and mental distress. Further, a positive correlation exists between age, years of formal education, and performance on cognitive tests. Moreover, an individual's cultural background may influence testing attitudes, thus consequently affecting their performance on cognitive tests. As such, clinicians must consider these factors when interpreting scores on the Logical Memory subtest and others.

References

Ahn, Y. D., Yi, D., Joung, H., Seo, E. H., Lee, Y. H., Byun, M. S. et al. (2019). KBASE Research Group. Normative data for the logical memory subtest of the Wechsler Memory Scale-IV in middle-aged and elderly Korean people. Psychiatry Investigation, 16(11): 793. doi:10.30773/pi.2019.0061.

Anastasi, A. and Urbina, S. (1997). Psychological Testing. Prentice Hall/Pearson Education.

Bortnik, K. E., Boone, K. B., Marion, S. D., Amano, S., Ziegler, E., Victor, T. L. et al. (2010). Examination of various WMS-III Logical Memory scores in the assessment of response bias. The Clinical Neuropsychologist, 24(2): 344–357. https://doi.org/10.1080/13854040903307268.

Bouman, Z., Elhorst, D., Hendriks, M. P., Kessels, R. P. and Aldenkamp, A. P. (2016a). Clinical utility of the Wechsler Memory Scale—Fourth Edition (WMS-IV) in patients with intractable temporal lobe epilepsy. Epilepsy & Behavior, 55: 178–182. doi:10.1016/j.yebeh.2015.11.022.

Bouman, Z., Hendriks, M. P., Schmand, B. A., Kessels, R. P. and Aldenkamp, A. P. (2016b). Indicators of suboptimal performance embedded in the Wechsler Memory Scale–Fourth Edition (WMS–IV). Journal of Clinical and Experimental Neuropsychology, 38(4): 455–466. doi:10.1080/13803395.2015.1123226.

Brooks, B. L., Holdnack, J. A. and Iverson, G. L. (2011). Advanced clinical interpretation of the WAIS-IV and WMS-IV: Prevalence of low scores varies by level of intelligence and years of education. Assessment, 18(2): 156–167. doi:10.1177/1073191110385316.

Chapman, K. R., Bing-Canar, H., Alosco, M. L., Steinberg, E. G., Martin, B., Chaisson, C. et al. (2016). Mini-Mental State Examination and Logical Memory scores for entry into Alzheimer's disease trials. Alzheimer's Research & Therapy, 8(1): 1–11. doi:10.1186/s13195-016-0176-z.

Chey, J., Park, K., Hwang, S. and Hong, S. (2012). Korean Wechsler Memory Scale IV. Daegu: Korea Psychology.

Cohen, N. J. and Eichenbaum, H. (1993). Memory, Amnesia, and the Hippocampal System. Massachusetts Institute of Technology, Cambridge, Massachusetts.

Golden, C. J., Espe-Pfeifer, P. and Wachsler-Felder, J. (2000). Neuropsychological Interpretation of Objective Psychological Tests. Springer Science and Business Media.

Gonçalves, C., Pinho, M. S., Cruz, V., Gens, H., Oliveira, F., Pais, J. et al. (2017). The Portuguese version of the Wechsler Memory Scale is the 3rd edition's utility with demented elderly adults. Applied Neuropsychology: Adult, 24(3): 212–225. doi:10.1080/23279095.2015.1135440.

Gonzalez, L. M., Anderson, V. A., Wood, S. J., Mitchell, L. A. and Harvey, A. S. (2007). The localization and lateralization of memory deficits in children with temporal lobe epilepsy. Epilepsia, 48(1): 124–132. https://doi.org/10.1111/j.1528-1167.2006.00907.x.

Gross, A. L., Khobragade, P. Y., Meijer, E. and Saxton, J. A. (2020). Measurement and structure of cognition in the Longitudinal Aging Study in India–Diagnostic Assessment of Dementia. Journal of the American Geriatrics Society, 68: S11–S19. doi:10.1111/jgs.16738.

Helmstaedter, C., Wietzke, J. and Lutz, M. T. (2009). Unique and shared validity of the "Wechsler Logical Memory Test," the "California Verbal Learning Test," and the "Verbal Learning and Memory Test" in patients with epilepsy. Epilepsy Research, 87(2-3): 203–212.

Hoelzle, J. B., Nelson, N. W. and Smith, C. A. (2011). Comparison of Wechsler Memory Scale–Fourth Edition (WMS–IV) and Third Edition (WMS–III) dimensional structures: Improved ability to evaluate auditory and visual constructs. Journal of Clinical and Experimental Neuropsychology, 33(3): 283–291.

Jones-Gotman, M., Smith, M. L., Risse, G. L., Westerveld, M., Swanson, S. J., Giovagnoli, A. R. et al. (2010). The contribution of neuropsychology to diagnostic assessment in epilepsy. Epilepsy & Behavior, 18(1-2), 3–12. doi:10.1016/j.yebeh.2010.02.019.

Kertesz, A. and Clydesdale, S. (1994). Frontal lobe deficits prominent in vascular dementia. Archives of Neurology, 51: 1226–1231. doi:10.1001/archneur.1994.00540240070018.

Lacritz, L. H., Barnard, H. D., Van Ness, P., Agostini, M., Diaz-Arrastia, R. and Cullum, C. M. (2004). Qualitative analysis of WMS-III Logical Memory and Visual Reproduction in temporal lobe epilepsy. Journal of Clinical and Experimental Neuropsychology, 26(4): 521–530. https://doi.org/10.1080/13803390490496650.

Li, M., Ng, T. P., Kua, E. H. and Ko, S. M. (2006). Brief informant screening test for mild cognitive impairment and early Alzheimer's disease. Dementia and Geriatric Cognitive Disorders, 21: 392–402. doi:10.1159/000092808.

Lo, A., Humphreys, M., Byrne, G. and Pachana, N. (2012). Test-retest reliability and practice effects of the Wechsler Memory Scale-III. Journal of Neuropsychology, 6: 212–231. doi:10.1111/j.1748-6653.2011.02023.x.

Mathias, J. L. and Burke, J. (2009). Cognitive functioning in Alzheimer's and vascular dementia: A meta-analysis. Neuropsychology, 23: 411–423. doi:10.1037/a0015384.

Matioli, M. and Caramelli, P. (2010). Limitations in differentiating vascular dementia from Alzheimer's disease with brief cognitive tests. Arquivos de Neuropsiquiatria, 68: 185–188. doi:10.1590/s0004-282201000200006.

Nolan, M. A., Redoblado, M. A., Lah, S., Sabaz, M., Lawson, J. A., Cunningham, A. M. et al. (2004). Memory function in childhood epilepsy syndromes. Journal of Paediatric and Child Health, 40: 20–7. doi:10.1111/j.1440-1754.2004.00284.x.

O'Bryant, S. E., Edwards, M., Johnson, L., Hall, J., Gamboa, A. and O'jile, J. (2018). Texas Mexican American adult normative studies: Normative data for commonly used clinical neuropsychological measures for English-and Spanish-speakers. Developmental Neuropsychology, 43(1): 1–26. doi:10.1080/87565641.2017.1401628.

Pliskin, J. I., DeDios Stern, S., Resch, Z. J., Saladino, K. F., Ovsiew, G. P., Carter, D. A. et al. (2021). Comparing the psychometric properties of eight embedded performance validity tests in the Rey Auditory Verbal Learning test, Wechsler Memory Scale Logical Memory, and Brief Visuospatial Memory Test–revised recognition trials for detecting invalid neuropsychological test performance. Assessment, 28(8): 1871–1881. doi:10.1177/1073191120929093.

Raspall, T., Doñate, M., Boget, T., Carreño, M., Donaire, A., Agudo, R. et al. (2005). Neuropsychological tests with lateralizing value in patients with temporal lobe epilepsy: Reconsidering material-specific theory. Seizure, 14(8): 569–576. doi:10.1016/j.seizure.2005.09.007.

Soble, J. R., Eichstaedt, K. E., Waseem, H., Mattingly, M. L., Benbadis, S. R., Bozorg, A. M. et al. (2014). Clinical utility of the Wechsler Memory Scale—Fourth Edition (WMS-IV) in predicting laterality of temporal lobe epilepsy among surgical candidates. Epilepsy & Behavior, 41: 232–237. https://doi.org/10.1016/j.yebeh.2014.10.014.

Soble, J. R., Bain, K. M., Bailey, K. C., Kirton, J. W., Marceaux, J. C., Critchfield, E. A. et al. (2018). Evaluating the accuracy of the Wechsler Memory Scale-(WMS-IV) Logical Memory embedded validity index for detecting invalid test performance. Applied Neuropsychology: Adult. doi:10.1080/23279095.2017.1418744.

Sugishita, M. (2001). Manual for the Japanese edition of the Wechsler Memory Scale-Revised. Tokyo: Nihon Bunka Kagakusha (in Japanese).

Takuya, Y., Daisuke, I., Daisuke, S., Satoko, I., Hajime, T., Mika, K. et al. (2016). Diagnostic accuracy of neuropsychological tests for classification of dementia. Neurology Asia, 21(1): 47–54.

Tierney, M., Black, S., Szalai, J., Snow, G., Fischer, R., Nadon, G. et al. (2001). Recognition memory and verbal fluency differentiate probable Alzheimer's disease from subcortical ischemic vascular dementia. Archives of Neurology, 58: 1654–1659. doi:10.1001/archneur.58.10.1654.

Wechsler, D. (2009a). WMS-IV: Wechsler Memory Scale-Fourth Edition. San Antonio, Tex: Pearson.

Wechsler, D., Pearson Education Inc, and PsychCorp. (2009b). WMS-IV: Technical and Interpretive Manual. Pearson.

Wood, A. G., Saling, M. M., O'Shea, M. F., Berkovic, S. F. and Jackson, G. D. (2000). Components of verbal learning and hippocampal damage assessed by T2 relaxometry. Journal of the International Neuropsychological Society, 6: 525–534. doi:10.1017/s1355617700655029.

CHAPTER 11

Purdue Pegboard

*Rebecca Aronson** and *Ryan Bennett*

The Purdue Pegboard is a widely used assessment tool for measuring manual dexterity and fine motor skills in clinical and research settings. The test requires the participant to place small metal pegs into a series of holes on a board, using dominant hand and then nondominant, as well as perform similar tasks involving assembly, sorting, and placing pegs into designated areas. The test is scored based on the number of pegs placed in a given time and the number of errors made during the task. The Purdue Pegboard is a reliable and valid measure of fine motor skills and is often used to assess brain injury, dementia, and other neurological disorders. As the literature suggests, batteries within neuropsychology have shifted from using the Purdue Pegboard to the Grooved Pegboard.

Normed Population

Norms are available for individuals aged 5 to 89 (Lafayette Instrument Company 2015).

Adults

Yeudall and colleagues (1986) conducted a study to establish normative data for the Purdue Pegboard assessment in adults. The sample was stratified based on age (15–40 years) and gender. Exclusion criteria included evidence from interviews of forensic involvement, prenatal or birth complications, psychiatric disorders, or substance abuse problems. Hand preference was determined by the hand used to write with, and the administration consisted of one trial per subtest.

Agnew and colleagues (1988) conducted a study to provide data on the Purdue Pegboard assessment based on a sample of 212 healthy, well-educated individuals aged 40 to 85 years who were screened for cognitive impairment. The subtest scores

Nova Southeastern University, Fort Lauderdale, Florida, USA.
Email: rb1934@nova.edu
* Corresponding author: ra1258@mynsu.nova.edu

were calculated as the average of three trials per subtest, and the difference between dominant and nondominant hands was also calculated. The manual difference was found to be greater for women than for men. There was a trend for this difference to increase with age, but it did not reach statistical significance.

DesRosiers and colleagues (1995) also conducted a study to provide normative data for the Purdue Pegboard assessment in a random sample of 360 individuals drawn from the electoral pool of a city in Quebec. The sample was stratified for age and gender and consisted of individuals aged 60 to 89 years who were lucid and independent in activities of daily living, had no impairment affecting upper limb functioning, and could see sufficiently well. Hand preference was determined by the Edinburgh Handedness Inventory, with 92% of participants classified as right-handed.

Lastly, McCurry and colleagues (2001) directed a study to present data on the Purdue Pegboard assessment based on a sample of Japanese-American adults aged 70 years and older who were enrolled in a prospective study of aging and dementia in King County, Washington. None of the participants were diagnosed with dementia based on clinical and screening neuropsychological examinations. Hand preference was determined by asking participants which hand they preferentially used, with 94% of the sample classified as right-handed. Participants completed two 30-second trials for each subtest.

Children

Gardner and Broman (1979) provided normative data for the Purdue Pegboard in children aged 5 years to 15 years and 11 months. The sample consisted of 1,334 schoolchildren (663 boys and 671 girls) in regular classes in a New Jersey suburb. The participants were primarily in the 95 to 110 IQ range and scored in the middle range on national achievement tests. Children in special education classes or those with a history of grade repetition were not included in the study. Similar findings were reported for Brazilian children by Brito and Santo-Morales (2002), as both studies noted that the performance difference between hands was equivalent in boys and girls.

Mathiowetz and colleagues provided normative data based on a three-trial administration for 176 subjects aged 14 to 19 years (Mathiowetz et al. 1986). The adolescents had no history of neuromuscular or orthopedic dysfunction that would interfere with finger dexterity. Unfortunately, hand preference was not reported. The scores are higher than those reported by Gardner and Broman (1979), reflecting the influence of practice effects afforded by the additional trials.

Test Procedure

Golden and colleagues (2000) provided a detailed overview of the Purdue Pegboard test procedures. They reported this test consists of a board with two parallel rows of holes into which the examinee places cylindrical pins (pegs). Each row contains 25 holes. The top of the board has four spaces in which pegs and other components of the instrument are placed. The pegs are placed in the extreme right and extreme left cups of the board. In the center, two cups, metal collars, and washers are placed. The test involves a total of four trials. Each of the first three trials is 30 seconds long. During each trial, the examinee places as many pegs as possible into the holes on the board. In the first trial, the client is required to use only the preferred (dominant) hand when placing pegs into the holes. During the second trial, the nonpreferred (non-dominant) hand is tested, and in the third trial, both hands are used. The fourth trial is 60 seconds long, and the examinee is asked to build assemblies consisting of a peg, a washer, a collar, and an additional washer using both hands and placing them on the board.

Errors

Common errors made on the Purdue Pegboard Test include inserting pegs into the wrong holes, dropping pegs or parts, and taking too long to complete the task. Other errors may include using the wrong hand during a specific subtest or failing to follow the designated pattern when assembling objects. The test instructions should be followed carefully to minimize errors and ensure accurate results. Test-takers may also experience fatigue or frustration during the test, which can negatively affect their performance.

Administration and Scoring

Golden and colleagues (2000) noted the administration of this test begins with a demonstration of each of the four trials. The examinee is then allowed to practice each trial until the examiner is confident in their understanding. Generally, only a single practice trial is required for each of the four trials. The first trial used the dominant hand, the second trial used the nondominant hand, and the third trial assessed both hands simultaneously. When the examinee is using their right hand, pegs are pulled from the extreme right-side cup and placed as quickly as possible down the right-side column. When the examinee is using their left hand, pegs are pulled from the extreme left-side cup and placed as quickly as possible down the left-side column. For both hands, the examinee is told to start at the top and work downward without skipping any holes. The trials are stopped at 30 seconds. Before the third trial, the pegs from both columns are removed and placed back in their respective cups. In the third trial, both hands are used simultaneously. The examinee selects pegs with each hand from the same side cup and places them in the respective side's column. Again, the examinee begins at the top of each column and works downward for 30 seconds. Following the end of the trial, the pegs are removed and placed back in their respective cups.

The fourth trial, the assemblies trial, also requires the use of both hands. In this trial, the examinee is asked to use both hands in a continuous alternating motion, such that the first hand picks up a peg, the second hand picks up a washer, the first hand picks up a collar, and so on, in order to build the assemblies. The examinee constructs the assembly and then places it on the board, repeating the sequence as quickly as possible within a 60-second time limit.

In practical use, many administer and score only the first two trials. When all four trials are administered, scores are obtained for each of them. The number of pegs placed on the board in the holes during the 30 seconds is the score for each of the first two trials. The score for the third trial, during which both hands are used, is the number of peg pairs placed on the board. For the fourth and final trial, the total number of parts assembled comprises the score. The scores are compared to the average scores of the appropriate normed population. It should be noted that practice effects have been found on this measure. The practice effect is greater in younger populations (ages 25–33) than in the older populations (Golden et al. 2006).

Reliability and Validity

Test-Retest Reliability and Practice Effects

The Lafayette Instrument Company (2015) user instruction manual denotes the number of trials allowed per subtest affects reliability. For one-trial administration over intervals of 1 to 2 weeks, correlation coefficients ranging from .37 to .82 have been obtained for normal individuals (Buddenberg and Davis 2000; DesRosiers et al. 1995; Reddon et al. 1988; Tiffin 1968). Three-trial administration yields higher reliabilities (.76 to .89) after retest intervals of 1 week (.81 to .89) and 6 months (.76 for peg-placing trials). Right-left difference scores or ratios tend to be unreliable, with correlations ranging from .22 to .61 (Reddon et al. 1988; Sappington 1980). Reddon and colleagues noted that, when normal right-handed adults were tested weekly over five occasions, the right-hand was greater than the left-hand score on average 50% of the time in men. In women, the right-hand score was greater than the left-hand score on the average 62.9% of the time. Because changes in performance occur commonly in normal adults, considerable caution should be exercised in interpreting any changes in between-hand asymmetry (Lafayette Instrument Company 2015).

There are practice effects, with scores improving in subsequent trials (DeRosiers et al. 1995; Feinstein et al. 1994; Reddon et al. 1988; Wilson et al. 1982). For example, Feinstein and colleagues examined the effects of practice in healthy volunteers tested at 2- to 4-week intervals over eight test sessions. Performance improved with time and was still apparent at the eighth session. Age also appears to interact with practice. The improvement was marked for younger subjects, aged 25 to 33 years, who performed better than older subjects, aged 41 to 57 years, and who continued to improve for a great length of time. The Purdue Pegboard Test has been shown to have good construct validity, suggesting it accurately measures manual dexterity and fine motor skills.

Relationships With Other Measures

The Purdue Pegboard instruction manual (Lafayette Instrument Company 2015) reported that factor-analytic studies (Fleishman and Ellison 1962; Fleishman and Hempel 1954) have shown that the Purdue Pegboard Test loads on a finger dexterity factor defined as "the ability to make rapid, skillful, controlled manipulative movements of small objects, where the fingers are primarily involved." However, the assembly test appears to measure something besides finger dexterity and also loads on a manual dexterity factor defined as "the ability to make skillful, controlled arm-hand manipulations of larger objects." Strenge and colleagues also highlighted the importance of attention as a key factor in the assembly and nondominant hand tasks (2002).

Interpretation

Developed in the 1940s as a test of manipulative dexterity for personnel selection, the Purdue Pegboard measures unimanual and bimanual finger and hand dexterity (Lafayette Instrument Company 2015). In addition, the Purdue Pegboard has been employed in neuropsychological assessment to assist in localizing cerebral lesions and deficits. Although it can provide valuable information when used by itself, it is most commonly used as a part of a battery. The Purdue Pegboard Test is a good screening method for brain damage owing to its brief administration and because it is unlikely to fatigue the client. It is generally seen as requiring more fine motor control than Finger Tapping (Golden et al. 2000).

**The following interpretations were primarily derived from the 'Neuropsychological Interpretation of Objective Psychological Tests' by Charles Golden, Patricia Espe-Pfeifer, and Jana Wachsler-Felder (2000).

1. The Purdue Pegboard Test scores reflect an individual's ability to produce rapid, competent, controlled, manipulative handling of small objects using fingers. They also reflect the individual's capacity to coordinate arm-hand motions to maneuver larger objects. Generally, individuals perform 10% better on the preferred hand trial than on the nonpreferred hand trial. The Purdue Pegboard is scored as the number of pegs placed in 30 seconds.
2. Patterns of performance in which the dominant hand is slower than the nondominant hand suggest clear deficits in the dominant hand.
3. Patterns of performance in which the nondominant hand is less than 80% of the dominant hand indicate slowness in the nondominant hand.
4. Results should be coordinated with scores from the Finger Tapping Test (FTT), the Tactual Performance Test (TPT), Grip Strength, and other lateralized motor and sensory examinations. If consistent findings are found on one side of the body, then a lesion of the contralateral hemisphere is suggested. Inconsistent findings may suggest a subcortical disorder or motivational problems, which must be considered in the interpretation.
5. Performance improves during childhood and slows with advancing age (Agnew et al. 1988; Brito and Santos-Morales 2002; DesRosiers et al. 1995; Gardner and Broman 1979; Mathiowetz et al. 1986; McCurry et al. 2001; Wilson et al. 1982).
6. Females tend to perform better than males. Gender differences in fine manual dexterity may be confounded by gender differences in finger size. For most men, the fingers are of a size that is relatively unsuitable for this task. With larger-sized pegs, men may no longer be at a disadvantage.

7. In general, performance is better with the preferred than with the nonpreferred hand. There is evidence that left-handers perform more proficiently on the assembly component (Judge and Stirling, 2003).
8. In cases where there is evidence of dominant side problems, valuable information may be gained by comparing the Purdue Pegboard (PP) and TPT performance using the following formula:

$$\frac{\text{DOM[PP]} \times \text{DOM [TPT]}}{\text{ND [PP]} \times \text{ND [TPT]}}$$

9. Where PP scores are expressed in total pegs in 30 seconds and TPT scores in time per block (Note: in cases where zero blocks are placed on a single trial, we assign an arbitrary score of 10 minutes).
10. In cases where the D-RATIO defined in number 8 is between 1.35 and 1.65, there are equal deficits in the dominant hand on the two tests.
11. In cases where the D-RATIO is greater than 1.65, this suggests greater impairment on the TPT dominant hand, which indicates more posterior dominant hemisphere involvement.
12. In cases where the D-RATIO is less than 1.35, this suggests greater impairment on the PP dominant hand, which indicates more anterior dominant hemisphere involvement. In cases in which there is evidence of nondominant motor and sensory problems on the PP and TPT, the ND-RATIO is used to compute whether there is more anterior or posterior involvement. This is the reverse of the D-RATIO (number 8) and expressed as:

$$\frac{\text{ND[TPT]} \times \text{ND[PP]}}{\text{DOM [TPT]} \times \text{DOM [PP]}}$$

13. When the ND-RATIO is between 1.5 and 1.8, more TPT impairment is indicated, which is suggestive of a more posterior focus.
14. When the ND-RATIO is less than 1.5, there is more impairment on PP, suggesting a more anterior focus.
15. Overall, poorer performance on Finger Tapping compared to the Purdue Pegboard indicated speed problems without fine motor coordination problems. Overall poorer performance on the Purdue Pegboard compared to the Finger Tapping Test suggests less speed impairment and greater problems in fine motor control. Poorer performance is defined by T-scores for one test that is 10 points or more below the T-scores for the other test.
16. Lateralized deficits on Finger Tapping, which are greater than the lateralized deficit on the Purdue Pegboard, indicate more speed than fine motor problems in the affected hand. Similarly, greater lateralized deficits on the Purdue Pegboard than on Finger Tapping indicate greater problems with fine motor control as opposed to basic speed.
17. A greater lateralization deficit can be calculated by computing the following ratio:

$$\frac{\text{FT (DOM)/FT(NON-DOM)}}{\text{PP(DOM)/PP(NON-DOM)}}$$

Finger Tapping (FT) is expressed as average taps per 10 seconds, and Purdue Pegboard (PP) is expressed as pegs per 30 seconds.

18. In cases where DOM hand scores are higher than NON-DOM scores, a ratio of 1.2 or more indicates more lateralized Finger Tapping Performance, while a ratio less than .83 indicates more lateralized Purdue Pegboard performance.
19. In cases where NON-DOM scores are higher than DOM scores for both tests, a ratio of 1.2 indicates more lateralized performance on Purdue Pegboard, while a ratio less than .83 indicates more lateralized performance on the Finger Tapping Test.
20. Lateralized dominant hand deficits on Purdue Pegboard (and Finger Tapping) or generalized slowing will affect all visual-motor tasks in a test battery. Profiles in which there is a motor deficit and on which all deficits are seen on motor-dependent tasks must be interpreted with caution for deficits other than motor speed.
21. The degree of impairment on this measure and sensory measures must be compared. If there are greater sensory than motor deficits, a lesion of the sensory system is suggested, while greater deficits on the Purdue Pegboard suggest a focus on the motor system.
22. In all cases, peripheral motor and other peripheral causes for any deficits must be considered. In some cases, clients with heavily callused hands may have trouble picking up the small pegs, as will clients with arthritis or peripheral neuropathies.
23. Overall, poorer performance on Finger Tapping compared to the Purdue Pegboard indicates speed problems without fine motor coordination problems. Overall poorer performance on the Purdue Pegboard is defined by T-scores for one test that is 10 points or more below the T-scores for the other test.
24. Lateralization deficits on Finger Tapping, which are greater than the lateralization deficits on the Purdue Pegboard, indicate more speed than fine motor problems in the affected hand. Similarly, greater lateralized deficits on the Purdue Pegboard than on Finger Tapping indicate greater problems with fine motor control as opposed to basic speed.
25. Impairments on two-hand scores, as well as impairments on scores of both single-hand trials, are indicative of nonlateralized, more diffuse brain damage. Studies have shown that individuals with cerebellar disease, Parkinson's disease, and Huntington's disease have difficulty producing two-hand movements on the Purdue Pegboard.
26. Overall, poorer performance on the Purdue Pegboard compared to Grip Strength indicates speed or fine motor problems without strength or larger muscle problems. Overall poorer performance on Grip Strength compared to Purdue Pegboard suggests less speed or fine motor impairment and greater problems in gross motor strength. Poorer performance is defined by T-scores for one test that is 10 points or more below the T-scores for the other test.
27. Lateralized deficits on the Purdue Pegboard that are greater than the lateralized deficit on Grip Strength indicate more speed or fine motor than strength problems in the affected hand. Similarly, greater lateralized deficits on Grip Strength than

on Purdue Pegboard indicate greater problems with strength as opposed to basic speed or coordination.

28. A greater lateralized deficit can be calculated by computing the following ratio:

$$\frac{\text{PP(DOM)/PP(NON-DOM)}}{\text{GS(DOM)/GS(NON-DOM)}}$$

29. Purdue Pegboard (PP) is expressed as average taps per 10 seconds, and Grip Strength (GS) is expressed as average strength.
30. In cases where DOM hand scores are higher than NON-DOM scores, a ratio of 1.2 or more indicates more lateralized Purdue Pegboard performance, while a ratio less than .83 indicates more lateralized Grip Strength performance.
31. In cases where NON-DOM scores are higher than DOM scores for both tests, a ratio of 1.2 indicates more lateralized performance on Grip Strength, while a ratio less than .83 indicates more lateralized performance on the Purdue Pegboard.

References

Agnew, J., Bolla-Wilson, K., Kawas, C. H. and Bleeker, M. L. (1988). Purdue Pegboard age and sex norms for people 40 years old and older. Developmental Neuropsychology, 4: 29–35.

Asikainen, L., Nybo, T., Mueller, K., Sarna, S. and Kaste, M. (1999). Speed performance and l ong-term functional and vocational outcome in a group of young patients with moderate or severe traumatic brain injury. European Journal of Neurology, 6: 179–185.

Baron, I-S. (2004). Neuropsychological Evaluation of the Child. New York: Oxford University Press.

Braun, C. M. J., Archambault, M-A., Daigneault, S. and Larocque, C. (2000). Right body side performance decrement in congenitally dyslexic children and left body side performance decrement in congenitally hyperactive children. Neuropsychiatry, Neuropsychology, and Behavioral Neurology, 13: 89–100.

Brito, G. N. O. and Santos-Morales, T. R. (2002). Developmental norms for the Gardner Steadiness Test and the Purdue Pegboard: A study with children of a metropolitan school in Brazil. Brazilian Journal of Medical and Biological Research, 35: 931–949.

Brown, R. G., Jahanshahai, M. and Marsden, D. C. (1993). The execution of bimanual movements in patients with Parkinson's, Huntington's, and cerebellar disease. Journal of Neurology, Neurosurgery and Psychiatry, 56: 295–297.

Buddenberg, L. A. and Davis, C. (2000). Test-retest reliability of the Purdue Pegboard Test. American Journal of Occupational Therapy, 54: 555–558.

Costa, L. D., Vaughan, H. G., Levita, E. and Farber, N. (1963). Purdue Pegboard as a predictor of the presence and laterality of cerebral lesions. Journal of Consulting Psychology, 27: 133–137.

Costa, L. D., Scarola, L. M. and Rapin, I. (1983). Purdue Pegboard scores for normal grammar school children. Perceptual and Motor Skills, 18: 748.

DesRosiers, J., Hebert, R., Bravo, G. and Dutil, E. (1995). The Purdue Pegboard Test: Normative data for people aged 60 and over. Disability and Rehabilitation, 17: 217–224.

Doyen, A-L. and Carlier, M. (2002). Measuring handedness: A validation study of Bishop's reaching card test. Laterality, 7: 115–130.

Feinstein, A., Brown, R. and Ron, M. (1994). Effects of practice of serial tests of attention in healthy subjects. Journal of Clinical and Experimental Neuropsychology, 16: 436–447.

Fleishman, E. A. and Ellison, G. D. (1962). A factor analysis of fine manipulative tests. Journal of Applied Psychology, 46: 96–105.

Fleishman, E. A. and Hempel, W. E. Jr. (1954). A factor analysis of dexterity tests. Personnel Psychology, 7: 15–32.

Flyckt, L., Sydow, O., Bjerkenstedt, L., Edman, G., Rydin, E. and Wiesel, F-A. (1999). Neurological signs and psychomotor performance in patients with schizophrenia, their relatives and healthy controls. Psychiatry Research, 86:113–129.

Gardner, R. A. and Broman, M. (1979). The Purdue Pegboard: Normative data on 1334 school children. Journal of Clinical Child Psychology, 8: 156–162.

Golden, C. J., Espe-Pfeifer, P. and Wachsler-Felder, J. (2006). Neuropsychological Interpretation of Objective Psychological Tests. Springer Science & Business Media

Judge, J. and Stirling, J. (2003). Fine motor skill performance in left- and right-handers: Evidence of an advantage for left-handers. Laterality, 8: 297–306.

Lafayette Instrument Company. (2015). Catell Ab - Startsida - Catell AB. Purdue Pegboard Test - User Instructions. https://www.catell.se/images/1.59.2009221614/purdue-pegboard.pdf.

Lehoux, C., Everett, J., Laplante, L., Emond, C., Trepanier, J., Brassard, A. et al. (2003). Fine motor dexterity is correlated to social functioning in schizophrenia. Schizophrenia Research, 62: 269–273.

Mathiowetz, V., Rogers, S. L., Dowe-Keval, M., Donahoe, L. and Reline's, C. (1986). The Purdue Pegboard: Norms for 14- to 19-year-olds. The American Journal of Occupational Therapy, 40: 174–179.

McCurry, S. M., Gibbons, L. E., Uomoto, J. M., Thompson, M. L., Graves, A. B., Edland, S. D. et al. (2001). Neuropsychological test performance in a cognitively intact sample of older Japanese American adults. Archives of Clinical Neuropsychology, 16: 447–459.

Nybo, T. and Koskiniem, M. (1999). Cognitive indicators of vocational outcome after severe traumatic brain injury (TBI) in childhood. Brain Injury, 13: 759–766.

Pernat, K., Kfitikos, A., Phillips, J. G., Bradshaw, J. L., Iansek, R., Kempster, P. et al. (1996). The association between clinical and quantitative indexes of Parkinsonian symptomatology. Neuropsychiatry, Neuropsychology and Behavioral Neurology, 9: 234–241.

Peters, M. (1990). Subclassification of non-pathological left-handers poses problems for theories of handedness. Neuropsychologia, 28: 279–289.

Peters, M., Servos, P. and Day, R. (1990). Marked sex differences on a fine motor skill task disappear when finger size is used as a covariate. Journal of Applied Psychology, 75: 87–90.

Rapin, I., Tourk, L. M. and Costa, L. D. (1966). Evaluation of the Purdue Pegboard as a screening test for brain damage. Developmental Medicine and Child Neurology, 8: 45–54.

Reddon, J. R., Gill, D. M., Gauk, S. E. and Maerz, M. D. (1988). Purdue Pegboard: Test-retest estimates. Perceptual and Motor Skills, 66: 503–506.

Roy, M-A., Lehoux, C., Emond, C., Laplante, L., Bouchard, R. H., Everett, J. et al. (2003). A pilot neuropsychological study of Kraepelinian and non-Kraepelinian schizophrenia. Schizophrenia Research, 62: 155–163.

Sappington, T. J. (1980). Measures of lateral dorninrce: Interrelationships and temporal stability. Perceptual and Actor Skills, 50: 783–790.

Sattler, J. M. and Engelhardt, J. (1982). Sex differences on Purdue Pegboard norms for children. Journal of Clinical Child Psychology, 11: 72–73.

Schmidt, R., Fazekas, F., Offenbacher, H., Dusek, T., Zac, E., Reinhart, B. et al. (1993). Neuropsychologic correlations of MR1 white matter hyperintensities: A study of 150 normal volunteers. Neurology, 43: 2490–2492.

Stanford, M. S. and Barratt, E. S. (1996). Verbal skills, finger tapping, and cognitive tempo define a second-order factor of temporal information processing. Brain and Cognition, 31: 35–45.

Stewart, W. F., Schwartz, B. S., Simon, D., Bola, K. I., Todd, A. C. and Links, J. (1999). Neurobehavioral function and tibial and chelatable lead levels in 543 former organolead workers. Neurology, 52: 1610–1617.

Strenge, H., Niederberger, U. and Seelhorst, U. (2002). Correlation between tests of attention and performance on Grooved and Purdue Pegboards in normal subjects. Perceptual and Motor Skills, 95: 507–514.

Tiffin, J. (1968). Purdue Pegboard: Examiner Manual. Chicago: Science Research Associates. Tiffin, J. and Asher, E. I. (1948). The Purdue Pegboard: Norms and studies of reliability and validity. Journal of Applied Psychology, 32: 234–247.

Tiffin, J. and Asher, E. J. (1948). The Purdue Pegboard: norms and studies of reliability and validity. Journal of Applied Psychology, 32(3): 234–247. https://doi.org/10.1037/h0061266.

Triggs, W. J., Calvanio, R., Levine, M., Heaton, R. K. and Heilman, K. M. (2000). Predicting hand preference with performance on motor tasks. Cortex, 36: 679–689.

Uitti, R. J., Wharen, R. E., Turk, M. F., Lucas, J. A., Finton, M. J., Graff- Radford, N. R. et al. (1997). Unilateral pallidotomy for Parkinson's disease: Comparison of outcome in younger versus elderly patients. Neurology, 49: 1072–1077.

Vaughan, H. G. and Costa, L. D. (1962). Performance of patients with lateralized cerebral lesions: II. Sensory and motor tests. Journal of Nervous and Mental Disease, 134: 237–243.

Verdino, M. and Dingman, S. (1998). Two measures of laterality in handedness: The Edinburgh Handedness Inventory and the Purdue Pegboard test of manual dexterity. Perceptual and Motor Skills, 86: 476–478.

Wilson, B. C., Iacovello, J. M., Wilson, J. J. and Risucci, D. (1982). Purdue Pegboard performance of normal preschool children. Journal of Clinical Neuropsychology, 4: 19–26.

Yeudall, L. T., Fromm, D., Reddon, 1. R. and Stefanyk, W. O. (1986). Normative data stratified by age and sex for 12 neuropsychologi-cal tests. Journal of Clinical Psychology, 42: 918–946.

Zakzanis, K. K., Leach, L. and Freedman, M. (1998). Structural and functional meta-analytic evidence for fronto-subcortical system deficit in progressive supranuclear palsy. Brain and Cognition, 38: 283–296.

CHAPTER 12

Stroop Color and Word Test

*Kayla Thompson** and *Ryan Bennett*

The Stroop Color and Word Test (SCWT), also known as the Stroop test, is a neuropsychological test used clinically and experimentally to assess inhibition of cognitive interference. The test was originally proposed in 1935 by John Ridley Stroop, although many versions of the test have been created that slightly depart from the original. These include but are not limited to the Comalli version (Comalli et al. 1962), the Golden version (Golden and Freshwater 1978), the Victoria version (Regard 1981), the Delis-Kaplan Executive Function System Stroop task (Delis et al. 2001), and the Cognitive Assessment System Stroop task (Naglieri and Das 1997). Herein, only the Golden version of the Stroop test will be discussed, as it remains the most common version that is used today.

Normed Population

The Golden SCWT aimed to incorporate a normative sample of 100 subjects, ranging in age from 15–90 years and education 2–20 years (Golden 1978). In 2002 (Golden and Freshwater), an additional 300 normal controls were added to the sample. At this time, Golden discovered the association of gender and education with Stroop scores. This finding resulted in the updated normative data adjusted for age and education (Ivnik et al. 1996). Thus far, the SCWT has been normed for various populations, including but not limited to Latin American Spanish (Rivera et al. 2015), Dutch (van der Elst et al. 2006), and elder African Americans (Moering et al. 2004).

Nova Southeastern University, Fort Lauderdale, Florida, USA.
Email: rb1934@mynsu.nova.edu
* Corresponding author: kt986@mynsu.nova.edu

Test Description

The SCWT comprises three sections: Color, Word, and Color-Word. Each has five columns containing 20 items that subjects are required to read as fast as possible. The first section lists color names (e.g., RED, GREEN, and BLUE) printed in black ink and arranged in random order. The second section consists of a nonmeaningful pattern (e.g., XXXX) printed in the corresponding color from the color names in section one. In contrast, the Color-word section represents the incongruent condition as color-words are printed in an inconsistent color ink while subjects are asked to name the ink color rather than the written word. Thus, for example, the word RED will be printed in green or blue ink, but never red, to allow for the processing of one stimulus feature to affect the processing of another stimulus attribute (Stroop 1935). As such, the items feature a random pattern where no word nor color can follow itself. The congruent condition are automated tasks, while the incongruent condition requires inhibiting interference from the automated task of word reading, to perform the less automated task of naming ink color. In this regard, color naming is often less automatic than word naming.

Test Procedure

Administration of the SCWT is intended for ages 5 to 90 and is appropriate for all populations except the visually impaired. The test is well-recognized as simple and, on average, is completed in 5 minutes. The measure directs the subject to read aloud as many items from each page accurately and swiftly in 45 seconds until they are instructed to stop. Instructions for each page are unique to the section. Instructions on the first page state, “Read as many words as quickly as possible until you are stopped.” Instruction for the second page asks the examinee to “Name as many colors as quickly as possible.” On the third page, the client is told, “On each of these items, you are to ignore the word and name only the color of the ink in which the word is printed. For example, the first item is the word RED printed in blue. Your answer would be blue for the color of the ink. Remember, name as many colors as you can as quickly as possible until I tell you to stop.” Once the examiner is ready, each section is presented to the subject and placed at eye level on a flat surface. Upon the examiner saying “Go,” the 45-second timer begins until the subject is instructed to stop. The number of items completed in the 45-second period is recorded. If the subject reads all items before the 45-second timer ends, they are to return to the first column and begin again. While subjects are permitted to rotate the cards 45 degrees in either direction, lifting the card off the surface is prohibited. It is essential for the examiner to attend to items carefully. In the event the subject makes an error, they are instructed by the examiner to reread the item; however, errors are not counted or necessary to record. During corrections, the penalty for errors is additional time taken to identify the item correctly.

Task Demands

Traditionally, the SCWT has been thought to measure executive function; however, the three conditions have been revealed to measure varying aspects of cognitive functioning. The word and color tasks are suggested measures of processing speed (Golden et al. 2000). In the Color-Word task, there is a demand of selective attention, cognitive flexibility, and cognitive inhibition (Rosselli et al. 2002; Straus et al. 2006; van der Elst et al. 2006; Wecker at al. 2000). Other studies have suggested that the SCWT task also measures working memory, verbal fluency, and semantic activation (Straus et al. 2006; Periáñez et al. 2021). Despite this, the exact constructs which underlie the neuropsychological measure have been widely debated.

Scoring

Each section is scored by the number of items completed in 45 seconds. Accordingly, the test generates three scores: the number of items completed on word reading in 45 seconds, the number of colors identified on color naming in 45 seconds, and the number of items completed on color-word in 45 seconds. In adults, adjusted scores are calculated based on the subject's age and education, to determine normal performance in each section. The adjusted score is then subtracted from the raw score to yield a score that is converted to a T-score. In addition, an interference score is derived to assess the interference of word naming on the color naming process. There are various methods to calculating the interference score which have been controversial over the years. Respectively, the two methods most commonly used will be discussed. One method evaluates the decline in performance due to interference by subtracting the color score from the Color-Word score. However, limitations to this method have been identified by Golden et al. (2000) due to not taking word naming into account, thereby skewing the interference score for those who perform strongly on word naming. According to Golden (1978), the preferred method is based on a formula to obtain an expected color-word score, (color * word)/(color + word), which is then subtracted from the actual color-word score. The formula is as follows: $(I = CW - [(W \times C)/(W + C))$. Currently as it stands, the preferred method is the most commonly used and widely accepted method.

Reliability

Evaluation of test-retest reliability showed no significant differences when evaluating intervals of three minutes, one day, and one week. Jensen (1965) reported reliabilities of .88, .79, and .71, respectively, for raw scores of word, color, and color-word. Similarly, reliabilities of .73–.86 were reported by Golden (1975). Those evaluated at intervals of 1–2 weeks reported reliabilities of .67–.83 (Franzen et al. (1987). While the tests demonstrated reliability, Straus et al. (2006) deemed them marginally acceptable and suggested heeding with caution when used for clinical diagnosis. According to Chafetz and Matthew (2004), there are moderate to high correlations among the three sections, suggesting they measure similar domains of cognitive abilities.

Validity

Regarding construct validity, there has been a lack of consensus about the underlying constructs of the test. Interference scores have been demonstrated to be measures of inhibition and attention while exhibiting good concurrent validity compared to other measures of inhibition and attention (May and Hasher 1998). In addition, processing speed and semantic knowledge have also been attributed to the interference score (Straus et al. 2006). In order to address years of inconsistency, the most recent study evaluated five cognitive processes most commonly stated as constructs of the test over the past 85 years, including speed of visual search, phonemic verbal fluency, working memory, cognitive flexibility and conflict monitoring (Periáñez et al. 2021). Results revealed that word reading was a measure of speed of visual search, color naming was a measure of working memory and speed of visual search, color-word reflected conflict monitoring, working memory, and speed of visual search, while the interference score represented working memory and conflict monitoring. In addition to this, findings have cohesively supported word reading and color naming to be related to verbal fluency and speed (Protopapas et al. 2007; Lanham et al. 1999). Similarly, color word has been demonstrated to represent cognitive control and interference control (Ríos et al. 2004; Spikman et al. 2001).

Recent studies have examined the performance validity of the test across all indices (word, color, and color-word scores). Lee and colleagues (2019) identified that the test can differentiate between valid and invalid performance presentations in a mixed clinical (i.e., anxiety, depression and PTSD) and forensic sample. Of the indices, the word and color trial scores were found to have robust classification accuracy of 0.83 and 0.81. Although within acceptable ranges, the color-word trial demonstrated lower classification accuracy with an area under the curve (AUC) of 0.71. These results can be explained by the fact that more complex tasks innately result in lower performance, and easier tasks are better markers of performance validity. In a mild traumatic brain injury sample, Guise et al. (2014), similarly showed the tests ability to differentiate malingering and non-malingering individuals, although discriminability was relatively lower. Respectively, there was an AUC of 0.72 (Word), 0.69 (color), and 0.68 (color-word). Taken together, these findings, in conjunction with support from others (Khan et al. 2022), suggest the word index is an effective measure with good classification accuracy across populations.

Technical Aspects of Computerized Tests

Considering the increasing demand for computerized tests, the reliability and validity of the computerized test were evaluated. There have been considerable discrepancies in findings relative to computerized tests in adults and children. When examining the computerized and manual test on children, Basu (2021) showed that those between the ages of 8 and 13 had an absence of correlational relationships and low internal consistency, although reliability was established. On the contrary, Periáñez et al.

(2021) found significant correlations between computerized and manual versions of the Stroop test in an adult sample. Due to the lack of research using the version of the test discussed herein, the credibility of the computerized test remains obscure. Hence, the computerized version of the test warrants further investigation and, therefore, should not be used clinically for diagnoses.

Clinical Applications

The Stroop test is best used with other cognitive tests as part of a comprehensive neuropsychological battery; however, the test can be used as a stand-alone screener to differentiate populations. The test is well regarded as a sensitive measure for impaired concentration, high distractibility, and delayed processing, given that reading is an automatic process in healthy, literate individuals. In the word and color task individuals with speech motor dysfunction or learning disability typically exhibit diminished performance (Golden et al. 2000). Specific to the color task, performance may be affected by color blindness or individual/s inability to name colors. Given the nature of the task and the interference control component, the test is invaluable when assessing those with attention deficit hyperactivity disorder (ADHD), who are usually affected by the task's demand of selective attention and task set coordination. Noteworthy, is that the test is indicative of frontal lobe dysfunction however poor performance is not sufficient to make a diagnosis (Homack and Riccio 2004; King et al. 2004). It is increasingly recognized that the test is a good measure of frontal lobe injury due to the brain areas involved in the task such as the inferior frontal, dorsolateral prefrontal, and anterior cingulated cortices (Egner and Hirsh 2005; Harrison et al. 2005; Peterson et al. 1999). In a 1976 study, the Stroop was found to have 88.9% accuracy in differentiation between those with traumatic brain injury (TBI) and those without (Golden 1976). Similarly, the SCWT is often used to assess selective attention in those with TBI. In the elder population, the test is useful to assess deteriorate of cognitive functioning such as executive functioning, attentional control, and processing speed (Brink and McDowd 1999; West 1999b; Comalli et al. 1962; Milham et al. 2001).

Interpretation

Interpretation of the SCWT for all three sections is followed by a general rule of thumb, whereby T-scores of 40 or less are considered low, whiles scores above 40 are considered normal. In order to establish a difference between scores, there must be a 10-point difference or greater. According to Golden et al. (1978; 2000) the following interpretations correspond to T-scores of a given section.

1. Specifically, T-scores of less than 40 on word reading indicate motor speech problems, poorly developed reading skills, developmental learning disorder, having English as a second language, or an injury to the posterior region of the left hemisphere, which results in poor reading skills.
2. T-scores of less than 40 on color may indicate injury to the temporal-occipital area in the right hemisphere; however, if this is in combination with a T-score

above 40 on word reading, it may be a result of color blindness or an inability to identify color names. In contrast if the scores are in combination with T-scores of 40 or less this may suggest speech impairment, low intelligence, or a lack of effort (i.e., malingering).

3. Color-word T-scores of 40 or less that are accompanied by word and color scores above 40 suggest prefrontal pathology or an acute emotional turmoil. Good ability to inhibit conflicting responses is denoted by a color-word T-score that is at least 10 points above the color naming and word reading scores.
4. Interference scores above 40 typically suggest good cognitive flexibility. Low interference scores in the presence of normal Color and Word scores indicate prefrontal disorders.
5. In the event of mixed scores that diminish across sections, such as high color-word scores, normal color scores, and low word scores, this may suggest acquired or developmental dyslexia. Similar scores are also seen in left parietal-temporal brain injuries.
6. In the event of low scores on word and color-word, while color scores are high, this may indicate an individual displaying a lack of motivation or malingering.
7. The color-word score cannot be interpreted when either Color or Word score are below a T-score of 35.
8. When there is a consistent pattern of low scores across color, word, and color-word that are below 30, this may suggest severe cognitive dysfunction, left hemisphere injury, or diffuse brain injury.

References

Basu, S. (2022). Examining the reliability and validity of computerized stroop test in children aged 5–13 years: a preliminary study. Quality & Quantity, 1–9.

Brink, J. M. and McDowd, J. M. (1999). Aging and selective attention: An issue of complexity or multiple mechanisms? Journal of Gerontology: Psychological Sciences, 54B(1): 30–33.

Chafetz, M. D. and Matthews, L. H. (2004). A new interference score for the Stroop test. *Archives of* Clinical Neuropsychology, 19(4): 555–567.

Comalli P. E. Jr., Wapner S. and Werner H. (1962). Interference effects of Stroop Color-Word Test in childhood, adulthood, and aging. Journal of Genetic Psychology, 100(1): 47–53.

Comalli, P. E., Wapner, S. and Werner, H. (1962). Interference effects of Stroop color-word test on childhood, adulthood, and aging. Journal of Genetic Psychology, 100: 47–53.

Delis, D. C., Kaplan, E. and Kramer, J. H. (2001). San Antonio, TX: The Psychological Corporation. Delis-Kaplan Executive Function System. San Antonio, TX: The Psychological Corporation.

Egner, T. and Hirsch, J. (2005). The neural correlates and functional integration of cognitive control in a Stroop task. Neuroimage, 24(2): 539–547.

Franzen, M. D., Tishelman, A. C., Sharp, B. H. and Friedman, A. G. (1987). An investigation of the testretest reliability of the stroop colorword test across two intervals. Archives of Clinical Neuropsychology, 2(3): 265–272.

Golden C. J. and Freshwater S. M. (2002). Stroop Color and Word Test: Revised Examiner's Manual, Wood Dale, IL: Stoelting Co.

Golden, C. J. and Freshwater, S. M. (1978). Stroop color and word test.

Golden, C. J., Espe-Pfeifer, P. and Wachsler-Felder, J. (2000). Neuropsychological Interpretation of Objective Psychological Tests. Springer Science and Business Media.

Guise, B. J., Thompson, M. D., Greve, K. W., Bianchini, K. J. and West, L. (2014). Assessment of performance validity in the S troop C olor and W ord T est in mild traumatic brain injury patients: A criterion-groups validation design. Journal of Neuropsychology, 8(1): 20–33.

Harrison, B. J., Shaw, M., Yücel, M., Purcell, R., Brewer, W. J., Strother, S. C. et al. (2005). Functional connectivity during Stroop task performance. Neuroimage, 24(1): 181–191.

Homack, S. and Riccio, C. A. (2004). A meta-analysis of the sensitivity and specificity of the Stroop Color and Word Test with children. Archives of clinical Neuropsychology, 19(6): 725–743.

Jensen, A. R. (1965). Scoring the Stroop test. Acta Psychologica, 24(5): 398–408.

Khan, H., Rauch, A. A., Obolsky, M. A., Skymba, H., Barwegen, K. C., Wisinger, A. M. et al. (2022). A comparison of embedded validity indicators from the Stroop Color and Word Test among adults referred for clinical evaluation of suspected or confirmed attention-deficit/hyperactivity disorder. Psychological Assessment.

King, J. A., Colla, M., Brass, M., Heuser, I. and von Cramon, D. (2007). Inefficient cognitive control in adult ADHD: evidence from trial-by-trial Stroop test and cued task switching performance. Behavioral and brain functions : BBF, 3: 42. https://doi.org/10.1186/1744-9081-3-42.

Lanham, R. A., Vanderploeg, R. D. and Curtiss, G. (1999). The lack of construct validity of the Stroop color and word test with traumatic brain injury. Archives of Clinical Neuropsychology, 14(8): 782–783.

Lee, C., Landre, N. and Sweet, J. J. (2019). Performance validity on the Stroop Color and Word Test in a mixed forensic and patient sample. The Clinical Neuropsychologist, 33(8): 1403–1419.

May, C. P. and Hasher, L. (1998). Synchrony effects in inhibitory control over thought and action. Journal of Experimental Psychology: Human Perception and Performance, 24(2): 363.

Milham, M. P., Erickson, K. I., Banich, M. T., Kramer, A. F., Webb, A., Wszalek, T. et al. (2002). Attentional control in the aging brain: insights from an fMRI study of the stroop task. Brain and Cognition, 49(3): 277–296.

Naglieri J. A. and Das J. P. (1997). Cognitive assessment systems interpretive handbook, Itaska, IL: Riverside.

Periáñez, J. A., Lubrini, G., García-Gutiérrez, A., and Ríos-Lago, M. (2021). Construct validity of the stroop color-word test: influence of speed of visual search, verbal fluency, working memory, cognitive flexibility, and conflict monitoring. Archives of Clinical Neuropsychology, 36(1): 99–111.

Peterson, B. S., Skudlarski, P., Gatenby, J. C., Zhang, H., Anderson, A. W. and Gore, J. C. (1999). An fMRI study of Stroop word-color interference: evidence for cingulate subregions subserving multiple distributed attentional systems. Biological Psychiatry, 45(10): 1237–1258.

Protopapas, A., Archonti, A. and Skaloumbakas, C. (2007). Reading ability is negatively related to Stroop interference. Cognitive Psychology, 54(3): 251–282.

Regard, M. (1981). Cognitive rigidity and flexibility: A neuropsychological study. Unpublished Ph.D. dissertation, University of Victoria.

Ríos, M., Periáñez, J. A. and Muñoz-Céspedes, J. M. (2004). Attentional control and slowness of information processing after severe traumatic brain injury. Brain Injury, 18(3): 257–272.

Rosselli, M., Ardila A., Santisi M. N., del Rosario Arecco, M., Salvatierra, J. et al. (2002). Stroop effect in Spanish–English bilinguals. Journal of the International Neuropsychological, 8(06): 819–827.

Spikman, J. M., Kiers, H. A., Deelman, B. G. and van Zomeren, A. H. (2001). Construct validity of concepts of attention in healthy controls and patients with CHI. Brain and Cognition, 47(3): 446–460.

Strauss E., Sherman E. and Spreen O. (2006), A Compendium of Neuropsychological Tests: Administration, Norms, and Commentary, (3rd ed.). New York: Oxford University Press.

Stroop, J. R. (1935). Studies of interference in serial verbal reactions. Journal of Experimental Psychology, 18(6): 643.

Van der Elst W., Van Boxtel M. P., Van Breukelen G. J. and Jolles J. (2006). The stroop color-word test: Influence of age, sex, and education; and normative data for a large sample across the adult age range. Assessment, 13(1): 62–79.

Rivera, D., Perrin, P. B., Stevens, L. F., Garza, M. T., Weil, C., Saracho, C. P. et al. (2015). Stroop color-word interference test: normative data for the Latin American Spanish speaking adult population. NeuroRehabilitation, 37(4): 591–624.

Wecker, N. S., Kramer, J. H., Wisniewski, A., Delis, D. C. and Kaplan, E. (2000). Age effects on executive ability. Neuropsychology, 14(3): 409.

West, R. (1999b). Age differences in lapses.

CHAPTER 13

Symbol Digit Modalities Test (SDMT)

Melissa Ferrer

The Symbol Digit Modalities Test (SDMT) is a widely used paper-pencil assessment that measures psychomotor speed, encompassing processing speed and motor speed (Smith 1982). The test requires the examinee to substitute digits for abstract symbols using a reference key. The examinee's performance on the SDMT is dependent on several cognitive functions, including attention, visual scanning, tracking, and working memory abilities. The SDMT is a brief and easy-to-administer test that has high validity and reliability, which contributes to its widespread use in research (Sheridan et al. 2006).

History and Normative Sample

The Symbol Digit Modalities Test (SDMT) was first developed in the early 20th century by Guy Montrose Whipple and William Henry Pyle as a symbol digit substitution task to examine school children (Benedict et al. 2017; Pyle 1913). The United States Army later adopted this task to screen recruits for mental deficiency (Yerkes et al. 1921). A similar version of the SDMT emerged in the 1930s, requiring examinees to write symbols in accordance with target numbers. This later evolved into the digit symbol coding or digit symbol substitution test used in the Weschler intelligence test (Benedict et al. 2017). In the 1960s, researchers began using the original number response method of the SDMT in studies of cognitive aging and neuropsychology (Benedict et al. 2017). Smith later published the SDMT as a commercially available test in 1982, measuring information processing speed and efficiency through the symbol/digit substitution task (Benedict et al. 2017). Currently

Nova Southeastern University, Fort Lauderdale, Florida, USA.
Email: mf2096@mynsu.nova.edu

owned by Western Psychological Services (WPS), the SDMT has been included in the Brief Repeatable Battery of Neuropsychological Test (BRB) and the Minimal Assessment of Cognitive Function in Multiple Sclerosis (MACFIMS).

The Symbol Digit Modalities Test (SDMT) manual provides separate norms for written and oral administration. Norms for children are separated by sex and age, while the norms for adults are separated by age group and level of education. The test includes normative data for students and adults with various disorders; however, no data is presented for adults without a pre-existing disorder (Sheridan et al. 2006). Research on the SDMT's age and gender breakdowns, as well as its associations with socioeconomic status and education, is limited (Sheridan et al. 2006). In 1975, Centofani published supplemental adult norms by providing means and standard deviations for non-clinical adults aged 18–75 years, but gender breakdowns were not reported (Sheridan et al. 2006). Cutler also reported mean SDMT scores for college students in 1968, but no age or gender breakdowns were given. Although no systematic effects have been found across normal younger individuals, research studies suggest a decrease in performance on the SDMT for individuals over the age of 55 (Sheridan et al. 2006).

Test Procedures

As previously noted, The SDMT is a paper-pencil measure that requires examinees to substitute digits for abstract symbols using a reference key of nine different abstract symbols, each paired with a number (Smith 1968). Before starting the actual administration, the examiner explained the task and asked the examinee to complete the ten-item practice exercises located in the first row. The examinee writes or orally provides the corresponding number on the empty boxes under the randomized geometric figures, and the examiner provides feedback and answers any questions.

During the actual administration, the examinee is given 90 seconds to complete as many items as possible out of 110 items without erasing any mistakes. The examiner does not correct any errors or provide feedback during the administration. The examinee is encouraged to complete the task as fast as possible, without skipping any items, and from left to right until each row is completed. The total administration time for the SDMT is under 5 minutes. Individuals aged eight years and above must undergo the same administration procedure, as there are no age-appropriate starting points (Benedict et al. 2017).

Task Demands and Strategies

The SDMT is a test that assesses psychomotor speed and key neurocognitive functions such as attention, visual scanning, and motor speed (Ryan et al. 2020). The examinee's psychomotor speed will be assessed during this task by having them actively maintain and manipulate information over a brief period. This test will require the examinee to identify quickly the numbers associated with the corresponding symbol and write down the number or orally state them. Examinees may employ different strategies to complete the SDMT task. Some may attempt to memorize the matching pairs, allowing them to complete the task without referring to the coding key. However, others may resort to guessing, as the test is timed, and there may be perceived pressure to complete as many items as possible. In this scenario, accuracy might not be prioritized over speed, potentially leading to errors.

Scoring

The SDMT is scored by tallying the number of correct responses the examinee produced within the 90-second timeframe. The examiner can verify correct responses using the SDMT manual or WPS Auto Score Test Form. While the SDMT manual does not provide standardized scores, Western Psychological Services recommends examiners use a formula recognized by statisticians to produce standardized scores (Western Psychological Services). To obtain these standardized scores, the examiner can subtract the examinee's raw score from the mean score, divide the result by the standard deviation, and multiply the answer by 15. Adding 100 to this result yields the final standardized score, which can be rounded to the nearest whole number. The SDMT manual includes age-based means and standard deviations to aid score interpretation.

Reliability

Research has shown that the Symbol Digit Modalities Test (SDMT) has good to excellent test-retest reliability in healthy individuals. For the oral response version, the reliability coefficient was found to be 0.76 (Benedict 2005). Moreover, a study investigating the effects of using alternative forms during repeated neuropsychological testing in patients with multiple sclerosis found that the reliability coefficient for the SDMT was 0.97, considerably higher than the coefficient reported in the manual (Benedict 2005). Studies examining the reliability of the SDMT have demonstrated its consistency over short and long intervals, as well as across different languages. For instance, reliability coefficients for the Persian, Portuguese, and Spanish translations of the SDMT were 0.79, 0.86, and 0.95, respectively (Benedict et al. 2017).

Validity

The Symbol Digit Modalities Test (SDMT) has been established as a reliable and valid measure of processing speed and is considered the most sensitive neuropsychological test for multiple sclerosis (Benedict et al. 2017; Ryan et al. 2020). While computerized versions of the SDMT have been developed, none have been validated in patients with multiple sclerosis (Akbar et al. 2010). A study by Akbar and colleagues aimed to validate a new computerized version of the SDMT for use in patients with multiple sclerosis. The study involved 119 patients with multiple sclerosis and 38 healthy controls, and a comparison was made between the paper and computerized versions of the SDMT. Results indicated that patients with multiple sclerosis performed significantly worse than the control group on both test versions, with greater impairment observed on the computerized version (37%) compared to the paper version (29%). The study also found good test-retest reliability for the computerized version of the SDMT, suggesting that it is a sensitive measure of cognitive dysfunction in patients with multiple sclerosis (Akbar et al. 2010).

The construct validity of the SDMT has been investigated in a study by Benedict and colleagues, which involved 278 individuals with multiple sclerosis (2017). Results showed that the SDMT loaded on a general processing factor in the relapsing-remitting multiple sclerosis analysis. There was a split loading in the secondary-progressive multiple sclerosis group on both a speed function and memory factor. These findings are important because the SDMT was originally developed as a learning and processing efficiency test, assuming that as the administration proceeds, the examinee will learn the symbol/digit associations (Benedict et al. 2017).

Clinical Applications in Research

Correlations have been noted between the SDMT and instrumental activities of daily living and employability in multiple sclerosis patients, with a decline in SDMT performance being a predictor of work disability (Benedict et al. 2020). A study by Sheridan and colleagues (2006) examined the effects of age, education, gender, and income on SDMT performance in a community-dwelling control sample. Based on previously published studies, the authors generated means and standard deviations for oral and written SDMT administrations for adults under 30, adults aged 30–55, and adults over 55. The sample included 238 participants without major medical or psychiatric illnesses. Results from this study suggested that age, education, gender, and income did not significantly affect SDMT performance, indicating that the test is robust to these variables. This finding supports using the SDMT as a measure of neuropsychological impairment in non-clinical samples (Sheridan et al. 2006).

Interpretation

The Symbol Digit Modalities Test (SDMT) is a valid measure of psychomotor speed; however, it should not be used in isolation to determine the examinee's level of cognitive functioning. Poor performance on the SDMT is not necessarily indicative of specific neurological conditions but rather highly sensitive to the presence of cognitive impairment. Therefore, caution should be taken in interpreting the results of the SDMT, as it is not a definitive diagnostic tool for neurological conditions (Ryan et al. 2020).

1. In the written version of the SDMT, examinees are required to write down numbers under corresponding geometric figures. As such, fine motor skills play a role in the examinee's performance on the test. If there is reason to suspect poor motor skills, such as information gathered during the clinical interview or poor performance on other motor tests like Finger Tapping and Grooved Pegboard, it is recommended to administer the oral version of the SDMT instead. This would provide a more accurate representation of the examinee's cognitive abilities without the influence of motor skills (Benedict et al. 2017).
2. The SDMT is a timed test, and the examinee may need to be encouraged to work faster to complete as many items as possible within the allotted time. If the

examinee is experiencing anxiety during the test, they may tend to overthink their responses and focus more on accuracy rather than speed, which can negatively impact their performance (Benedict et al. 2017).

3. To complete the SDMT more quickly, examinees may rely on memorizing the coding key instead of referring to it for each item. In such cases, the examiner should administer other assessments to evaluate the examinee's visual memory abilities, such as the Visual Reproduction and Design subtests of the WMS.
4. processing speed is observed with traumatic brain injury, multiple sclerosis, strokes, and various other neurodegenerative diseases. Therefore, if the examinee performs poorly on the SDMT, it is then important for the examiner to obtain a detailed medical history from the examinee to rule out or consider possible causes for the performance.
5. Examinees with a history of hyperactivity and/or inattention symptoms may perform poorly on the SDMT, as this test requires the examinee to pay close attention to the pairs of numbers and symbols. An examinee who is hyperactive or inattentive may sacrifice accuracy for speed of completion. If symptoms of hyperactivity and/or inattention are suspected, the examiner should administer a continuous performance test, such as CPT-3 and CATA, to assess for possible attentional deficits that may be hindering the examinee's performance on the SDMT.
6. As performance on the SDMT can be influenced by visual acuity and ocular motor functions, it is then essential for the examiner to obtain information during the clinical interview about any possible visual issues the examinee may have.

References

Akbar, N., Honarmand, K., Kou, N. and Feinstein, A. (2011). Validity of a computerized version of the Symbol Digit Modalities Test in multiple sclerosis. Journal of Neurology, 258(3), 373–379.

Benedict, R. H. B. (2005, January 1). Effects of Using Same-versus Alternate-Form Memory Tests during Short-Interval Repeated Assessments in Multiple Sclerosis. Journal-International Neuropsychological Society, 11(6): 727–736.

Benedict, R. H. B., DeLuca, J., Phillips, G., LaRocca, N., Hudson, L. D. and Rudick, R. (2017). Multiple Sclerosis Outcome Assessments Consortium. (2017). Validity of the Symbol Digit Modalities Test as a cognition performance outcome measure for multiple sclerosis. Multiple Sclerosis Journal, 23(5): 721–733. https://doi-org.ezproxylocal.library.nova.edu/10.1177/1352458517690821.

Benedict, R. H. and Smerbeck, A. (2022). Construct validity of the symbol-digit modalities test. Multiple Sclerosis (Houndmills, Basingstoke, England), 13524585221112380. https://doi-org.ezproxylocal.library.nova.edu/10.1177/13524585221112381.

Normative Data for the Symbol Digit Modalities Test in Older White Australians and Americans, African-Americans, and Hispanic/Latinos. (2020).

Pyle, W. H. (1913). The examination of school children: A manual of directions and norms. New York: Macmillan.

Ryan, J., Woods, R. L., Britt, C. J., Murray, A. M., Shah, R. C., Reid, C. M., Wolfe, R., Nelson, M. R., Orchard, S. G., Lockery, J. E., Trevaks, R. E., Storey, E. (2020). Behalf of the ASPREE Investigator Group on. Normative Data for the Symbol Digit Modalities Test in Older White Australians and Americans, African-Americans, and Hispanic/Latinos. J Alzheimers Dis. Rep. 2020 August 4: 4(1): 313–323. doi: 10.3233/ADR-200194.

Sheridan, L. K., Fitzgerald, H. E., Adams, K. M., Nigg, J. T., Martel, M. M., Puttler, L. I. et al. (2006). Normative Symbol Digit Modalities Test performance in a community-based sample. Archives of Clinical Neuropsychology, 21(1): 23–28.

(SDMT) symbol digit modalities test. Educational & Psychological Assessments for Clinicians & Educators. (n.d.). Retrieved from https://www.wpspublish.com/sdmt-symbol-digit-modalities-test.

Smith, A. (1968). The symbol-digit modalities test: a neuropsychologic test of learning and other cerebral disorders. pp. 83–91. *In*: J. Helmuth (Ed.). Learning Disorders. Seattle: Special Child Publications.

Smith, A. (1982). Symbol Digits Modalities Test. Los Angeles: Western Psychological Services.

Waldmann, B. W., Dickson, A. L., Monahan, M. C. and Kazelkis, R. (1992). The relationship between intellectual ability and adult performance on the Trail Making Test and the Symbol Digit Modalities Test. Journal of Clinical Psychology, 48(3): 360–363.

Yerkes, R.M. Psychological examining in the United States Army. Washington, DC: Government Printing Office, 1921.

CHAPTER 14

Trail Making Test (TMT)

*Patricia Ordóñez** and *Cooper Dunn*

Originally created as part of the Army Individual Test Battery (1944), a measure of general mental ability used to predict military performance, the Trail Making Test (TMT) (1946) is a neuropsychological measure used to evaluate visual scanning, graphomotor speed, and mental flexibility. The TMT is also capable of detecting elements of various neurocognitive disorders such as Alzheimer's disease and other forms of dementia. It is a simple test that can be quickly administered. It was found that the skills required by both Part A and Part B of the TMT are significantly impacted by brain injury and, therefore, affect performance (Reitan and Wolfson 1995); thus, the TMT serves as a measure of various cognitive functions as well as the interplay between them in adolescents, adults, and older adults. It places demands on various cognitive domains, requiring mental flexibility and motor function abilities. It also requires the ability to recognize letters and numbers, which is highly dependent on the functions of the dominant cerebral hemisphere, and visual scanning, which is dependent on those of the non-dominant hemisphere. Processing speed and the brain's ability to integrate and synthesize the information presented visually are also highly involved in completing this measure, in addition to the ability to correctly sequence the numbers and/or letters; thus, the TMT has been called an especially useful measure of the overall integrity of the brain (Corrigan and Hinkeldey 1987).

Test Procedure

The TMT consists of two parts: Trails A (TMT-A) and Trails B (TMT-B). TMT-A is a numerical sequencing task, including circles containing the digits 1–25. Part A can be considered an effort measure as part of the instructions include the directions to "Draw the lines as fast as you can [and] do not lift the pencil from the paper" (Bowie and Harvey 2006). To complete Trails A, an examinee must employ processing and

Nova Southeastern University, Fort Lauderdale, Florida, USA.
Email: bd946@mynsu.nova.edu
* Corresponding author: po179@mynsu.nova.edu

graphomotor speed, attention, visual scanning, motor skills, and memory processes to quickly and accurately sequence the digits. TMT-B requires alternate sequencing between letters and numbers (letters from A–L; digits from 1–13) and measures processing speed, attention, visual scanning, motor skills, memory, and cognitive flexibility involving inhibition. For an examinee to correctly alternately sequence the letters and numbers, they must first master each of the sequences (alphabetical and numerical) and be able to access those sequences when prompted. Further, the examinee must be able to employ the frontal task of inhibition, allowing them to employ the sequence of A-1-B instead of A-B-C or 1-2-3, for example. The completion time for TMT-B is typically expected to be about double that for TMT-A, given the additional complexity of TMT-B and the two alternating sequences required within the measure. Part B requires maintaining two response sets simultaneously (Kortte et al. 2002). Further, a ratio score of TMT-B to TMT-A may serve as a measure of cognitive efficiency and/or dissimulation in individuals without a traumatic brain injury (Martin et al. 2003).

Scoring

The scoring procedures for TMT-A and TMT-B consist of time to completion and number of errors. The most common error identified is an incorrect connection (e.g., connecting 1 to 3 instead of 1 to 2). The total time in seconds is then used as the raw score, which is converted to a Heaton T-score. T-scores between 40 and 60 are within the average range.

Reliability and Validity

In Reitan's validation study (1955), TMT was administered to groups (N = 27) of brain-damaged and hospitalized control subjects who were paired based on sex, race, age, and education. Reitan found highly significant intergroup mean differences ($p < .001$) on both parts of the TMT, individually and summed, confirming Armitage's findings (1946) that this readily accessible and easily administered measure may be a valid tool to detect brain damage. It is important to consider that subsequent research found that the validity of TMT decreases for older, less intelligent patients; it was found that as intelligence increases, TMT performance increases, but that performance is expected to decrease as age increases (Goul and Brown 1970).

Smith et al. (2008) used clinical and non-clinical samples (N = 74) to investigate the validity and reliability of the TMT. In order to examine convergent validity, correlational data using other measures of visuospatial processing speed and nonverbal reasoning were compared to findings of TMT, and the researchers were able to find a statistically significant discriminant validity value, suggesting that the TMT was able to differentiate between clinical and non-clinical patients at a rate of .80, meaning it can accurately classify 80% of the research participants (Smith et al. 2008).

Sánchez-Cubillo et al. (2009) conducted a literature review focused on the cognitive abilities that underlie performance on the TMT and found that TMT-A had high construct validity primarily related to visuospatial ability while TMT-B showed high construct congruence with working memory and task-switching capabilities. Overall, the researchers concluded that when parts A and B were combined, executive control capability was the main construct being measured (Sánchez-Cubillo et al. 2009).

Interpretation

Interpretation of the Trail Making Test is generally a function of the patient's completion speed rather than a tally of correct versus incorrect responses. Slow completion speeds indicate the presence of some disturbance, whereas average or above-average completion speeds would lead the clinician to find little to no brain dysfunction. However, observation and/or tallying of incorrect responses can provide quality clinical utility. Further, behavioral observations during administration can be highly useful: an examinee may exhibit a tremor or visual field neglect, which may be noted by the clinician for further assessment or to explain the performance-based score. As mentioned, TMT-A is generally understood to be a measure of visual scanning and graphomotor speed, primarily because it does not require a mental shift between numbers and letters. Because the participant must switch between letters and numbers on TMT-B, this part is considered mainly to evaluate mental flexibility and switching. A summary of key interpretation guidelines is as follows:

1. Reitan originally classified normal Trails A and Trails B completion times as less than 40 or 91 seconds, respectively. However, older individuals are expected to perform slower, so age-adjusted norms should be used when interpreting results.
2. While Reitan does not adjust for age or education, Heaton et al. norms (1990) adjust for age, education, and gender, adding race as well. Heaton's scores are expressed as T-scores, with scores below 40 seen as impaired.
3. The ratio of Trails B divided by Trails A can provide a useful measure of comparative performance on the two test sections. A ratio less than 1.5 suggests that the individual has some impairment in the skills required for Trails A (i.e., motor skills/visual scanning impairment).
4. Impairment on Trails B is indicated by a ratio higher than 3. Impairment on Trails B is usually caused by a lack of alphabetic knowledge and/or an inability to switch between letters and numbers cognitively.
5. Poor performance on Trails B caused by poor alphabetic knowledge indicates lifelong problems that can be evaluated through the patient's history.
6. Poor performance on Trails A, as indicated by a completion time over the cutoff and/or a ratio less than 1.5, is usually caused by motor or visual construction impairment.
7. Poor number awareness or poor counting ability may result in high-time completion or incomplete test administrations. This is usually caused by damage to the posterior dominant hemisphere or an intellectual disability of a moderate or severe nature. In such cases, assess whether the individual can repeat the alphabet quickly and count to 30. (Formal measures of counting and alphabet are assessed in the Wechsler Memory Scale measures.)

8. Good performance on the TMT, specifically Trails B, is uncommon in brain-injured individuals. Therefore, the TMT is capable of detecting many forms of brain injury. However, brain injury may be more difficult to detect in highly intelligent individuals.
9. Depressed individuals may perform slower on Trails B. Furthermore, due to the cognitive effects of aging, depressed elderly individuals may require much more time to complete the test than their healthy counterparts or younger depressed individuals.
10. The TMT should not be exclusively used as a diagnostic tool in psychiatric settings as false positives may be too high, especially in acute or more impaired psychiatric populations.

References

Armitage, S. G. (1946). An analysis of certain psychological tests used for the evaluation of brain injury. Psychological Monographs, 60(1), i–48. https://doi.org/10.1037/h0093567

Corrigan, J. D. and Hinkeldey, M. S. (1987). Relationships between parts A and B of the Trail Making Test. J. Clin. Psychol., 43(4), 402–409.

Golden, C. J., Espe-Pfeifer, P. and Wachsler-Felder, J. (2002). Neuropsychological Interpretation of Objective Psychological Tests (Critical Issues in Neuropsychology). Springer.

Goul, W. R. and Brown, M. (1970). Effects of age and intelligence on Trail Making Test performance and validity. Perceptual and Motor Skills, 30(1): 319–326. https://doi.org/10.2466/pms.1970.30.1.319.

Kortte, K. B., Horner, M. D. and Windham, W. K. (2002). The trail-making test, part B: cognitive flexibility or ability to maintain set? Applied Neuropsychology, 9(2): 106–109. https://doi.org/10.1207/S15324826AN0902_5.

Martin, T. A., Hoffman, N. M. and Donders, J. (2003). Clinical utility of the trail making test ratio score. Applied Neuropsychology, 10(3): 163–169. https://doi.org/10.1207/S15324826AN1003_05.

Reitan, R. M. and Wolfson, D. (1995). Category test and trail making test as measures of frontal lobe functions. The Clinical Neuropsychologist, 9(1): 50–56. https://doi.org/10.1080/13854049508402057.

Sánchez-Cubillo, I., Periáñez, J. A., Adrover-Roig, D., Rodríguez-Sánchez, J. M., Ríos-Lago, M., Tirapu, J. and Barceló, F. (2009). Construct validity of the Trail Making Test: Role of task-switching, working memory, inhibition/interference control, and visuomotor abilities. Journal of the International Neuropsychological Society: JINS, 15(3): 438–450. https://doi.org/10.1017/s1355617709090626.

Smith, S. R., Servesco, A. M., Edwards, J. W., Rahban, R., Barazani, S., Nowinski, L. A., Little, J. A., Blazer, A. L. and Green, J. G. (2008). Exploring the validity of the comprehensive trail making test. The Clinical Neuropsychologist, 22(3): 507–518. https://doi.org/10.1080/13854040701399269.

CHAPTER 15

Tests of Variables of Attention (TOVA)

Kayley Slicer

The Test of Variables of Attention (TOVA) is a computerized continuous performance assessment developed to measure the key components of attention and inhibitory control (Leark et al. 2008). The test is divided into auditory and visual tasks that consist of two halves: target infrequent and target frequent. The TOVA is primarily used by psychologists to assist other healthcare professionals when evaluating attention deficits, including ADHD, in child and adult populations. It is normed for use with people ages 4 to 80+ years, and all norms are stratified by age and gender (Leark et al. 2008). The administration time for the TOVA varies based on age with those 5.6 years and older completing the assessment in 21.6 minutes, and those aged 4 to 5.5 years completing the assessment in 10.8 minutes. The TOVA measures an examinee's response time variability, response time, commissions, and omissions. It may be used as an aid for clinicians to diagnose and establish effective treatment plans for individuals with an attention deficit disorder (Leark et al. 2008).

Normed Population

The TOVA Professional Manual outlines the collection of normative data for visual and auditory tests (Leark et al. 2008). In the visual test, 769 children aged 6–16 years (grades 1, 3, 5, 7, and 9) were randomly selected from suburban public schools in or near Minneapolis, MN (Greenberg and Waldman 1993). Notably, 99% of the sample comprised Caucasian children, with the remaining 1% categorized as "other" ethnicities. Stringent exclusionary criteria excluded children on psychoactive medication, those receiving Special Education services, or with an identified deviant behavior rating 2 standard deviations above the norm from teacher rating scales.

Nova Southeastern University, Fort Lauderdale, Florida, USA.
Email: ks2999@mynsu.nova.edu

Additional normative data was collected and comprised 571 children, with 73 subjects aged 4–5 and 498 subjects aged 12–19 (Greenberg and Crosby 1992A). These children were randomly selected from suburban public schools and a rural high school in Minnesota. The sample again was 99% Caucasian and 1% other. The exclusion rules were the same as the ones described above for the original normative sample. Testing occurred in the morning to mitigate diurnal effects. The subjects aged 4–5 were administered the shorter version of the TOVA.

Adult normative data for the visual test involved 250 participants, mainly college undergraduates from Minnesota and local communities, aged 20 and above. Like the child sample, 99% were Caucasian and 1% were classified as "other" ethnicities. Exclusion criteria identified adults on psychoactive medication or with a history of central nervous system disorders or injuries.

Regarding the auditory test, the normative sample included 2,551 children from Minneapolis suburban schools (ages 6 to 19), with 99% being Caucasian. Similar exclusion criteria applied, and testing was conducted in the morning to control diurnal effects. Attempts to norm the test for ages 4 to 5 indicated that the task was too difficult for this population.

For the auditory test's adult sample (129 participants, ages 20 and above), normative information is pending completion, as testing is still in the experimental phase. Results for adult normative data will be available upon conclusion. Currently, the auditory test is normed for use with people aged 6–29 years. Normative data for test variables was obtained for both auditory and visual tests by using two-year age groups. Age and gender differences for each variable were examined.

Test Procedures

The following test procedures were derived from the TOVA Company User's Manual (2020). To administer the TOVA, examiners begin by creating a new session for an existing or new respondent. This involves adding the participant's name, date of birth, gender, and favorite color. Once saved, information about the test session is added and the test administration may be launched.

Examiners choose between administering a visual or auditory test and must ensure the accuracy of the participant's date of birth and gender, as the results are compared to gender and age group norms. The examiner may select the language for test instructions, and upon launching the test, the instructions are presented. After reviewing the instructions, a practice test is conducted, followed by the full TOVA administration. Prompting is permitted during the practice test, but not during the actual test administration. Once the participant completes the test a summary of their results appears on the screen. If this information looks appropriate, their results are saved, and a report is generated containing the test results.

The TOVA is a visual continuous performance test (CPT) where subjects are presented with visual targets and nontargets on screen (Leark et al. 2008). The subjects are instructed to press the microswitch as quickly as possible each time they see a target. They are instructed to refrain from pressing the microswitch when they are presented with a nontarget. The targets and nontargets are presented in two conditions or halves: stimulus frequent and stimulus infrequent.

The TOVA-Auditory is an auditory CPT that mimics the structure of the visual portion with auditory targets (Leark et al. 2008). The auditory target is a G note and the nontarget sound is a middle C note. Similar to the visual test there are two stimulus conditions or halves: stimulus frequent and stimulus infrequent.

As the TOVA was normed for its use in the morning before 1 p.m., it should be administered in the morning to avoid possible diurnal variations. It should also be administered first before other tests, to ensure optimal attention and to reduce interference with other tests.

Reliability

To examine internal reliability of the TOVA a Pearson's *r* correlation coefficient was used; due to the timed nature of the task Cronbach's alpha was not appropriate. The authors examined between variable reliability coefficients across two conditions: stimulus frequent and stimulus infrequent (Leark et al. 2008). The authors found that between variable reliability coefficients were not as robust as the within variable coefficients. The between variable coefficients supports the notion that the variables capture different aspects of variance. As expected, the authors reported the greatest closeness in variables of response time and response time variability ($r = .7 - .8$).

Llorente et al. (2001) examined the internal consistency of the TOVA with 49 children aged 6–12 years with a preexisting diagnosis of ADHD. The researchers analyzed the total number of correct target responses from both halves of the assessment. Pearson product moment correlations were derived using subjects scores from initial performance and performance 16 weeks (about 3 and a half months) later. Results showed high internal consistency across both halves, between both halves, and the total.

In addition, Llorente and colleagues (2001) examined the test/retest reliability of the TOVA with the same sample of children described above. The children were evaluated three times over four months to assess for temporal stability and reproducibility of test scores. Pearson product moment correlations were calculated across three separate time intervals for all four variables of the TOVA. The results provided evidence for moderate test-retest reliability across several test periods. Due to the observed variability, the researchers used a Bland-Altman procedure with the data to determine the limits of agreement between scores. They found less agreement than previously observed and attributed this to natural variability in individual's attention and concentration that occurs in ADHD itself.

Leark et al. (2004) investigated the test-retest reliability of the TOVA with a sample of healthy school children aged 6–14.2 years. Participants were excluded if they had a history of CNS impairment, loss of consciousness, or psychiatric disorder, or if they used any prescribed medication that may affect attention. The children were administered the TOVA and then underwent a second administration at 90 minutes. The results indicated adequate test-retest reliability for the 90-minute interval.

The researchers conducted a second study with 33 children aged 6–14.5 years randomly selected from private and public schools in Southern California. The same exclusionary criteria as described above was applied. The participants were administered the TOVA once and then readministered the test again approximately seven days later at the same time of day. The results of the study found positive and significant correlations between the two administrations on all TOVA variables.

Validity

To examine criterion validity, Greenberg and Waldman (1993) selected individuals with ADHD, undifferentiated ADD, Conduct Disorder, and healthy controls. They examined their performance on the visual stimulus version of the TOVA. They examined disparities in group performance across various variables in five distinct approaches: (1) Assessing group performance differences; (2) Evaluating group performance while controlling for gender and age; (3) Exploring group performance in relation to age; (4) Investigating group performance differences based on test conditions; and (5) Analyzing group performance differences with respect to test quarters. They found significant differences on most variables between the ADHD and ADD group, and the ADHD and CD and control groups respectively. When examining the effects of age and gender, the researchers found that the number of omission errors varied as a function of age. There were larger differences observed between younger children than in older children. Overall, the ADHD group had the highest scores across all groups on the TOVA. Forbes (1998) also documented significant between group differences on the variables of the TOVA in a sample of 117 children with ADHD/ADD and healthy controls.

The TOVA has evidence for discriminative validity in its ability to differentiate between adults and children diagnosed with ADHD and healthy controls (Greenberg and Crosby 1992B, Greenberg and Crosby 1992C). The TOVA has found to be highly predictive in accurately classifying those individuals with and without attention problems. The TOVA has also been found to be sensitive to caffeine usage on two of the four test variables (Bernstein et al. 1994).

Factor analysis was employed to derive validity data for the auditory segment of the TOVA. The auditory portion exhibited loadings on five distinct factors: response time, percentage of commission errors in the stimulus frequent condition, percentage of omissions in the stimulus frequent condition, percentage of commission errors in the stimulus infrequent condition, and percentage of omission errors in the stimulus infrequent condition. In aggregate, these five factor loadings from the analysis explained 86% of the variance.

Scoring

As the test is computerized, scores are automatically generated based on the performance of each respondent. Specific preset formulas are employed for each variable to derive their scores. Each formula, tailored to a particular variable, generates a distinct score by considering the respondent's performance. For example, the response time variability formula is as follows: A sum of the correct response times subtracted by the mean correct response time, squared, and then divided by the number of correct responses. This computation results in a score specific to response time variability. The scores, obtained through these formulas, are presented at various intervals, including quarter, half, and total scores. These intervals offer a comprehensive overview of the respondent's performance on the TOVA.

The response time variable is the average time the subject takes to respond correctly to a target. This is calculated by summing the correct response times and then dividing by the number of targets. The Errors of Commission variable is calculated as the ratio of the incorrect responses to nontargets to the number of nontargets presented to the subject. The Errors of Omissions variable is calculated as the ratio of correct responses to targets divided by the number of targets presented, subtracted by the number of anticipatory responses to targets.

The TOVA also produces a D Prime score which is the response discriminability score that represents the ratio of hits to "false alarms". The TOVA calculates a total ADHD score that compares the subject's performance to that an identified ADHD sample's performance.

Types of Errors

The TOVA evaluates four variables designed to identify errors in a respondent's performance: omission, commission, response speed, and response time variability. An omission error arises when the respondent fails to react to the correct stimulus, indicating a lapse in attention or an inability to recognize and respond appropriately to the target stimulus.

Conversely, a commission error occurs when the respondent responds to an incorrect stimulus, suggesting difficulties in inhibiting impulsive responses or distinguishing between relevant and irrelevant stimuli.

Additionally, the TOVA measures response speed, gauging how quickly the respondent reacts after the correct stimulus presentation. Slowed response speed indicates delays or prolonged response times following the appearance of the correct stimulus. This may imply challenges in processing and initiating a prompt response. Lastly, response time variability reflects inconsistencies in response times throughout the entire test. High variability in response times suggests fluctuations in attention and reaction speed, indicating difficulties in sustaining attention or maintaining consistent attention throughout.

Clinical Applications in Research

Forbes (1998) investigated the TOVA's ability to differentiate between children with ADHD and those with "other" clinical diagnoses. Results indicated significant differences in the TOVA variables between the ADHD group and the group with "other" diagnoses. Specifically, the TOVA accurately identified 80% of the ADHD sample and 72% of the non-ADHD sample, showcasing its potential as a tool for distinguishing between these groups in a clinical setting.

Similarly, Semrud-Clikeman and Wical (1999) conducted a study focusing on differentiating between groups of children with complex partial seizures (CPS), comparing four groups: CPS with ADHD, CPS without ADHD, ADHD alone, and a control group. Results revealed that the CPS and ADHD group performed the poorest on the TOVA, highlighting significant attentional challenges. Treatment with methylphenidate improved performance in both ADHD groups, indicating its effectiveness in enhancing attention functioning in children with CPS and ADHD.

Parasnis et al. (2003) explored TOVA performance in prelingually deaf young adults compared to hearing young adults without ADHD. Deaf participants exhibited lower d' scores and increased commission errors, indicating reduced perceptual sensitivity and heightened impulsivity during response initiation. Factor analysis showed similar structures for both groups, suggesting homogeneous construct validity. The study emphasized the necessity for TOVA norms tailored to the deaf population to prevent overdiagnosis of ADHD.

Chae et al. (2003) investigated the correlation between intelligence and TOVA performance in gifted children. Gifted children demonstrated fewer omission and commission errors, and more consistent responses on the TOVA, with significant positive correlations between intelligence and these variables. The study suggested the need for developmental norms for younger ages when assessing gifted individuals with the TOVA. In addition, Weyandt and colleagues (2002) explored the relationship between intelligence and TOVA performance in a sample of young adults. In contrast to Chae and colleagues, they found no significant correlation between FSIQ and TOVA performance.

Regarding memory, Braverman et al. (2010) explored the use of the TOVA in predicting attention complaints and memory impairments using the Weschler Memory Scale-Third Edition (WMS-III) in a clinical setting. The results indicated a consistent correlation between decreased TOVA performance and attention and memory impairments. In a sample of children, Riccio et al. (2007) examined the relationship between the TOVA and the Children's Memory Scale (CMS), and found significant correlations between subscales of the CMS and the TOVA. In particular, there were significant correlations between TOVA Omissions, reaction time, and reaction time variability, but not commissions. By incorporating the TOVA into attention deficit diagnostic evaluations, a clinician may be able to gain valuable insights into impairments across other tests of cognitive functioning, for a more accurate understanding of the patient.

The TOVA has also been evaluated for its use in identifying credible performance. Pollock et al. (2021) assessed adults using the TOVA, identifying three distinct profiles: low TOVA performance indicating attention-related difficulties, self-reported ADHD symptoms suggesting subjective attention difficulties, and higher rates of failure on validity tests indicating potential exaggeration. The study highlighted the value of analyzing TOVA performance patterns in gauging the credibility of reported difficulties.

Interpretations

As with any neuropsychological assessment, a clinician should not conclude a diagnosis following the administration of only one assessment. This criterion applies to the TOVA as well, and a diagnosis of ADHD should not be given solely based on this test. It is important to consider additional factors such as behavioral functioning, academic functioning, medical history, etc., when interpreting the data from the TOVA. Of note, this interpretative process should only be conducted by a professional who has had sufficient training in TOVA administration and psychological assessment. The following guidelines were derived from the TOVA Professional Manual and may be used to assist with interpreting results (Leark et al. 2008).

1. The test result is considered invalid if the Response Time (RT) or the Response Time Variability (V) equals 0.
2. If the test procedure is interrupted and needs to be paused, it is important for the clinician to note that the results following this break will be considered invalid.
3. If an examinee's anticipatory response rate is greater than 10% then the results are considered invalid. This type of response style negatively impacts the accuracy for identifying commission and omission errors.
4. If an examinee's Commission or Omission error rate is equal to 100% then the results are invalid.
5. Performance during the first half of the assessment helps identify individuals who are "under aroused", or have more difficulty sustaining attention.
6. Performance during the second half of the assessment helps identify individuals who are "over stimulated" and may be easily distracted.
7. In addition to examining the first and second halves of the TOVA, the intra-half quarters should also be addressed. For example, if an examinee demonstrates poorer performance in quarter 1 compared to quarter 2, they may be experiencing elevated levels of anxiety.
8. If an examinee demonstrates poorer performance in quarter 3 compared to quarter 4, they may also be experiencing anxiety with elevated levels of obsessive-compulsive traits.
9. In conclusion, when interpreting the TOVA, it is important to identify the section labeled, "Notes to the Clinician". This section will provide an individualized interpretation of the examinee's performance which can further guide the clinician with treatment planning.

References

Burnstein, M. D., G., Carroll, PhD, M., Crosby, PhD, R., Perwien, B. A., A., Go, M.D., F. and Benowitz, M.D., N. (1994). Caffeine effects on learning, performance, and anxiety in normal school-age children. Journal of American Academy of Child & Adolescent Psychiatry, 33(3): 407–415.

Braverman, E. R., Chen, A. L., Chen, T. J., Schoolfield, J. D., Notaro, A., Braverman, D. et al. (2010). Test of variables of attention (TOVA) as a predictor of early attention complaints, an antecedent to dementia. Neuropsychiatric Disease and Treatment, 6: 681–690. https://doi.org/10.2147/NDT.S12243.

Forbes G. B. (1998). Clinical utility of the Test of Variables of Attention (TOVA) in the diagnosis of attention-deficit/hyperactivity disorder. Journal of Clinical Psychology, 54(4): 461–476. https://doi.org/10.1002/(SICI)1097- 4679(199806)54:4<461::AID-JCLP8>3.0.CO;2-Q.

Golden, C. J., Espe-Pfeifer, P. and Wachsler-Felder, J. (2000). Neuropsychological interpretation of objective psychological tests. Springer Science & Business Media.

Greenberg, M. D., L. M. and Crosby, PhD, R. D. (1992a). A Summary of Developmental normative Data on the T.O.V.A. Ages 4 to 80+. Unpublished manuscript.

Greenberg, M. D., L. M. and Crosby, PhD, R. D. (1992b). The assessment of Medication Effects in Attention Deficit Disorder Using the Test of Variables of Attention (T.O.V.A.) Manuscript submitted for publication.

Greenberg, M. D., L. M. and Crosby, PhD, R. D. (1992c). Specificity and Sensitivity of the Test of Variables of Attention (T.O.V.A.). Manuscript submitted for publication.

Greenberg, L. M. and Waldman, I. D. (1993). Developmental normative data on the Test of Variables of Attention (T.O.V.A.). Journal of Child and Adolescent Psychiatry, 34(6): 1019–1030.

Greenberg, L. M., Kindschi, C. L., Dupuy, T. R. and Hughes, S. J. (1994). Test of Variables of Attention continuous performance test. Los Alamitos, CA: Universal Attention Disorders.

Leark, R. A., Wallace, D. R. and Fitzgerald, R. (2004). Test-retest reliability and standard error of measurement for the Test of Variables of Attention (T.O.V.A.) With Healthy School-Age Children. Assessment, 11(4): 285–289. https://doi.org/10.1177/1073191104269186.

Leark, R. A., Greenberg, L. M., Kindschi, C. L., Dupuy, T. R. and Hughes, S. J. (2008). TOVA professional manual. Los Alamitos, CA: TOVA Company.

Leark, R., Greenberg, L., Kindschi, C., Dupuy, T. and Hughes, S. (2008, February 20). Test of Variables of Attention Professional Manual. TOVA - Test of Variables of Attention. https://files.tovatest.com/documentation/7.3/professional_manual_844.pdf.

Llorente, A. M., Voigt, R., Jensen, C. L., Fraley, J. K., Heird, W. C. and Rennie, K. M. (2008). The Test of Variables of Attention (TOVA): internal consistency (Q_1 vs. Q_2 and Q_3 vs. Q_4) in children with attention deficit/hyperactivity disorder (ADHD). Child Neuropsychology: A Journal on Normal and Abnormal Development in Childhood and Adolescence, 14(4): 314–322. https://doi.org/10.1080/09297040701563578.

Parasnis, I., Samar, V. J. and Berent, G. P. (2003). Deaf adults without attention deficit hyperactivity disorder display reduced perceptual sensitivity and elevated impulsivity on the Test of Variables of Attention (T.O.V.A.). Journal of Speech, Language, and Hearing Research, 46(5): 1166–1183. https://doi.org/10.1044/1092-4388(2003/091).

Pollock, B., Harrison, A. G. and Armstrong, I. T. (2021). What can we learn about performance validity from TOVA response profiles? Journal of Clinical and Experimental Neuropsychology, 43(4): 412–425. https://doi.org/10.1080/13803395.2021.1932762.

Reddy, L. A., Newman, E., Pedigo, T. K. and Scott, V. (2010). Concurrent validity of the Pediatric Attention Disorders Diagnostic Screener for children with ADHD. Child Neuropsychology, 16(5): 478–493. https://doi.org/10.1080/09297041003705479.

Riccio, C. A., Garland, B. H. and Cohen, M. J. (2007). Relations Between the Test of Variables of Attention (TOVA) and the Children's Memory Scale (CMS). Journal of Attention Disorders, 11(2): 167–171. https://doi.org/10.1177/1087054706295653.

Semrud-Clikeman, M. and Wical, B. (1999). Components of attention in children with complex partial seizures with and without ADHD. Epilepsia, 40(2): 211–215. https://doi.org/10.1111/j.1528-1157.1999.tb02077.x.

The TOVA Company. (2020). T.O.V.A. 9.1 User's Manual. https://files.tovatest.com/documentation/9/User's%20Manual.pdf.

Weyandt, L. L., Mitzlaff, L. and Thomas, L. (2002). The Relationship Between Intelligence and Performance on the Test of Variables of Attention (TOVA). Journal of Learning Disabilities, 35(2): 114–120. https://doi.org/10.1177/002221940203500203.

CHAPTER 16

Visual Puzzles

*Kayley Slicer** and *Ryan Bennett*

The Weschler Adult Intelligence Scale (WAIS-IV) is a comprehensive assessment tool with several subtests to measure cognitive abilities. In the latest version of the WAIS, introduced in 2008, the Visual Puzzles subtest replaced the Object Assembly subtest as a core subtest within the Perceptual Reasoning Index (Weschler 2008).

Visual Puzzles are a visual analog of the Object Assembly subtest and assess an individual's ability to analyze and synthesize abstract visual stimuli and measure nonverbal reasoning (Weschler 2008). This subtest requires individuals to identify the missing pieces in a complex visual image, testing their visual-spatial abilities and problem-solving skills.

Overall, the Visual Puzzles subtest is a valuable tool in assessing an individual's perceptual reasoning abilities and provides insight into their nonverbal reasoning skills.

Test Procedures

The Visual Puzzles subtest is a timed measure that assesses an individual's ability to analyze and synthesize abstract visual stimuli (Wechsler 2008). It comprises one demonstration item, one sample, and 26 test items. During this subtest, the examinee is presented with a whole puzzle and must select three out of six presented pieces that fit together to create the puzzle shown. Depending on the item, the examinee is given 20 or 30 seconds to respond.

The test begins with a demonstration item in which the examiner gives verbal instructions on completing the task and explains the rationale for accurately selecting a puzzle piece (Wechsler 2008). Next, the examinee is given a sample item to practice what they have learned and to check for understanding of the task. If the examinee answers incorrectly, they receive feedback on correctly selecting a puzzle piece. The

Nova Southeastern University, Fort Lauderdale, Florida, USA.
Email: rb1934@nova.edu
* Corresponding author: ks2999@mynsu.nova.edu

appropriate starting item for this subtest is based on the individual's age and cognitive ability. Those aged 16–90 start with item 5, while individuals suspected of having an intellectual disability or intellectual deficit start with item 1 (Wechsler 2008).

Scoring

The Visual Puzzles subtest on the WAIS-IV utilizes a scoring system in which one point is awarded for a correct answer within the specified time limit, and zero points are awarded for an incorrect response or a response outside the time limit (Wechsler 2008). If the examinee initially gives an incorrect answer but corrects themselves within the time limit, the examiner may provide clarification, and full points can be awarded for a correct answer. However, if the examinee fails to choose three pieces, the first time they can be corrected and awarded full points, but any subsequent occurrence is considered incorrect. The raw score is then converted into a scaled score, which is factored into the Perceptual Reasoning Index score and the Full Scale IQ (Wechsler 2008). Scaled scores have a mean of 10 and a standard deviation of 3, with scores of 8–12 considered average, scores of 7 are low average, scores of 5–6 are borderline, and scores of 4 and below are extremely low. Conversely, scores of 13 and above are high average to very superior. When converting raw scores to scaled scores, the examiner must use the norm tables provided in the WAIS-IV manual, which were created based on scores earned by the representative sample of individuals in specific age groups. These norm tables are divided into age groups of 16–19 in 2-year intervals, 20–34 and 65–90 in 5-year intervals, and 35–64 in 10-year intervals (Wechsler 2008).

Reliability and Correlations

The Visual Puzzles subtest on the WAIS-IV has fair internal consistency with an average reliability coefficient of .86 and below-average to average test-retest reliability with an average coefficient of .69 (Wechsler 2008). Test-retest reliability was assessed by retesting 298 individuals from the 13 age groups in the standardization sample.

The Visual Puzzles subtest is a fair measure of g (overall intelligence), accounting for 45% of the variance in overall intelligence (Wechsler 2008). On the Perceptual Reasoning Index, it has a substantial factor loading of .81 across all 13 age groups, and it has the highest intercorrelation with the Block Design subtest (.64) and a moderately high correlation with FSIQ (.70). However, it has relatively low correlations with the Verbal Comprehension Scale, the Working Memory Scale, and the Processing Speed Scale.

A retrospective study was conducted on a database of 44 veterans who were administered the WAIS-IV and other neuropsychological measures, such as the Boston Naming Test and the Controlled Oral Word Association Test (Chen et al. 2016). The results showed a significantly high correlation of Visual Puzzles with the Perceptual Reasoning Index (r = .87), moderate correlations with FSIQ (r = .43), General Abilities Index (r = .39), and Processing Speed Index (r = .41). In addition, the Visual Puzzles subtest is significantly correlated with other subtests of the WAIS, such as the Block Design subtest (r = .60), Matrix Reasoning (r = .49), Symbol Search (r = .56), and Digit Symbol Coding (r = .37). Visual Puzzles is also moderately correlated with other neuropsychological measures, including CVLT-II Long Delay Free Recall (r = .49), RCF Delayed Recall (r = .46), and TMT Part B (r = .45).

Overall, the Visual Puzzles subtest on the WAIS-IV has fair internal consistency, below-average to average test-retest reliability, and is a fair measure of g. It has the highest intercorrelation with the Block Design subtest and a moderate correlation with FSIQ. It is also statistically significantly correlated with other subtests of the WAIS and several other neuropsychological measures.

Validity

The Visual Puzzles subtest on the WAIS-IV has evidence for construct validity, convergent validity, and discriminant validity. Construct validity was examined in a study by Fallows and Hislebeck (2012), which found that Visual Puzzles had adequate construct validity, as it was significantly correlated with other measures of nonverbal reasoning, such as the Block Design and Matrix Reasoning subtests, and had a lower correlation with measures of verbal ability, such as the Vocabulary subtest. Convergent validity has been demonstrated by the substantial correlation between Visual Puzzles and the Perceptual Reasoning Index, which measures nonverbal cognitive processes such as perceptual organization, visual-motor integration, and spatial reasoning (Wechsler 2008). Discriminant validity has been demonstrated by the relatively low correlation of Visual Puzzles with the Verbal Comprehension Scale, the Working Memory Scale, and the Processing Speed Scale on the WAIS-IV (Wechsler 2008). In terms of predictive validity, the Visual Puzzles subtest has been found to predict job performance in certain professions that require good visual problem-solving skills (Schretlen et al. 2010). Additionally, the Visual Puzzles subtest on the WAIS-IV has ample specificity for most norm sample age groups and adequate specificity for ages 18–19 and 80–90 (Wechsler 2008).

Interpretation

The Visual Puzzles subtest on the WAIS-IV measures spatial visual-perceptual reasoning, as the examinee must analyze a figure and mentally break it down into parts to assemble three presented pieces that form the whole puzzle (Wechsler 2008). In addition to nonverbal reasoning, this subtest measures cognitive factors such as nonverbal fluid reasoning, mental transformation, speed of spatial visual-perceptual reasoning, spatial ability, visual-perceptual discrimination, attention and concentration, and ability to analyze and synthesize puzzles. The subtest also requires the examinee to be motivated and persistent, work under time pressure, and have sufficient visual acuity to see the pieces and puzzle accurately.

1. A scaled score of more than 1.5 standard deviations below the mean suggests deficits in nonverbal reasoning. If there are also similar deficits in Block Design

and Matrixes, then there are likely general nonverbal reasoning and spatial visual-perceptual reasoning deficits.

2. Normal scores on Visual Puzzles can rule out severe deficits in spatial visual-perceptual reasoning and nonverbal reasoning, but because there is a verbal component to the task, there may be opportunities to miss mild disorders.
3. Visual Puzzles have a verbal component, similar to Matrix Reasoning and Block Design. If an examinee is of average intelligence, they may use more verbal mediation skills and cover up poor analytic skills. This is accompanied by strong performance on verbal measures in general.
4. In the case of Visual Puzzles, as stated earlier, the examinee must be motivated to complete the mental abstraction as necessary. The examinee must also be persistent in their answers by trying to complete the puzzles as they get more difficult. If an examinee does not perform well on this task, then it is possible they do not have adequate motivation or persistence, which may stem from an overall lack of motivation or from psychological disorders like depression or anxiety.
5. A person with visual acuity issues may make errors in choosing pieces if they are not seeing them accurately. It is important to ensure the examinee does not require visual aids such as glasses or contact lenses and is trying to complete testing without them.
6. The examinee may choose two pieces instead of three due to poor attention and concentration during the instruction period. When this happens the first time, it is corrected, but if it happens again after the correction, the examinee may have deficits in attention or trouble following instructions. It is also possible that the examinee does not understand the instructions at all and will continue to make errors in choosing just three pieces.
7. The Visual Puzzles subtest is found to be sensitive in detecting poor performance in individuals with traumatic brain injury (TBI), specifically in populations of complicated mild, moderate, and severe TBI patients (Carlozzi et al. 2015). While significantly low performance on this subtest is associated with brain injury, it may not indicate a specific area of the brain that has been affected.
8. If an individual shows poor performance on both the Block Design and Visual Puzzles subtests, it may indicate a deficit in their analysis and synthesis abilities since both tests require these skills to complete the tasks successfully. In order to perform well on these subtests, the examinee must be able to analyze the Block Design or puzzle and synthesize it into its components. Furthermore, poor performance on both subtests may suggest deficits in the functioning of the brain's right hemisphere, which plays a crucial role in visual-spatial abilities.
9. Good performance on Visual Puzzles but poor performance on Block Design may indicate problems of motor functioning, as Block Design requires motor skills to create the presented designs. If there are issues with other tests requiring average motor functioning, such as drawing tasks and tests like Grooved Pegboard or Finger Tapping, then it is more likely a dysfunction of motor abilities rather than visual-perceptual reasoning.
10. Good performance on Block Design and poor performance on Visual Puzzles may suggest a deficit in mental abstraction and rotation. An examinee must be

able to take the pieces in their mind and fit them together to create the puzzle without any physical or visual representation of it in front of them. This is unlike Block Design, where the examinee can physically put the blocks together and see if they reflect the picture or not and work to manipulate the blocks by hand.

11. If an individual shows poor performance on both the Visual Puzzles and Matrix Reasoning subtests, it may indicate difficulties in attending to the details of a picture, as these subtests require more attention to detail than Block Design, for example. Such difficulties may be manifested as good performance on the Block Design subtest but below-average scores on the Visual Puzzles and Matrix Reasoning subtests. This pattern of test performance may suggest deficits in the functioning of the brain's left hemisphere.
12. Slow performance or time failures on Visual Puzzles may suggest an issue with following time limits or anxiety around time constraints, which would correlate with performance on other timed measures such as Block Design. If an individual is given extra time or if testing of limits is done without the time constraint and an individual performs well, then it may be a matter of time pressure.
13. There is an aspect of learning sets of rules to complete this task, and poor performance on Visual Puzzles may suggest deficits in learning rules and sets, similar to skills needed to complete the WCST or Category test.
14. In cases where the examinee has unilateral neglect, they may ignore puzzle pieces to the left side of the page and will then make errors when the correct pieces are on that side. If this is suspected, the examiner may ask the client to describe what they see on the page and can present the stimulus page to the side where they are not experiencing visual neglect.
15. If the examinee has a loss of the visual field, such as that seen in homonymous hemianopsia, they may not be able to scan the full array of puzzle piece options. This may reflect errors in choosing pieces or missing certain pieces entirely. It is important that the examinee has a full field of vision before administering this task.

References

Fallows, R. R. and Hilsabeck, R. C. (2012). WAIS-IV visual puzzles in a mixed clinical sample. The Clinical Neuropsychologist, 26(6): 942–950. https://doi.org/10.1080/13854046.2012.697193.

McCrea, S. M. and Robinson, T. P. (2011). Visual Puzzles, Figure Weights, and Cancellation: Some Preliminary Hypotheses on the Functional and Neural Substrates of These Three New WAIS-IV Subtests. ISRN Neurology, 2011, 123173. https://doi.org/10.5402/2011/123173.

Molinari, M., Petrosini, L., Misciagna, S. and Leggio, M. G. (2004). Visuospatial abilities in cerebellar disorders. Journal of Neurology, Neurosurgery and Psychiatry, 75(2): 235–240.

Sattler, J. M. and Ryan, J. J. (2009). Assessment with the WAIS-IV. Jerome M Sattler Publisher.

Wechsler, D. (2008). Wechsler Adult Intelligence Scale–Fourth Edition. Technical and Interpretive Manual. San Antonio, TX: NCS Pearson, Inc.

Wechsler, D. (2008). WAIS-IV technical and interpretive manual. Pearson.

Zipf-Williams, E. M., Shear, P. K., Strongin, D., Winegarden, B. J. and Morrell, M. J. (2000). Qualitative block design performance in epilepsy patients. Archives of Clinical Neuropsychology: the Official Journal of the National Academy of Neuropsychologists, 15(2): 149–157.

CHAPTER 17

WMS-IV Visual Reproduction

*Ines Tchienga** and *Ryan Bennett*

Unlike Logical Memory and Verbal Paired Associates, which primarily measure auditory and verbal memory, Visual Reproduction (VR) assesses memory for nonverbal visual stimuli and requires fine motor skills. Further, it comprises VR-I (immediate recall) and VR II (delayed recall) and is among the subtests for the Visual Memory index. Contrary to the Design subtest, which examines similar constructs as VR, it is only included in the adult battery. Further, VR was among the Visual Memory subtests included in the first version of the Wechsler Memory Scale (WMS) published in 1945. However, revisions have been made over the years regarding its content and scoring. For example, the authors simplified the scoring procedures of VR, a significant issue in the previous version (Groth-Marnat 2009). Nonetheless, the VR task has consistently correlated with visuospatial problem-solving and Visual Memory tests, particularly with the delay trial (Leonberger et al. 1991).

History and Normative Sample

The Wechsler Memory Scale (WMS) was first developed by David Wechsler in 1945. The WMS was one of the earliest comprehensive memory assessment tools that was designed to assess various aspects of memory function. Over the years, the WMS underwent several revisions to improve its psychometric properties and keep up with advancements in neuropsychology. The WMS underwent its fourth major revision in 2009, which aimed to provide a more comprehensive memory assessment with an updated normative sample. The current normative sample for the WMS-IV includes individuals aged 16 to 90 years and represents the general

Nova Southeastern University, Fort Lauderdale, Florida, USA.
Email: rb1934@nova.edu
* Corresponding author: it212@mynsu.nova.edu

population across characteristics of age, gender, ethnicity, and education level. The Visual Reproduction (VR) subtest is a component of the WMS-IV that measures Visual Memory and visual perception. The WMS-IV VR subtest has been widely used in both clinical and research settings. It is often used to assist with diagnosing memory impairments, tracking changes in memory function over time, and planning appropriate interventions for individuals with memory difficulties.

Test Procedures

Prior to administration, the examiner will need the WMS-IV Technical and Interpretive Manual, WMS-IV Record Form, and the Visual Reproduction Stimulus Book. Administration of the VR subset begins with the examiner reading the instruction of VR-I to the examinee. VR-I consists of five total pages, each containing one or two designs. The first three pages have one design for the examinee to encode. Each stimulus page is presented to the examinee for 10 seconds. Immediately following the presentation, the examinee draws the item from memory in the Record Form. The fourth and fifth pages each consist of two designs. The examinee is shown the stimulus page for 10 seconds and is then prompted to draw both designs in the Record Form. The examiner should note the time when the examinee completes the last item. There is a 20-to-30-minute delay prior to administering the delayed condition, VR II. The delayed condition assesses long-term visual-spatial memory via free recall, recognition, and an optional copy task. Free recall is assessed as the examinee is asked to draw the original designs previously shown to them from memory in no particular order. The examinee assesses visual recognition by choosing which of the six designs on a page matches designs from VR I. The copy task is assessed as the examinee is asked to draw designs while looking at them.

Per the administration manual, clinicians must not penalize or mistake poor motor control for memory or orientation issues. However, this may cause greater confusion because clinicians must rely on clinical judgment to discern when scoring each design, even when scoring templates are used. Additionally, since clinical judgment is sometimes needed when scoring each design, it may result in under/over-scoring depending on the clinician's experience. Lastly, though the manual provides instructions, exposing the examinee to the wrong stimuli or exposing a stimulus for over/under 10 seconds may consequently affect the individual's performance on VR.

Scoring

The Technical and Interpretive Manual outlines the specific scoring criteria for the WNS-IV VR subtest. In general, the VR subtest has a complex scoring system and will be scored by the examiner after the testing session. Each design is comprised of a unique criteria set that reflects the accuracy and completeness of the examinee's drawings. Each item criterion is scored either 0 or 1. The total raw scores for VR I and VR II are then converted to scaled scores, which go on to make up the Visual Memory, Immediate Memory, and Delayed Memory indices.

Reliability and Validity

Overall, the WMS-IV seems to have good reliability compared to its predecessor. For example, both VR I (0.93) and VR II (0.97) were among the subtests with the highest internal consistency (Wechsler 2009). Further, the internal consistency was equally high in clinical samples specifically, individuals with Alzheimer's (VR I–0.96; VR II–0.99), Traumatic Brain Injury (VR I–0.97; VR II–0.98), Autism (VR I–0.97; VR II–0.97), etc. (Wechsler 2009). Furthermore, the stability coefficients for VR I and II were 0.67 and 0.64. Though VR was among the subtests with the highest internal consistency, the current edition did not observe significant differences from the previous version. As such, scores ranged from .98 for Visual Memory (standard error of measurement [SEM] = 3.04) to a low of .93 for Visual Working Memory (SEM = 3.71) (Wechsler 2009). However, independent factor analytic studies for the WMS-III and WMS-IV in clinical groups yielded inconsistent results among subtests. For instance, Tulsky and Price found that Visual Reproduction of the WMS-III provided a better model fit on the Visual Memory factor than Faces (2003).

Relatedly, Holdnack et al. (2011) observed that the VR I loaded more strongly with a visuospatial ability factor defined by Block Design than Logical Memory and Verbal Paired Associates. Furthermore, the Auditory Memory and Visual Memory (i.e., Visual Reproduction) indices were moderately correlated (0.64), suggesting that the auditory and Visual Memory components of the WMS-IV are adequately differentiated (Groth-Marnat 2009; Wechsler 2009). However, the intercorrelation between VR I, DE I spatial, VR II, and DE II spatial were 0.37, 0.30, 0.27, and 0.30, respectively, and relatively low. Notably, there is controversy as to whether the WMS-IV assesses Visual Memory, though the Technical and Interpretive Manual cites high inter-factor correlations for all four indexes.

Clinical Utility

Clinicians commonly employ Visual Reproduction to assess cognitive impairments in individuals. Further, it is also used to discern between neurological illnesses. For example, Hori and colleagues (2013) used VR to assess performance among three Japanese native groups- healthy participants, Mild Cognitive Impairment, and Alzheimer's disease (AD). As expected, the MCI group performed significantly lower than the control group, but only on VR II, thus suggesting that the decline in Visual Memory occurs first in VR II, followed by a decline in immediate recall (2013). Similarly, the AD group performed lower on VR I and II than the healthy group. Markedly, the authors reported that though the MCI group scores were significantly lower than the control groups, their scores were relatively higher than American participants with MCI, which was attributed to educational and linguistic factors; and their findings are consistent with previous work (Tabert et al. 2009; Teng et al. 2009; Sugishita and Omura 2001). Carolozzi et al. (2013) also utilized the WMS-IV to examine memory functioning in individuals with traumatic brain injury (TBI). As anticipated, the severe and moderate group performed significantly lower than the healthy group on all subtests; the moderate TBI group performed more poorly on the Visual Memory index, including VR I and VR II, with a large effect size.

Further, results indicated a significant relationship between time since injury and VR II (Carolozzi et al. 2013; West et al. 2011; Fisher et al. 2000; Hawkins 1998).

Similarly, Soble and colleagues (2014) also assessed the clinical utility of the WMS-IV in predicting temporal lobe epilepsy (TLE) in participants. Their results suggest that VR II significantly predicted left temporal lobe epilepsy in subjects. Markedly, there is mixed evidence on the diagnostic utility of VR in discriminating seizure laterality in TLE because previous findings provided inconsistent results (Schoenberg et al. 2013; Schoenberg et al. 2012; Wilde et al. 2003; Lee et al. 2002). Additionally, Rzezak and colleagues (2017) argued that VR scores did not correlate with an ecologically valid test of memory functioning, though a measure of story memory correlated strongly in a sample of patients with TLE. Conversely, Whipple and Cullum (2011) examined the relationship between memory ability and performance on the Texan Functional Living Scale (TFLS). They observed a moderate correlation between VR I (0.63) and II (0.63) and TFLS in the clinical sample, thus suggesting good sensitivity and utility. Specifically, the correlation was high among the following clinical groups: Alzheimer's disease, TBI, and Moderate Intellectual Disability. However, mixed results were observed when other subtests of the WMS-IV were examined.

Clinical Interpretation

Visual Reproduction contributes to the overall Visual Memory Index on the WMS-IV, which clinicians have used over the years. Interpretation of scores can be challenging at times if scores are inconsistent.

1. High scores on VR-I indicate individuals' abilities to recall immediate visual stimuli and understand novel tasks. Conversely, low scores on VR-I demonstrate the inability to retrieve immediate visual stimuli or a poor understanding of novel tasks.
2. Low scores on VR II suggest poor retrieval of delayed visual stimuli. In contrast, high scores on VR II indicate good retrieval of delayed visual stimuli.
3. High scores on VR I and II indicate individuals' abilities to retain and manipulate visual information for an immediate and extended period. Everyday examples might include completing visual tasks with great ease and navigating familiar and unfamiliar settings.
4. Low performance on VR I and II is expected for individuals with low formal education because although education is not needed for VR, studies have shown a strong correlation between education and intelligence, which may, in return, influence performance.
5. While low scores on VR I and II may indicate poor retrieval of visual stimuli, it does not ultimately mean memory impairment, especially when VRII is better than or equal to VRI. Clinicians are advised to examine scores on tests with similar constructs such as Design, Bender-Visual Motor Gestalt Test, and Visual Puzzles.
6. Low VR I and II scores can also be attributed to impaired vision. That said, clinicians must ensure participants have corrective lenses or accurate vision.

Further, low performance is also expected for individuals with Hemisphere Neglect due to impaired lateralization, which affects the left visual field in return. Additionally, individuals with Alzheimer's disease tend to produce excessive errors on VR, so a poor performance on the test would support a suspicion of AD (Selden 2000).

7. Because of the motor component of the drawings, scores are uninterpretable in many cases of motor disorder due to stroke, Parkinson's disease, and other conditions that impact the dominant drawing hand. In such cases, the optional ecognition score may be a better alternative.
8. In summary, research suggests that VR has good construct validity; however, the main focus of interpretation should be at the index level, which represents robust, psychometrically sound measures (Groth-Marnat 2009).

References

Fisher, D. C., Ledbetter, M. F., Cohen, N. J., Marmor, D. and Tulsky, D. S. (2000). WAIS-III and WMS-III profiles of mildly to severely brain-injured patients. Applied Neuropsychology, 7(3): 126–132.

Groth-Marnat, G. (2009). Handbook of Psychological Assessment. John Wiley & Sons.

Hawkins, K. A. (1998). Indicators of brain dysfunction derived from graphic representations of the WAIS-III/WMS-III technical manual clinical samples data: A preliminary approach to clinical utility. The Clinical Neuropsychologist, 12(4): 535–551.

Holdnack, J. A. and Drozdick, L. W. (2009). WMS-IV technical and interpretive manual. San Antonio, TX: Pearson

Lee, T. M., Yip, J. T. and Jones-Gotman, M. (2002). Memory deficits after resection from left or right anterior temporal lobe in humans: a meta-analytic review. Epilepsia, 43(3): 283–291.

Leonberger, F. T., Nicks, S. D., Goldfader, P. R. and Munz, D. C. (1991). Factor analysis of the Wechsler Memory Scale-Revised and the Halstead-Reitan neuropsychological battery. The Clinical Neuropsychologist, 5(1): 83–88.

Noelle E. Carlozzi, Julie Grech and David S. Tulsky (2013) Memory functioning in individuals with traumatic brain injury: An examination of the Wechsler Memory Scale–Fourth Edition (WMS–IV), Journal of Clinical and Experimental Neuropsychology, 35:9, 906–914, DOI: 10.1080/13803395.2013.833178.

Rzezak, P., Lima, E. M., Gargaro, A. C., Coimbra, E., de Vincentiis, S., Velasco, T. R. et al. (2017). Everyday memory impairment in patients with temporal lobe epilepsy caused by hippocampal sclerosis. Epilepsy & Behavior, 69, 31–36.

Schoenberg, M. R., Eichstaedt, K. E., Rinehardt, E., Mattingly, M., Benbadis, S. R., Bozorg, A. M. et al. (2013). Predictors of pre-operative side of epilepsy surgery and predicting post-surgical memory outcome following temporal lobe epilepsy. In Clinical Neuropsychologist, 27(4): 599–599. 325.

Schoenberg, M. R., Eichstaedt, K. E., Rinehardt, E., Mattingly, M. L., Benbadis, S. R., Bozorg, A. M. et al. (2012). Emerging evidence based practice for use of the WMS-IV in the pre-surgical evaluation for patients with right and left temporal lobe epilepsy. In Clinical Neuropsychologist, 26(3): 429–429. 325.

Soble, J. R., Eichstaedt, K. E., Waseem, H., Mattingly, M. L., Benbadis, S. R., Bozorg, A. M. et al. (2014). Clinical utility of the Wechsler Memory Scale—Fourth Edition (WMS-IV) in predicting laterality of temporal lobe epilepsy among surgical candidates. Epilepsy & Behavior, 41: 232–237.

Sugishita, M. and Omura, K. (2001). Learning Chinese characters may improve visual recall. Percept Mot Skills, 93, 579–594.

Tabert, M. H., Manly, J. J., Liu, X., Pelton, G. H., Rosenblum, S., Jacobs, M. et al. (2006). Neuropsychological prediction of conversion to Alzheimer's disease in patients with mild cognitive impairment. Archives of General Psychiatry, 63(8): 916–924.

Teng, E., Tingus, K. D., Lu, P. H. and Cummings, J. L. (2009). Persistence of neuropsychological testing deficits in mild cognitive impairment. Dementia and Geriatric Cognitive Disorders, 28(2): 168–178.

Wechsler, D. (2009). Wechsler Memory Scale–Fourth Edition (WMS–IV): Technical and Interpretive Manual. San Antonio, TX: Pearson Clinical Assessment.

West, L. K., Curtis, K. L., Greve, K. W. and Bianchini, K. J. (2011). Memory in traumatic brain injury: The effects of injury severity and effort on the Wechsler Memory Scale-III. Journal of Neuropsychology, 5(1): 114–125.

Wilde, N. J., Strauss, E., Chelune, G. J., Hermann, B. P., Hunter, M., Loring, D. W. et al. (2003). Confirmatory factor analysis of the WMS-III in patients with temporal lobe epilepsy. Psychological Assessment, 15(1): 56.

Whipple Drozdick, L. and Munro Cullum, C. (2011). Expanding the ecological validity of WAIS-IV and WMS-IV with the Texas Functional Living Scale. Assessment, 18(2): 141–155.

CHAPTER 18

WAIS-IV Arithmetic

Christina Nunez

The arithmetic subtest is the sixth subtest in the Wechsler Adult Intelligence Scale Fourth Edition (WAIS-IV), a widely used assessment tool to measure intelligence and cognitive abilities in adults aged 16 to 90. The arithmetic subtest is part of the Working Memory Index and is specifically designed to measure quantitative reasoning and mental manipulation. In this subtest, the individual is required to solve word problems that are verbally presented to them. The examinee must then retain the information in their working memory and solve the problem within a strict time limit of thirty seconds. Thus, the arithmetic subtest is important for assessing an individual's working memory, quantitative reasoning, and problem-solving abilities.

History and Normative Sample

The arithmetic subtest has been a part of the Wechsler Intelligence Scale since the first publication of the Wechsler-Bellevue Intelligence Scale in 1939. The subtest has undergone several revisions since then, and the most recent version is the fourth edition of the arithmetic subtest in the Wechsler Adult Intelligence Scale (WAIS-IV). The original arithmetic subtest in the Wechsler-Bellevue Intelligence Scale consisted of simple arithmetic problems such as addition, subtraction, multiplication, and division. However, the current version of the arithmetic subtest in the WAIS-IV is designed to measure more quantitative reasoning and mental manipulation skills. Over time, the arithmetic subtest has become an essential tool for assessing an individual's working memory, problem-solving abilities, and quantitative reasoning skills. With the advent of the WAIS-IV, the arithmetic subtest has undergone further refinement and standardization, making it a more reliable and valid measure of adult cognitive abilities.

The WAIS-IV was normed on 2,200 healthy adults. This sample comprised individuals without a clinical presentation, ages 16 to 90, and were English speakers.

Nova Southeastern University, Fort Lauderdale, Florida, USA.
Email: cn584@mynsu.nova.edu

Individuals were excluded if there was evidence of sensory or motor impairments and those with medication or a diagnosis that may impact test performance. In this most recent revision, the test developers were interested in having a more representative sample. To accomplish this, they divided the United States into four regions and sampled individuals from them. The proportion of ethnicity representation in the sample was based on the proportion of Whites, African Americans, Hispanics, Asians, and other racial groups in the corresponding population. The normative sample is considered more diverse than the previous sample on characteristics of geographic region, ethnicity, education, age, and sex.

Test Procedures

The examiner begins by introducing the test, where the individual is informed of the task and informed the examiner can repeat the word problem only one more time. The examiner then reads the sample item, begins timing for thirty seconds, and records the individual's response and completion time. The examiner then proceeds to the appropriate starting point. The examiner reads each word problem, begins the timer, and records the individual's responses and completion time. The examiner continued administering until the individual produced three incorrect responses in a row. If the individual incorrectly responds to either of the first two items, then the examiner is to reverse to previous items, which require the stimulus book, until the individual produces two consecutive perfect scores or item one is reached. Each item is allotted 30 seconds; the examiner may prompt the individual if they have an answer after twenty seconds. If the individual asks the examiner to repeat the word problem, the examiner immediately reads the word problem but does not stop the timer.

Item Difficulty and Types of Errors

Items on the WAIS-IV arithmetic subtest become progressively more difficult as the individual continues. The easiest item on the arithmetic subtest requires the individual to count. The subtest then moves from basic addition and subtraction to more complex addition and subtraction. Then, the individual is asked to perform more complex problems that require multiplication, division, and mental manipulation of information.The arithmetic subtest of the WAIS-IV can pose several challenges for individuals being assessed. Computation errors are the most common mistake made on this subtest. Additionally, some individuals may struggle to attend to the word problem being read by the examiner, which may require the examiner to repeat the problem. Misinterpretation of the word problem, errors in computation, or use of incorrect values can also occur due to the individual's difficulty in retaining all the incoming information from the problem. Asking the examiner to repeat the problem may lead to time failure as the timer continues running during the repetition. Furthermore, taking too much time on a problem can result in time failure. It is essential for the examiner to be aware of these challenges and take appropriate measures to support individuals in performing their best on the arithmetic subtest.

Task Demands and Strategies

In the most recent edition, the arithmetic subtest was revised to decrease the need for math knowledge and verbal comprehension and rely more on the demands of working memory. This subtest requires the individual to listen to a word problem, hold the information in their mind, and then mentally manipulate the information by performing calculations to generate the correct response. The arithmetic subtest is part of the Working Memory Index. Therefore, the emphasis is placed on working memory and complex attention. The subtest also relies on the individual's ability to carry out mental math. The individual is not permitted to have a calculator, paper, or pen, which requires them to rely on their working memory. The strategy individuals use to complete the task is to mathematically compute the information as quickly as possible to relieve their working memory. Another strategy used is attending to keywords in the word problem. If the individual can attend to the keywords of the word problem, then they can compute the responses with less taxing information.

Scoring

Correct responses that are given within the 30-second time allotment are scored a value of one point. Correct responses outside the designated 30-second allotment are considered a time-fail and should be scored a zero. It is important that the examiner records both the completion time and the individual's response. Many examiners allow the individual to exceed the designated time to maintain rapport and make behavioral observations. Incorrect responses, regardless of time, are scored a zero. The examiner then sums the total points and records the arithmetic total raw score. Scoring conversion tables, provided in the WAIS-IV manual, convert raw scores into scaled scores.

Reliability

Internal Consistency

The overall WAIS-IV was evaluated for reliability using a split-half technique to compute internal consistency reliability coefficients. The overall reliability estimate across age groups for the WAIS-IV Full Scale IQ was .98. The reliability of the Working Memory Index was .94. The reliability of the arithmetic subtest was .88. When considering special populations, such as individuals with various intellectual abilities, ADHD, traumatic brain injuries, major depression, or mild cognitive impairment the arithmetic reliability coefficients were above .80 for all considered groups—the average reliability coefficient across special populations was .89 for the arithmetic subtest.

Test-Retest Reliability

To investigate test-retest reliability, the test developers administered the WAIS-IV with an interval between 8 and 82 days. The average interval was 22 days. The overall sample had a reliability coefficient of .95 for the Full Scale IQ, which was then corrected to .96 due to the sample's variability. The reliability coefficient for the Working Memory Index was .87, then corrected to .88. The reliability for the arithmetic subtest was .80, which was then corrected to .83.

Validity

Construct Validity

In the most recent edition, the test developers revised the arithmetic subtest to have a measure more dependent on working memory than math abilities and verbal comprehension. The subtests within each index score were correlated to provide evidence of convergent validity. The subtests were then correlated with other subtests from different index scores to measure discriminate validity. Subtests that attributed to the same factor were more closely related than subtests that attributed to a different factor. Structural equation modeling was used to assess the model to data fit. The arithmetic subtest was cross-loaded on the working memory and verbal comprehension variables. This suggests arithmetic has some verbal components associated with the outcomes, as the model showed a good model to data fit. The WAIS-IV was also correlated with other measures to assess construct validity, including the WAIS-III, WISC-IV, WMS-III, CMS, WIAT-II, Brown ADD, D-KEFS, CVLT-II, and RBANS.

Diagnostic Validity

Diagnostically, the arithmetic subtest significantly differentiated individuals from various special populations compared to a control group. The subtest significantly distinguished those considered intellectually gifted from controls, with a standard difference of -1.06. Those with mild and moderate intellectual disability performed significantly differently than the controls on arithmetic, with a standard difference of 2.69 and 3.58, respectively. Individuals with borderline intellectual functioning performed significantly differently on arithmetic compared to controls, with a standard difference of 1.67. Those with a reading and math disorder performed significantly differently than the control condition on arithmetic, with a standard difference of .97 and 1.26, respectively.Individuals with ADHD performed significantly differently than the control group, with a standard difference of .47. For individuals with a traumatic brain injury, the arithmetic subtest was able to significantly differentiate their performance from a control group, with a standard difference of .87. Those with autism spectrum disorder and Asperger's disorder performed significantly difference from the control group with a standard difference of 1.46 and .43 respectively. Those with mild cognitive impairment and Alzheimer's disease performed significantly differently on the arithmetic subtest than the control group, with a standard difference of .49 and 1.18, respectively. Performance on the arithmetic subtest was not significantly different than a control group for those with major depressive disorder.

Clinical Application in Research

Studies have investigated the role of education in arithmetic performance (Brooks et al. 2011). These studies found a relationship between WAIS-IV arithmetic scores and education. This suggests that the arithmetic subtest may be more sensitive to school-based knowledge acquisition than a true measure of working memory. The test developers were aware of this potential conflict and revised the current arithmetic edition to be less dependent on verbal comprehension and math abilities. Studies have also found sensitivity to math performance anxiety (Buelow and Frakey 2013). The study found that math anxiety predicted performance on the arithmetic subtest in a sample of college students but not on the other WAIS-IV measures of working memory. Math anxiety is predicted over and above other variables such as general test anxiety, math performance level, and gender. These findings suggest that letter-number sequencing may be a more appropriate measure of working memory in individuals with high math anxiety.

Another area of interest was the influence of demographic features on the arithmetic performance. One area of interest was evaluating performance on WAIS-IV arithmetic by gender. One study found a large effect in favor of men on the arithmetic subtest and the Working Memory Index (Pezzuti et al. 2020). This study further investigated gender bias using a multi-group confirmatory factor analysis and found gender bias in arithmetic in both the WAIS-R and the WAIS-IV editions. The study did note that gender differences were present in both editions but more pronounced in the WAIS-R. Regarding ethnicity and language, studies have investigated the normative data of the WAIS-R in a sample of Spanish-speaking individuals from the US-Mexico border region (Scott et al. 2020). The researchers in this study aimed to improve the normative data and develop demographically adjusted interpretive norms for this population. The participants completed the WAIS-R block design and arithmetic in Spanish, and the adjusted scoring was applied. The study found that education was positively associated with performance in arithmetic, and men in this sample outperformed women. The study also noted a higher rate of detected impairment in this sample of the population, stating that norms for English speakers underestimated impairment in this section of the population. The Spanish norm adjustment may have overestimated impairment in this section of the population.

Interpretation

Interpreting the arithmetic subtest score of the WAIS-IV requires consideration of several factors. The arithmetic subtest score can provide insight into the individual's ability to manipulate numbers mentally and perform calculations accurately and efficiently. It can also reflect the individual's working memory capacity, as the subtest requires the retention of information while solving the problem within a limited time frame. When interpreting the arithmetic subtest score, it is essential to consider the individual's overall cognitive profile and any relevant background information, such as educational or cultural background. A low score on the arithmetic subtest alone may not necessarily indicate a deficit in mathematical ability but may be influenced by factors such as anxiety or unfamiliarity with the test format. Possible interpretative analyses include:Discrepancies in scores between WAIS-IV arithmetic and digit span suggest incongruent measures of working memory. The addition of letter-number sequencing may help clarify scores.Low arithmetic scores may be due to high math anxiety or low math abilities, especially for individuals who struggle in math or have a suspected specific learning disorder in math. As math disorders are common, this score should never be used to indicate working memory impairment.

1. Low scores on arithmetic may be due to poor verbal comprehension as the arithmetic subtest is cross-loaded on the Verbal Comprehension Index.
2. When individuals cannot pass simple counting items, no attempt should be made to use this as a working memory score.
3. Individuals who simply need more time to solve word problems (exceeding the allowed time limit) are more likely not to have mathematic problems rather than working memory issues.Individuals with poor verbal memory may show significant impairment in Arithmetic word items.
4. Working memory deficits and attentional deficits are often confounded, so there is a need to evaluate sustained attentional skills carefully.
5. Working Memory scores that are lower than all other scores are rare, suggesting that other external factors may affect test results. This can include emotional issues, distractions, confusion, and preoccupations.

References

Brooks, B. L., Holdnack, J. A. and Iverson, G. L. (2011). Advanced clinical interpretation of the WAIS-IV and WMS-IV: Prevalence of low scores varies by level of intelligence and years of education. Assessment, 18(2): 156–167.

Buelow, M. T. and Frakey, L. L. (2013). Math anxiety differentially affects WAIS-IV arithmetic performance in undergraduates. Archives of Clinical Neuropsychology, 28(4), 356–362. https://doi.org/10.1093/arclin/act006

Lynn, R. and Irwing, P. (2008). Sex differences in mental arithmetic, digit span, and g defined as working memory capacity. Intelligence, 36(3): 226–235.

Pezzuti, L., Tommasi, M., Saggino, A., Dawe, J. and Lauriola, M. (2020). Gender differences and measurement bias in the assessment of adult intelligence: Evidence from the Italian WAIS-IV and WAIS-R standardizations. Intelligence, 79: 101436.

Scott, T. M., Morlett Paredes, A., Taylor, M. J., Umlauf, A., Artiola i Fortuny, L., Heaton, R. K. et al. (2021). Demographically-adjusted norms for the WAIS-R Block Design and Arithmetic subtests: Results from the Neuropsychological Norms for the US-Mexico Border Region in Spanish (NP-NUMBRS) project. The Clinical Neuropsychologist, 35(2): 419–432.

Wechsler, D. (2008). Wechsler Adult Intelligence Scale-Fourth Edition, Technical and Interpretive Manual. Bloomington MN. PsychCorp.

CHAPTER 19

WAIS-IV Index Scores

Brittny Arias

The Weschler Adult Intelligence Scale-Fourth Edition (WAIS-IV) is an individually administered clinical instrument designed to assess cognitive performance as a multidimensional construct, containing numerous indices assessing qualitatively different types of intellectual functioning (Lezak et al. 2012). The test includes a simplified four-factor structure with an increased emphasis on index scores, which reflect the examinee's performance in more discrete domains of cognitive functioning. The WAIS-IV measures cognitive abilities such as verbal comprehension, fluid intelligence, working memory, and processing speed through a reduced testing time, additional demonstration items, enlarged visual stimuli, simplified verbal instructions, little emphasis on time bonuses, and reduced motor demands (Weschler 2008; Weiss et al. 2010). The simplified test structure and attention to more discrete domains of cognitive functioning allow for measuring intellectual capacity with sensitivity, precision, and economy of time (Lezak et al. 2012). Overall, the WAIS-IV is a valuable tool for assessing the multidimensional nature of intelligence in adults and has demonstrated strong psychometric properties, clinical utility, and user-friendliness (Weschler 2008).

History and Normative Sample

The development of the WAIS-IV began with the Weschler-Bellevue (WB) Intelligence Scale, which was first introduced in the 1930s (Weschler 2008). The original WB scale defined intelligence as a global entity, but subsequent revisions of the WAIS recognized the multidimensional nature of intelligence and assessed distinct cognitive abilities, such as verbal comprehension, perceptual reasoning, working memory, and processing speed (Weschler 2008). The concept of intelligence has evolved from a unitary construct to a multidimensional construct comprised of distinct cognitive abilities (Lezak et al. 2012). The Weschler Adult Intelligence Scale

Nova Southeastern University, Fort Lauderdale, Florida, USA.
Email: ba717@mynsu.nova.edu

(WAIS) has undergone several revisions to reflect this evolution. The WAIS-IV, the latest edition of the WAIS, is a comprehensive cognitive assessment tool designed for use with adults aged 16–69 (Weschler 2008).

The WAIS-IV was released in 2008 to provide comprehensive and contemporary norms, improve psychometric properties, and increase clinical utility and user-friendliness (Weschler 2008). As a result, the WAIS-IV includes four index scores, each of which assesses a specific cognitive ability: verbal comprehension, perceptual reasoning, working memory, and processing speed (Weschler 2008). These index scores provide a more nuanced understanding of an individual's cognitive profile and can aid in the diagnosis and treatment of cognitive disorders (Lezak et al. 2012).

Despite the advancements of the WAIS-IV, intelligence testing has been a source of controversy. Some critics question the ethical or moral implications of intelligence testing, while others argue that there is insufficient empirical support to continue using intelligence tests in applied clinical settings (Weschler 2008). Given these concerns, it is important to conceptualize intelligence as a performance variable and focus on evaluating cognitive abilities and how individuals acquire and demonstrate essential intellectual functions (Lezak et al. 2012).

The normative sample information for the WAIS-IV is based on a national sample representative of the United States English-speaking population from March 2007 to April 2008 (Wechsler 2008). This sample included individuals from diverse demographic backgrounds, including age, sex, race, ethnicity, self or parent education level, and geographic region, per the October 2005 United States census data (Wechsler 2008). The normative sample comprised 2,200 examinees, divided into 13 age groups ranging from 16 to 90 years of age, with 200 participants in the nine younger age groups and 100 participants in each of the four older age groups. Most of the normative sample consisted of an equal number of female and male examinees in each age group, with five older age groups having more women than men (Wechsler 2008). The proportions of Caucasians, African Americans, Hispanics, Asians, and other racial groups in the normative sample were based on the proportions of individuals within the corresponding age group of the United States population. Furthermore, the normative sample was divided into five education levels: ≤ 8 years, 9–11 years, 12 years, 13–15 years, and ≥ 16 years, according to census reports. The United States was divided into four major geographic regions: Northeast (NE), Midwest (MW), South (S), and West (W) for sampling purposes (Wechsler 2008). Therefore, the current test scores of the WAIS-IV are based on normative information that is both contemporary and representative of the relevant United States population, allowing for an accurate interpretation of cognitive functioning (Wechsler 2008). It is important for clinical neuropsychologists to be aware of these norms when administering and interpreting the WAIS-IV.

Test Components

Understanding the structure and organization of the WAIS-IV intelligence assessments is essential to interpreting cognitive function accurately. The WAIS-IV comprises 15 subtests that are organized into four index scales, which represent significant components of intelligence: Verbal Comprehension Index (VCI),

Perceptual Reasoning Index (PRI), Working Memory Index (WMI), and Processing Speed Index (PSI), contributing to the Full-Scale Intelligence Quotient (FSIQ) (Wechsler 2008).

The revised nomenclature accurately reflects the configuration of the contributing subtests and the cognitive abilities assessed for each composite score (Wechsler 2008). The VCI measures verbal acquired knowledge and verbal reasoning, including three core subtests (i.e., Similarities [SI], Vocabulary [VC], and Information [IN]) and one supplemental subtest (i.e., Comprehension [CO]).The PRI assesses fluid reasoning in the perceptual domain with tasks that assess nonverbal concept formation, visual perception and organization, visual-motor coordination, learning, and the ability to separate figures and visual stimuli. This second index scale incorporates three core subtests (i.e., Block Design [BD], Matrix Reasoning [MR], and Visual Puzzles [VP]) and two supplemental subtests (i.e., Figure Weights [FW] and Picture Completion [PCm]).The WMI comprises two core subtests (i.e., Digit Span [DS] and Arithmetic [AR]) and one supplemental subtest (i.e., Letter-Number Sequencing [LN]). This index scale measures nonverbal reasoning skills and taps into more fluid thinking, requiring visual perceptual abilities. It reflects a person's ability to take in and hold information in immediate awareness and perform a mental operation on that information.

The PSI has two core subtests (i.e., Symbol Search [SS] and Coding [CD]) and one supplemental subtest (i.e., Cancellation [CA]). It measures a person's ability to scan, sequence, or discriminate simple visual information and short-term memory, attention, and visual-motor coordination quickly and correctly.The FSIQ, which is derived from the combination of the four index scores, provides an overall estimate of general intellectual functioning (Wechsler 2008).

Test Procedures

Following the recommended administration order of the Wechsler Adult Intelligence Scale-Fourth Edition (WAIS-IV) subtests, as outlined in the Administration and Scoring Manual. Deviation from the standard administration order may sometimes be necessary to meet the clinical needs of a particular examinee. However, such deviation can result in several administration issues that may affect the scale's validity and reliability, including subtest administration order, subtest selection, and substitution (Wechsler 2008).

It is worth noting that the normative information for composite scores is based on the ten core subtests. Therefore, substituting supplemental subtests and using prorated sums of scaled scores may introduce additional measurement errors into composite scores (Wechsler 2008). Limiting substitution and proration may be beneficial in reducing possible sources of measurement error while allowing for the derivation of interpretable composite scores. Adhering to the recommended administration order of the WAIS-IV subtests may help ensure the test's validity and reliability in assessing cognitive function accurately. When deviation from the standard administration order is necessary, it is crucial to be mindful of the potential measurement errors that may arise and take steps to minimize these errors.

Reliability

The reliability coefficients for WAIS-IV composite scores, which utilize the split-half and Cronbach's alpha methods, are generally higher than those for the individual subtests that make up the composite scores (Weschler 2008). The composite score reliability coefficients are equal to or higher than the previous edition, WAIS-III (Weschler 2008). While subtests represent only part of a person's intellectual functioning, the composite scores summarize performance on a broader sample of abilities. The average reliability coefficient for the Processing Speed Index (PSI) is slightly lower than the other composite scores due to its reliance on test-retest subtest reliabilities, which tend to be lower than split-half or alpha reliabilities.Notably, reliability data for specific populations supports the generalizability of the WAIS-IV, with evidence of internal consistency reliability obtained from a range of special populations, including those with intellectual disability, reading and mathematics disorders, ADHD, traumatic brain injury, and dementia (Weschler 2008). However, previous research has found discrepancies in reliability between WAIS-IV indices, specifically in the discrepancy score reliability, which is based on the internal consistency reliability of each score and the correlation between two tests (Glass et al. 2010). A lower reliability coefficient may suggest measurement error, precluding any hypotheses or clinical interpretations based on the discrepancy score. Internal consistency reliabilities ranged from .55 to .88 for subtest discrepancy scores and .80 to .91 for index discrepancy scores (Glass et al. 2010). While none of the subtest discrepancy score comparisons and only four index discrepancy score comparisons met the desired level of reliability, index discrepancy score reliabilities of the WAIS-IV represented notable improvements, with reliabilities of ≥ .80, making it more suitable for developing clinical hypotheses (Guilford and Fruchter 1978; Ponterotto and Ruckdeschel 2007; Salvia and Ysseldyke 1988; Sattler 2008). Examiners should, therefore, be cautious when interpreting any WAIS-IV discrepancy scores.

Validity

In the context of neuropsychological evaluation, the WAIS-IV is typically administered as part of a broader battery of tests for assessing psychological and cognitive functioning. Evidence of the convergent validity of the WAIS-IV provided correlational studies with the following instruments: Weschler Individual Achievement Test Second Edition (WIAT-II), Weschler Memory Scale Fourth Edition (WMS-IV), Delis-Kaplan Executive Function System (D-KEFS), and Repeatable Battery for the Assessment of Neuropsychological Status (RBANS).Evidence supports using the WAIS-IV with the WIAT-II, a comprehensive measure of academic achievement, to provide information on cognitive ability and academic achievement in high school students ages 16–19. Canivez (2013) examined the incremental validity of the WAIS-IV factor index scores in predicting academic achievement on the WIAT-III and the WIAT-II beyond that predicted by the WAIS-IV FSIQ. Results indicated that FSIQ accounted for statistical significance and most of the WIAT-II and WIAT-III subtest and composite score variance (Canivez 2013). The WAIS-IV factor index scores provided statistically significant variance in most WIAT-II and WIAT-III subtests and composite scores over and above the FSIQ; however, the effect size ranged from trivial to medium compared to other intelligence tests (Canivez 2013). The WAIS-IV factor index scores offered minor unique contributions to predicting WIAT-II and WIAT-III scores. Further, Weschler (2008) confirmed that the WAIS-IV composites, except for PSI, correlated highly with WIAT-II Total Achievement. Beyond this, VCI correlated most highly with the Reading and Oral Language composites and least with the Written Language composite. The PRI and PSI correlated most highly with the mathematics composite, and WMI most highly correlated with the Mathematics and Reading Composite. In educational settings, intelligence tests extensively evaluate specific cognitive deficits that may contribute to low academic achievement and predict future academic achievement (Weschler 2008). These results demonstrated the relations between the WAIS-IV and WIAT-II and that specific WAIS-IV composite scores relate differently to specific achievement domains.The WAIS-IV and WMS-IV pairing enhances the clinical utility of the WAIS-IV by including complete information on memory function. Weschler (2008) has proven a moderate correlation between the WAIS-IV VCI and PRI scales and the WMS-III auditory and visual memory indices and relatively higher correlations between the VCI and the WMS-III auditory indices and between PRI and the WMS-III visual indices. The other WAIS-IV composite scores correlated moderately with the WMS-IIII, as evidenced by a WMI of .35 and a PSI of .69 (Weschler 2008). Some modalities were specific to certain indices. VCI correlated more highly with the auditory memory indexes than visual memory indexes. Conversely, PRI generally correlated more highly with the visual memory indices than the VCI (Weschler 2008). The results indicated that intellectual impairment would influence a person's memory, mainly working memory, immediate visual memory, and immediate auditory memory. Although the effects of visual memory tasks might be less obvious if intellectual impairment were to affect memory performance, an examiner could effectively compare an examinee's intelligence and memory scores to determine impairment and cognitive weaknesses relative to the general ability level. In addition, Ryan and colleagues (2022) examined whether a significant scatter in WAIS-IV GAI will reduce its validity in predicting performance on WMS-IV indexes. The findings demonstrated a considerable index variability scatter with extreme VCI> PRI (59%) and VCI<PRI (48.3%) discrepancies within the GAI for the overall WAIS-IV normative sample; however, the Pearson correlations between the GAI and each WMS-IV index did not differ significantly from the GAI- Index correlation from the WMS-IV Technical and Interpretive Manual (Weschler 2008b; Ryan et al. 2022). Thus, the memory ability measures both co-varied in a similar magnitude of the coefficients, suggesting that the GAI should be as effective a predictor of memory scores for clinical clients as in the normative sample. Such findings indicate that the subtest scatters, defined by the VCI-PRI discrepancy, did not reduce the validity of the FSIQ for predicting WMS-IV indexes.D-KEFS consists of nine tests that measure a broad spectrum of verbal and nonverbal executive functions to determine how deficits in abstract and creative thinking may impact an individual's daily functioning. Delis et al. (2001) published correlations of the WAIS-IV with D-KEFS Trail Making and Verbal Fluency ranges, suggesting moderate to significant correlations for most WAIS-IV subtests. Specifically, Trail Making Letter-Number switching correlates with FSIQ at .77 for

the normative sample and PSI at .88. In comparison, Weschler (2008) investigated the validity between the WAIS-IV and two specific tests from the D-KEFS, Trail Making and Verbal Fluency, that measure multiple aspects of verbal abilities and cognitive flexibility. Results indicated that the WAIS-IV mean composite scores ranged from 98.2 (WMI) to 103.3 (PSI), with correlations ranging from .22 (PRI with Category Fluency) to .77 (FSIQ with Trail Making Number-Letter Switching-Completion Time) (Weschler 2008). Individually, the VCI demonstrated higher correlations with the letter fluency and category fluency scores, suggesting a similarity between tasks that involve generating novel responses that do not use overlearned information. PSI displayed the highest correlation with the D-KEFS Trail Making completion time scores.The RBANS is a brief, individually administered test that provides index scores for Immediate Memory, Visuospatial/Constructional Abilities, Language, Attention, and Delayed Memory, as well as a Total Score. Rudolph (1998) suggested that the RBANS Total Score correlated with the WAIS-IV FSIQ at .75. The correlations between the FSIQ and the RBANS scores ranged from .38 (Delayed Memory) to .75 (RBANS Total Score), in which the FSIQ correlated most highly with the RBANS Total Score (Weschler 2008). The PSI correlated most highly with the Visuospatial/Constructional Abilities Index compared to the other RBANS scores, which may reflect the working memory component inherent in fluid reasoning tasks. As expected, the WMI correlated most highly with the RBANS Attention Index and moderately with the Immediate Memory Index (Weschler 2008).

Clinical Applications in Research

In addition to its function as a widely used intelligence scale, the WAIS-IV indices have shown promise in assessing cognitive functioning across various clinical domains. Although Weschler did not initially intend to use his index scales as neuropsychological tools, they have become recognized as integral to neuropsychological batteries (Weschler 2008). Individuals referred for assessment in clinical settings often present complex problems requiring a comprehensive assessment using intellectual, functional, and neuropsychological instruments.

The WAIS-IV indices have also been used to evaluate the impact of Traumatic Brain Injuries (TBIs) on cognitive functioning. Memory, attention, processing speed, language skills, and executive function commonly affect individuals with complicated mild, moderate, and severe TBI (Carlozzi et al. 2015; Weschler 2008). Carlozzi and colleagues (2015) investigated the clinical utility of the WAIS-IV in 100 individuals with complicated mild, moderate, or severe TBI, comparing them to 100 control participants who met the normative sample criteria for the WAIS-IV. Univariate analysis showed that individuals with severe TBI performed significantly worse than the control group on all index scores and subtests, except for Matrix Reasoning (Carlozzi et al. 2015). Those with complicated mild to moderate TBI performed poorly compared to controls on the Working Memory Index (WMI), Processing Speed Index (PSI), and Full-Scale Intelligence Quotient (FSIQ). Only the FSIQ and PSI scores differed significantly between individuals with severe and complicated mild to moderate TBI. Overall, the index and subtest scores demonstrated small to moderate effect sizes for individuals with complicated mild to moderate

TBI and moderate to large effect sizes for those with severe TBI. The PSI exhibited good sensitivity and specificity for classifying individuals with severe TBI but not for those with memory impairments from severe TBI. These findings support using the WAIS-IV as a valuable tool for evaluating cognition and intellectual function in individuals with complicated mild, moderate, or severe TBI.

Cognition declines with age in typically developed (TD) adults, particularly in memory and overall cognitive functioning. Research suggests that age-related differences in other cognitive abilities may be related to a decline in processing speed. Tse et al. (2019) compared the cognitive and memory abilities of 28 older adults with autism and 29 without autism over 50. The results indicated that the older adults with autism performed similarly to TD adults in all other domains except for poorer processing speed and visual working memory performance. Deficits in processing speed in individuals with autism may be due to difficulties in focusing on details and individual parts of the whole, as well as differences in executive functioning, which are associated with top-down processing and set-shifting difficulties. Jenkins and colleagues (2000) have also demonstrated that tasks involving working memory decline less precipitously with age, particularly verbal tasks, which are included in the WAIS-IV working memory tasks. Visuospatial tasks show a more significant decline with age than verbal tasks in healthy aging adults.

Efforts have been made to shorten the duration of cognitive assessments to maximize efficiency in completing a comprehensive evaluation. Meyers and colleagues (2013) used seven subtests of the WAIS-IV to predict the full FSIQ and the VCI, PRI, WMI, and PSI. Results showed that it is possible to use seven subtests to diagnose effectively. In addition, short-form subtest administration should follow the order recommended in the Administration and Scoring Manual. Ryan and colleagues (2015) indicated that some WAIS-IV short forms could be highly effective in situations where time is of top choice and classification of the individuals as either intellectually impaired or not is sufficient. The WAIS-IV has proven effective in ruling out subnormal intelligence, with hit rates ranging from 84% to 95%. Nevertheless, the ability to classify an examinee based on an FSIQ estimate of ≤ 69 or ≤ 79 using the WAIS-IV as a screening tool does not replace the need for an informed clinical judgment. Thus, examiners should consider determining base interest rates in their clinical practice to inform decision-making.

Interpretation

1. The WAIS-IV is a useful tool for identifying intellectual disability, intellectual giftedness, and cognitive strengths and weaknesses in various neurological conditions. It can provide differential diagnosis, guide intervention planning, estimate premorbid intelligence, and offer reliable data for research purposes. The FSIQ is reported as a deviation IQ with a norming sample mean FSIQ of 100, and the current classification system ranges from "Very Superior" to "Extremely Low" based on IQ scores.
2. VIQ is considered least impacted by brain injury and age, showing less decline as it measures largely overlearned skills with no timing requirements. The VCI will often be the highest score after a brain injury or the onset of dementia and

similar disorders. However, it is also the highest score for verbal individuals who work in areas where verbal skills are predominant.

3. PSI is a good measure of processing speed and is often impaired by both neurological and psychiatric disorders as well as age. Thus, it cannot be used as an indicator of brain injury but more as a measure of cognitive distress. WMI should be in the normal range in anyone who can function normally on a day-to-day basis at home and work. Impairment can arise through problems working with numbers or arithmetic processes. Arithmetic is likely not a working memory measure when impaired, but Digit Span is not. However, in some number phobic individuals, both may be impaired, with Digit Span backward and sequencing showing more impairment. Valid WMI deficits are generally associated with acute or chronic cognitive disorders.
4. PRI is generally sensitive to cognitive changes but less sensitive than PSI to attentional and psychiatric problems. This score is most reliable when Matrixes is the highest, followed by the other two scales with time and speed limitations. It is useful for clients to go over time limits to see if they can do a task versus more serious visual construction or visual-spatial problems that suggest posterior nondominant hemisphere injuries.

References

Canivez, G. L. (2013). Incremental Criterion Validity of WAIS-IV Factor Index Scores: Relationships with WIAT-II and WIAT-III Subtest and Composite Scores. Psychological Assessment, 25(2): 484–495. https://www.doi.org.10.1037/a0032092.

Carlozzi, N. E., Kirsch, N. L., Kisala, P. A. and Tulsky, D. S. (2015). An Examination of the Weschler Adult Intelligence Scales, Fourth Edition (WAIS-IV) in Individuals with Complicated Mild, Moderate, and Severe Traumatic Brain Injury (TBI). The Clinical Neuropsychologist, 29(1): 21–37. https://dx.doi.org/10.1080/13854046.2015.1005677.

Delis, D. C., Kaplan, E. and Kramer, J. H. (2001). Delis-Kaplan executive function system. San Antonio, TX: Harcourt Assessment.Etherton, J. L. (2014). Cold Pressor-Induced Pain Does Not Impair WAIS-IV Processing Speed Index or Working Memory Index Performance. Applied Neuropsychology: Adult, 21: 14–20. https://doi.org.10.1080/09084282.2012.718017.

Etherton, J. (2015). WAIS-IV Verbal Comprehension Index and Perceptual Reasoning Index Performance are Unaffected by Cold-Pressor Pain Induction. Applied Neuropsychology: Adult, 22, 54–60. https://doi.org.10.1080/23279095.838166Glass, L. A., Ryan, J. J., and Charter, R. A. (2010). Discrepancy Score Reliabilities in the WAIS-IV Standardization Sample. Journal of Psychoeducational Assessment, 28(3): 201–208. https://www.doi.org.10.1177/0734282909346710.

Guilford, J. P. and Fruchter, B. (1978). Fundamental statistics in psychology and education (6th ed.). New York: McGraw-Hill.

Jenkins, L., Myerson, J., Joerding, J. A. and Hale, S. (2000). Converging evidence that visuospatial cognition is more age-sensitive than verbal cognition. Psychology and Aging, 15(1): 157–175. https://doi.org/10.1037/0882-7974.15.1.157.

Meyers, J. E., Zellinger, M. M., Kockler, T., Wagner M. and Miller, R. M. (2013). A Validated Seven-Subtest Short Form for the WAIS-IV. Applied Neuropsychology: Adult, 20, 249–256. https://www.doi.org.10.1080/09084282.2012.710180

Moore, R. A., Lippa, S. M., Brickell, T. A., Louis, M. Lange, F., and Lange, R. T. (2020) Clinical Utility of WAIS-IV 'excessive decline from premorbid functioning' scores to detect invalid test performance following traumatic brain injury. The Clinical Neuropsychologist, 34(3): 512–528. https://doi.org/10.1080/13854046.2019.1668059.

Ponterotto, J. G. and Ruckdeschel, D. E. (2007). An overview of coefficient alpha and a reliability matrix for estimating the adequacy of internal consistency coefficients with psychological research measures. Perceptual and Motor Skills, 105: 997–1014.

Randolph, C. (1998). Repeatable Battery for the assessment of neuropsychological status. San Antonio, TX: The Psychological Corporation.

Ryan, J. J., Kreiner, D. S., Gontkovsky, S. T., Golden, C. J. and Teichner, G. (2022). Does high scatter on the Weschler Adult Intelligence Scale-Fourth Edition general ability index reduce validity in predicting Weschler Memory Scale-Fourth Edition indexes? Applied Neuropsychology: Adult. https://doi.org/10.1080/23279095.2021.2021412.

Ryan, J. J., Kreiner, D. S., Gontkovsky, S. T. and Umfleet, L. G. (2015). Classification Accuracy of Sequentially Administered WAIS-IV Short Forms. Applied Neuropsychology: Adult, 22: 409–414. https://doi.org/10/1080/23279095/2014/953677.

Salvia, J. and Ysseldyke, J. (1988). Assessment in special and remedial education (4th ed.). Boston: Houghton Mifflin.

Sattler, J. M. (2008). Assessment of children: Cognitive foundations (5th ed.). La Mesa, CA: Jerome M. Sattler, Publisher.

Tse, V. W. S., Crabtree, J., Islam, S., and Stott, S. (2019). Comparing Intellectual and Memory Abilities of Older Autistic Adults with Typically Developing Older Adults Using WAIS-IV and WMS-IV. Journal of Autism and Developmental Disorders, 49: 4123–4133. https://doi.org.10.1007/s10803-019-04122-w.

Weiss, L. G., Saklofske, D. H., Coalson, D. L. and Raiford, S. E. (2010). WAIS-IV Clinical use and Interpretation. (First Edition). Elsevier Inc.

Weschler, D. (2008). Weschler Adult Intelligence Scale- Fourth Edition (WAIS-IV) [Database record]. APA PsycTests. https://doi.org/10.1037/t15169-000.

CHAPTER 20

Wisconsin Card Sorting Test (WCST)

Rebecca Aronson and *Ryan Bennett**

The Wisconsin Card Sorting Test (WCST) consists of four stimulus cards and a response deck. The previous administration consisted of two response decks, each consisting of 64 cards; as of 1999, the administration of the WCST became manualized, resulting in one response deck with 128 cards. The cards contain geometric shapes that vary according to form (e.g., circle, square, triangle, or cross), color (e.g., red, green, blue, or yellow), and number (e.g., one, two, three, or four).

The WCST is now a computerized test unusual to clients because little information about how to do the task is given. The client is asked to match each card at the bottom of the screen (response cards) to one of the four Key Cards (stimulus cards). Using the mouse, the client points to the Key Card that they believe matches the response card displayed at the bottom of the screen. Once the client has made their choice, they are asked to press either the left or right mouse button to make their selection. The computer will place the response card under the Key Card the client has selected, and a new card will appear at the bottom of the screen. The client does have the option to change their answer before the card stops moving. If desired, the client can immediately click on the Key Card, or anywhere on the screen a second time, to stop the response card from moving toward the selected Key Card. The client will then be permitted to select again. Once the card stops moving, the client's response is locked, and they can no longer change their answer. The administrator cannot tell the client how to match the cards; however, the computer screen will show whether they are right or wrong each time. It is explained to the client that if they are wrong, they must try to match the next card correctly and then continue matching the cards until the test ends. The test has no time limit; administration takes 15–20 minutes.

Nova Southeastern University, Fort Lauderdale, Florida, USA.
Email: rb1934@nova.edu
* Corresponding author: ra1258@mynsu.nova.edu

Once completed, the computer system generates a score report for each client. Raw scores, standard scores, t-scores, and percentiles are all generated for the following categories: trials administered, total correct, total errors, percent errors, perseverative responses, percent perseverative responses, perseverative errors, percent perseverative errors, non-perseverative errors, percent non-perseverative errors, conceptual level responses, percent conceptual level responses, categories completed, trials to complete first category, failure to maintain set, and learning to learn. The total number of errors, the total number of correct responses, and the number of categories completed are then totaled. Perseverative responses are then identified. A perseverative response is an answer that would have been correct under a previous criterion principle. Scoring rules for perseverative response are many and complex and should be attended to carefully.

Normed Population

The revised WCST was normed on a group of 899 normal subjects between the ages of 6 years, 6 months, and 89 years, 11 months. The 899 subjects were drawn from six distinct samples. One group of 150 subjects was described as being in the original WCST manual and normative study published in 1991 by Heaton and his colleagues, whereas another was a group of 124 commercial airline pilots participating in a study of computerized neuropsychological testing (Bowden et al. 1998). According to the manual, the majority of subjects in the norming groups were selected from the southeastern and southwestern/Rocky Mountain regions of the United States. Data pertaining to race were reported in only one sample, a group of 379 children from an urban setting in the southeast. No race data were provided for the remaining subjects, and no socioeconomic data were included for any subjects. Gender data were provided and, for the most part, evenly distributed (Bowden et al. 1998). Age and education data were also provided; however, the mean age of the child and adolescent samples was not given.

The mean age of the 384 adult subjects was noted to be 49.89 years, with a standard deviation of 17.94 years. The data were compared to the 1995 census data and showed an underrepresentation of younger adults and an overrepresentation of older adults. This, however, does not mean that all groups of older adults are adequately represented in the normative sample. In fact, only four subjects comprise the 85 years and older group. The mean adult education level was 14.95 years (Bowden et al. 1998). Comparing this with the 1987 U.S. Census data showed that the WCST sample education mean was three years higher. Although it would have been preferred to equate education, the analyses of the normative data showed that the demographic variable with the greatest relationship to WCST performance was age. According to regression analyses, performance on the WCST steadily increases from 6.5 through about 19 years of age. Performance remains stable from the 20s through the 50s, at which point performance declines. The data indicate individuals with higher levels of education perform better on the WCST (Bowden et al. 1998).

Reliability and Validity

Reliability data reported in the manual pertaining to interscorer and intrascorer agreement for the child/adolescent and adult samples, and generalizability coefficients and standard error of measurement values for the child and adolescent data only (Bowden et al. 1998) The interscorer and intrascorer reliability studies reported in the manual were conducted with 30 adult psychiatric inpatients. The first study used experienced clinicians and showed a range of interscorer reliability between .88 and .93 and intrascorer coefficients between .91 and .96. Coefficients found for novice examiners were also adequate and ranged from .75 to .97 (Heaton et al. 1993; Bowden et al. 1998). Similar data were obtained for a sample of children and adolescents. With the exception of the learning-to-learn score, interscorer coefficients ranged from .90 to 1.00 (the learning-to-learn coefficient was .66) (Heaton et al. 1993; Bowden et al. 1998). Intrascorer coefficients for the same set of data ranged from .83 to 1.00. Generalizability coefficients for 46 subjects ranged from .39 to .72, with an average of .57 (Heaton et al. 1993; Bowden et al. 1998).

Several valid studies of correlational and discriminant functional analyses support the use of the WCST for various neurological and psychological problems in a variety of populations (Bowden et al. 1998). The WCST is valid and useful for assessing executive functions among individuals who have suffered closed head injuries, demyelinating diseases, seizure disorders, and schizophrenia. In a pediatric context, the WCST has shown strong validity following traumatic brain injuries, learning disabilities, and attention deficit hyperactivity disorders. Although some correlational data have shown that the WCST is sensitive to frontal lesions, data provided in the manual and the research suggest that the WCST is also sensitive to dysfunction in other areas of the brain (Heaton et al. 1993; Bowden et al. 1998).

Interpretation

The WCST is widely used in neuropsychological assessment to measure executive dysfunction. Executive functioning is often referred to as problem-solving and abstraction, which incorporate initiating appropriate sets of responses, maintaining responses, and shifting responses when required. The WCST has become the gold standard for frontal lobe disorders or executive functioning (Eling et al. 2008). However, recent studies have shown that the WCST has some limitations. Although the sensitivity of WCST to frontal disease is high, the test's specificity is low. Controlled studies show that the test is sensitive to lesions in a wide variety of lesions (Bowden et al. 1998). The extent to which the WCST adequately assesses frontal lobe and executive functioning is up for question. Modern imaging studies have shown that frontal lobes are functionally seen and diverse, suggesting that the WCST can only reveal specific aspects of frontal lobe processing (Eling et al. 2008). The WCST, at best, may only tap specific aspects of frontal lobe functioning, such as the shift from using an old rule to a new rule (Eling et al. 2008). Studies examining the mechanisms involved with shifting have demonstrated that perseverance is not the primary factor causing errors, but learned irrelevance is. Learned irrelevance refers to the phenomenon in which a subject has learned irrelevant in a specific discrimination task and takes longer to become detected as the relevant feature after a shift. (Eling et al. 2008).

Performance on the WCST has been examined concerning the subject's age, stress, anxiety, psychiatric disorder, and neurological status. Through the investigation of such researchers as Milner (1963), Drewe (1974), and Nelson (1976), the sensitivity of the WCST to frontal lobe lesions was demonstrated (Heaton et al. 1993). Other investigations found the WCST to be sensitive to the cognitive changes of chronic alcoholism. To alleviate the comparability of research findings across studies, Heaton and colleagues provided a standard method of administration and scoring of the WCST based on the original systematic card configuration developed by Grant and Berg (1948) (Heaton et al. 1993).

Interpretation

1. The complexity of the WCST creates difficulty in interpreting a specific cause or lesion. The WCST is a test of frontal lobe function. However, it has been identified that many nonfrontal functions are involved, including understanding the instructions, verbal memory, visual analysis, visual memory, attention, concentration, and frustration analysis, in addition to the more frontal skills of sequencing, learning from experience, hypothesis formation, behavioral evaluation, planning, and conceptualization. Interpretation of frontal deficits is stronger when the deficit occurs despite an average performance on tests of language comprehension, Block Design, Digit Span, Visual Memory Testing, and Picture Completion (Golden et al. 2002).
2. For diagnostic purposes, it is recommended to use the demographically corrected normative scores (Heaton et al. 1993). These scores provide information about the client's performance relative to the client's age or age and education peers in the normative sample. When considering the categories associated with the normative score ranges, the clinician should remember that the focus of interpretation is the client's performance. That is, it is the client's performance on the WCST, rather than the client per se, that may be experiencing deficits or be impaired. This distinction is fundamental when evaluating children and older adults because of the greater variability in WCST performance found among neurologically intact individuals within this age range (Heaton et al. 1993).
3. When administered to individuals with schizophrenia, the WCST has excellent test-retest reliability. Specifically, "perseverative responses" and "perseverative errors" showed good test-retest reliability. "Non-perseverative errors" and "failure to maintain set" demonstrate lower levels of consistency in scores over repeated assessments, suggesting caution is necessary when using the assessment for diagnosing schizophrenia (Chiu and Lee 2019). People with schizophrenia cannot find and maintain the rules referring simultaneously to three parameters (i.e., form, number, and color). This leads to many guessing the answer, which increases instability. One possible reason for low scores on the WCST in those with schizophrenia is their frustration with negative feedback from the computer program, which may impact their results (Chiu and Lee 2019).

4. When administered to individuals with seizure disorders, clients with nondominant temporal lobe seizures make more errors, perseverative errors, and perseverative responses than those with dominant temporal lobe seizures (Heaton et al. 1993). Impairment in frontal lobe function may be attributed to neural noise created by the seizure disorder and propagated through the pathways connecting the anterior temporal lobe and hippocampal area with the frontal cortex (Heaton et al. 1993).
5. The WCST has been used in several studies that examine the cognitive deficits associated with Parkinson's disease (PD). Results demonstrate impaired performance on the WCST in patients with PD. Performance in individuals with PD is comparable to those with focal lesions involving the frontal lobes and is associated with poor performance on the mental status exam (Heaton et al. 1993).
6. Evidence from studies of children, adolescents, and adults suggests the WCST is a valid measure of executive function in neurologically impaired populations. In addition, studies of physiological correlates of WCST performance and the performance of groups of focal brain lesioned clients suggest that the WCST is particularly sensitive to frontal lobe dysfunction (Heaton et al. 1993).
7. Results of research studies that examined WCST performance in children and adolescents who have been diagnosed with ADHD, learning disability in reading, seizure disorder, or TBI suggest that the WCST may help evaluate executive function in these conditions (Heaton et al. 1993).
8. Clients with high intelligence may perform poorly, making the task more difficult. They attempt to discover the combination of color, form, and number being used. When faced with negative feedback, they adopt a more difficult plan, which furthers their poor performance.
9. Individuals diagnosed with Anorexia Nervosa (AN) make significantly more perseverative errors during the WCST. There is no significant difference between children and adults diagnosed with AN. However, with a medium effect size, adults with AN may have greater difficulty with set-shifting than young people with AN, supporting previous research (Westwood et al. 2016).
10. Compared to adults and children with autism spectrum disorder (ASD), adults with ASD made significant perseverative errors, indicating significant difficulties with set-shifting. When studying the WCST on children diagnosed with ASD, a similar finding was discovered, as children with ASD demonstrate difficulties with set-shifting (Westwood et al. 2016).
11. When the WCST is impaired, but the category test, COWAT, Stroop, and Trails B are not impaired, this suggests the client has figured out the intent of the WCST. On the other tests mentioned, the client is told when instructions change; however, on the WCST, the client is tasked with figuring out the change based on the feedback provided by the computer system (Golden et al. 2002). Individuals with mild frontal lobe concerns can handle the other tests; however, they react poorly to the sudden change in feedback on a task like the WCST. They may also be confused as they may place the response card correctly on accident following an old category when the card matches more than one category (Golden et al. 2002).

12. When the WCST is not impaired, but tests like the Category Tactual Performance Test (TPT) are impaired, a visual-spatial impairment must be considered. There is a visual component to the WCST; no spatial component exists (Golden et al. 2002).
13. Due to the length of the WCST, it demands more sustained attention than other memory tasks. Problems in sustained attention may correlate with poor performance. If this is the case, poor performance will also be observed on the category test (Golden et al. 2002).

References

Arffa, S., Lovell, M., Podell, K. and Goldberg, E. (1998). Wisconsin Card Sorting Test Performance in Above Average and Superior School Children Relationship to Intelligence and Age. Archives of Clinical Neuropsychology, 13(8): 713–720. https://doi.org/10.1016/s0887-6177(98)00007-9.

Boone, K. B., Ghaffarian, S., Lesser, I. M., Hill-Gutierrez, E. and G. Berman, N. (1993). Wisconsin card sorting test performance in healthy, older adults: Relationship to age, sex, education, and IQ. Journal of Clinical Psychology, 49(1): 54–60. https://doi.org/3.0.co;2-6">10.1002/1097-4679(199301)49:1<54::aid-jclp2270490108>3.0.co;2-6.

Bowden, S. C., Fowler, K. S., Bell, R. C., Whelan, G., Clifford, C. C., Ritter, A. J. et al. (1998). The Reliability and Internal Validity of the Wisconsin Card Sorting Test. Neuropsychological Rehabilitation, 8(3): 243–254. https://doi.org/10.1080/713755573.

Chelune, G. J. and Baer, R. A. (1986). Developmental norms for the wisconsin card sorting test. Journal of Clinical and Experimental Neuropsychology, 8(3): 219–228. https://doi.org/10.1080/01688638608401314.

Chiu, E.-C. and Lee, S.-C. (2019). Test-retest reliability of the Wisconsin Card Sorting Test in people with Schizophrenia. Disability and Rehabilitation, 43(7): 996–1000. https://doi.org/10.1080/09638288.2019.1647295.

Demakis, G. J. (2003). A meta-analytic review of the sensitivity of the Wisconsin Card Sorting Test to frontal and lateralized frontal brain damage. Neuropsychology, 17(2): 255–264. https://doi.org/10.1037/0894-4105.17.2.255.

Eling, P., Derckx, K. and Maes, R. (2008). On the historical and conceptual background of the Wisconsin Card Sorting Test. Brain and Cognition, 67(3): 247–253. https://doi.org/10.1016/j.bandc.2008.01.006.

Golden, C., Espe-Pfeifer, P. and Wachsler-Felder, J. (2002). Neuropsychological Interpretation of Objective Psychological Tests. Boston Kluwer Academic Publishers.

Grant, D. A. and Berg, E. A. (1948). Wisconsin Card Sorting Test. PsycTESTS Dataset. https://doi.org/10.1037/t31298-000.

Heaton, R. K., Chelune, G. J., Talley, J. L., Kay, G. G. and Curtiss, G. (1993). WCST: Wisconsin Card Sorting Test. Psychological Assessment Resources.

Hedge, C., Powell, G. and Sumner, P. (2017). The reliability paradox: Why robust cognitive tasks do not produce reliable individual differences. Behavior Research Methods, 50(3): 1166–1186. https://doi.org/10.3758/s13428-017-0935-1.

Huizinga, M. and van der Molen, M. W. (2007). Age-Group Differences in Set-Switching and Set-Maintenance on the Wisconsin Card Sorting Task. Developmental Neuropsychology, 31(2): 193–215. https://doi.org/10.1080/87565640701190817.

King, J. H., Sweet, J. J., Sherer, M., Curtiss, G. and Vanderploeg, R. D. (2002). Validity Indicators Within the Wisconsin Card Sorting Test: Application of New and Previously Researched Multivariate Procedures in Multiple Traumatic Brain Injury Samples. The Clinical Neuropsychologist, 16(4): 506–523. https://doi.org/10.1076/clin.16.4.506.13912.

Kopp, B., Lange, F. and Steinke, A. (2019). The Reliability of the Wisconsin Card Sorting Test in Clinical Practice. Assessment, 28(1): 248–263. https://doi.org/10.1177/1073191119866257.

Kopp, B., Maldonado, N., Scheffels, J. F., Hendel, M. and Lange, F. (2019). A Meta-Analysis of Relationships between Measures of Wisconsin Card Sorting and Intelligence. Brain Sciences, 9(12): 349. https://doi.org/10.3390/brainsci9120349.

Kopp, B., Steinke, A., Bertram, M., Skripuletz, T. and Lange, F. (2019). Multiple Levels of Control Processes for Wisconsin Card Sorts: An Observational Study. Brain Sciences, 9(6): 141. https://doi.org/10.3390/brainsci9060141.

Lichtenstein, J. D., Erdodi, L. A., Rai, J. K., Mazur-Mosiewicz, A. and Flaro, L. (2016). Wisconsin Card Sorting Test embedded validity indicators developed for adults can be extended to children. Child Neuropsychology, 24(2): 247–260. https://doi.org/10.1080/09297049.2016.1259402.

Nyhus, E. and Barceló, F. (2009). The Wisconsin Card Sorting Test and the cognitive assessment of prefrontal executive functions: A critical update. Brain and Cognition, 71(3): 437–451. https://doi.org/10.1016/j.bandc.2009.03.005.

Riccio, C. A., Hall, J., Morgan, A., Hynd, G. W., Gonzalez, J. J. and Marshall, R. M. (1994). Executive function and the Wisconsin card sorting test: Relationship with behavioral ratings and cognitive ability. Developmental Neuropsychology, 10(3): 215–229. https://doi.org/10.1080/87565649409540580.

Romine, C., Lee, D., Wolfe, M., Homack, S., George, C. and Riccio, C. (2004). Wisconsin Card Sorting Test with children: a meta-analytic study of sensitivity and specificity. Archives of Clinical Neuropsychology, 19(8): 1027–1041. https://doi.org/10.1016/j.acn.2003.12.009.

Snow, J. H. (1998). Developmental Patterns and Use of the Wisconsin Card Sorting Test for Children and Adolescents with Learning Disabilities. Child Neuropsychology, 4(2): 89–97. https://doi.org/10.1076/chin.4.2.89.3180.

Tate, R. L., Perdices, M. and Maggiotto, S. (1998). Stability of the Wisconsin Card Sorting Test and the Determination of Reliability of Change in Scores. The Clinical Neuropsychologist, 12(3): 348–357. https://doi.org/10.1076/clin.12.3.348.1988.

CHAPTER 21

Wide Range Achievement Test Fifth Edition

Saba Verani

The Wide Range Achievement Test (WRAT) is a comprehensive assessment tool designed to measure reading skills, math skills, spelling, and comprehension for individuals aged 5 to 85+. With a history dating back to 1936 and multiple revisions, the newest edition, WRAT-Fifth Edition (WRAT-5), is a reliable and well-established assessment tool for evaluating academic performance. The WRAT-5 is a versatile assessment that can be used in various settings, including schools, clinics, hospitals, and private practices. It is a compressive psychoeducational or neuropsychological assessment that can be used for a variety of purposes, including evaluating students' academic skill levels, determining grade placement, or placement within specific reading groups. (Wilkinson and Robertson 2017). The results can be used for older individuals to determine the level of training required or for preparatory purposes. Overall, the WRAT-5 is an assessment tool that can provide valuable information about an individual's academic performance and support the development of educational and training plans.

History and Normative Sample

The Wide Range Achievement Test (WRAT) was first introduced in 1936 and has undergone multiple revisions. In order to standardize the assessment, a sample of 5,600 individuals aged 5 years 0 months to 74 years 11 months were included in the study (Reynolds 1986). The sample was classified based on variables, including age, race, region of residence, and sex. A limitation found within this stratification was that there was not an equal number of individuals within each variable. This stems

Nova Southeastern University, Fort Lauderdale, Florida, USA.
Email: sv746@mynsu.nova.edu

from the fact that the percentage of Black individuals in the United States varied by age at the time (Reynolds 1986). The authors faced difficulty in incorporating non-White racial groups, such as Blacks, Hispanics, American Indians, Asian Americans, and other minority groups, into the normative data sampling (Reynolds 1986).

The National Center for Health Statistics collected the normative sample for the WRAT. The sample was selected to represent the general population in terms of age, sex, region of location, race, and a few other characteristics (Silverstein 1978). Two sets of raw score data were collected through testing groups aged 6 to 13 ½ at six-month intervals, as well as ages 14, 15, and 16–17 (Silverstein 1978). The results from this sample yielded corresponding data to the current norms. For example, the reading subtest scores within the sample were 70, which corresponded with the norm standard score of 74 (Silverstein 1978).

The WRAT underwent significant revision with its Fourth Edition release (WRAT-4) in 2006. The WRAT-4 featured updated norms with an extended age range, including a Sentence Comprehension Subtest, increased words in the reading and spelling subtests, and two different forms (blue and green) (Wilkinson and Robertson 2006). The WRAT-4 and subsequent editions are based on both age and grade-based norms.

To standardize the WRAT-4, a sample of 3,000 individuals was included, with about 100 to 150 individuals assigned to 19 different groups based on factors such as age, gender, race/ethnicity, education level, and geography (Pearson 2006). This resulted in the creating of 43 norm groups, providing age-based standard scores. In order to accommodate the greater developmental growth seen in the youngest ages, 5:0–5:2 to 7:9–7:11, 12 groups were created at 3-month intervals (Pearson 2006). In contrast, for the less exponential growth seen in older ages, 25–34 and 85–94, there were seven groups created at 10-year intervals (Pearson 2006).

The normative sample for the Wide Range Achievement Test Fifth Edition (WRAT-5) was comprised of examinees in kindergarten to 12th grade and adults aged 19 to 85. These examinees were not institutionalized and had no physical or perceptual impairments that would prevent them from completing the WRAT-5 subtests (Wilkinson and Robertson, 2017). As with the WRAT-4, the green and blue forms were administered to all samples. The age norm sample consisted of 2,355 participants and focused on ages 5 years 0 months to 85 years 11 months. The grade norm sample included 2,150 participants in grades K-12 (Wilkinson and Robertson 2017). These samples provided a representative cross-section of the population regarding age and grade level, allowing for the creation of valid and reliable norms for the WRAT-5.

Reliability

The test-retest reliability of the Wide Range Achievement Test (WRAT) has been investigated in various studies. In a study by Woodward et al. (1975), the reliability of the WRAT was evaluated in a sample of children with emotional disturbances or slow learning difficulties who were placed in special education classes. The WRAT was administered twice to two groups, and the results showed that the test-retest reliability coefficients for all subtests were significant, with the highest correlation found in the reading subtest. Although the lowest test-retest reliability was found in the arithmetic subtest, it was still highly significant. The study concluded that the WRAT is a consistent and stable measure of academic achievement for children.

In a study by Ashendorf et al. (2009), the stability of the WRAT-3 reading subtest was evaluated in a sample of cognitively normal adults, adults with mild cognitive impairment, and adults with Alzheimer's Disease. The sample consisted of 200 cognitively normal controls, 73 participants with mild cognitive impairment, and 41 participants diagnosed with Alzheimer's Disease. The reading subtest of the WRAT-3 was administered during a single neuropsychological testing session at baseline and one year later. The results showed that the reading subtest scores differed based on diagnosis, with participants diagnosed with Alzheimer's Disease performing worse than those with mild cognitive impairment and the control group. The study also found that Caucasian participants performed better than African-American participants, with no gender differences. The test-retest reliability of the WRAT-3 was 0.90 ($p < 0.001$), with a stability of 0.84 for non-Hispanic Caucasian participants and 0.96 for African Americans ($p < 0.001$). The results of these studies suggest that the WRAT Reading subtest has high test-retest reliability and stability, making it a useful tool for evaluating literacy levels and dementia. The test-retest reliability was found to be consistent for most groups, with a higher rate of stability observed in participants with Alzheimer's Disease.

Validity

After the 1936 and 1946 editions of the WRAT, the 1963 edition changed to Level 1 and Level II. Level I was catered toward ages 5–11, and Level II was for ages 12 and older. In this validation study, Level I was administered to 342 boys and 341 girls in grades 1 through 6, and to avoid bias, students were selected from different counties. The results demonstrated that the revised WRAT has reasonably good concurrent and diagnostic validity (Schaie et al. 1970). The validity coefficients across grade levels and regions of residence ranged from 0.41 to 0.87 for the reading subtest and 0.49 to 0.78 for the arithmetic subtest (Schaie et al. 1970). Based on these results, the correlation between the criterion measures of age was high and serves as a satisfactory assessment for school achievement. This study also found that the WRAT Reading and Arithmetic subtest overestimated the actual grade level when compared to the Stanford Achievement Test (SAT) (Schaie et al. 1970).

The WRAT-4 and WRAT-5 have been used in various studies to assess individuals' academic achievement and cognitive abilities. A study by Abreu-Mendoza and colleagues was conducted in Mexico and Columbia to evaluate the Math Computation subtest of the WRAT-4 for its internal reliability, concurrent validity, and normative data (2019). The sample consisted of 1,318 Mexican adolescents, and the results showed good internal consistency, with the average score being 25.58 ($SD = 5.66$). The concurrent validity was acquired through a sample of 466 students, and the results indicated that the WRAT Math Computation subtest was suitable for assessing individuals' mathematical abilities.

In a validation study of the WRAT-3, the test was administered to 342 boys and 341 girls in grades 1 through 6 and was found to have reasonably good concurrent and diagnostic validity (Schaie et al. 1970). The median reliability coefficient for the WRAT-4 ranges from 0.87 to 0.93 for the four subtests with similar reliability between the green and blue forms (Pearson 2006). The WRAT-4 was found to have concurrent validity with several achievement and cognitive ability assessments, with a higher correlation found with verbal indices of academic achievement tests (Pearson 2006).

Compared With Other Instruments

To compare the correlations between WRAT-4 and WRAT-5, 105 examinees aged 5–18 were administered the WRAT-4 and WRAT-5 (Wilkinson and Robertson 2017). The correlation between the two versions of Word Reading is $r = 0.83$, Spelling is $r = 0.88$, Math Computation is $r = 0.87$, Sentence Comprehension is $r = 0.83$, and Reading Composite is $r = 0.87$ (Wilkinson and Robertson 2017). The correlation between the WRAT-4 and WRAT-5 subtest scores was found to be consistently high (~0.80); however, the mean scores were higher on the WRAT-4, specifically Spelling and Math Computation (Wilkinson and Robertson 2017). The high correlational consistency indicates that the fourth and fifth editions of the WRAT have the same constructs of measurements (Wilkinson and Robertson 2017).

Administration

The materials required for administering the WRAT-5 include the WRAT manual, a norms book, two Record Forms, a Response Booklet, a Word Reading List, a Spelling List Card, and a Sentence Comprehension Card. The WRAT-5 consists of four subtests: Word Reading, Spelling, Math Computation, and Sentence Comprehension. The Word Reading subtest assesses an individual's ability to recognize and identify letters and words, and it is not timed. The spelling subtest measures an examinee's ability to write letters and words from dictation. The Math Computation subtest measures an individual's mathematical abilities and arithmetic skills, including their ability to perform basic arithmetic operations, such as addition, subtraction, multiplication, and division. The Sentence Comprehension Subtest focuses on the individual's ability to understand the meaning of words and comprehend the information and ideas presented in a sentence. The standard scores from the Word Reading and Sentence Comprehension subtests are combined to form the Reading Composite.

The Word Reading subtest of the WRAT-5 assesses the examinee's ability to recognize and identify letters and words. The subtest is divided into Part 1: Letter Reading and Part 2: Word Reading. In Part 1, the examinee reads a list of 15 letters. For grades K-2, the starting point is Part 1: Letter Reading, Item 1. In Part 2, the examinee reads from a list of 55 words, with the starting point for grades 3–12+ being Part 2: Word Reading, Item 1. The subtest is not timed and is designed to measure the individual's ability to read words accurately.

The WRAT-5 Spelling subtest consists of two parts: Letter Writing and Spelling. In Part 1: Letter Writing, the examinee is asked to write their name followed by writing 13 letters as they are dictated. In Part 2: Spelling, the examinee is asked to spell up to 42 words that are dictated. The starting point for K-2 grade students is Part 1: Letter Writing, Item 1, and for grades 3–12, the starting point is Part 2: Spelling, Item 1.

The Math Computation subtest of the WRAT-5 consists of two parts: Oral Math and Math Computation. In the Oral Math section, the examinee is required to respond orally to 15 mathematical items, whereas in the Math Computation section, the examinee is given 15 minutes to solve 40 arithmetic problems in the Response Booklet. For grades K-2, the start point is Part 1: Oral Math, Item 1, and for grades 3–12 and above, the start point is Part 2: Math Computation, Item 1.

Lastly, in Sentence Completion, the examinee is asked to read one or two sentences with a fill-in-the-blank representing a missing word. The examinee is then asked to respond with one or more words to demonstrate an understanding of the text and context. This subtest is not administered to the Kindergarten grade. After completing Samples Items 1–3, the start point for grades 1–4 is Item 1, the start point for grades 5–7 is Item 10, and the start point for grades 8–12+ is Item 10.

Scoring

The WRAT-5 is scored by comparing the individual's performance on each subtest to the performance of a standardized sample of individuals of the same age. The scores are then transformed into standard scores, which are reported as T-scores, with a mean of 50 and a standard deviation of 10. These T-scores provide a standardized way of comparing an individual's performance to others of the same age and allow for easy interpretation of the results. In addition to T-scores, the WRAT-5 also provides percentiles, indicating the percentage of individuals in the standardized sample who scored lower than the individual being evaluated. For example, if an individual's score is at the 70th percentile, this means that they scored higher than 70% of individuals in the standardized sample. The WRAT-5 also provides Age Equivalents (AE), which indicate the average age at which the individual's performance on the subtest is typical. For example, if an individual's AE on a subtest is 14 years, this means that their performance on that subtest is typical of an average 14-year-old. Overall, the WRAT-5 results provide a comprehensive report with a detailed summary of the individual's performance on each subtest.

Interpretation

Using the examinee's raw scores and converting them to standard scores based on the normative samples is the best way to interpret the individual's performance. Subtest scores can range from 55 to 145, including a mean of 100 and a standard deviation of 15. Scores above 100 are considered above the mean, and scores below 100 are considered below the mean. Scores in between:

1. 55–69 are considered Lower Extreme
2. 70–79 are considered Low
3. 80–89 are considered Below Average
4. 90–110 are considered Average

5. 110–119 are considered Above Average
6. 120–129 are considered Superior
7. 130–145 are considered Upper Extreme

Scores that are below average should be evaluated in areas of weaknesses. If an individual is consistently performing poorly in reading, a learning disability, specifically for reading, should be considered. These scores can help determine where an individual's performance is weak as well as assess for areas of need within places of work or education.

Applications in Research

The WRAT 5 is a neuropsychological assessment tool used to measure academic abilities and is validated for use with individuals of varying ages and abilities. The WRAT 5 measures skills such as reading, spelling, arithmetic, and math computations. The overall clinical applications of the WRAT-5 have evolved with the assessment modifications. For example, in a study of 71 undergraduate students, the WRAT-4 Math Computations subtest was found to be a statistically significant predictor of final grades in college science classes (Zagar et al. 2018). Another study evaluated the test-retest reliability of the reading, spelling, and arithmetic subtests of the WRAT-3 over two administrations for individuals with autism spectrum disorder (Jantz et al. 2005). The study found that the subtests had acceptable test-retest stability, but the reading subtest may not be the best measure for individuals with autism due to possible communicative deficits.

Saperstein and colleagues explored how to assess cognitive health in early psychosis. The study aimed to put together a toolkit comprising a clinician manual, an assessment, decision-making tools, and a menu of cognitive health service options (Saperstein et al. 2020). Also, 933 individuals were administered the WRAT-5 reading test. They found that there were similar competition times among the measures, and the rate of impairment suggested lower cognitive health (Saperstein et al. 2020).

To evaluate the premorbid functioning and intellect, the WRAT and the Barona, an IQ assessment, were administered to 93 patients with mild to moderate Huntington's disease (O'Rourke et al. 2011). Ninety-three participants with confirmed Huntington's disease were administered a combination of the reading subtest of WRAT-3 and WRAT-4. The mean WRAT Reading score was 92.9 (SD = 11.2), and the mean Barona score was 107.5 (SD = 7.54) (O'Rourke et al. 2011). Based on the analysis, the WRAT Reading subtest scores yielded a lower estimated IQ than the Barona in a majority (89%) of the participants (O'Rourke et al. 2011). The study found that the WRAT Reading performance had a stronger relationship with clinical features of Huntington's disease than the Barona assessment. Lower or poorer performance on the WRAT reading was linked to greater motor dysfunction and overall influencing progressive neural degeneration (O'Rourke et al., 2011). It may be likely that deficits in motor and speech caused lower scores and performance on the reading subtest. Furthermore, lower memory functioning was associated with lower scores on the WRAT reading subtest, suggesting a positive relationship between delayed memory and WRAT scores (O'Rourke et al. 2011). This study's findings suggest that subcortical dementia, which influences cognitive dysfunction in individuals with Huntington's disease, also influences irregular abilities of Word Reading, which is also consistent with Alzheimer's disease patients (O'Rourke et al. 2011).

Another study by Casaletto and colleagues evaluated HIV individuals to understand and identify neurocognitive decline as well as their premorbid levels of cognitive functioning. One hundred fifty individuals who were HIV positive (HIV+) and 76 individuals who were HIV negative (HIV-) were administered the WRAT-4 Reading subtest. In order to evaluate premorbid functioning, 48 HIV+ individuals were reassessed at a second visit. The 70-item oral reading test was administered to assess their ability to read letters and assess any irregularly pronounced words (Caseletto et al. 2014). In order to determine the relationship between neuropsychological performance, it was correlated with WRAT-4 Reading ($p = 0.36$, $p = 0.001$) as well as weak motor performance ($p = 0.34$, $p = 0.002$). Caseletto and colleagues found that WRAT-4 reading performance varied with HIV-associated participants regarding their neurocognitive impairments. When comparing the results for the group of participants that were administered WRAT-4 twice, they found that between HIV+ and HIV- individuals, HIV+ individuals demonstrated significantly worse neurocognitive functioning currently (Caseletto et al. 2013). However, the results between the two test results were not significant for reading performance (Caseletto et al. 2013).

The WRAT reading subtest has also been used to evaluate premorbid functioning and intellect in individuals with Huntington's disease (O'Rourke et al., 2011). Results showed that the WRAT Reading subtest had a strong relationship with clinical features of Huntington's disease and was linked to greater motor dysfunction and delayed memory. In a study of a 17-year-old female with Moyamoya Disease and a specific learning disorder, the WRAT-5 was administered and found to indicate a specific learning disorder in mathematics (Mikula et al. 2022).

Interpretation

The Wide Range Achievement Test Fifth Edition (WRAT-5) is a useful clinical tool for a variety of purposes, including:

1. Identification of Learning Disabilities: The WRAT-5 can help identify the presence of a possible learning disability by evaluating an individual's performance in areas such as reading, math, spelling, and comprehension. The WRAT is a screening test, so low scores in any area should be followed by more comprehensive educational testing. Generally, scores in the lower 25% of the population are considered indicative of possible impairment, which may require educational remediation (T-scores below 43, IQ scores below 90).
2. Evaluating one's overall academic performance: The WRAT-5 can be used to evaluate an individual's academic skill level, which can be useful for determining grade placement or placement within specific educational groups. Again, since this is a screening instrument, low WRAT scores should be confirmed by more detailed educational evaluations.

3. Monitoring academic progress and development: The WRAT-5 can be used to monitor an individual's progress over time, providing valuable information about their academic growth and development.
4. Preparing for educational or training programs: The WRAT-5 can be used to determine the level of training required for older individuals, including adolescents and adults, who are preparing for educational or training programs.
5. Assisting in the development of educational plans: The results of the WRAT-5 can be used to assist in developing educational plans, including individualized education plans (IEPs) and remediation plans.
6. The reading score is considered a good measure of premorbid function after a brain injury in adults. It is most useful in cases where there is no substantial language impairment (such as left hemisphere strokes or some forms of dementia). In these latter cases, it may underestimate premorbid levels. It is also not a good measure in individuals with a premorbid learning disability in reading. As such, the WRAT-5 can be used as part of a comprehensive neuropsychological evaluation, providing valuable information about an individual's cognitive and academic abilities.
7. Left hemisphere injuries are most associated with reading and spelling disorders, while right hemisphere posterior injuries may impact mathematical skills.

References

Abreu-Mendoza, R. A., Chamorro, Y. and Matute, E. (2019). Psychometric properties of the WRAT Math Computation Subtest in Mexican adolescents. Journal of Psychoeducational Assessment, 37(8): 957–972. https://doi.org/10.1177/0734282918809793.

Ashendorf, L., Jefferson, A. L., Green, R. C. and Stern, R. A. (2009). Test-retest stability on the WRAT-3 reading subtest in geriatric cognitive evaluations. Journal of Clinical and Experimental Neuropsychology, 31(5): 605–610.

Casaletto, K. B., Cattie, J., Franklin, D. R., Moore, D. J., Woods, S. P., Grant, I.,... and HNRP Group. (2014). The Wide Range Achievement Test–4 reading subtest "holds" in HIV-infected individuals. Journal of Clinical and Experimental Neuropsychology, 36(9): 992–1001.

Jantz, P. B., Froehlich, A. L., Cariello, A. N., Anderson, J., Prigge, M. B. D., Lange, N. et al. (2015, January 1). Wide Range Achievement Test in Autism Spectrum Disorder: Test-retest Stability. Psychological Reports, 116(3): 674–684.

Mikula, C., Kim, J. H., Phenis, R. and Kiselica, A. (2022). Specific learning disorder in mathematics and moyamoya disease: A case report. Applied Neuropsychology: Child, 1–8. https://doi.org/10.1080/21622965.2022.2033745.

O'Rourke, Justin, J.F., William, H. Adams, Kevin Duff, Joanne Byars, Peg Nopoulos, Jane S. Paulsen, and Leigh J. Beglinger. (2011). Estimating premorbid functioning in Huntington's disease: the relationship between disease progression and the wide range achievement test reading subtest. Archives of clinical neuropsychology, 26(1): 59–66. https://doi.org/10.1080/13854046.2016.1186224.

Oyedeji, C.I., Hall, K., Luciano, A. et al. (2020). Geriatric assessment for older adults with sickle cell disease: protocol for a prospective cohort pilot study. Pilot Feasibility Stud, 6: 131z. https://doi.org/10.1186/s40814-020-00673-3.

Philip Sayegh, Alyssa Arentoft, Nicholas S. Thaler, Andy C. Dean, April D. Thames, Quality of Education Predicts Performance on the Wide Range Achievement Test-4th Edition Word Reading Subtest, Archives of Clinical Neuropsychology, Volume 29, Issue 8, December 2014, Pages 731–736, https://doi.org/10.1093/arclin/acu059.

Reynolds, C. R. (1986). Wide Range Achievement Test (WRAT-R) 1984 Edition. Journal of Counseling & Development, 64(8): 540. https://doi-org.ezproxylocal.library.nova.edu/10.1002/j.1556-6676.1986.tb01196.x.

Reynolds, C. R., Altmann, R. A. and Allen, D. N. (2021). Achievement Tests in the Era of High-Stakes Assessment. In Mastering Modern Psychological Testing (pp. 291–330). Springer, Cham.

Robertson, G. J. (2010). Wide-Range Achievement Test. The Corsini encyclopedia of psychology, 1–2. https://doi.org/10.1002/9780470479216.corpsy1038.

Saperstein, A. M., Medalia, A., Malinovsky, I., Bello, I. and Dixon, L. B. (2021). Toolkit for assessing and addressing cognitive health in early psychosis: Evaluation of feasibility and utility in a coordinated specialty care setting. Early Intervention in Psychiatry, 15(5): 1376–1381. https://doi.org/10.1111/eip.13070.

Schaie, K. W., Roberts, J. and Health Services and Mental Health Administration, D. B., MD. (1970). School Achievement of Children 6–11 Years as Measured by the Reading and Arithmetic Subtests of the Wide Range Achievement Test.

Silverstein, A. B. (1978). Note on the norms for the WRAT. Psychology in the Schools, 15(2): 152–153. https://doi.org/10.1002/1520-6807(197804)15:2<152::AID-PITS2310150202>3.0.CO;2-H.

Test, R. A. (2009). Wide range achievement test 4 (wrat4. J. Occup. Psychol., Employment Disabil., 11(1): 49.

Wilkinson, G. S. and Robertson, G. J. (2006). Wide Range Achievement Test 4. Lutz, FL: Psychological Assessment Resources.

Wilkinson, G. S. and Robertson, G. J. (2017). Wide Range Achievement Test, Fifth Edition (WRAT5). Pearson Inc.

Woodward, C. A., Santa-Barbara, J. and Roberts, R. (1975). Test-Retest Reliability of the Wide Range Achievement Test. Journal of Clinical Psychology, 31(1): 81–84. https://doi-org.ezproxylocal.library.nova.edu/10.1002/1097-4679(197501)31:1<81::AID-JCLP2270310124>3.0.CO;2-H

Zagar, R. J., Kovach, J. W., Lakhani, A., Stone, T., Singh, I., Portela, M. et al. (2018). Can the WRAT-4 Math Computation Subtest Predict Final Grade in College-Level Science. Rev. Eur. Stud., 10: 144.

Section II
Effort Tests

CHAPTER 22

Medical Symptom Validity Test (MSVT)

Hayley Herndon

The Medical Symptom Validity Test (MSVT) (Green 2004) is a short, computerized test that gauges cognitive effort and memory. The test is a short-form version of the Word Memory Test (WMT) (Green 2004). The MSVT displays common word pairs throughout two consecutive trials, like the WMT. During this test, Immediate Recognition (IR), Delayed Recognition (DR), and Consistency (CNS) between the two scores are measured to assess effort, the cut-offs of which can be viewed in the test manual. Free recall (FR) and paired associates (PA) tests are also included to assess memory. While patients with severe neurological conditions can easily pass the effort subtests of the MSVT, it is designed to appear to be a real memory test (Carone 2009).

Normed Population

Normative data for MSVT are drawn from more than 1,000 patients from different clinical groups, including patients with neurological disorders, severe and mild traumatic brain injury, psychological disorders, children and adults with learning disabilities (and/or an IQ below 70), chronic pain patients, and normal controls (e.g., healthy volunteers). As described in the test manual, the author, other clinicians, and researchers tested these patients and replicated the ease with which they completed the tasks. According to the manual and computer program for the MSVT, people with severe TBI or neurological diseases can pass it easily. These results also show that the scores of adult subjects asked to fake memory impairment are below those of patients with advanced dementia, including those who have been institutionalized (Carone 2009).

Nova Southeastern University, Fort Lauderdale, Florida, USA.
Email: hh644@mynsu.nova.edu

Reliability

MSVT is partly easy because the subtests recognize each other, and the pairs represent one concept. However, visual cues, like text length, can help determine the correct answer. Due to these subtle cues, even patients who speak a foreign language can pass the MSVT (Richman et al. 2006). There is also a "stealth" version of the MSVT, which is similar to the MSVT but contains word pairs that are harder to associate and subtests with different psychometric properties, meant to prevent coaching. This is very useful, for example, if the examiner has reason to suspect that an examinee may have been coached to do well on any 50/50 forced-choice tasks administered by a computer but to perform poorly on other types of memory tests. Since the stealth version is more difficult, it can demonstrate the patient has adequate memory abilities in such a situation (Carone 2009).

As a final point, it is important to note that the MSVT measures both effort and memory. Thus, it does not directly assess malingering. Apart from malingering, oppositional behavior stemming from a dislike of testing is another explanation for poor effort. Nonetheless, the MSVT test manual presents data on multiple groups of malingerers who were instructed to fake memory impairment. Based on a study by Merten et al. (2005), one group showed that all simulators failed the MSVT (100% sensitivity) and that effort subtests proved between 97% and 100% accurate in differentiating the simulating group from volunteers who were asked to try their best. For the DR and CNS subtests, the specificity rate was 100%, while for the IR subtests, the specificity rate was 94%. Overall, the MSVT has high sensitivity and specificity in evaluating effort but should be used in conjunction with the WMT rather than as a replacement unless there are significant time constraints (Carone 2009).

Validity

The MSVT is easier than the WMT, consistent with the theory behind its construction, and is, therefore, not as sensitive. Test author Dr. Green and his colleague, Dr. Roger Gervais, evaluated 279 MSVT and WMT patients involved in disability or compensation claims (Green 2007). A total of 37% of the patients failed the WMT, while 29% failed the MSVT, resulting in 80.3% agreement between the two tests. Also, 14% of cases had passed the MSVT but failed the WMT. It may reflect the inconsistent effort that 5.75% of cases failed the MSVT when the WMT passed. Additionally, the differences between the two tests can provide information about the consistency of test-taking efforts since MSVT scores should be higher than WMT scores. The MSVT is a useful alternative to the WMT when time is of the essence; however, the WMT is recommended when time permits due to its enhanced sensitivity (Carone 2009).

The MSVT can also be administered to children, another useful feature. Test manual data shows that children can pass the MSVT with a mean age of 12 and a mean Full-Scale Intelligence Quotient of 88 (n = 50), by children aged 6 to 10 (n = 36), by children in second grade (Gill et al. 2007) (n = 20), and by children with a mean full-scale IQ of 65 (n = 7). The study by Gill et al. also shows that children with a Verbal IQ of 70 or below (n = 23) can easily pass the MSVT. The MSVT computer program shows that other pediatric groups tested by Dr. Lloyd Flaro easily passed the MSVT efforts subtests, such as children with attention deficit hyperactivity disorder (ADHD), fetal alcohol syndrome, and children with a mean Verbal IQ of 64. All these findings illustrate that if children (and adults) with significant neurological impairments can pass the MSVT, then adults with mild neurological injuries/dysfunction who perform below-established cut-offs are not making the necessary effort. This makes the finding that 62% of adults presenting for an independent psychiatric evaluation under personal injury litigation or insurance protection claims failed their MSVT even more astonishing, especially when viewed in the context of the fact they were not suffering from severe neurological conditions (Gill et al. 2007). Similarly, Richman et al. (2006) found a 42% MSVT failure rate in adult independent medical evaluations, and Chafetz et al. (2007) found a 50% to 60% MSVT failure rate during adult and child Social Security Disability evaluations (Carone 2009).

Patients with dementia routinely score poorly on measures of effort (Green et al. 1996; Green 2003; Green 2004; Patton et al. 2004; Teichner and Wagner 2004). Teichner and Wagner (2004) reported that individuals with dementia scored significantly poorer on all trials of the TOMM than either normal or cognitively impaired individuals. Green (2004) reported that half of the early dementia patients scored below the 85% cut-off in Immediate Recognition (IR), Delayed Recognition (DR), and Consistency Tasks of the MSVT, while 80% of the advanced dementia patients scored below the cut-off on all three subtests. Green (2003) and Patton et al. (2004) both reported similar findings with the WMT (Covert 2008).

Even though demented patients perform poorly on tests of effort, they are assumed to fail due to extreme memory deficits rather than a lack of motivation to do well (Green 2004). Also, as Feehan and colleagues (1991) reported, demented patients are generally believed to be largely unaware of their cognitive deficits, further accrediting the belief that this group would have no reason to put forth poor effort (Covert 2008).

Individuals with dementia often fall into the Dementia Profile. The Dementia Profile (DP) consists of guidelines designed to validate an individual's test results by demonstrating their better performance on easier aspects of the MSVT compared to the more challenging ones. As explained by Howe and Loring (2009), the primary objective of the DP is to minimize false positive results in MSVT by distinguishing those individuals who failed the test due to neurological conditions from those exhibiting genuine symptom validity issues.

In their study involving individuals with dementia, Howe and Loring (2009) discovered that out of 20 subjects who failed the MSVT, 17 met the DP criteria, indicating an 85% sensitivity rate for the DP. Similarly, Frerichs (2006) reported that 37.5% of his clinical sample, consisting of 16 individuals with mild cognitive impairment, and 51.5% of his sample with dementia (comprising 33 individuals) failed the MSVT. Remarkably, with the exception of one patient, all individuals who failed the MSVT met the DP criteria (Whitney et al. 2009).

These subtests have proven to be highly responsive to detecting compromised symptom validity while generally remaining unresponsive to genuine cognitive impairment, even in cases of severe impairment. Richman et al. (2006) illustrated the simplicity of these assessments by revealing that the average scores on these measures consistently fell within the range of 95% to 99% correct, whether administered to adults or children in their native language or to individuals, both adults and children, in a foreign language they were not proficient in. It is worth noting that the study's participants included adults with severe traumatic brain injuries (TBI) or neurological conditions, as well as children with below-average IQs.

In addition, Richman et al. (2006) referenced data provided by Flaro, which indicated that children with a full-scale IQ of 70 or lower achieved an average score of 95% correct on the primary symptom validity subtests. In contrast, these researchers highlighted the MSVT's sensitivity to diminished symptom validity by demonstrating that 33% of individuals with soft tissue injuries or fibromyalgia who were undergoing independent medical examinations for disability evaluations failed one or more of these indices. The overall outcome patterns among individuals with soft tissue injuries or fibromyalgia who failed the MSVT closely resembled those of individuals attempting to simulate symptoms rather than those with genuine neurological dysfunction (Whitney et al. 2009).

The available data strongly suggests that, among groups presumed to be making their best effort during testing, only patients with advanced dementia score below the specified cut-off on the primary symptom validity subtests, as Green (2004) noted.

Test Procedures

The examinee is presented with a learning phase involving two presentations of ten different word pairs, one every six seconds, representing one concept (e.g., belly button) rather than two concepts (e.g., cookie and milk). The test includes foils, which are more obviously incorrect, during the IR and DR subtests. The learning phase is followed by an Immediate Recognition trial (IR). During the IR trial, the examinee must select a previously viewed word from a list of twenty-word pairs. After a ten-minute delay, the examinee is administered a delayed recognition trial (DR), during which they must select words viewed during the initial two learning trials from a second, different set of 20-word pairs. Administered next is the Paired Associate (PA) trial, which involves providing the first word of each presented word pair and requires the examinee to give the correct matching word. Finally, during free recall (FR), the examinee is required to freely recall as many words as possible from the initial word pairs in any order (Macciocchi 2017).

Scoring

During the IR trial, the examinee is credited for correctly selecting a previously viewed word from a list of twenty-word pairs. If the examinee does not select the correct word from the list, they are incorrect and given no credit. After a ten-minute delay, the examinee is administered a delayed recognition trial (DR), during which they are awarded credit for selecting words viewed during the initial two learning trials from a second, different set of 20-word pairs. Once the IR and DR trials are complete, a Consistency Index (CNS) is computed. The CNS metric reflects the degree to which the examinee correctly or incorrectly chose words during IR and DR. CNS does not reflect accuracy but reflects the consistency of correct responding during the IR and DR trials (Green 2004). In addition to IR, DR, and CNS scores, the MSVT has two other metrics. During the Paired Associate (PA) trial, examinees are awarded credit for correctly providing the first word of each initially presented word pair and the correct matching word. Finally, during free recall (FR), the examinee is awarded credit by freely recalling as many words as possible from the initial word pairs in any order (Macciocchi 2017). Individuals scoring below the 85% cut-off on IR, DR, or CNS, below 70% on PA, or below 50% on FR are considered to exhibit poor effort (Howe and Loring 2008).

Item Difficulty and Types of Errors

As mentioned previously, even patients with severe neurological conditions can easily pass the effort subtests of the MSVT. Nevertheless, unlike many other effort tests, the MSVT is unique in that it combines multiple subtests with variable difficulty levels, allowing profile analysis. Profile analysis is an important tool for determining whether a failure is due to poor effort or severe cognitive impairment. A severe impairment profile, or Dementia Profile, is characterized by the following: no scores below chance, the mean of the easy subtests (IR, DR, and CNS) being at least 20 points higher than the harder subtests (PA and FR), and clinical correlations indicating dementia or severe cognitive impairment. However, other authors (Howe et al. 2007; Howe and Loring 2009; Whitney et al. 2009) added that there should be no order violations in which the patient performs worse on easier subtests than difficult subtests. In genuine neurological illness, patients perform worse on difficult tests than on easy tests, so the IR, DR, and PA scores should not be lower than the FR scores. An individual who performs below the cut-offs on the effort indexes but meets all the criteria of the severe impairment profile would not be regarded as having a false positive. Accordingly, the severe impairment profile can be conceptualized as a configurational safeguard of the test that ensures severely impaired patients who perform below the cut-offs are correctly classified as having made a good effort (Carone 2009).

Task Demands and Strategies

As previously mentioned, the MSVT is a computerized test gauges cognitive effort and memory. The test relies on individuals putting forth their best effort to perform well. The MSVT requires a forced selection of answers and an integrated effort measure. The MSVT effort indices can be easily passed with mean scores well above the pass/fail cut-off by English- and non-English-speaking children and adolescents with a reading level greater than second grade who put forth adequate effort. Studies have reported that 96%–98% of healthy children from Germany, Brazil, and Canada passed the MSVT (Blaskewitz et al. 2008; Green 2004). Furthermore, ~95% of children with moderate-to-severe brain injury or developmental disability scored above the recommended pass/fail cut-off (Carone 2008; Green et al. 2012).

Clinical Applications in Research

Evidence suggests that the MSVT is potentially a valuable tool in determining those patients who might not be putting forth full effort or performance validity. However, in a study of 405 participants, 81.2% passed the MSVT. This supports the findings of other research (e.g., Carone 2008) that a substantial majority can pass the MSVT without difficulty, even in a heterogeneous sample of tertiary neuropsychological referrals, some of whom had significant and complex neurological cognitive or psychological impairment. The same study estimated an unexplained failure rate of at least 5.2%, broadly in line with the false positive base rate of 4.8% found in a previous study (Howe et al. 2007) and a specificity of 0.95. This suggests that the MSVT alone might not be as specific to clinically significant poor performance validity as some studies have suggested (Suesse et al. 2015).

Interpretation

The literature suggests that the MSVT is a symptom validity test that shows promise for use in various populations when interpreted correctly. The interpretation of MSVT test results is typically completed in a few steps.

1. The first step in interpreting the MSVT involves assessing the client's effort through the examination of the two primary symptom validity subtests, Immediate Recognition (IR) and Delayed Recognition (DR), as well as a third subtest Consistency (CNS) that evaluates the consistency in the patient's responses to the primary symptom validity subtests.
2. A test-taker is considered to have failed the examination if they scored below specified cut-offs on any of these three indices. A cut-off score of 85 or less is suggested for these indices, and performance at or below a score of 85 indicates a failure of the symptom validity subtests, and further analysis of the profile and clinical factors must be considered (Whitney et al. 2009).
3. The next step of interpretation involves assessing the client's memory by examining a free recall (FR) test and paired associates (PA) test. Individuals scoring below the 70% cut-off on PA or below 50% on FR are considered to exhibit poor effort.
4. When a patient's scores fall below the designated cut-off values, the examiner advances to the next phase of test interpretation, known as profile analysis. This step is implemented because, in cases where a patient has not met the specified cut-off criteria in the MSVT, their data may still be deemed reliable if their test results align with the Dementia Profile (DP).
5. The final step is determining if the client's scores are invalid due to lack of effort.
6. As Green (2004) asserts, once dementia has been ruled out, it is rare for individuals to score below the 85% cut-off when they are genuinely putting in their best effort. In most instances, individuals scoring below 90% on the primary effort measures (IR, DR, and CNS) do so because they are not genuinely exerting full effort to perform well on these tests.

7. Alternatively, they may intentionally be performing poorly to present themselves as more impaired than they are. In either scenario, the results of the MSVT do not accurately reflect the individual's true capabilities, and the validity of their results on other tests becomes questionable.

References

Armistead-Jehle, P. and Gervais, R. O. (2011). Sensitivity of the Test of Memory Malingering and the Nonverbal Medical Symptom Validity Test: A Replication Study. Applied Neuropsychology, 18(4): 284–290. https://doi.org/10.1080/09084282.2011.595455.

Blaskewitz, N., Merten, T. and Kathmann, N. (2008). Performance of children on symptom validity tests: TOMM, MSVT, and FIT. Archives of Clinical Neuropsychology, 23(4): 379–391.

Carone, D. A. (2008). Children with moderate/severe brain damage/dysfunction outperform adults with mild-to-no brain damage on the Medical Symptom Validity Test. Brain Injury, 22(12): 960–971.

Carone, D. A. (2009). Test review of the medical symptom validity test. Applied Neuropsychology, 16(4): 309–311. https://doi.org/10.1080/09084280903297883.

Chafetz, M. D., Abrahams, J. P. and Kohlmaier, J. (2007). Malingering on the Social Security disability consultative exam: A new rating scale. Archives of Clinical Neuropsychology, 22(1): 1–14.

Conder, R., Allen, L. and Cox, D. (1992). Manual for the computerized assessment of response bias. Durham, NC: Cognisyst.

Covert, Julie Hart. (2008). Neurocognitive Variables Underlying Group Performance on a Measure of Effort: The Medical Symptom Validity Test (MSVT). Doctor of Philosophy (Health Psychology and Behavioral Medicine), 88 pp., 31 tables, 2 figures, references, 92 titles.

Feehan, M., Knight, R.G. and Partridge, F.M. (1991). Cognitive complaint and test performance in elderly patients suffering from depression or dementia. International Journal of Geriatric Psychiatry, 6: 287–293.

Frerichs, R. (2006). Effort testing in older adults: Poor effort or poor memory? Poster presented at the 26th Annual National Academy of Neuropsychology Conference, San Antonio, TX, October 25–28. Archives of Clinical Neuropsychology, 21: 551.

Gervais, R., Green, P. and Allen, L. (1999). Differential sensitivity to symptom exaggeration of verbal, visual, and numerical symptom validity tests. Archives of Clinical Neuropsychology, 14: 746–747.

Gill, D., Green, P., Flaro, L. and Pucci, T. (2007). The role of effort testing in independent medical examinations. Medico-Legal Journal, 75(Pt 2): 64–71.

Green, P. (2003). Green's Word Memory Test for Windows: User's manual. Edmonton, Canada: Green's Publishing.

Green, P. (2004). Green's Medical Symptom Validity Test (MSVT) for Microsoft Windows (user manual). Edmonton, Canada: Green's Publishing.

Green, P. (2007). Spoiled for choice: Making comparisons between forced-choice effort tests. In K. B. Boone (Ed.). Assessment of feigned cognitive impairment: A neuropsychological perspective (pp. 55–77). New York, NY: Guilford Press.

Green, P., Allen, L. and Astner, K. (1996). Manual for the Word Memory Test (DOS.) Durham, N.C., Cognisyst.

Green, P., Berendt, J., Mandel, A. and Allen, L. M., III. (2000). Relative sensitivity of the Word Memory Test and Test of Memory Malingering in 144 disability claimants. Archives of Clinical Neuropsychology, 15: 841.

Green, P., Flaro, L., Brockhaus, R. and Montijo, J. (2012). Performance on the WMT, MSVT, and NV-MSVT in children with developmental disabilities and in adults with mild traumatic brain injury. In Reynolds C. R. Horton A. M. (Eds.), Detection of malingering during head injury litigation (2nd ed., pp. 201–219). New York: Springer.

Howe, L. L. S., Anderson, A. M., Kaufman, D. A. S., Sachs, B. C. and Loring, D. W. (2007). Characterization of the Medical Symptom Validity Test in evaluation of clinically referred memory disorders clinic patients. Archives of Clinical Neuropsychology, 22: 753–761.

Howe, L.S.L. and Loring, D.W. (2008). Classification accuracy and predictive ability of the medical symptom validity test's dementia profile and general memory impairment profile. The Clinical Neuropsychologist, in press.

Howe, L. L. S. and Loring, D. W. (2009). Classification accuracy and predictive ability of the Medical Symptom Validity Test's dementia profile and general memory impairment profile. The Clinical Neuropsychologist, 23: 1–14.

Macciocchi, S. N., Seel, R. T., Yi, A. and Small, S. (2017). Medical Symptom Validity Test Performance Following Moderate-Severe Traumatic Brain Injury: Expectations Based on Orientation Log Classification. Archives of Clinical Neuropsychology, 32(3): 339–348. https://doi.org/10.1093/arclin/acw112.

Mareike Suesse, Vivien W. C. Wong, Laura L. Stamper, Katherine N. Carpenter and Richard B. Scott (2015). Evaluating the Clinical Utility of the Medical Symptom Validity Test (MSVT): A Clinical Series, The Clinical Neuropsychologist, 29(2): 214–231, DOI: 10.1080/13854046.2015.1022226.

Merten, T., Green, P., Henry, M., Blaskewitz, N. and Brockhaus, R. (2005). Analog validation of German-language symptom validity tests and the influence of coaching. Archives of Clinical Neuropsychology, 20(6): 719–726. https://doi.org/10.1016/j.acn.2005.04.004.

Patton, C., Mittenberg, W., Loewenstein, D. and Roberts, D. (2004). Validation of the Oral Word Memory Test in dementia and psychiatric disorders. Presented at the National Academy of Neuropsychology, Seattle, Washington.

Richman, J., Green, P., Gervais, R., Flaro, L., Merten, T. and Brockhaus, R. et al. (2006). Objective tests of symptom exaggeration in independent medical examinations. Journal of Occupational and Environmental Medicine, 48(3): 303–311.

Slick, D. J., Hopp, G., Strauss, E. and Thompson, G. (1996). The victoria symptom validity test. Lutz, FL: Psychological Assessment Resources.

Tan, J. E., Slick, D. J., Strauss, E. and Hultsch, D. F. (2002). How'd they do it? Malingering strategies on symptom validity tests. The Clinical Neuropsychologist, 16: 495–505.

Teichner, G. and Wagner, M.T. (2004). The Test of Memory Malingering (TOMM): Normative data from cognitively intact, cognitively impaired, and elderly patients with dementia. Archives of Clinical Neuropsychology, 19: 455–464.

Tombaugh, T. N. (1996). The test of memory malingering. Los Angeles, CA: Western Psychological Services.

Whitney, Kriscinda, Shepard, Polly, Williams, Amanda, Davis, Jeremy and Adams, Kenneth. (2009). The Medical Symptom Validity Test in the evaluation of Operation Iraqi Freedom/Operation Enduring Freedom soldiers: A preliminary study. Archives of clinical neuropsychology: the official journal of the National Academy of Neuropsychologists, 24: 145–52. 10.1093/arclin/acp020.

CHAPTER 23

Structured Interview of Reported Symptoms, Second Edition (SIRS-2)

D'Shawn Harrigan

The Structured Interview of Reported Symptoms, Second Edition (SIRS-2), is used to assess whether an individual is credibly reporting their symptoms of psychopathology (Rogers et al. 2010). The SIRS-2 is comprised of 172 items that were developed to assess for feigned and honest responses, including data on strategies the client uses to provide noncredible responses. The structure of the SIRS-2 encompasses two parallel sequences composed of detailed inquiries, repeated inquiries, and general inquiries, which use a variety of detection strategies.

Normed Population

The most recent revision of the SIRS-2 attempted to compile a representative sample of the United States population. Feigning groups were procured from mental health units housed in correctional facilities (Rogers et al. 2004), a clinical forensic group (Wang et al. 1997), and a corrections base inpatient psychiatric hospital (Jackson et al. 2005). For the clinical group (general), 16% of the population were male, while 84% were female. Regarding ethnicity, 8.9% were African Americans, 81.4% were European American, 2.5% were Hispanic American, 3.8% were Biracial, and 3.4% were unknown. The clinical population's ethnicity comprised 18.7% African Americans, 76.3% European American, 2.5% Hispanic American, 0.9% Biracial, and 1.6% Unknown. The clinical group (forensic) was 77.4% male, while 22.6% were female. Ethnicity in the nonclinical group (correctional) was 8.9% African American, 81.4% European American, 2.5% Hispanic American, 3.8% Biracial,

Nova Southeastern University, Fort Lauderdale, Florida, USA.
Email: dh1701@mynsu.nova.edu

and 3.4% unknown. In the nonclinical (community/college) group, 47.9% of the population were male, while 52.1% of the population were female. Regarding ethnicity, 3.2% were African Americans, 74.7% were European American, 17.1% were Hispanic American, 4.2% were Biracial, and 0.9% were unknown (Rogers et al. 2010).

Task Demands and Strategies

Detailed inquiries are used to aggregate information on plausible symptomatology using four detection strategies. The first detection strategy includes the Selectivity of Symptoms (SEL) scale, which consists of the total number of symptoms reported by the client. The second strategy incorporates the Severity of Symptoms (SEV) scale containing the number of characterized symptoms with extreme severity. The third strategy consists of the Blatant Symptoms (BL) scale, entailing the total symptoms identifiable as significant psychopathology. Finally, the fourth strategy involves the Subtle Symptoms (SU) scale, which is characterized by the total number of item responses classified as typical problems not associated with severe psychopathology.

Repeated inquiries sequence analyzes discrepancies in a client's report on the Inconsistency of Symptoms (INC) scale. The sequence achieves this by diverting the feigning client's attention from common detection strategies achieved by increasing their cognitive load as they attempt to recall the nature and severity of their previous responses.

The general inquiries phase consists of the SIRS-2 primary scales, each utilizing unlikely detection strategies whose items consist of content rarely endorsed by clinical populations. The scales are as follows: Rare Symptoms (RS) scale contains items that gauge symptoms infrequently observed in psychiatric samples—the Symptom Combination (SC) scale inquires about the presence of psychiatric symptoms that rarely occur together. The Improbable or Absurd Symptoms (IA) scale consists of implausible and outrageous symptoms that are exceedingly unlikely to be valid. The Reported versus Observed Symptoms scale probes the client about specific behaviors comprising of physical movements and speech to be compared with the examiner's behavioral observations.

In addition, the general inquiries phase includes four supplementary scales providing the examiner with pertinent qualitative information. The Direct Appraisal of Honesty (DA) scale investigates how clients report their transparency with mental health professionals and their willingness to depict their symptoms accurately without overreporting or fabrication. The Defensive Symptoms (DS) scale is designed to investigate common psychological problems by reducing the transparency of the scales by asking questions most honest examinees can relate to. The DS scale also provides information regarding the denial or minimization of common symptoms in clinical populations. The Improbable Failure (IF) assesses for feigned cognitive impairment with examinee's suspected of having low average or higher intelligence and redirects the examinees focus from the primary detection strategies. Finally, the Overly Specified Symptoms (OS) scale comprises symptoms reported with an unrealistic degree of precision.

Item Difficulty and Types of Errors

Given the nature of the structured questionnaire, item difficulty is designed to be consistent and simple to avoid introducing confounds in the examinees' reporting of symptoms. There are no errors in this measure, given that the examinee's response is taken verbatim (Rogers et al. 2010).

Administration and Scoring

The SIRS-2 is a fully structured interview that prohibits the examiner from asking questions or probes. Examiners can only read the questions to the examinee verbatim. The time requirements of the SIRS-2 are contingent upon the population to which the examinee belongs. Examinees who are high-functioning and cooperative can finish the measure in approximately 30 minutes. Those who are impaired or are attempting to feign may require 30 to 45 minutes for administration. An administration time that exceeds an hour should be cautioned as standardized administration may not have been followed.

Examinees who respond to an inquiry with a "Definite Yes" response will score two points. Responses of "Qualified Yes/Sometimes" are provided one point, and a response of "No" is scored zero points. If the examinee does not respond to an inquiry, the item is scored as "X." The totality of scores is calculated and is categorized into three categories: "genuine," "probable feigning," or "definite feigning" (Rogers et al. 1992).

Reliability

The SIRS-2 demonstrates good reliability as indicated by an adequate to high internal consistency for the primary scales ranging from .77 to .92 (Rogers et al. 2010). Adequate reliability was further supported by the test's standard error of measurement. Test-retest reliability was robust, as demonstrated by a coefficient of $r = .82$ for the Total Score. Test-retest reliability was adequate for the majority of scales denoted by a mean Pearson r coefficient of .77. Significant variability of test-retest coefficients was found for the Symptom Combinations (SC), Improbable or Absurd Symptoms (IA), and Reported versus Observed Symptoms (RO) scales. Variability for test-retest reliability is expected as the feigning of symptoms is motivated by contextual factors such as primary and secondary gain. Consistency across repeated testing is most reliable for the categorization of examinees into "feigning" or "non-feigning" designations (Becke et al. 2019).

Validity

Regarding validity, the SIRS-2 demonstrates good convergent validity and exhibits moderate associations with other measures using simulator samples. Measures showing good convergent validity with the SIRS-2 include the Minnesota Multiphasic Personality Inventory (Butcher 2009), the Personality Assessment Inventory (Morey

1991), the Structured Inventory of Malingered Symptomatology (Widows and Smith 2005), and the Miller Forensic Assessment of Symptoms Test (Miller 2004).

Clinical Applications in Research

The SIRS-2 provides a variety of different clinical applications regarding medical symptoms pertaining to dizziness, nausea, fatigue, pain, and shortness of breath (Wygant et al. 2022). Moreover, mood and behavioral changes are assessed, ranging from depressive and anxiety disorders, chronic obstructive pulmonary disease (COPD), irritable bowel syndrome (IBS), and diabetes mellitus type 2 (DM2). As the role of psychologists shifts to a "Health Service Psychologist" paradigm, increased applications of the validity of mental and medical disorders are crucial (Bell et al. 2020). Given the SIRS-2 expansive utilization of various detection strategies of reported responses such as rare symptoms, symptom combinations, improbable symptoms, indiscriminate symptom endorsement, symptom severity, obvious symptoms, common (subtle) psychological problems, and reported vs. observed symptoms, the measure may be used as a proxy or initial screener for the aforementioned disorders and others above and beyond its utilization as a measure of feigning.

Previous studies have attempted to determine if the SIRS-2 is an appropriate measure of detecting feigned Attention-Deficit Hyperactivity Disorder using the decision model delineated in the manual. Findings of one study found that the decision model provided poor classification accuracy for genuine cases of ADHD and simulators (Becke et al. 2019). While the majority of genuine participants were classified correctly, a significant minority was classified as Indeterminant. The study also found that 19.3% of the simulators were detected, and 59.1% of the simulators were misclassified as honest responders. Thus, the SIRS-2 is not an appropriate measure to rely on for detecting feigned ADHD.

Dissociative Identity Disorder

Up to 88% of SCID-D-R diagnosed individuals with Dissociative Identity Disorder endorsed at least one of the items that make up the Rare Symptoms (RS) scale referencing dissociative experiences. Over 57% of DID participants scored above the genuine range on the SIRS-2 profile (Brand et al. 2014). Individuals with DID tend to endorse items on the "amplified detection strategy" scales in the SIRS-2. The scales include the Subtle Symptoms (SU), Selectivity of Symptoms (SEL), and Severity of Symptoms (SEV) scales that are indicative of anxiety and depression (Brand et al. 2009). Moreover, individuals with DID fail to demonstrate elevations on the "unlikely detection strategies" scales associated with items not typically endorsed in any genuine psychiatric condition (Rodgers et al. 2009). High scores on the "amplified detection strategy" scales and low scores on the "unlikely detection strategies" scales suggest that it is the DID participant's trauma not the feigning of symptoms that contributes to elevations on the SIRS-2. Previous studies have found many cases where individuals with complex trauma histories have an increased risk of being misclassified as feigning due to the influence of trauma (Brown 2009; Klotz et al. 2003).

Cognitive Feigning

Intellectual disabilities (ID) are commonly feigned in forensic settings. Despite the similarities between psychiatric symptoms and cognitive impairments, they are distinct constructs (Gottfried and Glassmire 2016). The Improbable Failure (IF) scale on the SIRS-2 was designed to detect feigned gross cognitive impairment via simple cognitive tasks. A study using pretrial defendants found that defendants with an IQ below an FSIQ of 80 demonstrated an increase in the likelihood that they would be classified as being a feigner on the IF scale than defendants with higher IQs.

A study conducted by Weiss et al. (2011) found that the primary scales measuring amplified symptoms misclassified individuals who fell in the Definite and Probable ranges, demonstrating a higher likelihood of acquiescence and suggestibility among individuals with an intellectual disability. The Symptom Combinations (SC) and Improbable or Absurd (IA) scales measuring unlikely symptoms classified all the participants as Honest or Indeterminate indicating that individuals with ID are not likely to acquiescence when endorsing symptoms that are unfamiliar.

Clinical Interpretations

1. The SIRS-2 utilizes a decision-tree classification strategy to determine whether an examinee is feigning or not (Rogers et al. 2010).
2. The first classification step uses the Primary Scale scores, where test-takers can fall into any of the three categories: Feigners (FGN), Indeterminant (IND), or Genuine (GEN).
3. To be classified as a feigner, three or more scales must be in the probable range or one scale in the definite range. Additionally, the RS Total scale must be greater than four. Moreover, if one or two scales fall in the probable range and the MT index exceeds 45, the test-taker is classified as a feigner.
4. To be classified as indeterminant, one or two scales must fall in the probable range, zero scales fall in the probable range, and six or fewer scales must fall in the genuine range.
5. If the examinee's MT index ranges from 22 to 45, they receive the additional classification of Indeterminant-Evaluate, where the examiner should administer additional tests to make a determination.
6. If the examinee's MT index ranges from 13 to 21, they receive the supplementary classification of Indeterminant-General, indicating when the measure is unable to determine an appropriate classification.
7. For an examinee to be classified as genuine, zero scales must fall in the probable range, and more than six scales must fall in the genuine range. Additionally, the SS index must be greater than four to be classified as a genuine responder.
8. If the SS index has a score of less than four, the examinee receives a disengagement classification, indicating that the examinee made attempts not to answer the probing questions to disrupt the evaluation.

References

Becke, M., Fuermaier, A., Buehren, J., Weisbrod, M., Aschenbrenner, S., Tucha, O. et al. (2019). Utility of the Structured Interview of Reported Symptoms (SIRS-2) in detecting feigned adult attention-deficit/hyperactivity disorder. Journal of Clinical and Experimental Neuropsychology, 41(8): 786–802.

Bell, D. J., Self, M. M., Davis, C., Conway, F., Washburn, J. J. and Crepeau-Hobson, F. (2020). Health service psychology education and training in the time of COVID-19: Challenges and opportunities. The American Psychologist, 75(7): 919–932.

Brand, B. L., Tursich, M., Tzall, D. and Loewenstein, R. J. (2014). Utility of the SIRS-2 in distinguishing genuine from simulated dissociative identity disorder. Psychological Trauma: Theory, Research, Practice, and Policy, 6(4): 308–317.

Brand, B. L., Classen, C., Lanius, R., Loewenstein, R. J., McNary, S., Pain, C. et al. (2009). A naturalistic study of dissociative identity disorder and dissociative disorder not otherwise specified patients treated by community clinicians. Psychological Trauma: Theory, Research, Practice, and Policy, 1: 153–171.

Brown, L. S. (2009). True Drama or True Trauma? Forensic Trauma Assessment and the Challenge of Detecting Malingering. In: P. F. Dell and J. A. O'Neil (Eds.). Dissociation and the dissociative disorders: DSM-V and beyond (pp. 585–594). New York, NY: Routledge.

Butcher, J. N. (2009). Minnesota multiphasic personality inventory. Corsini Encyclopedia of Psychology, 21(1–3), 2010.

Gottfried, E. and Glassmire, D. (2016). The Relationship Between Psychiatric and Cognitive Symptom Feigning Among Forensic Inpatients Adjudicated Incompetent to Stand Trial. Assessment, 23(6): 672–682.

Jackson, R. L., Rogers, R. and Sewell, K. W. (2005). Forensic applications of the Miller Forensic Assessment of Symptoms Test (M-FAST): Screening for feigned disorders in competency to stand trial evaluations. Law and Human Behavior, 29: 199–210.

Klotz Flitter, J. M., Elhai, J. D. and Gold, S. N. (2003). MMPI-2 F scale elevations in adult victims of child sexual abuse. Journal of Traumatic Stress, 16: 269–274.

Miller, H. A. (2004). Examining the use of the M-FAST with criminal defendants incompetent to stand trial. International Journal of Offender Therapy and Comparative Criminology, 48(3): 268–280.

Morey, L. C. (1991). Personality assessment inventory: Professional manual. Odessa, FL: Psychological Assessment Resources.

Rogers, R., Bagby, R. M. and Dickens, S. E. (1992). Structured interview of reported symptoms: Professional manual (1st ed.). Lutz, FL: Psychological Assessment Resources.

Rogers, R., Jackson, R. L., Sewell, K. W. and Harrison, K. S. (2004). An examination of the ECST-R as a screen for feigned incompetency to stand trial. Psychological Assessment, 16: 139–145.

Rogers, R., Sewell, K. W. and Gillard, N. D. (2010). Structured Interview of Reported Symptoms (SIRS), 2nd Edition, Professional Manual. Lutz, FL: Psychological Assessment Resources, Inc.

Wang, E. W., Rogers, R., Giles, C. L., Diamond, P. M., Herrington-Wang, L. E. and Taylor, E. R. (1997). A pilot study of the Personality Assessment Inventory (PAI) in corrections: Assessment of malingering, suicide risk, and aggression in male inmates. Behavioral Sciences & the Law, 15(4): 469–482.

Weiss, R. A., Rosenfeld, B. and Farkas, M. R. (2011). The utility of the structured interview of reported symptoms in a sample of individuals with intellectual disabilities. Assessment, 18(3): 284–290.

Widows, M. R. and Smith, G. P. (2004). SIMS: Structured Inventory of Malingered Symptomatology Professional Manual. Lutz, FL: Psychological Assessment Resources, Inc.

Wygant, D. B., Tylicki, J. L., Disney, L. F. and Connelly, A. I. (2022). Structured Interview of Reported Symptoms-(SIRS-2): Use and Admissibility in Forensic Mental Health Assessment. Journal of Personality Assessment, 104(2): 265–280.

CHAPTER 24

The Test of Memory Malingering (TOMM)

*Ryan Bennett** and *Sharvan Chhabria*

The Test of Memory Malingering (TOMM) is a 50-item visual memory recognition test for adults aged 16–84 that provides a systematic method in distinguishing malingering from genuine memory impairments. The test consists of two learning trials and a Retention Trial. In the learning trials, participants are shown 50 line drawings of common objects, each displayed for three seconds with a one-second interval between them. Afterward, the participant is presented with pairs of drawings, one being an original target picture and the other a new image. The participant is tasked to identify the correct target picture from each pair. The TOMM is effective for detecting malingering as the large number of visual stimuli makes the perception that the test is much more difficult than it is (Tombaugh 1996). For the purpose of this assessment, the term malingering was defined as a spectrum ranging from mild exaggeration of symptoms to the flagrant fabrication of symptoms (Millis 1992; Heubrock and Petermann 1998). While the TOMM is sensitive to malingering, it is insensitive to neurological impairments (Tombaugh 1996). The majority of individuals, even those with neurological impairments, possess a strong ability to store and recall images of everyday objects, like those employed in the TOMM. This consistent effect allows the TOMM to provide norm-based criteria for detecting malingering.

Normative Data and Validation

Normative non-clinical data for the TOMM was gathered in two phases. In the initial phase, 405 individuals aged between 16 and 84 were given a four-choice version of the TOMM without feedback. This sample consisted of 53% females with an average education level of 13.1 years. Phase one results concluded that 94% of

Nova Southeastern University, Fort Lauderdale, Florida, USA.
Email: sc9220@mynsu.nova.edu
* Corresponding author: rb1934@nova.edu

the targets were correctly identified on Trial 1, and 99% were correctly identified on the remaining two trials. There was a notable discrepancy during this phase regarding the participants' perceived low expectation and their extremely high levels of performance. Thus, it was concluded the TOMM could effectively measure malingering without its intention being overtly apparent. During phase two, 70 independent community-dwelling individuals aged between 17 and 73 took the two-choice version of the test, where they received feedback regarding the accuracy of their responses. This sample consisted of 63% males with an average education level of 12.7 years. Phase two results indicated that 95.6% of the targets were correctly identified on Trial 1, and 99% were correctly identified on the remaining two trials. The overall findings were very similar to the initial phase, and both concluded that neurologically intact individuals demonstrate excellent accuracy and performance on the TOMM.

The continued efforts for the development and validation of the TOMM were achieved by exploring the accuracy and performance within a clinical sample. Data were obtained from 138 consecutive neuropsychological evaluations of inpatients and outpatients at the Veterans Administration Medical Center in Boston, MA. Additionally, information from 23 head-injured subjects was derived from a recent Ph.D. thesis (Rees 1996). The clinical sample was then divided into five main diagnostic groups: No Cognitive Impairment ($n = 20$), Cognitive Impairment ($n = 42$), Aphasia ($n = 21$), Traumatic Brain Injury ($n = 45$, and Dementia ($n = 40$). Based on the overall performance of the clinical sample, a cutoff score of 45 on Trial 2 was established. This cutoff score correctly classified 95% of all patients without dementia and 91% of all clinical patients as not malingering.

Lastly, the validation of the TOMM was assessed via a simulated malingerer group and an "at risk" malingerer group (Rees and Tombaugh 1996). The simulated malingerers consisted of 27 undergraduate students who were given a motor vehicle accident scenario and instructed to "look like [they] are still suffering from brain damage." Reese and Tombaugh's study concluded that there was virtually no overlap between the simulated malingerers and the control group. All individuals in the control group scored 49 or greater (100% specificity), while 93% of the simulated malingerers scored lower than 49 with 93% sensitivity (Rees and Tombaugh 1996). These findings support that the TOMM discriminates effectively between individuals who put forth adequate effort and those who intentionally malinger.

An additional study aimed to validate the TOMM with patients who sustained a traumatic brain injury (TBI). Gansler and colleagues (1995) divided participants into four groups to investigate the validation of the TOMM: 17 TBI patients considered "not at risk" for malingering, 11 TBI patients classified as "at risk" for malingering, 11 cognitively intact controls, and 12 patient controls exhibiting significant focal neuropsychological impairment. In Trial 1, TBI patients classified as "not at risk" for malingering showed slightly lower performance compared to both control groups. However, their performance in the other two trials was comparable. In stark contrast, the "at risk" TBI group demonstrated significantly lower performance across all trials.

Reliability and Validity

In 2004, Teichner and Wagner contributed to the psychometric validation of the TOMM by including data from a sample of elderly patients, encompassing those who were cognitively intact, those with cognitive impairment, and individuals with dementia. Their findings revealed significant differences between the dementia and the other two groups. However, there was no statistically significant difference between the cognitively intact and cognitively impaired groups. Moreover, fewer than five errors were observed in the cognitively intact group and 93% of those with cognitive impairment during Trial 2 and the Retention Trial (Teichner and Wagner 2004).

Another frequently used performance validity test is the Rey 15-Item Memory Test (Rey II), which was examined compared to the TOMM by Whitney and colleagues in 2008. Rey's scoring methods, both qualitative and quantitative, were found to be discriminative, but they exhibited relatively low positive and negative predictive power, with values of only .62 and .64, respectively (Whitney et al. 2008). Interestingly, despite being considered a more complex test than the seemingly "easier" Rey test, the TOMM holds greater face validity (Tracy 2014).

Additionally, the TOMM was compared to the Word Memory Test (WMT) for detecting invalid performance in disability claimants, as demonstrated by Bhowmick and colleagues in 2019. The WMT had higher sensitivity than the TOMM, and both assessments have been well-validated for assessing performance validity (Bhowmick et al. 2019). Furthermore, the TOMM assesses visual memory, while the WMT focuses on verbal memory, making them commonly used tools in forensic settings. Another study by O'Bryant and colleagues (2007) reported individuals who passed the TOMM but failed the WMT exhibited lower overall performance in academic/achievement testing, visuospatial tasks, and global intellectual functioning. Conversely, those who passed the TOMM but failed the WMT reported more depressive symptoms and memory complaints.

The TOMM is highly referred to as an independent "one and done" performance validity test (PVT). In 2018, Webber and colleagues conducted a study to investigate the role of cognitive impairment, focusing specifically on the utility of the TOMM (Trial 1) as an independent performance validity test (PVT) in comparison to the Word Choice Test, Word Memory Test, and WAIS Reliable Digit Span. The study included 127 veterans, and the findings revealed that TOMM Trial 1 displayed outstanding sensitivity and specificity, with values of 83% and 93%, respectively. The overall findings suggested that using Trial 1, along with a cutoff score of 40, in combination with one or more additional PVTs, could prove advantageous in identifying instances of invalid or poor test performance (Webber et al. 2018).

Test Procedures

The TOMM is comprised of two learning trials and one Retention Trial. The administration of Trial 1 and Trial 2 are mandatory, while the administration of the

Retention Trial is optional. The examiner introduces the TOMM, who places the Trial 1 test booklet before the examinee. The examiner will then read the manualized instruction, presenting the assessment as a memory test. A sample trial is presented before Trial 1 to ensure the examinee's full understanding of the task by the examinee. During Trial 1, the examiner shows each target picture for three seconds, with a one-second interval between items. Of note, if the examinee requests the images be shown at a faster or slower rate, the examiner can state that they must present each item for three seconds. Following the administration of the 50 target pictures, the examiner presents the recognition panel, which consists of the target picture and one new picture. The examinee is instructed to point at the picture they had previously been shown. If the examinee does not respond within approximately 10 seconds, the examiner encourages them to make their best guess. The examiner gives feedback by stating "Correct" or "No, that is not right. It was this one," following the examinee's response for each item. After completing the recognition portion, the examiner immediately administers Trial 2 (the second learning trial), which consists of the same procedure as Trial 1. The optional Retention Trial is administered 15 minutes after the completion of Trial 2. It is imperative there is no interference during the 15-minute delay; therefore, no visual tests should be administered until the TOMM has been fully completed. The Retention Trial booklet is then placed in front of the examinee, and they are instructed to identify which picture they had previously seen. The administration procedure of the Retention Trial is similar to the recognition portion of both learning trials. Malingerers are readily identified during this trial, as they perform lower due to the assumption that the previously shown pictures should have been forgotten. The total administration time for the TOMM, excluding the Retention Trial, is approximately 15 minutes (Tombaugh 1996).

Scoring

Scoring the TOMM is an additive and straightforward process. A single point is awarded for every correct answer on both the recognition and Retention trials. Consequently, the minimum score attainable on each trial is 0, signifying no correct answers. In contrast, the highest achievable score is 50. A cutoff score of 45 or lower on Trial 2, which corresponds to 90% or fewer correct responses, suggests the possibility of malingering.

Task Demands and Strategies

The TOMM has proven to be an effective tool for assessing efforts in various clinical populations among adults, including individuals with traumatic brain injuries (TBIs), chronic pain, psychosis, and depression (Schneider et al. 2014). More recently, researchers have extended their examination of the TOMM to pediatric samples, and the previously established cutoff scores have remained consistent. This consistency has been demonstrated in pediatric samples from the United States and Germany (Schneider et al. 2014). It is worth noting that in these pediatric samples, approximately 90% of the children successfully passed Trial 2. However, children who performed poorly were often identified as having Attention-Deficit/Hyperactivity Disorder

(ADHD). Their difficulty sustaining attention had likely impacted their performance and possibly led to impulsivity during a timed visual memory task. It is important to recognize that acquiring basic recognition memory skills is an essential tool for performing well on the TOMM. Additionally, various factors such as attention, motor speed, and language expression can influence children's performance (Schneider et al. 2014).

Clinical Applications in Research

As previously noted, the primary clinical application of the TOMM is to identify individuals who may be exaggerating or feigning cognitive deficits, often for secondary gain, such as in legal or compensation cases. The TOMM is frequently used as a clinical assessment tool and adds value to comprehensive neuropsychological batteries, forensic evaluations, physical pain assessments, psychiatric conditions, treatment planning, and test development.

When conducting assessments to determine validity, clinicians may encounter cases where malingering or a lack of effort is suspected, even in the presence of chronic pain. Chronic pain is often associated with elevated levels of psychological distress. It is well-established that psychological conditions can disrupt memory, attention, processing speed, and overall quality of life. Consequently, Iverson and colleagues (2007) investigated TOMM scores in individuals with fibromyalgia. Interestingly, their study revealed that none of the patients with fibromyalgia scored close to the cutoff point on the TOMM, effectively ruling out the possibility of poor effort among this group. Despite these patients facing numerous challenges in various aspects of functioning, the TOMM appeared to be a relatively straightforward task (Iverson et al. 2007). An important takeaway from this research is that individuals coping with both chronic pain and substantial psychological distress can still perform well on the TOMM.

Research has also delved into the connection between validity indicators on the PAI and cognitive effort measures on the TOMM. Individuals displaying an elevated Negative Impression Management (NIM) scale on the PAI and endorsing atypical emotional symptoms were found to be at an increased risk of exhibiting suboptimal cognitive effort as indicated by performance on the TOMM (Whiteside et al. 2009). Despite their primary clinical focus on personality, these assessments serve as valuable supplementary tools that aid in detecting inadequate cognitive effort.

Walter and colleagues (2014) administered the TOMM alongside the Repeatable Battery for Assessment of Neuropsychological Status (RBANS) to a cohort of participants, including those who were cognitively intact, individuals with mild neurocognitive impairment, and those with moderate to severe dementia. Their findings align with prior research, indicating that the TOMM appears relatively stable in individuals with varying degrees of cognitive impairment. However, it may present challenges when attempting to differentiate malingering in individuals with modern-day, moderate to severe Major Neurocognitive Disorder.

When it comes to neurodevelopmental disorders, there is a limited body of literature addressing the relationship between performance on the TOMM and ADHD. Closely examining this connection is crucial, particularly considering that such evaluations can lead to accommodations and medication decisions (Shura et al. 2017). Shura and colleagues (2017) conducted a study investigating veterans seeking treatment for ADHD and their performance on the TOMM. Of note, only Trial 1 of the TOMM was employed. Their findings concluded veterans who did not perform well on the TOMM tended to report a higher number of symptoms associated with ADHD (Shura et al. 2017).

In 2019, Denning and Shura explored performance on the TOMM among a cohort of veterans who were appealing for disability benefits, particularly those seeking financial assistance. This study aimed to address concerns about the potential over-exaggeration of cognitive complaints, including issues related to attention, memory, and somatic symptoms following mild traumatic brain injuries (Denning and Shura 2019). The conclusions drawn from this study indicated that nearly one-third to one-half of the veterans were malingering their cognitive deficits.

Grant and Werner (2020) further explored clinical applications of the TOMM by focusing on patients with intractable epilepsy and low estimated premorbid functioning. Their findings revealed a remarkable level of specificity for the TOMM, making it a practical tool for use with similar patient populations. As expected, they found that scores across the TOMM trials showed strong correlations with scores on tests assessing memory (Grant and Werner 2020).

Interpretation

In conclusion, it is important to recognize that no single TOMM score can definitively confirm that a patient exerted full effort during testing. In order to ensure a thorough assessment and enhance accuracy, it is recommended that clinicians incorporate multiple Performance Validity Tests (PVTs) into the evaluation process. The interpretation of the TOMM should be approached with great caution, as there are great consequences for misinterpreting in either direction. Based on one's overall performance on the TOMM, several interpretations can be inferred:

1. An examinee will likely be malingering if they score below chance (50%) on any of the TOMM trials. Siegel and colleagues (1957) identified the 95% confidence interval for chance ranges from 18 to 32. Therefore, scores below 18 indicate the examinee knows that some of the target pictures were correct and intentionally chose the incorrect picture (Messick 1957).
2. Any score lower than 45 on Trial 2 or the Retention Trial indicates the possibility of malingering (Tombaugh 1996).
3. Lower scores on the TOMM (Trial 2 < 45) raise significant concerns regarding low motivation, suboptimal effort, and/or poor performance on other tests that were administered. If a low TOMM score is identified, the validity of all other assessments is questioned and must be thoroughly reviewed.
4. In most cases, a TOMM score below 45 makes it virtually impossible for the clinician to arrive at a clinical diagnosis (Tombaugh 1996).
5. Although the DSM-5 has excluded malingering as a diagnosis, it remains a V-Code. When considering the malingering V-Code, it is imperative that this conclusion is not exclusively made based on the TOMM score. Malingering

must demonstrate that the symptoms are false or exaggerated, intentionally produced, and motivated by external incentives. Low effort cannot be confused with malingering, which is deliberate and an attempt to mislead.

References

Ashendorf, L., Constantinou, M. and McCaffrey, R. J. (2004). The effect of depression and anxiety on the Tomm in community-dwelling older adults. Archives of Clinical Neuropsychology, 19(1): 125–130. https://doi.org/10.1093/arclin/19.1.125.

Bhowmick, C., Hirst, R. and Green, P. (2019). Comparison of the word memory test and the test of memory malingering in detecting invalid performance in neuropsychological testing. Applied Neuropsychology: Adult, 28(4): 486–496. https://doi.org/10.1080/23279095.2019.1658585.

Denning, J. H. and Shura, R. D. (2019). Cost of malingering mild traumatic brain injury-related cognitive deficits during compensation and pension evaluations in the Veterans Benefits Administration. Applied Neuropsychology: Adult, 26(1): 1–16. https://doi.org/10.1080/23279095.2017.1350684.

Grant, A. F. and Werner, N. J. (2020). Retrospective analysis of the Test of Memory Malingering in a low intellectual quotient intractable epilepsy sample. Archives of Clinical Neuropsychology, 35(6): 726–734.

Heubrock, D. and Petermann, F. (1998). Neuropsychological assessment of suspected malingering: Research results, evaluation techniques, and further directions of research and application. European Journal of Psychological Assessment, 14(3): 211–225. https://doi.org/10.1027/1015-5759.14.3.211.

Iverson, G. L., Page, J. L., Koehler, B. E., Shojania, K. and Badii, M. (2007). Test of memory malingering (TOMM) scores are not affected by chronic pain or depression in patients with fibromyalgia. The Clinical Neuropsychologist, 21(3): 532–546. https://doi.org/10.1080/13854040600611392.

Messick, S. (1957). Nonparametric Statistics for the Behavioral Sciences. Sidney Siegel. McGraw-Hill, New York, 1956. 312 pp. $6.50. Science, 126(3267): 266–266.

Millis, S. R. (1992). The Recognition Memory Test in the detection of malingered and exaggerated memory deficits. Clinical Neuropsychologist, 6(4): 406–414. https://doi.org/10.1080/13854049208401867.

O'Bryant, S. E., Finlay, C. G. and O'Jile, J. R. (2006). Tomm performances and self-reported symptoms of depression and anxiety. Journal of Psychopathology and Behavioral Assessment, 29(2): 111–114. https://doi.org/10.1007/s10862-006-9034-9.

Rees, L. M. (1997). The test of memory malingering; simulation studies and clinical validation (Doctoral dissertation, Carleton University).

Rees, L. M., Tombaugh, T. N., Gansler, D. A. and Moczynski, N. P. (1998). Five validation experiments of the Test of Memory Malingering (TOMM). Psychological Assessment, 10(1): 10.

Ryan, J. J., Glass, L. A., Hinds, R. M. and Brown, C. N. (2010). Administration order effects on the test of memory malingering. Applied Neuropsychology, 17(4): 246–250. https://doi.org/10.1080/09084282.2010.499802.

Schneider, H. E., Kirk, J. W. and Mahone, E. M. (2014). Utility of the test of memory malingering (TOMM) in children ages 4–7 years with and without ADHD. The Clinical Neuropsychologist, 28(7): 1133–1145. https://doi.org/10.1080/13854046.2014.960004.

Shura, R. D., Denning, J. H., Miskey, H. M. and Rowland, J. A. (2017). Symptom and performance validity with veterans assessed for attention-deficit/hyperactivity disorder (ADHD). Psychological Assessment, 29(12): 1458–1465. https://doi.org/10.1037/pas0000436.

Siegel, S. (1957). Nonparametric statistics. The American Statistician, 11(3): 13–19.

Slotnick, S. D., Thompson, W. L., and Kosslyn, S. M. (2011). Visual memory and visual mental imagery recruit common control and sensory regions of the brain. Cognitive Neuroscience, 3(1): 14–20. https://doi.org/10.1080/17588928.2011.578210.

Teichner, G. (2004). The test of Memory malingering (tomm): Normative data from cognitively intact, cognitively impaired, and elderly patients with dementia. Archives of Clinical Neuropsychology, 19(3): 455–464. https://doi.org/10.1016/s0887-6177(03)00078-7.

Tombaugh, T. N. (1997). The Test of Memory Malingering (TOMM): Normative data from cognitively intact and cognitively impaired individuals. Psychological Assessment, 9(3): 260.

Walter, J., Morris, J., Swier-Vosnos, A. and Pliskin, N. (2014). Effects of severity of dementia on a symptom validity measure. The Clinical Neuropsychologist, 28(7): 1197–1208. https://doi.org/10.1080/13854046.2014.960454.

Webber, T. A., Bailey, K. C., Alverson, W. A., Critchfield, E. A., Bain, K. M., Messerly, J. M. et al. (2018). Further validation of the test of memory malingering (TOMM) trial 1 performance validity index: Examination of false positives and convergent validity. Psychological Injury and Law, 11(4): 325–335. https://doi.org/10.1007/s12207-018-9335-9.

Whiteside, D. M., Dunbar-Mayer, P. and Waters, D. P. (2009). Relationship between tomm performance and pai validity scales in a mixed clinical sample. The Clinical Neuropsychologist, 23(3): 523–533. https://doi.org/10.1080/13854040802389169.

Whitney, K. A., Hook, J. N., Steiner, A. R., Shepard, P. H. and Callaway, S. (2008). Is the Rey 15-item memory test II (Rey II) a valid symptom validity test? Comparison with the Tomm. Applied Neuropsychology, 15(4): 287–292. https://doi.org/10.1080/09084280802325215.

Section III
Screening Tests

CHAPTER 25

Mini-Mental Status Examination (MMSE)

Casey Morocho

The Mini-Mental Status Examination (MMSE) is a widely used cognitive screening tool to assess an individual's cognitive functioning, particularly in attention, memory, language, and visuospatial skills (Folstein et al. 1975). The measure consists solely of items that focus on the cognitive aspect of mental functioning (Folstein et al. 1975). It typically includes tasks such as orientation (e.g., identifying the current date and location), registration and recall of a series of words, attention and calculation (e.g., serial subtraction or spelling a word backward), language abilities (e.g., naming objects, following verbal commands), and visual-spatial skills (e.g., copying a geometric figure). Items on mood, abnormal mental experiences, and forms of thinking are excluded (Folstein et al. 1975).

Normed Population

The normative data originally developed for the MMSE consisted of two sample groups. Sample A comprised 132 individuals in a private hospital (Folstein et al. 1975). Of this sample, 63 participants were considered healthy elderly individuals, while the others were elderly individuals diagnosed with clinical conditions (Folstein et al. 1975). The clinical conditions included dementia syndromes from a variety of brain diseases, uncomplicated affective disorder, and affective depressed type with clinically recognizable cognitive impairment (Folstein et al. 1975). Sample B was formed of 137 elderly patients who were admitted to the hospital (Folstein et al. 1975). These individuals had diagnoses of dementia, affective disorder, schizophrenia, personality disorder with drug abuse, and neurosis (Folstein et al. 1975).

Nova Southeastern University, Fort Lauderdale, Florida, USA.
Email: cm3318@mynsu.nova.edu

Since its publication, the MMSE has been a topic of interest among researchers in developing normative data for different clinical groups. Examples of these clinical groups include individuals with Alzheimer's disease, Parkinson's disease, and those who have experienced a stroke. Normative data has also been gathered for healthy adults and the elderly population. Creating specific datasets based on clinical conditions allows for a better comparison of MMSE scores and the detection of possible cognitive impairment.

Updated versions of the MMSE were developed as part of the Mini-Mental Status Examination Second Edition (MMSE-2) (MMSE-2, n.d.). The goal of the MMSE-2 was to expand the usefulness of the original version among other populations with milder forms of cognitive impairment (MMSE-2, n.d.). Three versions were developed: MMSE-2 Standard Version (MMSE-2:SV), Mini-Mental Status Examination-2 Brief Version (MMSE-2:BV), and the Mini-Mental Status Examination-2 Expanded Version (MMSE-2: EV) (MMSE-2, n.d.). Examiners must consider several factors when choosing which updated MMSE-2 version is best for their clients (MMSE-2, n.d.). These versions are available in ten languages, including Spanish, Russian, and Simplified Chinese (MMSE-2, n.d.).

Test Procedures

For the administration of the MMSE, the examiner is instructed to read the 11 items on the administration form in the order they are presented (Folstein et al. 1975). Certain items are required to administer the MMSE, including a pencil, a watch, a blank piece of paper, and a paper with the phrase "close your eyes" (Folstein et al. 1975). These objects are necessary for items 6, 8, and 9. The examiner will write the examinee's response for each item (Folstein et al. 1975). There is no time limit for each item or the completion of the administration (MMSE n.d.). The administration is estimated to last 10 to 15 minutes (MMSE, n.d.). Of note, there may be instances where individuals completing the MMSE may have difficulty completing serial 7's task in the "Attention and Calculation" section (Folstein et al. 1975). The designated task requires an individual to count backward by seven from 100. The examinee is expected to do five correct subtractions. Due to the item difficulty and frustration tolerance of the examinee, it is possible for the examiner to substitute an alternative task of spelling the word "world" backward (Folstein et al. 1975).

Scoring

After the administration is completed, the examiner can score the individual's responses based on the guidelines presented on the administration form. The estimated time for scoring is five minutes (MMSE, n.d.). Each correct answer is allocated one point (Folstein et al. 1975). The examiner must add all the points to calculate the individual's total raw score (Folstein et al. 1975). The MMSE has a maximum possible total raw score of 30 points (Folstein et al. 1975). After calculating the total raw score, an examiner can gather a T-score from the Appendix in the MMSE Clinical Guide (MMSE, n.d.). The Appendix in the MMSE Clinical Guide has normative data available based on age and education (MMSE, n.d.). Using the individual's age and educational profile, the examiner will reference the associated T-score based on their raw score. The t-scores can be viewed as a supplemental interpretation, as the traditional method for interpretation is based on the raw MMSE scores (MMSE, n.d.). In addition, the examiner will assess the individual's level of consciousness on a continuum (Folstein et al. 1975). This continuum is described as going from fully alert to in a coma (Folstein et al. 1975).

Reliability and Validity

Regarding the measure's reliability, the MMSE is reliable for 24-hour and 48-hour retesting with a reliability coefficient of 0.88 (Folstein et al. 1975). Different examiners can also administer the measure twice and yield similar results (Folstein et al. 1975). When assessing interrater reliability, the overall reliability coefficient was 0.827 (Folstein et al. 1975). Internal consistency of the MMSE was deemed moderate (Mitchell 2013). The measure's validity was examined by comparing scores of patients before and after appropriate treatment for their conditions (Folstein et al. 1975). It was hypothesized that the patients with dementia that could not be corrected with medical interventions would not show much change in cognitive functioning, whereas other patients with conditions that could be improved would see a considerable change (Folstein et al. 1975). As expected, the MMSE scores of patients with dementia did not significantly change (Folstein et al. 1975). The patients diagnosed with depression who received a type of intervention saw a small, significant change (Folstein et al. 1975). In addition, a large, significant change from baseline to after intervention was found among patients with depression characterized by cognitive difficulty (Folstein et al. 1975).

Folstein and his team examined the concurrent validity of the MMSE with an intelligence measure in their publication study (Folstein et al. 1975). Specifically, they wanted to see if the MMSE scores were correlated with the Weschler Adult Intelligence Scale (WAIS) Verbal and Performance Intelligence Quotients (IQs) (Folstein et al. 1975). The Verbal IQ and Performance IQ were strongly correlated to the MMSE scores with validity coefficients of 0.77 and 0.66, respectively (Folstein et al. 1975). The association between the MMSE and the Mattis Dementia Scale Rating Scale (MDRS) was also examined (Freidl et al. 1996). Their results showed poor concurrent validity with a coefficient of 0.29 (Freidl et al. 1996). More comparisons were made, especially with measures focused on specific clinical populations. When comparing the MMSE to the Montreal Cognitive Assessment (MoCA), the convergent validity was deemed adequate among healthy controls with a coefficient value of 0.43 (Trzepacz et al. 2015). This differed from the excellent convergent validity among participants with mild cognitive impairment ($r = 0.60$) (Trzepacz et al. 2015). Excellent convergent validity was also found among a mixed sample of healthy controls and participants with either dementia or mild cognitive impairment ($r = 0.84$) (Trzepacz et al. 2015).

Strong convergent validity was found between the Standardized Mini-Mental State Examination (SMMSE) and the Global Deterioration Scale (GDS) (Mougias et al. 2018). Another study found that excellent convergent validity existed between the MMSE and the number of incorrect items on the Six Item Screener completed by 651 individuals who were referred to the Alzheimer's disease Center (r = 0.87) (Callahan et al., 2002). Other measures, such as the Dementia Rating Scale and the Addenbrooke's Cognitive Examination, were highly correlated with the MMSE (Aarsland et al. 2004; Kaszás et al. 2012). Researchers found the MMSE scores were associated with the Frontal Assessment Battery, Barthel Index (BI), Zung Depression Scale, and the Montgomery-Asberg Depression Scale (MADRS) (Kaszas et al. 2012; Agrell and Dehlin 2000).

Clinical Applications in Research

The MMSE allows for screening cognitive impairment and estimating the severity of impairment at a given time (Folstein et al. 1975). It can also be used serially to document a patient's response to treatment and has been recommended for the screening of cognition in depressed patients (Folstein et al. 1975). MMSE scores tended to be lower for patients with more severe forms of cognitive impairment, like dementia and depression with cognitive impairment (Folstein et al. 1975). It is important to note that the MMSE does not perform well as a confirmatory measure for certain clinical conditions like dementia, mild cognitive impairment, and delirium (Mitchell 2013). It was also not considered a useful screening tool for memory issues or cognitive impairment after a stroke (Blake et al. 2002). In addition, the MMSE was not recommended for detecting dementia among older adults and adults with Parkinson's disease (Dujardin et al. 2010; Aarsland et al. 2001).

Although research has found trends associated with the severity of cognitive difficulty experienced by the patient, there are other significant factors to consider (Folstein et al. 1975). Normally, MMSE norms decline with age (Grigoletto et al. 1999). Yet, MMSE scores tend to increase with years of education (Grigoletto et al. 1999). Language is another factor to consider clinically since the MMSE can influence scores (Bravo and Hébert 2007). It has been found that English-speaking participants receive higher MMSE scores than French-speaking participants (Bravo and Hébert 2007). The measure may also not capture language disorders like aphasia (Myrberg et al. 2020).

Interpretation

The MMSE is a valuable tool for screening possible cognitive impairment among individuals. It should not be solely used as a diagnostic tool, as reliance on cut-off scores for detecting cognitive impairment may result in misdiagnoses. It has been recommended that MMSE scores be used solely as a screener to assess if the client needs no further cognitive evaluation or a more extensive evaluation (Lopez et al. 2005). The examiner should take other factors into consideration when assessing an individual's cognitive functioning.

Although the suggested cut-off score in the MMSE manual for cognitive impairment is 22 or 23, other research teams have found other cut-off scores highly associated with specific clinical disorders. For example, a commonly used cut-off score for dementia is 23 or 24 (Mitchell 2009). This was further supported by the literature suggesting scores less than 23 were associated with a diagnosis of dementia in at least 79% of cases (Lancu and Olmer 2006).

There are highly associated groups of MMSE scores for different levels of cognitive impairment. Normal cognition was found to be associated with scores ranging from 24 to 30, whereas scores between 18 to 24 were associated with mild cognitive impairment (Tombaugh and McIntyre 1992). Low MMSE scores between 0 and 17 are indicative of severe cognitive impairment (Tombaugh and McIntyre 1992).

Education has been found to be a factor that can lead to biased MMSE scores (Jacqmin-Gadda 1997). High scores may be related to one's educational level (Jacqmin-Gadda 1997). For example, it is possible for individuals with a neurocognitive disorder who have obtained a high level of education to score relatively high on the MMSE. It is also possible for a healthy individual who did not learn how to read to obtain a relatively low MMSE score, indicating cognitive impairment.

1. Injury to the frontal cortex or cerebellum may lead to difficulty answering items involving motor responses. Items 8, 9, 10, and 11 involve hand and mouth movement to complete the assigned task.
2. Damage to the occipital lobe can result in different levels of visual impairment. An individual who has a visual disturbance may not be able to perform well on items 6, 9, and 11.
3. Lesions in Broca's and Wernicke's area may lead to issues for an individual when completing the "Language" section.
4. The MMSE may miss milder cases of dementia as well as more severe cases in highly educated individuals.
5. While sensitive to education, MMSE scores are not predictive of IQ.
6. Poor performance in any area should be considered a possible indicator of specific focal deficits in milder cases.
7. Low scores may reflect premorbid impairment rather than an ongoing or new disorder in clients with lower education.

References

Agrell, B. and Dehlin, O. (2000). Mini-mental state examination in geriatric stroke patients. Validity, differences between subgroups of patients, and relationships to somatic and mental variables. Aging (Milan, Italy), 12(6): 439–444. https://doi.org/10.1007/BF03339874.

Aarsland, D., Andersen, K., Larsen, J. P., Lolk, A., Nielsen, H. and Kragh-Sørensen, P. (2001). Risk of dementia in Parkinson's disease: a community-based, prospective study. Neurology, 56(6): 730–736. https://doi.org/10.1212/wnl.56.6.730.

Aarsland, D., Andersen, K., Larsen, J. P., Perry, R., Wentzel-Larsen, T., Lolk, A. et al. (2004). The rate of cognitive decline in Parkinson disease. Archives of Neurology, 61(12): 1906–1911.

Blake, H., McKinney, M., Treece, K., Lee, E. and Lincoln, N. B. (2002). An evaluation of screening measures for cognitive impairment after stroke. Age and Ageing, 31(6): 451–456. https://doi.org/10.1093/ageing/31.6.451.

Bravo, G. and Hébert, R. (1997). Age- and education-specific reference values for the Mini-Mental and modified Mini-Mental State Examinations derived from a non-demented elderly population. International journal of geriatric psychiatry, 12(10): 1008–1018. https://doi.org/10.1002/(sici)1099-1166(199710)12:10<1008::aid-gps676>3.0.co;2-a.

Brugnolo, A., Nobili, F., Barbieri, M. P., Dessi, B., Ferro, A., Girtler, N. et al. (2009). The factorial structure of the mini mental state examination (MMSE) in Alzheimer's disease. Archives of Gerontology and Geriatrics, 49(1): 180–185. https://doi-org.ezproxylocal.library.nova.edu/10.1016/j.archger.2008.07.005.

Callahan, C. M., Unverzagt, F. W., Hui, S. L., Perkins, A. J. and Hendrie, H. C. (2002). Six-item screener to identify cognitive impairment among potential subjects for clinical research. Medical Care, 771–781.

Dujardin, K., Dubois, B., Tison, F., Durif, F., Bourdeix, I., Péré, J. J., Duhamel, A. and EXECUTIVE study group. (2010). Parkinson's disease dementia can be easily detected in routine clinical practice. Movement disorders : official journal of the Movement Disorder Society, 25(16): 2769–2776. https://doi.org/10.1002/mds.23391.

Folstein, M. F., Folstein, S. E. and McHugh, P. R. 1975. 'Mini-mental state: a practical method for grading the cognitive state of patients for the clinician. J. Psychiatr. Res., 12: 189–198.

Freidl, W., Schmidt, R., Stronegger, W. J., Fazekas, F. and Reinhart, B. (1996). Sociodemographic predictors and concurrent validity of the Mini Mental State Examination and the Mattis Dementia Rating Scale. European Archives of Psychiatry and Clinical Neuroscience, 246(6): 317–319. https://doi.org/10.1007/BF02189025.

Grigoletto, F., Zappala, G., Anderson, D.W. and Lebowitz, B. D. (1999). Norms for the Mini-Mental State Examination in a healthy population. Neurology, 53(2): 315–320.

Jacqmin-Gadda, H., Fabrigoule, C., Commenges, D. and Dartigues, J. F. (1997). A 5-year longitudinal study of the Mini-Mental State Examination in normal aging. American Journal of Epidemiology, 145(6): 498–506.

Kaszás, B., Kovács, N., Balás, I., Kállai, J., Aschermann, Z., Kerekes, Z. et al. (2012). Sensitivity and specificity of addenbrooke's cognitive examination, mattis dementia rating scale, frontal assessment battery and mini mental state examination for diagnosing dementia in Parkinson's disease. Parkinsonism and Related Disorders, 18(5): 553–556.

Lopez, M. N., Charter, R. A., Mostafavi, B., Nibut, L. P. and Smith, W. E. (2005). Psychometric Properties of the Folstein Mini-Mental State Examination. Assessment, 12(2): 137–144. https://doi.org/10.1177/1073191105275412.

Lancu, I. and Olmer, A. (2006). The minimental state examination—an up-to-date review. Harefuah, 145(9), 687–90.

Mitchell, A. J. (2009). A meta-analysis of the accuracy of the mini-mental state examination in the detection of dementia and mild cognitive impairment. Journal of Psychiatric Research, 43(4): 411–431.

Mitchell, A. J. (2013). The Mini-Mental State Examination (MMSE): an update on its diagnostic validity for cognitive disorders. pp. 15–46. In: Cognitive Screening Instruments. Springer, London.

Mougias, A. A., Christidi, F., Kiosterakis, G., Messinis, L. and Politis, A. (2018). Dealing with severe dementia in clinical practice: A validity and reliability study of Severe Mini-Mental State Examination in Greek population. International Journal of Geriatric Psychiatry, 33(9): 1236–1242.

MMSE Mini-Mental Status Examination. PAR. (n.d.). https://www.parinc.com/Products/Pkey/237.

MMSE-2 Mini-Mental Status Examination, 2nd edition. Psychological Assessment Resources. (n.d.). https://www.parinc.com/products/pkey/238.

Myrberg, K., Hydén, L. C. and Samuelsson, C. (2020). The mini-mental state examination (MMSE) from a language perspective: an analysis of test interaction. Clinical Linguistics and Phonetics, 34(7): 652–670.

PAR (n.d.). MMSE-2 Presentation [PowerPoint slides]. Psychological Assessment Resources, Inc. https://www.parinc.com/products/pkey/238.

Tombaugh, T. N. and McIntyre, N. J. (1992). The mini-mental state examination: a comprehensive review. Journal of the American Geriatrics Society, 40(9): 922–935.

Trzepacz, P. T., Hochstetler, H., Wang, S., Walker, B., Saykin, A. J. and Alzheimer's Disease Neuroimaging Initiative. (2015). Relationship between the Montreal Cognitive Assessment and Mini-mental State Examination for assessment of mild cognitive impairment in older adults. BMC geriatrics, 15: 107. https://doi.org/10.1186/s12877-015-0103-3.

CHAPTER 26

Montreal Cognitive Assessment (MoCA)

Rachel Geller and *Kayley Slicer**

The Montreal Cognitive Assessment (MoCA) is a neuropsychological battery that is used to measure cognitive functioning and decline. The MoCA is recommended to be administered every three months or less and is normed for people ages 55–85 (Nasreddine 2021). The full-length exam, MoCA Full (version 8.1), is scored on a 30-point basis and can be administered in 10 minutes. The creators of the MoCA require examiners to take a one-hour certification training in order to be qualified to administer and interpret this test. The MoCA Full assesses short-term memory, visuospatial/executive functioning, attention, concentration, working memory, language, and orientation to place and time (Nasreddine 2021).

Normed Population

The most current and commonly used form of the test is the MoCA 8.1, which is available in over 100 languages and has been adapted to accommodate different needs. The MoCA Basic is similar to the MoCA Full but is adapted to screen for mild cognitive impairment in people with less than five years of education. The MoCA Blind/Telephone is also available for people who are visually impaired and is adapted to 5-minute and 10-minute versions. There is a MoCA Hearing Impairment that is available as well. The MoCA Audiovisual can be administered via teleconference, allowing people to take the assessment remotely. The MoCA is also available in five languages via an app and can be administered via telehealth/video conference.

The MoCA has been normed for each version and divides populations into three categories: Normal Controls (NC), Mild Cognitive Impairment (MCI), and Alzheimer's disease (AD). In trials conducted with these three groupings (n = 277),

Nova Southeastern University, Fort Lauderdale, Florida, USA.
Email: rg1318@mynsu.nova.edu
* Corresponding author: ks2999@mynsu.nova.edu

the average MoCA score for normal controls (M = 27.4, S.D. = 2.2), mild cognitive impairment (M = 22.1, S.D. = 3.1), and Alzheimer's disease (M = 16.2, S.D. = 4.8) (Nasreddine et al. 2005). Thus, the cutoff score for mild cognitive impairment and Alzheimer's disease is a total score of < 26 points.

Educational Level

In examining norms for different education levels, Gagnon et al. (2013) sampled 25 outpatient individuals with dementia and 39 individuals with amnestic mild cognitive impairments, accounting for educational levels. This study reported that applying corrections for education can have a detrimental effect and decrease the test's sensitivity by 80% in detecting cognitive impairments.

Cecato et al. (2014) studied a sample of 136 individuals (39 healthy controls, 45 mild cognitive impairment, and 52 Alzheimer's disease). After administering the MoCA, this study reported that it serves as a good screening measure to distinguish between mild cognitive impairment and Alzheimer's disease. The researchers also noted that this tool is more effective in assessing elderly populations with four or more years of education. Still, differences in education years between the three groups were not statistically significant.

Luo et al. (2020) used Item Response Theory (IRT) to see if this analysis would reduce the effects of confounding factors, including education. In a sample of 1,873 older adults, this study divided participants into two educational categories: no formal education and some/formal education. Interestingly, the results of this study demonstrated that people without formal education tended to perform better on the cube, clock number, and clock hand items. Thus, researchers expressed the need for a more in-depth analysis of these items using IRT.

Age

In terms of norming based on age, Malek-Ahmadi et al. (2015) argued that the threshold for cognitive impairments should be lowered to below 26 points for older, less educated populations. In sample age groups of 70–79, 80–89, and 90–99, there were significant differences between age/education groups. Specifically, younger and more educated participants scored significantly higher than same-aged peers.

Elkana et al. (2019) similarly argued that the current MoCA cutoff is too high for highly educated and cognitively normal older adults. Through analysis of 27 patients ages 68–83, these researchers argue that the average MoCA total score was below the cutoff of 26/30 over five years. Compared to other neuropsychological exams, these participants scored within the normal range and even above average in some instances.

Additionally, Carson, Leach, and Murphy (2018) used a meta-analysis to study the norm cutoffs in age and concluded that the MoCA should lower the cutoff score from 26/30 to 23/30 to reduce the rate of false positives in diagnosing mild cognitive impairments. In a study with 67 HIV-positive patients 60 years or older, receiver operator characteristics determined that an optimal cutoff score would be ≲ 25/30

(Milanini et al. 2014). Milanini et al. (2014) highlighted that the MoCA has only moderate performance characteristics for screening HIV-positive elders.

Race

Rossetti et al. (2011) examined normative data for the MoCA in a population-based sample using 2,653 ethnically diverse participants with cardiovascular disease (Caucasian 34%, African American 52%, Hispanic 11%, and other 2%). This study reports that total scores were lower than previously published normative data, with 66% of the sample scoring ≲ 26 points. Nasreddine et al. (2012) commented on this study, claiming that Rossetti et al. (2011) used a substantially different population to conduct their study. Specifically, Nasreddine et al. (2012) claim that their study included a younger sample (52.9 versus 72.8) and only reported slightly lower mean MoCA scores (25.6 versus 26.9). Additionally, Nasreddine et al. (2012) claim that their sample had stricter criteria. With conflicting results, the researchers must be able to norm the MoCA using a more diverse, representative sample.

Milani et al. (2018) examined 3,895 individuals with 80.7% non-Hispanic White, 15.0% non-Hispanic Black, and 4.2% Hispanic. This study found optimal cutoffs for detecting mild cognitive impairment differed by race. Specifically, this study argued that optimal cutoffs for detection are 25 among non-Hispanic whites (19 points for detection of dementia), 24 points among Hispanics (16 points for dementia), and 23 points among non-Hispanic Blacks (16 points for dementia). Furthermore, this study explained that lower education levels produced lower optimal cutoffs for diagnosing mild cognitive impairment.

Goldstein et al. (2014) conducted research evaluating the MoCA's validity in a sample of 81 African-American patients ages 50 years and older. This study reports that the MoCA is a valid and cost-effective screener for cognitive impairments among African Americans. However, these researchers suggest that there is a higher likelihood of misclassifying African Americans with no cognitive impairments reported as having cognitive impairments.

Test Procedures

In terms of test administration, the test does not require the extensive use of outside materials and can be administered in about 10 minutes. The test is administered as follows:

1. Alternative Trail Making: The examinee must draw a line from a number to a letter in ascending order. The examinee must draw the pattern 1-A-2-B-3-C-4-D-5-E without drawing any lines that cross.
2. Visuoconstructional Skills (Cube): The examinee can copy the drawing of a cube as accurately as possible.
3. Visuoconstructional Skills (Clock): The examinee must draw a clock, put the numbers, and set the time to 10 past 11.
4. Naming: The examinee will tell the examiner the name of each animal in the picture (i.e., lion, rhinoceros, and camel).

5. Memory: The examiner reads a list of five words at a rate of one per second, giving the following instructions: "This is a memory test. I am going to read a list of words that you will have to remember now and later on. Listen carefully. When I am through, tell me as many words as you can remember. It doesn't matter in what order you say them." On this first trial, the examiner marks a check in the allocated space for each word the subject produces. The examiner may not correct the subject if they recall a deformed word or a word that sounds like the target word. When the subject indicates that they have finished (have recalled all words) or can recall no more words, the examiner reads the list a second time with the following instructions: "I am going to read the same list for a second time. Try to remember and tell me as many words as you can, including words you said the first time." The examiner puts a check in the allocated space for each word the subject recalls on the second trial. At the end of the second trial, the examiner informs the subject that they will be asked to recall these words again by saying: "I will ask you to recall those words again at the end of the test."
6. Attention:
    a. Forward Digit Span: The examiner reads the five-number sequence at a rate of one digit per second, and the examinee will repeat back to them exactly as they were said.
    b. Backward Digit Span: The examiner reads the five-number sequence at a rate of one digit per second, which the examinee will repeat back to them in the backward order.
    c. Vigilance: The examiner reads a list of letters at a rate of one per second and asks the examinee to tap their hand every time the examiner says the letter "A."
    d. Serial 7s: The examinee counts by subtracting 7 from 100 and then subtracts 7 until told to stop. This must be performed through mental calculation. The examinee is not permitted to use their fingers or paper and pencil/pens. If the subject asks what her/his last given answer was or what number (s)he must subtract from his/her answer, the examiner responds by repeating the instructions if not already done so.
7. Sentence Repetition: The examiner reads a sentence to the examinee, and the examinee must repeat it exactly as it is said.
8. Verbal Fluency: The examinee lists as many words as they can think of and will be told to stop after one minute. Proper nouns, numbers, and verb forms are not permitted as a correct response. If the examinee names two consecutive words that begin with another letter of the alphabet, the examiner should repeat the target letter if the instructions have not been repeated.
9. Abstraction: The examiner asks the examinee to explain what each pair of words has in common.
10. Delayed Recall: The words that were read to the examinee previously are to be repeated by recalling as many words the examinee can remember.
11. Orientation: The examinee is asked to tell the examiner today's date (i.e., year, month, exact date, and day of the week) and the name of their location and city they are in.

Item Difficulty and Types of Errors

Item difficulty does not necessarily increase as the test continues. In other words, each subtest/task requires different cognitive skills and does not increase in difficulty. Rather, each subtest assesses different cognitive domains: attention and concentration, executive functions, memory, language, visuoconstructional skills, conceptual thinking, calculations, and orientation.

Regarding accommodations, the MoCA explains the instructions on how the test can be adapted to fit different populations. For example, Nasreddine et al. (2022) explain that people diagnosed with Hemiplegia can still complete the test, and scores can be converted using the test's norms for this population. However, the MoCA does have strict instructions that must be followed for different sections. For example, participants must draw a complete circle when drawing a clock in the visuospatial/executive portion of the test.

For the attention subtest that requires participants to complete serial subtraction in 7s starting at 100, participants are not allowed to use a calculator or a pen/pencil and paper. Additionally, the list of words in the memory portion of the test must be completed in two trials, and examiners are not allowed to complete more trials if the participant does not correctly repeat the five words.

It is important to note that in populations with motor difficulties, the MoCA can be difficult to complete, and in this case, people with Hemiplegia can still be tested but must use the correct norms. Additionally, the test does not allow for accommodations during specific portions, including the Attention and memory subtests. In these instances, the examiner might choose to allow for the examinee to use accommodations and make a note of this as behavioral observations but should still score the subtests according to the scoring criteria.

Task Demands and Strategies

As mentioned previously, each subtest measures a different cognitive domain. This includes attention and concentration, executive functions, memory, language, visuoconstructional skills, conceptual thinking, calculations, and orientation. Different strategies may be used to accomplish a variety of tasks. Breaking down large amounts of information, also called chunking, may be used to help remember the series of numbers read aloud during the attention task.

Chunking and remembering the numbers in smaller sets (i.e., three numbers at a time) can improve the examinee's score. For verbal fluency, an examinee can choose to think of each word that begins with "F" in alphabetical order and may also look around the room for cues.

Scoring

Scores at or above 26/30 are deemed normal and demonstrate a lack of cognitive impairments. One point may be added to the score if the examinee has had 12 or fewer years of education. Subtests are scored as follows:

1. Alternating Trail Making: Any error that is not self-corrected immediately is given a score of 0, and if the examinee draws a line from the end (E) to the beginning (1), this is also given a score of 0.
2. Visuoconstructional Skills (cube): One point is allocated for the correctly executed drawing. In order to earn this point, the following criteria must be met, and if any of the criteria are missing, a score of 0 is given:
   a. The drawing must be three-dimensional.
   b. All lines are drawn.
   c. All lines meet with little or no space.
   d. No line is added.
   e. Lines are relatively parallel, and their length is similar (rectangular prisms are accepted).
   f. The cube's orientation in space must be preserved.
3. Visuoconstructional Skills (Clock): The points are divided into three criteria (i.e., contour, numbers, and hands). The following criteria must be met:
   a. Contour (1 pt.): The clock contour must be drawn (either a circle or a square). Only minor distortions are acceptable (e.g., slight imperfection on closing the circle). If the numbers are arranged circularly, but the contour is not drawn, then the contour is scored as incorrect.
   b. Numbers (1 pt.): All clock numbers must be present with no additional numbers. Numbers must be in the correct order, upright, and placed in the approximate quadrants on the clock face. Roman numerals are acceptable. The numbers must be arranged circularly (even if the contour is a square). All numbers must either be placed inside or outside the clock contour. If the subject places some numbers inside the clock contour and some outside the clock contour, they do not receive a point for numbers.
   c. Hands (1 pt.): There must be two hands jointly indicating the correct time. The hour hand must be clearly shorter than the minute hand. Hands must be centered within the clock face with their junction close to the clock center.
4. Naming: One point is given for each correct response.
5. Memory: No points are given for Trials One and Two.
6. Attention:
   a. Digit Span: One point is allocated for each correct sequence repeated.
   b. Vigilance: Each time the examinee correctly taps on the letter A, one point is allocated. No points are awarded for any taps on other letters or missed As.
   c. Serial 7s: This item is scored out of 3 points. Give no (0) points for no correct subtractions, 1 point for one correct subtraction, 2 points for two or three correct subtractions, and 3 points if the subject successfully makes four or five correct subtractions. Each subtraction is evaluated independently; that is, if the subject responds with an incorrect number but continues to subtract 7 from it correctly, each correct subtraction is counted.
7. Sentence Repetition: One point is allocated for each sentence correctly repeated. Repetitions must be exact. Be alert for omissions (e.g., omitting "only"), substitutions/additions (e.g., substituting "only" for "always"), grammar errors/altering plurals (e.g. "hides" for "hid"), etc.

8. Verbal Fluency: One point is allocated if the subject generates 11 words or more in 60 seconds. The examiner records the subject's responses in the margins or on the back of the test sheet.
9. Abstraction: Only the last two pairs are scored. One point is given for each pair correctly answered.
10. Delayed Recall: In the allocated space, the examiner makes a check mark (√) for each of the words correctly recalled spontaneously without any cues. One point is allocated for each word recalled without any cues. To calculate the Memory Index Score (MIS), the examiner provides a category (semantic) cue for each word the subject was unable to recall depending upon the type of cue (i.e., category cue or multiple-choice cue).
11. Orientation: One point is allocated for each correct response. The date and place must be exact, and no points are allocated if the subject makes an error of one day for the day and date.

Reliability

The MoCA is often compared to the Mini-Mental Status Examination (MMSE), as both tests detect cognitive deficits. Wong et al. (2018) argue that the MoCA is "psychometrically superior" to the MMSE and worked to convert scores from the MMSE to the MoCA and MoCA-5-minute protocol. Wong et al. (2018) found that by using an equipercentile method, scores from the MMSE can be converted to the MoCA, adjusting for age and education. Kopecek et al. (2017) highlighted that the MoCA could be used with the MMSE to establish 90% reliable change indices (RCI) in cognitively healthy older adults in a sample of 197 cognitively healthy volunteers ages 60–94 years old.

Similarly, Dharmasaroja et al. (2020) were able to correlate scores between the Thai Mental State Exam (TSME), an exam similar to the MMSE. Dharmasaroja et al. (2020) created a conversion table that successfully translated scores between the two exams in mild cognitive impairment and dementia patients. However, this study concluded that the MoCA was superior to the TMSE in patients with mild cognitive impairment.

Kim et al. (2018) also validated a conversion between the MMSE and the MoCA in Korea. Specifically, these researchers validated conversion to the MoCA for patients with Parkinson's disease. Kim et al. (2018) sampled 391 patients with Parkinson's disease and found conversion instruments successful regardless of patients' educational levels. Adamis et al. (2016) were also able to demonstrate this in an outpatient older patient community setting successfully. This study highlighted that Pearson's r was .89 after converting scores from the MMSE to the MoCA, demonstrating high correlations between accuracy in the MoCA in detecting cognitive impairments.

Pinto et al. (2018) claimed that the MoCA proves to be more accurate in tracking mild cognitive impairment and Alzheimer's disease compared to the MMSE. By using a systematic review, this study concluded that after evaluating the Quality Assessment of Diagnostic Accuracy Studies 2 (QUADAS-2), over 80% of published articles favored the MoCA over the MMSE. Specifically, this study highlighted the MoCA's ability to distinguish better mild cognitive impairment versus no cognitive impairment in patients. Similarly, Koski (2013) demonstrated through a literature review that the MoCA is superior to the MMSE in detecting mild cognitive impairments in patients with cerebrovascular disease. However, Koski (2013) highlighted the need for norming the MoCA in populations with cerebrovascular disease.

Additionally, the creators of the test claim that the test-retest period can be administered for one month and that alternative versions should be used to negate learning effects when the MoCA is administered repeatedly (Nasreddine 2022). Gomez et al. (2012) reported that the Spanish version of the MoCA, the MoCA-S, shows high test-retest reliability in lower-educated Colombians, but scores depended on the number of years of education. Similarly, Lee et al. (2020) reported that the MoCA has high test-retest reliability after examining a sample of 60 patients with dementia. The patients were assessed two weeks apart, and researchers determined that the test could appropriately monitor cognitive functioning.

Lam et al. (2013) compared the validity of the MoCA with the MMSE and Mattis Dementia Rating Scale (DRS) and determined that the MoCA is a valid measure in assessing cognition. Specifically, this study highlighted the MoCA's ability to use domain-specific subscores and reported that these scores aligned with other measures used for neuropsychological testing.

Validity

The MoCA website lists studies for over 45 different diseases and conditions that have been studied in correlation with the test. The test's creators mainly highlight its uses in diagnosing mild cognitive impairment and Alzheimer's disease (Nasreddine 2022). Research has overall shown that the MoCA is reliable in diagnosing mild cognitive impairment and Alzheimer's disease.

Cersonsky et al. (2022) highlighted that the MoCA can identify individuals with cognitive decline. This study used data from the Alzheimer's disease neuroimaging initiative and reported that the test had a 77.3% precision in diagnosing three main clusters: high-performing individuals, individuals with memory deficits, and individuals with compound deficits. Kang et al. (2018) demonstrated similar results, highlighting that the MoCA scores can accurately assess cognitive decline. These researchers also claim that the MoCA demonstrates better discriminative power for mild cognitive impairment than the MMSE in reflecting cognitive reserve.

Similarly, Koski (2013) demonstrated through a literature review that the MoCA demonstrated strong content validity, but demonstrated mixed evidence in its sensitivity to the specific kind of cognitive impairment in people with cerebrovascular disease. However, Koski (2013) reported that the MoCA was advantageous compared to the MMSE in its ability to detect milder forms of cognitive decline that was associated with cerebrovascular disease.

In a sample of 103 Persian participants aged ≥ 60 with at least six years of formal education, Badrkhahan et al. (2019) reported that the MoCA could screen for the detection of Parkinson's disease accurately. Similarly, Gill et al. (2008) demonstrated the MoCA's ability to detect early or mild cognitive impairment in patients with

Parkinson's disease in a sample of 48 participants with a mean age of 71.3 years old with 14.8 years of education.

Rosca et al. (2019) reported that the MoCA could detect cognitive impairments in patients with HIV-associated neurocognitive disorders. These researchers argued that the cognitive impairment threshold should be lowered to 26/30 points. They argue that this will decrease the rates of false-positive diagnoses of cognitive impairment and improve the test's accuracy.

Since COVID-19, telehealth has become a more popular platform for clinicians who cannot meet with patients in person. DeYoung and Shenal (2019) explained that the MoCA can still be reliable when administered over telehealth. Specifically, DeYoung and Shenal (2019) sampled veterans from rural areas and found that administering the MoCA via telehealth still allows for accurate diagnosing and is well received by patients. This study highlights the test's flexibility and adaptability to be administered to patients with difficulty accessing neurological evaluation. Phillips et al. (2020) warn clinicians to note the camera resolution, display size, and lighting conditions when administering the MoCA via videoconference.

Group Comparisons

The MoCA's creators report high levels of internal consistency in identifying and distinguishing between mild cognitive impairments and Alzheimer's disease. Specifically, Nasreddine (2022) states that the cutoff score of 18 is used to distinguish between mild cognitive impairment and Alzheimer's disease. Specifically, the average MoCA score for mild cognitive impairment is 22 and ranges from 19–25 points. The average score for Mild AD is 16, with a range of 11–21 points (Nasreddine 2022). However, the creators of the test do acknowledge that there is an overlap between the scores, but the loss of autonomy and cognitive impairments ultimately determine AD.

Freitas et al. (2012) demonstrated high sensitivity levels in distinguishing between mild cognitive impairment, Alzheimer's disease, and normal control patients in a sample of 830 participants. These researchers argue that the optimal cutoff for mild cognitive impairment patients is below 22 points, and for AD patients is below 17 points. This study also supported the MoCA's construct validity and that item analysis proved "psychometric adequacy." However, items regarding naming the lion, orientation to place and city, and the contour of the clock suggested lower levels of difficulty with lower correlations to the domains of cognitive functioning.

Similarly, Goldstein et al. (2018) reported similar findings in their study examining the MoCA's incremental validity. This study reported that in a sample of participants with normal cognition (n = 295), mild cognitive impairment (n = 471), and Alzheimer's disease (n = 150), effect sizes were large (>.80), showing that index scores were able to differentiate between normal and impaired cognitive functioning accurately. This study notes that the interpretation of the MoCA is more valid when the entire test is administered, especially in distinguishing between normal cognition and mild cognitive impairment.

Bruijnen et al. (2020) examined scores on the MoCA for healthy participants ages 18–70 and reported that age and education correlated with scores from the

MoCA-TS and MoCA-MIS. This study reported that norms should consider age, education, and premorbid intelligence to improve reliability in test-retest measures. This study concluded that the MoCA is a reliable cognitive measure but highlighted the need for future studies to collect more normative data to improve differentiation between cognitively impaired and normal cognitive functioning populations.

McDicken et al. (2019) also reported that the MoCA can measure episodic memory loss effectively to detect cognitive impairments. Tan et al. (2021) explained that the MoCA demonstrates high diagnostic accuracy in items including trail making and clock drawing that allows for assessing executive functioning impairments. These executive functioning impairments are often associated with frontotemporal dementia, Parkinson's disease, and dementia with Lewy Bodies.

Clinical Applications in Research

Diagnosis

Overall, research has supported using the MoCA to detect mild cognitive impairments and Alzheimer's disease in a wide range of populations. This test can be an important tool for clinicians working with older adults and tracking cognitive decline. This test has also been validated in distinguishing between mild cognitive impairments and Alzheimer's disease; however, the test lacks reliability in differentiating mild cognitive impairment and no cognitive impairment.

With over 100 languages and dialects and multiple test formats, the MoCA can be used across the globe as a quick and efficient measure of cognitive decline, along with over 45 diseases listed on the creator's website (Nasreddine 2021). More specifically, the MoCA has proven efficient in detecting neurodegenerative diseases among diverse populations, including Parkinson's disease, dementia, and vascular cognitive impairments.

As mentioned previously, researchers have demonstrated the need for the standard of 26/30 points to be considered healthy to be lowered to reduce the rates of a false-positive diagnosis of cognitive impairments. Thus, when interpreting the results of the MoCA, clinicians need to consider the age and education level of the patient. Additionally, clinicians should use test-retest to obtain baseline cognitive levels of functioning to measure cognition over time.

Interpretation

1. The MoCA divides populations into three categories based on total score: Normal Controls (NC), Mild Cognitive Impairment (MCI), and Alzheimer's Disease (AD). The cutoff score for mild cognitive impairment and Alzheimer's Disease is a total score of < 26 points.
2. The authors of the MoCA further break down cognitive impairment into three categories based on total score. Mild cognitive impairments are reported to range from 18-25 points, moderate is 10-17 points, and the severe range is 10 points or less.

3. Poor performance on the MoCA may be due to lower levels of education and have been found to be more common in certain racial/ethnic groups (Cecato et al., 2014; Gagnon et al., 2013; Gomez et al., 2012).
4. Total scores of the MoCA may be used to track cognitive decline among patients with suspected or diagnosed with Alzheimer's Disease, Parkinson's Disease, and other neurodegenerative disorders (Nasreddine, 2021).
5. The MoCA requires expressive speech and motor abilities and those who have experienced a stroke may perform poorer due to decreased motor abilities, aphasia, as well as impaired attention and concentration within the first three months following a stroke (Chiti & Pantoni, 2014).
6. Total scores on the MoCA for patients who have experienced a stroke, may be indicative of prognosis 3 and 6-months post-stroke (Chiti & Pantoni, 2014). Those who demonstrate poor performance on the MoCA 3 months post-stroke may experience significant long-term effects medically and cognitively.
7. Poor performance on the MoCA is correlated with poor performance on the Mini-Mental Status Exam (MMSE) for those patients meeting the cut-off score for MCI and dementia (Trzepacs et al., 2015).
8. The visuoconstructional tasks (cube and clock drawing) of the MoCA require visuospatial, motor, and executive functioning abilities. If a person has deficits in these areas they would perform poorer on these tasks.
9. A patient with impaired vision, such as a loss of the visual field, may have poor performance on the trail-making, cube drawing, clock drawing, and confrontation naming tasks (Stark et al., 2023).

As mentioned previously, the MoCA has been normed for each version and divides populations into three categories: Normal Controls (NC), Mild Cognitive Impairment (MCI), and Alzheimer's disease (AD). The cutoff score for mild cognitive impairment and Alzheimer's disease is a total score of < 26 points. The authors of the MoCA further break down cognitive impairment into three categories: mild, moderate, and severe cognitive impairments. Mild cognitive impairments are reported to range from 18–25 points, moderate is 10–17 points and severe range is 10 points or less. The test creators note that these specific ranges have not been established yet (Nasreddine 2021).

The MoCA also shows high levels of validity for diverse populations in terms of age, race, and education. However, recent research regarding the norming of the MoCA suggests that the cutoff for mild cognitive impairment should be decreased among populations with lower levels of education and highlights some discrepancies seen among different racial/ethnic groups. The MoCA has also shown high levels of reliability in administration through telehealth. This can be useful for clinicians in administering the MoCA in rural populations that do not have easy access to neuropsychological testing sites. However, it is important that when administering the MoCA via videoconference, the clinician can ensure the examinee can view the test without audio or video connectivity issues.

In differentiating mild cognitive impairments from healthy populations, the MoCA lacks validity and can often misdiagnose people with impairments when they are healthy. Reducing the cutoff for a diagnosis of mild cognitive impairment should decrease the false positives seen throughout different populations. Compared to the MMSE, the MoCA outperforms the MMSE when detecting mild cognitive impairment. However, more research should be conducted to distinguish a valid cutoff for healthy individuals compared to those with mild cognitive impairments.

Nevertheless, the MoCA has proven to be a reliable measure in detecting cognitive impairments in diverse populations. The test can track cognitive decline in patients with Alzheimer's disease, Parkinson's disease, and other neurodegenerative disorders. The MoCA has a high test-retest reliability and validity, making it a useful tool to track cognitive declines.

References

Adamis, D. et al. (2016). Agreement and equation between Mini Mental State Examination (MMSE) and Montreal Cognitive Assessment (MoCA) in an old age psychiatry outpatient clinic population. European Psychiatry, 33: S184.

Badrkhahan, S. Z., Sikaroodi, H., Sharifi, F., Kouti, L. and Noroozian, M. (2019). Validity and reliability of the Persian version of the Montreal Cognitive Assessment (MoCA-P) scale among subjects with Parkinson's disease. Applied Neuropsychology: Adult.

Bruijnen, C. J., Dijkstra, B. A., Walvoort, S. J., Budy, M. J., Beurmanjer, H., De Jong, C. A. et al. (2020). Psychometric properties of the Montreal Cognitive Assessment (MoCA) in healthy participants aged 18–70. International Journal of Psychiatry in Clinical Practice, 24(3): 293–300.

Chiti, G. and Pantoni, L. (2014). Use of Montreal Cognitive Assessment in patients with stroke. Stroke, 45(10): 3135–3140.

Carson, N., Leach, L. and Murphy, K. J. (2018). A re-examination of Montreal Cognitive Assessment (MoCA) cutoff scores. International Journal of Geriatric Psychiatry, 33(2): 379–388.

Cecato, J., Martinelli, J., Montiel, J., Bartholomeu, D. and Aramaki, F. (2014). Discriminative Power of Montreal Cognitive Assessment. JMED Research, 1–10. https://doi.org/10.5171/2014.547274.

Cersonsky, T. E. K., Mechery, S., Carper, M. M., Thompson, L., Lee, A., Alber, J. et al. (2022). Using the Montreal cognitive assessment to identify individuals with subtle cognitive decline. Neuropsychology. Advance online publication. https://doi.org/10.1037/neu0000820.

DeYoung, N. and Shenal, B. V. (2019). The reliability of the Montreal Cognitive Assessment using telehealth in a rural setting with veterans. Journal of Telemedicine and Telecare, 25(4): 197–203.

Dharmasaroja, P. A., Charernboon, T., Assanasen, J., Dejthevaporn, C., Limwongse, C. and Phantumchinda, K. (2020). The Correlation of Thai Mental State Examination (TMSE) and Montreal Cognitive Assessment (MoCA) and Conversion Table. Journal of the Medical Association of Thailand, 103(3): 66.

Elkana, O., Tal, N., Oren, N., Soffer, S. and Ash, E. L. (2020). Is the cutoff of the MoCA too high? Longitudinal data from highly educated older adults. Journal of Geriatric Psychiatry and Neurology, 33(3): 155–160.

Freitas, S., Simoes, M. R., Marôco, J., Alves, L. and Santana, I. (2012). Construct validity of the montreal cognitive assessment (MoCA). Journal of the International Neuropsychological Society, 18(2): 242–250.

Gagnon, G., Hansen, K.T., Woolmore-Goodwin, S., Gutmanis, I., Wells, J., Borrie, M. et al. (2013). Correcting the MoCA for education: effect on sensitivity. Can J. Neurol. Sci., 2013 Sep; 40(5): 678–83. doi:10.1017/s0317167100014918. PMID: 23968941.

Gill, D. J., Freshman, A., Blender, J. A. and Ravina, B. (2008). The Montreal cognitive assessment as a screening tool for cognitive impairment in Parkinson's disease. Movement Disorders: Official Journal of the Movement Disorder Society, 23(7): 1043–1046.

Goldstein, F. C., Ashley, A. V., Miller, E., Alexeeva, O., Zanders, L. and King, V. (2014). Validity of the montreal cognitive assessment as a screen for mild cognitive impairment and dementia in African Americans. Journal of Geriatric Psychiatry and Neurology, 27(3): 199–203.

Goldstein, F. C., Milloy, A., Loring, D. W. and Alzheimer's Disease Neuroimaging Initiative. (2018). Incremental validity of Montreal cognitive assessment index scores in mild cognitive impairment and Alzheimer disease. Dementia and Geriatric Cognitive Disorders, 45(1): 49–55.

Gómez, F., Zunzunegui, M. V., Lord, C., Alvarado, B. and García, A. (2013). Applicability of the MoCA-S test in populations with little education in Colombia. International Journal of Geriatric Psychiatry, 28(8): 813–820.

Kang, J. M., Cho, Y. S., Park, S., Lee, B. H., Sohn, B. K., Choi, C. H. et al. (2018). Montreal cognitive assessment reflects cognitive reserve. BMC Geriatrics, 18(1): 1–8.

Kim, R., Kim, H. J., Kim, A., Jang, M. H., Kim, H. J. and Jeon, B. (2018). Validation of the Conversion between the Mini-Mental State Examination and Montreal Cognitive assessment in Korean Patients with Parkinson's Disease. Journal of Movement Disorders.

Kopecek, M., Bezdicek, O., Sulc, Z., Lukavsky, J. and Stepankova, H. (2017). Montreal Cognitive Assessment and Mini-Mental State Examination reliable change indices in healthy older adults. International Journal of Geriatric Psychiatry, 32(8): 868–875.

Koski, L. (2013). Validity and applications of the Montreal cognitive assessment for the assessment of vascular cognitive impairment. Cerebrovascular Diseases, 36(1): 6–18.

Lam, B., Middleton, L. E., Masellis, M., Stuss, D. T., Harry, R. D., Kiss, A. et al. (2013). Criterion and convergent validity of the Montreal cognitive assessment with screening and standardized neuropsychological testing. Journal of the American Geriatrics Society, 61(12): 2181–2185.

Lee, Y. C., Lin, Y. T. and Chiu, E. C. (2021). A comparison of test-retest reliability of four cognitive screening tools in people with dementia. Disability and Rehabilitation, 1–6.

Luo, H., Andersson, B., Tang, J. Y. and Wong, G. H. (2020). Applying Item Response Theory Analysis to the Montreal Cognitive Assessment in a Low-Education Older Population. Assessment, 1073191118821733.

Malek-Ahmadi, M., Powell, J. J., Belden, C. M., O'Connor, K., Evans, L., Coon, D. W. and Nieri, W. (2015). Age-and education-adjusted normative data for the Montreal Cognitive Assessment (MoCA) in older adults age 70–99. Aging, Neuropsychology, and Cognition, 22(6): 755–761.

McDicken, J. A., Elliott, E., Blayney, G., Makin, S., Ali, M., Larner, A. J. and VISTA-Cognition Collaborators. (2019). Accuracy of the short-form montreal cognitive assessment: systematic review and validation. International Journal of Geriatric Psychiatry, 34(10): 1515–1525.

Milani, S. A., Marsiske, M., Cottler, L. B., Chen, X. and Striley, C. W. (2018). Optimal cutoffs for the Montreal Cognitive Assessment vary by race and ethnicity. Alzheimer's and Dementia: Diagnosis, Assessment and Disease Monitoring, 10: 773–781.

Milanini, B., Wendelken, L. A., Esmaeili-Firidouni, P., Chartier, M., Crouch, P. C. and Valcour, V. (2014). The Montreal Cognitive Assessment (MoCA) to screen for cognitive impairment in HIV over age 60. Journal of Acquired Immune Deficiency Syndromes (1999), 67(1): 67.

Nasreddine, Z. (2021, December 8). Cognitive assessment. MoCA. Retrieved June 14, 2022, from https://www.mocatest.org/.

Nasreddine, Z. (2021, June 17). References: MOCA - cognitive assessment. MoCA. Retrieved June 16, 2022, from https://www.mocatest.org/reference/.

Nasreddine, Z. (2022, February 15). *FAQ:* MOCA - Cognitive Assessment. MoCA. Retrieved June 16, 2022, from https://www.mocatest.org/faq/#:~:text=The%20MoCA%20has%20been%20validated,section%20of%20the%20MoCA%20website.

Nasreddine, Z. S., Phillips, N., Chertkow, H. Normative data for the Montreal Cognitive Assessment (MoCA) in a population-based sample. Neurology. 2012 Mar 6; 78(10): 765–6; author reply 766. doi: 10.1212/01.wnl.0000413072.54070.a3. PMID: 22391608.

Nasreddine, Z. S., Phillips, N. A., Bédirian, V., Charbonneau, S., Whitehead, V., Collin, I. et al. (2005). The Montreal Cognitive Assessment, MoCA: a brief screening tool for mild cognitive impairment. Journal of the American Geriatrics Society, 53(4): 695–699.

Phillips, N. A., Chertkow, H., Pichora-Fuller, M. K. and Wittich, W. (2020). Special issues on using the Montreal Cognitive Assessment for telemedicine assessment during COVID-19. J. Am. Geriatr. Soc., 68(5): 942–944.

Pinto, T. C., Machado, L., Bulgacov, T. M., Rodrigues-Júnior, A. L., Costa, M. L., Ximenes, R. C. et al. (2019). Is the Montreal Cognitive Assessment (MoCA) screening superior to the Mini-Mental State Examination (MMSE) in the detection of mild cognitive impairment (MCI) and Alzheimer's Disease (AD) in the elderly?. International Psychogeriatrics, 31(4): 491–504.

Rosca, E. C., Albarqouni, L. and Simu, M. (2019). Montreal cognitive assessment (MoCA) for HIV-associated neurocognitive disorders. Neuropsychology Review, 29(3): 313–327.

Rossetti, H. C., Lacritz, L. H., Cullum, C. M. and Weiner, M. F. (2011). Normative data for the Montreal Cognitive Assessment (MoCA) in a population-based sample. Neurology, 77(13): 1272–1275.

Stark, Z., Morrice, E., Murphy, C., Wittich, W. and Johnson, A. P. (2023). The effects of simulated and actual visual impairment on the Montreal Cognitive Assessment. Aging, Neuropsychology, and Cognition, 30(4): 523–535.

Tan, J. P., Wang, X., Zhang, S., Zhao, Y., Lan, X., Li, N. et al. (2021). Accuracy of the Short-Form Montreal Cognitive Assessment Chinese Versions. Frontiers in Aging Neuroscience, 324.

Trzepacz, P. T., Hochstetler, H., Wang, S., Walker, B., Saykin, A. J. and Alzheimer's Disease Neuroimaging Initiative. (2015). Relationship between the Montreal Cognitive Assessment and Mini-mental State Examination for assessment of mild cognitive impairment in older adults. BMC Geriatrics, 15: 1–9.

Wong, A., Black, S. E., Yiu, S. Y., Au, L. W., Lau, A. Y., Soo, Y. O. et al. (2018). Converting MMSE to MoCA and MoCA-5-minute protocol in an educationally heterogeneous sample with stroke or transient ischemic attack. International Journal of Geriatric Psychiatry, 33(5): 729–734.

CHAPTER 27

The Repeatable Battery for the Assessment of Neuropsychological Status (RBANS)

Sophia G. Perez

The Repeatable Battery for the Assessment of Neuropsychological Status (RBANS) was originally developed by Christopher Randolph in 1998 to screen the geriatric population for suspected dementia (Shura et al. 2018). When developing the RBANS, Randolph wanted to ensure that the assessment would measure cognitive functions, take less than 30 minutes to administer to increase patient cooperation and decrease fatigue, have an appropriate difficulty level for impairment severity, and have alternate forms for progress monitoring (Randolph et al. 1998). It was designed to be a brief screener for the neurocognitive status of adults between 20 and 89 years old (Yang et al. 2009). However, its use has been expanded to evaluate various neurological and psychiatric conditions utilizing a wider age range (12 to 89 years) (Shura et al. 2018). In 2012, an RBANS Update version was developed to expand the age range to children and adolescents between the ages of 12 and 19 to screen for their neurocognitive status (Randolph 2012). The RBANS consists of 12 subtests across five domains (i.e., Immediate Memory, Visuospatial/Constructional, Language, Attention, and Delayed Memory), contributing to a total score (Shura et al. 2018). Scaled scores are utilized for the subtests (M = 10, SD = 15), and age-based standard scores are used for the index scores (M = 100, SD = 15) (Randolph 2012; Shura et al. 2018).

Nova Southeastern University, Fort Lauderdale, Florida, USA.
Email: sp1857@mynsu.nova.edu

Normed Population

Original RBANS (1998)

Normative scores were developed with a stratified nationally representative sample of 540 participants between the ages of 20 and 89, with each age group consisting of 90 participants (Randolph 2012). Sex, race/ethnicity (i.e., Whites, African Americans, Hispanics, Other), and geographic regions (i.e., northeast = 7.0%, north central = 62.4%, south = 23.7%, and west = 6.9%) were approximates based on the U.S. Census (Randolph 2012). In this sample, the southern region was overrepresented (Randolph 2012), and there were more Whites in comparison to other race/ethnic groups. The sample was stratified into three education levels (i.e., less than high school, equal to high school, and greater than high school) based on the number of years completed at school (Randolph 2012).

RBANS Update (2012)

The normative scores were also developed with a stratified nationally representative sample. The sample consisted of 690 adolescents and adults aged 12 to 89, with 50 participants comprising each age group. This sample had an approximately equal proportion of males and females (Randolph 2012). Race/ethnicity and geographic regions (i.e., northeast = 13.3%, north central = 24%, south = 30.7%, and west = 32%) were also approximated based on the U.S. Census (Randolph 2012). Like the original RBANS, the sample was stratified on three education levels; however, this was based on the parent's education level (Randolph 2012). Like the original version, the RBANS Update was comprised of more Whites than the other race/ethnic groups.

Reliability

Randolph (2012) reported the RBANS average index reliability coefficients ranging from .75 to .93. The reliability coefficients were higher among older adults, possibly due to more ceiling effects and decreased variability in the younger age groups (Randolph 2012). Regarding the 12 subtests of the RBANS, the average subtest reliabilities range from .50 to .85 (Randolph 2012). Subtest reliability is typically lower than index-level reliability (Randolph 2012). Because index scores are considered to be more reliable, the examinee's performance is interpreted with these scores (Randolph 2012).

One study found a strong internal consistency of 0.83 in a sample of moderate to severe Traumatic Brain Injury (TBI) (McKay et al. 2007). The reliability coefficients of the index scores ranged from 0.16 to 0.77, with Attention being the weakest and Delayed Memory being the strongest (McKay et al. 2007). The two weakest indices were Attention (0.16) and Language (0.32) (McKay et al. 2007). Among the Han elderly population with vascular cognitive impairment, the RBANS also exhibits good reliability, with its indices ranging between 0.61 and 0.84, while the total was 0.88 (Zhang et al. 2022). Yang et al. (2009) reported the overall reliability among a group of patients with Parkinson's disease (PD) to be 0.74. The reliabilities of the indices ranged from 0.03 to 0.70, where Language (0.03), Attention (0.13), and Visuospatial/Constructional (0.32) appeared to be the weakest (Yang et al. 2009). This may suggest that further research is needed on the utility of the RBANS for PD (Yang et al. 2009). De la Torre and colleagues (2016) assessed for cognitive impairment within a Spanish sample of healthy controls and participants diagnosed with schizophrenia. Overall, the Spanish-translated Form A of the RBANS produced a reliability coefficient of 0.79 (De la Torre et al. 2016).

Research translating the RBANS into different languages has also produced good internal consistency. Among a group of older adults in the Chinese community, the Chinese version of the RBANS produced an internal consistency of 0.80 (Cheng et al. 2009). Index scores on this version had coefficients ranging from 0.14 to 0.72, with the Language (0.14) and Attention (0.30) indices producing the weakest reliability (Cheng et al. 2009). Safaz and colleagues (2015) reported the internal consistency of their Turkish-translated RBANS to be 0.86. For the indices, test-retest coefficients ranged from 0.59 to 0.88 and from 0.45 to 0.93 for the subtests (Safaz et al. 2015). De la Torre and colleagues (2014) conducted a study to obtain psychometric properties of a Spanish-language adaptation of the RBANS Form A with healthy participants (N=336) and participants with Alzheimer's disease (AD) (N=50). The Spanish version of the RBANS produced an excellent reliability of 0.92 and a stability test coefficient of 0.90 (De la Torre 2014). Their research suggests their Spanish-language version of the RBANS has good overall internal consistency and reliability with acceptable psychometric properties (De la Torre 2014).

Validity

Zhang et al. (2022) found that the total scores of the RBANS and the Mini Mental State Exam (MMSE) were positively correlated. Each score on the MMSE was found to be positively correlated with the RBANS, while multiple dimensions from the RBANS were correlated to most of those in the MMSE. This indicates that this has good parallel validity, and the researchers found the measure to have overall good validity in the cognitive dysfunction of VCIs in the elderly population (Zhang et al. 2022). Their finding was similar to the study of Cheng et al. (2009), which also found the RBANS subtests had strong correlations with those of the MMSE. The Total Scale score of the RBANS was highly correlated with the total of the MMSE at 0.59 (Cheng et al. 2009). Randolph (2012) found a correlation of 0.78 between the RBANS Total Scale score and the Wechsler Adult Intelligence Scale-Revised (WAIS-R) Full Scale Intelligence Quotient among a sample consisting mostly of patients with dementia. It was indicated that in comparison to the WAIS-R, the RBAMS had greater sensitivity in acquired neurocognitive impairment (Randolph 2012).

Duff et al. (2010) noted there was good specificity but poor to moderate sensitivity, suggesting that because of its low sensitivity, there should be caution in utilizing the RBANS to diagnose mild cognitive impairment (MCI), such as amnestic MCI. De la Torre and colleagues (2014) found high specificity (95.54%), indicating that their version can be effective in identifying negative cases (individuals without AD). However, their sensitivity was low (30%), suggesting difficulty in identifying cases of those with AD (De la Torre 2014). Randolph has suggested that the RBANS is sensitive to AD as well as detecting and characterizing dementia, AD and Huntington's disease specifically (Randolph 1998; Randolph 2012). Duff and colleagues (2008) also supported the clinical utility of the measure in detecting the cognitive deficits related to AD. While in a sample of PD, the RBANS can help in identifying cognitive impairment patterns in AD and PD only if a dementia diagnosis is provided independently from the RBANS (Beatty 2003). The RBANS also demonstrated strong sensitivity (87.5%) and specificity (86.4%) in a study of schizophrenia, suggesting that it can correctly identify cases of schizophrenia and those without schizophrenia (De la Torre et al. 2016). In a moderate to severe traumatic brain injury sample, sensitivity was 82%, and specificity was 94% (McKay et al. 2008). The sensitivity of the RBANS' index scores was modest yet clinically adequate, whereas the specificity was acceptable (McKay et al. 2008).

Test Procedures

The 12 subtests of the RBANS should be administered in the order they appear on the Record Form. For the List Learning subtest, the examinee is required to recall a list of ten words (Randolph 2012). The examiner should read each word aloud every 1.5 seconds and is prohibited from providing feedback to the examinee (Randolph 2012). During the Story Memory subtest, examiners must read the story slightly slower than conversational speed and should refrain from providing the examinee with feedback (Randolph 2012). On the Figure Copy subtest, the examinee should reproduce an image in the stimulus book on the Record Form's appropriate page (Randolph 2012). With the Line Orientation subtest, examinees are provided only feedback for the sample items. They proceed to the remaining items once they understand the task but are prohibited from moving the stimulus book during the subtest (Randolph 2012). For the Picture Naming subtest, examinees must name each picture and are given a semantic cue if they misperceive the image (Randolph 2012). On Semantic Fluency, the examinee provides the appropriate answers based on the category provided to them (Randolph 2012). During Digit Span, examiners are required to provide the string of digits to the examinee at the rate of one second per number and are prohibited from repeating any digits (Randolph 2012). If the first string of digits was incorrect in any item, examiners should administer the second string. This subtest is the only one with a discontinue rule (i.e., failure of both strings within an item). On Coding, examiners should read instructions verbatim, demonstrate how to complete the first three items, and redirect the examinee to the task if they appear distracted (Randolph 2012). On the recall subtests (i.e., List Recall, List Recognition, Story Recall, Figure Recall), examiners should read the instructions on the Record Form and record the examinee's responses without providing feedback.

Scoring

For most subtests, one point is provided for each correct response that the examinee offers, where the total score of the subtest can be obtained by adding the totals of the items. The Figure Copy subtest scored 1 point on each portion of the figure, which is based on the exactness of the reproduced image as opposed to the time it takes the examinee to complete the task (Randolph 2012). For Semantic Fluency, four points get added to the examinee's total score if they were administered Stimulus Booklets B and C (Randolph 2012). Although the items correct on Digit Span are given one point, the first correct string is given two points (Randolph 2012). The Coding subtest requires a template to determine correct and incorrect items, but the overall score should be given only for responses provided within 90 seconds (Randolph 2012). Subtests measuring recall are also scored with one point per each correct item.

Clinical Applications

The RBANS can evaluate various neurological and psychiatric conditions of individuals between 12 and 89 years old (Shura et al. 2018). As previously mentioned, past studies have utilized the RBANS in clinical populations such as those diagnosed with AD, PD, TBI, and schizophrenia. Randolph suggested that the measure can be utilized as a screener for cognitive deficits in acute-care settings, tracking recovery throughout rehabilitation and progression of the condition, and it can be performed by non-neuropsychologists (Yang et al. 2009), demonstrating the measure's versatile functioning.

Interpretations

Almost 70% of examinees score between 85 and 115, which is considered to be one standard deviation below and above the mean (Randolph 2012). Also, 95% of examinees score in the 70 to 130 range, which is two standard deviations below and above the mean, and almost all of the examinees score 55 and 145 or three standard deviations (Randolph 2012). While interpreting the RBANS index scores, the examinee's education level should be considered, as low scores may suggest different things (Randolph 2012). For instance, low average scores may be consistent with an individual with limited education but may suggest concerns if someone with a higher education level obtains low scores (Randolph 2012).

1. Scores can be measured against the client's general intelligence results, such as the WAIS tests, or against an estimated premorbid intelligence. The RBANS Total Scale functioning can indicate cognitive functioning where low scores suggest difficulties with attention, memory, language, and constructional skills (Randolph 2012).
2. The Immediate Memory Index assesses the examinee's ability to encode and learn simple and complex information (Randolph 2012). Low scores may suggest challenges with verbal learning; however, language deficits can contribute to low scores as they impact processing and storage (Randolph 2012).
3. The Visuospatial/Constructional Index measures visuospatial perception and copying designs from models (Randolph 2012). Low scores in this index can signify problems with processing and utilizing visuospatial information but can

also be attributable to visual impairments or attentional disorders (Randolph 2012).

4. The Attentional Index of the RBANS examines simple auditory registration, visual scanning, and processing speed (Randolph 2012). Within this index, low scores can suggest issues with attention and the speed of information processing, and problems with language, auditory processing, and visual function can affect this (Randolph 2012).
5. The Language Index assesses expressive language with low scores suggesting difficulties in fluently using language or language impairment (Randolph 2012). Receptive language impairments can potentially influence the score of this index (Randolph 2012).
6. The Delayed Memory Recall Index measures delayed recall and the recognition of both verbal and visual information, with low scores indicative of difficulties in recognition and long-memory retrieval (Randolph, 2012). However, factors such as language, auditory processing, and visual functioning deficits can affect an examinee's score (Randolph 2012).
7. A difference of at least one standard deviation (15) from the client's global score should exist between individual scores before concluding that a weakness or strength may be present in a given area.

References

Cheng, Y., Li, C. and Wu, W. (2009). Reliability and validity of the chinese version of repeatable battery for the assessment of neuropsychological status (RBANS) in community elderly. Chinese Journal of Clinical Psychology, 17(5): 535–537.

Beatty, W. W., Ryder, K. A., Gontkovsky, S. T., Scott, J. G., McSwan, K. L. and Bharucha, K. J. (2003). Analyzing the subcortical dementia syndrome of Parkinson's disease using the RBANS. Archives of clinical neuropsychology: the official journal of the National Academy of Neuropsychologists, 18(5): 509–520.

De la Torre, G. G., Perez, M. J., Ramallo, M. A., Randolph, C. and González-Villegas, M. B. (2016). Screening of cognitive impairment in schizophrenia: Reliability, sensitivity, and specificity of the Repeatable Battery for the Assessment of Neuropsychological Status in a Spanish sample. Assessment, 23(2): 221–231.

De la Torre, G. G., Suárez-Llorens, A., Caballero, F. J., Ramallo, M. A., Randolph, C., Lleó, A. et al. (2014). Norms and reliability for the Spanish version of the Repeatable Battery for the Assessment of Neuropsychological Status (RBANS) Form A. Journal of Clinical and Experimental Neuropsychology, 36(10): 1023–1030. https://doi.org/10.1080/13803395.2014.965664.

Duff, K., Hobson, V. L., Beglinger, L. J. and O'Bryant, S. E. (2010). Diagnostic accuracy of the RBANS in mild cognitive impairment: limitations on assessing milder impairments. Archives of clinical neuropsychology: the official journal of the National Academy of Neuropsychologists, 25(5): 429–441. https://doi.org/10.1093/arclin/acq045.

Duff, K., Humphreys Clark, J.D., O'Bryant, S.E., Mold, J.W., Schiffer, R. and Sutker, P.B. (2008). Utility of the RBANS in detecting cognitive impairment associated with Alzheimer's disease: sensitivity, specificity, and positive and negative predictive powers. Archives of Clinical Neuropsychology: The Official Journal of the National Academy of Neuropsychologists, 23(5): 603–12.

McKay, C., Casey, J. E., Wertheimer, J. C. and Fichtenberg, N. L. (2007). Reliability and validity of the RBANS in a traumatic brain injured sample. Archives of Clinical Neuropsychology: The Official Journal of the National Academy of Neuropsychologists, 22(1): 91–8.

McKay, C., Wertheimer, J. C., Fichtenberg, N. L. and Casey, J. E. (2008). The Repeatable Battery for The Assessment of Neuropsychological Status (RBANS): Clinical utility in a traumatic brain injury sample. The Clinical Neuropsychologist, 22(2): 228–241. DOI:10.1080/13854040701260370.

Randolph, C., Tierney, M. C., Mohr, E. and Chase, T. N. (1998) The Repeatable Battery for the Assessment of Neuropsychological Status (RBANS): Preliminary clinical validity. Journal of Clinical and Experimental Neuropsychology, 20(3): 310–319, DOI: 10.1076/jcen.20.3.310.823.

Randolph, C. (2012). Repeatable Battery for the Assessment of Neuropsychological Status: Manual. The Psychological Corporation.

Safaz, I., Kurt, M., Cakir, G., Yasar, E. and Alaca, R. (2015). Test-retest reliability and practice effects of the Turkish version of repeatable battery for the assessment of neuropsychological status (RBANS) in healthy persons. Klinik Psikofarmakoloji Bülteni/Bulletin of Clinical Psychopharmacology, 25(3): 243–247. doi:https://doi.org/10.5455/bcp.20150207075550.

Shura, R. D., Brearly, T. W., Rowland, J. A., Martindale, S. L., Miskey, H. M. and Duff, K. (2018). RBANS validity indices: A systematic review and meta-analysis. Neuropsychology Review, 28(3): 269–284. https://doi.org/10.1007/s11065-018-9377-5.

Yang, C., Garrett-Mayer, E., Schneider, J. S., Gollomp, S. M. and Tilley, B. C. (2009). Repeatable battery for assessment of neuropsychological status in early Parkinson's disease. Movement Disorders, 24(10): 1453–1460. doi: 10.1002/mds.22552.

Zhang, C. Y., Deng, Y. M., Li, D. M., Shi, Q. Y., Yang, X. P., Zhao, Y. H. et al. (2022). Reliability and validity of the repeatable battery for assessment of neuropsychological status scale in evaluation of vascular cognitive impairment in elderly Han population. Noro Psikiyatri Arsivi, 59(2): 147–150. https://doi.org/10.29399/npa.27854.

Section IV
Computer Batteries

CHAPTER 28

CNS Vital Signs

Claire Stafford

CNS Vital Signs is a computerized neuropsychological assessment battery, lasting approximately 30 minutes, that evaluates a variety of cognitive processes. The "brief-core" battery consists of ten normed subtests: Verbal Memory (VBM), Visual Memory (VIM), Finger Tapping (FTT), Symbol Digit Coding (SDC), Stroop Test (ST), Shifting Attention Test (SAT) and the Continuous Performance Test (CPT). Three additional tests can be administered, including the Perception of Emotions (POET), Non-Verbal Reasoning (NVRT), and 4-Part Continuous Performance (FPCPT). These subtests automatically yield composite scores of assessed cognitive domains as well as a global neurocognitive test score. These five cognitive domains include memory, psychomotor speed, reaction time, cognitive flexibility, and complex attention. These stimuli are presented to individuals in a random order. CNS Vital Signs should not be used in isolation as they are not diagnostic. Patient history, physical examinations, and other neuropsychological assessment scores should be considered as well. The test can be administered by medical technicians, both in person and virtually, and is available in more than 50 languages.

Normed Population

CNS Vital Signs was normed using a large sample (N = 1662), ranging in age from 8 to 90. In the age-matched normative sample, subjects are in good health, have no previous or current neurological disorders, head injury, or learning disabilities, and are free of centrally acting medications. All individuals were based in the United States. For the purposes of comparison, normative data is presented in ten age groups: less than 10 years old, 10 to 14, 15 to 19, in deciles to 79, and 80 years and older. Standard scores have a mean of 100 and a standard deviation of 15. These age-matched norms help to determine the impairment status score, which evaluates the severity level. The severity classifications range from very low, indicating a high likelihood of deficit and impairment, to above average, indicating a high functioning

Nova Southeastern University, Fort Lauderdale, Florida, USA.
Email: cs3374@mynsu.nova.edu

and cognitive capacity level. The severity classifications are as follows: above average (greater than 74th percentile), average (25 to 74th percentile), low average (9 to 24th percentile), low (2 to 8th percentile), and very low (less than 2nd percentile).

Reliability

Studies looking at test-retest reliability showed that age and clinical status had little to no impact on reliability. Additionally, there is little ceiling and practice effect. Higher age is associated with lower scores on processing speed, psychomotor speed, reaction time, and cognitive flexibility but has little bearing on reliability. Individuals with higher levels of education performed better on tests of visual memory, processing speed, and cognitive flexibility when compared to individuals of middle and lower educational levels. Women were found to perform higher on tests of verbal memory, and men were found to perform higher on tests of psychomotor speed. Interpretations of CNS Vital Signs should be approached with caution due to the use of American norms and potential moderation of age, education, and sex (Rinjen et al. 2020).

Validity

CNS Vital Signs includes a validity indicator as part of the scored report. This measure helps alert the clinician whether the assessment may be invalid. Invalidity may be due to a lack of effort or other clinical conditions. It is important to note that this score does not determine validity but rather notifies the clinician that the scores should be reviewed and reevaluated if found to be necessary. When compared to PVTs, such as the TOMM, sensitivity on CNS Vital Signs embedded validity indicators was moderate, but there was often low sensitivity for identifying possible poor effort (Brooks et al. 2014).

Overall, the CNS Vital Signs were found to be fairly resistant to the effects of gender (Iverson et al. 2014). The only exception was the Finger Tapping Test, in which men scored significantly higher than women (64.73 versus 62.48) (Heaton et al. 2020). This may be due to differences in finger length, which can predict performance on this subtest. Rijnen et al. (2020) compared CNS Vital Signs normative data with healthy Dutch individuals and found significant performance disparities between the two groups on tests of processing speed, psychomotor speed, and cognitive flexibility. The Dutch individuals were found to perform higher on these subtests. Rijnen et al. (2020) found age, education, and sex to be significant predictors of performance on the CNS Vital Signs.

CNS Vital Signs is a computerized measure with competent test-retest reliability and concurrent validity with other computerized measures as well as conventional paper and pencil measures. Computer skills, however, have greatly developed over the past ten years, which may contribute to heightened performance on computerized assessments (Iverson et al. 2009).

In a sample of patients following brain injury, CNS Vital Signs yielded concurrent validity with other computerized cognitive assessments (Lanting et al. 2012). These tests included the Neuropsychological Assessment Battery, the Reynolds Intellectual Screening Test, and the Wechsler Test of Adult Reading. Test performance was compared in subjects on the CNS Vital Signs to performance on traditional neuropsychological assessments, such as the Rey Auditory Verbal Learning Test, Logical Memory and Facial Recognition from the Wechsler Memory Test, a mechanical finger tapper, the Stroop Test, Trails B and the Verbal Fluency Test, and computerized neurocognitive tests, including Finger Tapping, Switching Attention, and the Continuous Performance Test (Baker 1985). Moderate correlations were found between memory, perceptual-motor speed, and executive function tests on the traditional assessments and psychomotor speed and executive function on the computerized tests. Low correlations, however, were seen between the CPT in CNS Vital Signs and the computerized assessment.

CNS Vital Signs was found to be a valid screener for patients with COPD (Campman, van Ranst et al. 2017). Completion rates of the assessment were high, and scores were congruent to those of paper and pencil measures. Computer experience, however, was found to impede assessment performance. Clinicians should evaluate computer use prior to administration to avoid variability in scores.

As per the interpretation manual, certain factors can affect CNS Vital Signs scores. These factors include normal aging, education, special skills, and effort. In a discussion of ADHD diagnosis, CNS Vital Signs have been found to be a poor indicator. CNS Vital Signs include a continuous performance test (CPT); however, CPTs are measures of sustained attention and cannot be used to determine ADHD because they are not representative of all of the symptomology experienced by individuals with ADHD, such as changes in working memory, motor speed, and executive control.

Test Procedures

The "brief-core" battery of CNS Vital Signs consists of ten normed subtests: Verbal Memory (VBM), Visual Memory (VIM), Finger Tapping (FTT), Symbol Digit Coding (SDC), Stroop Test (ST), Shifting Attention Test (SAT) and the Continuous Performance Test (CPT). Three additional tests can be administered, including the Perception of Emotions (POET), Non-Verbal Reasoning (NVRT), and 4-Part Continuous Performance (FPCPT).

The Verbal Memory Test assesses how well subjects can recognize, remember, and retrieve words, with both an immediate and delayed portion. Fifteen words are presented, one at a time, on the screen every two seconds. During the learning phase or immediate recognition, the participant must identify those words confounded among 15 new words. Following six more tests, participants are administered a delayed recognition memory trial. The Visual Memory Test is similarly administered but measures how well the subject can recognize, remember, and retrieve 15 geometric figures while among distractor images. There is both a delayed and immediate portion of this test as well. During the immediate recognition phase, the participant must identify those figures confounded among 15 new figures. Five additional tests and a delayed recognition memory trial are administered.

The Finger Tapping test assesses motor speed and fine motor control. Participants are asked to tap the space bar as often as possible within a 10-second. Three rounds of tapping are completed with each hand while the speed and number of taps are measured. The Symbol Digit Coding test measures processing speed and other cognitive processes, such as visual scanning, perception, memory, and motor functions. This test consists of serial presentations of screens, each containing a bank of eight symbols above and eight empty boxes below. The participant types in the number on the number row corresponding to the symbol that is highlighted.

The Stroop Test assesses reaction times, inhibition, and attention. The Stroop Test has three parts. In the first part, the words red, yellow, blue, and green are printed in black and appear randomly on the screen. The participant is asked to press the space bar when they see the word. In the second part, the same words appear on the screen but are printed in color. The participant is asked to press the space bar when the color of the word matches what the word says. The same words appear on the screen in the third part, still printed in color. The participant is asked to press the space bar when the color of the word does not match the corresponding word.

The Shifting Attention Test assesses executive functioning and mental flexibility. Within this subtest, subjects are required to adjust their responses in accordance with changing rules. Participants are instructed to match geometric objects either by shape or by color. Three figures appear on the screen, one on top and two on the bottom. The top figure is either a square or a circle. The bottom figures are a square and a circle. The figures are either red or blue. The participant is asked to match one of the bottom figures to the top figure. The rules change randomly, and the participant is expected to adjust their responses accordingly.

The CPT measures vigilance or sustained attention or attention over time. Participants are asked to respond to the target stimulus "B" but not any other letter. The stimuli are presented at random. The POET assesses the participant's ability to perceive and identify specific emotions. Participants are asked to identify given emotional illustrations.

The NVRT measures how well a subject perceives and understands the meaning of visual or abstract information and recognizes relationships between visual and abstract concepts. The subtest consists of 15 visual analogies upon which the participants are asked to make conclusions. The analogies are progressively more difficult.

The 4PCPT is a four-part test that measures a subject's working memory and sustained attention. In part one, participants are administered a simple reaction time test. Part 2 is like the CPT, but the reaction times generated are choice reaction times with multiple stimuli. In Part 3, participants are told to respond to a figure only if the preceding figure is the same. In Part 4, participants are instructed to provide a response to a figure only if it matches the figure two positions back.

Scoring

Ten brief-core clinical domain scores are calculated following CNS Vital Signs administration. The neurocognition index (NCI), or a global score of neurocognition, is determined by taking the average of the five domain scores: composite memory, psychomotor speed, reaction time, complex attention, and complex flexibility. A composite memory score is calculated using the sum of VBM Correct Hits Immediate, VBM Correct Passes Immediate, VBM Correct Hits Delay, VBM Correct Passes

Delay, VIM Correct Hits Immediate, VIM Correct Passes Immediate, VIM Correct Hits Delay, and VIM Correct Passes Delay. A verbal memory score is calculated using the sum of VBM Correct Hits Immediate, VBM Correct Passes Immediate, VBM Correct Hits Delay, and VBM Correct Passes Delay. A visual memory score is calculated using the sum of VIM Correct Hits Immediate, VIM Correct Passes Immediate, VIM Correct Hits Delay, and VIM Correct Passes Delay. The sum of the FTT Right Taps Average, FTT Left Taps Average, and SDC Correct Responses determines a psychomotor speed score. A reaction time score is determined by the average of the ST Complex Reaction Time Correct and Stroop Reaction Time Correct. The sum of Stroop Commission Errors, SAT Errors, CPT Commission Errors, and CPT Omission Errors determines a complex attention score. A cognitive flexibility score is determined by SAT correct responses minus SAT errors minus Stroop Commission Errors. Processing speed scores are determined by the difference between SDC correct responses and SDC errors. Executive function scores are determined by the difference between SAT correct responses and SAT errors. A simple attention score is calculated using Continuous Performance (CPT) Correct Responses minus CPT commission errors. Motor function scores are calculated using the sum of the Finger Tapping Test Right Taps Average and Finger Tapping Test Left Taps Average.

Additional clinical domain scores can be calculated outside the brief-core battery, including working memory, sustained attention, social acuity, and non-verbal reasoning. Working memory scores differ between 4PCPT Part 4 Correct Responses and 4PCPT Part 4 Incorrect Responses. Sustained attention scores are calculated using the difference between the sum of 4PCPT Part 2 Correct Responses, 4PCPT Part 3 Correct Responses, and 4PCPT Part 4 Correct Responses and the sum of 4PCPT Part 2 Incorrect Responses, 4PCPT Part 3 Incorrect Responses, and 4PCPT Part 4 Incorrect Responses. Social acuity scores differ between POET Correct Responses and POET Commission Errors. Non-verbal reasoning scores are calculated using the difference between NVRT Correct Responses and NVRT Commission Errors.

Item Difficulty and Types of Errors

Errors in the Stroop subtest may result from impulsive tendencies, misperception, and confusion. Higher reaction times may indicate cognitive deficits. Errors in this subtest, like the Symbol Digit Coding test, may result from impulsive tendencies, misperception, and confusion. Optimal Shifting Attention Test scores have several high correct responses, a low number of errors, and short reaction times. Individuals with perfectionist tendencies may be accurate but have slow reaction times.

The Continuous Performance Test assesses sustained attention, vigilance, and reaction time. *C* on the CPT measures the subject's response style in tasks requiring prioritization of either speed or accuracy. Respondents will prioritize accuracy over speed, speed over accuracy, or appear unbiased toward either speed or accuracy. These priorities are important to note as they can affect scores, such as Commissions and Hit Reaction Time. The percentage of commissions or incorrect responses to non-targets, when combined with hit reaction times, can have clinical implications. High commission error rates combined with slow reaction times can indicate that the subject was inattentive to the stimulus type being presented and, as a result, responded to a high rate of non-targets. High commission error rates and fast reaction times may indicate that the subject was rushing to respond and was impulsive in responding to non-targets. Normal subjects usually score close to perfect on this subtest. Longer response times may indicate cognitive impairment. More than four errors indicate attentional dysfunction.

Task Demands and Strategies

Verbal memory requires verbal learning, word recognition, word memory, and immediate and delayed recall. Visual memory requires image memory and immediate and delayed recall. The Finger-Tapping test requires motor speed and fine motor control. The Symbol Digit Coding test requires information processing speed, complex attention, visual-perception speed, and information processing speed. The Stroop Test requires selective attention. The SAT requires executive functioning and sustained attention. CPT tasks demand sustained visual attention, choice reaction time, and impulsivity.

Clinical Applications in Research

Often, CNS Vital Signs is used in cases of concussion management. Consistent across several studies reporting high neurocognitive recovery outcomes of mild TBI cases, patients with MTBIs do not differ from controls 6 to 8 weeks following injury (Lanting et al. 2012). Headaches, a common symptom in concussions, are unrelated to CNS Vital Signs performance (Moreno et al. 2019). "Sandbagging," or purposefully obtaining low scores on baseline neurocognitive assessments so that it is easier to return to play, is a common issue that arises in assessments of concussion diagnosis and management. Anderson et al. (2019) examined the CNS validity indicator accuracy in detecting coached sandbagging compared to controls. The CNS invalidity criteria can detect most sandbagging behaviors, with 32% going undetected.

Further, CNS Vital Signs severity scores have been found to reliably aid in diagnosing Huntington's disease, with keen insight into the specific stage of disease development (King et al. 2011).

Interpretations

There are a variety of clinical interpretations that should be considered both overall and within each subtest. Baseline computer skills should be evaluated prior to administration to ensure that computer skills do not confound test performance.

1. Computer tests, in general, make qualitative observation more difficult. This is especially true if the session is not monitored by a clinician. In such cases, individual variations may occur due to environmental distractions, coughing, sneezing, pain, or other factors without the clinician recognizing that a score may be invalidated.

2. Moderately lower composite scores on psychomotor speed, processing speed, simple attention, and motor speed may suggest non-amnestic MCI.
3. Solely significantly lower composite verbal memory scores may indicate amnestic MCI.
4. Lower scores on visual memory and visual-spatial tasks, along with relatively intact verbal memory and processing speed, might suggest difficulties linked to conditions affecting visual-spatial processing or other perceptual disorders.
5. Low scores on the Finger Tapping test indicate slow motor function. Most individuals show slower motor functioning in their non-dominant hands.
6. Lower scores on motor speed and coordination tasks without significant deficits in other cognitive domains might reflect isolated motor impairment, which could be related to conditions affecting motor control or coordination.
7. Significantly lower composite processing speed, simple attention, and slightly lower psychomotor speed scores may indicate ADHD.
8. Lower scores in processing and motor speed tasks may indicate difficulties in quickly processing information and executing motor actions. This profile may be seen in conditions impacting cognitive and motor functions, such as neurological disorders or brain injuries.
9. Individuals with low SAT scores may have difficulty planning and organizing future tasks simultaneously and independently.
10. Lower scores in tasks assessing selective attention but relatively intact scores in other domains may indicate a deficit in one's ability to focus on relevant stimuli while filtering out distractions.
11. Low scores on the POET might indicate that the individual has a lower capability to interpret social and emotional cues in their environment (Arsalidou et al. 2011).
12. Relatively higher scores on NVRT, when compared to verbal reasoning scores, may suggest that an individual is better at comprehending visual information, such as pictures and diagrams.
13. Low scores on FPCPT may suggest that the individual has difficulty focusing on a task while in deep thought. These individuals may have difficulty planning and executing tasks that require immediate attention.

References

Anderson, M. N., Lempke, L. B., Bell, D. H., Lynall, R. C. and Schmidt, J. D. (2020). The ability of CNS vital signs to detect coached sandbagging performance during concussion baseline testing: a randomized control trial. Brain Injury, 34(3): 369–374.

Arsalidou, M., Morris, D. and Taylor, M. J. (2011). Converging evidence for the advantage of dynamic facial expressions. Brain Topography, 24(2): 149–163.

Baker, E. L. (1985). A computer-based neurobehavioral evaluation system for occupational and environmental epidemiology: methodology and validation studies. Neurobehavioral Toxicology and Teratology.

Bojar, I., Wójcik-Fatla, A., Owoc, A. and Lewiński, A. (2012). Polymorphisms of apolipoprotein Egene and cognitive functions of postmenopausal women, measured by battery of computer tests–Central Nervous System Vital Signs. Neuroendocrinology Letters, 33(4).

Brooks, B. L., Sherman, E. M. and Iverson, G. L. (2014). Embedded validity indicators on CNS vital signs in youth with neurological diagnoses. Archives of clinical neuropsychology : the official journal of the National Academy of Neuropsychologists, 29(5): 422–431.

Brooks, B. L., Plourde, V., Fay-McClymont, T. B., MacAllister, W. S. and Sherman, E. (2019). Factor structure of the CNS Vital Signs computerized cognitive battery in youth with neurological diagnoses. Child Neuropsychology: a Journal on Normal and Abnormal Development in Childhood and Adolescence, 25(7): 980–991. https://doi.org/10.1080/09297049.2019.1569609.

Campman, C., van Ranst, D., Meijer, J. W. and Sitskoorn, M. (2017). Computerized screening for cognitive impairment in patients with COPD. International Journal of Chronic Obstructive Pulmonary Disease, 3075–3083.

CNS Vital Signs, LLC. Frequently asked questions. https://www.cnsvs.com/FAQs.html.

Evers, A., Sijtsma, K., Lucassen, W. and Meijer, R. R. (2010). The Dutch review process for evaluating the quality of psychological tests: History, procedure, and results. International Journal of Testing, 10(4): 295–317.

Ford, C. B., Rodrigo, C. J., Guskiewicz, K. M. and Mihalik, J. P. (2017). Evaluation of domain and factor structure of CNS Vital Signs. Journal of Athletic Training, 52(6): S235.

Gualtieri, C. T. and Johnson, L. G. (2006). Reliability and validity of a computerized neurocognitive test battery, CNS Vital Signs. Archives of Clinical Neuropsychology, 21(7): 623–643.

Heaton, A., Gooding, A., Cherner, M., Umlauf, A., Franklin, D. R., Rivera Mindt, M. et al. (2021). Demographically-adjusted norms for the Grooved Pegboard and Finger Tapping tests in Spanish-speaking adults: Results from the Neuropsychological Norms for the U.S.-Mexico Border Region in Spanish (NP-NUMBRS) Project. The Clinical Neuropsychologist, 35(2): 396–418. https://doi.org/10.1080/13854046.2020.1713400

Iverson, G. L., Brooks, B. L. and Ashton Rennison, V. L. (2014). Minimal gender differences on the CNS vital signs computerized neurocognitive battery. Applied Neuropsychology: Adult, 21(1): 36–42.

Iverson, G. L., Brooks, B., Ashton, V., Johnson, L. and Gualtieri, T. (2009). Does familiarity with computers affect computerized neuropsychological test performance? Journal of Clinical and Experimental Neuropsychology 31(5): 594–604.

Iverson, G. L., Brooks, B. L., Weiss, M. D., Gualtieri, C. T. and Johnson, L. G. (2007). Clinical Usefulness of CNS Vital Signs for Assessing Neurocognition in ADHD. The Clinical Neuropsychologist, 21(4): 686.

Jones, R. (2011). Test-Retest Reliability and Effort on the CNS-Vital Signs Assessment. Regent University.

King, A. L. S., Valença, A. M., Cerqueira, A. C., Ferraz, L. M. C. and Nardi, A. E. (2011). Huntington's disease: Two-year observational follow-up of executive function evaluation with CNS vital signs test in an adult patient. Case Reports in Medicine, 2011.

Lanting, S. C., Iverson, G. L. and Lange, R. T. (2012, October). Concurrent validity of CNS Vital Signs in patients with mild traumatic brain injury. In American Congress of Rehabilitation Medicine Conference.

Lanting, S. C., Iverson, G. L. and Lange, R. T. (2012, October). Comparing patients with mild traumatic brain injury to trauma controls on CNS Vital Signs. In Poster presented at the American Congress of Rehabilitation Medicine Conference, Vancouver, British Columbia, Canada.

Littleton, A. C., Register-Mihalik, J. K. and Guskiewicz, K. M. (2015). Test-retest reliability of a computerized concussion test: CNS Vital Signs. Sports Health, 7(5): 443–447.

Moreno, C. C., Houck, Z., Svingos, A., Greif, S., Hromas, G., Jaffee, M. et al. (2019). Effects of Headache on CNS Vital Signs Performance in a Concussed Community Sample. Archives of Clinical Neuropsychology, 34(5): 783–783.

Rijnen, S., Meskal, I., Emons, W., Campman, C., van der Linden, S. D., Gehring, K. et al. (2020). Evaluation of Normative Data of a Widely Used Computerized Neuropsychological Battery: Applicability and Effects of Sociodemographic Variables in a Dutch Sample. Assessment, 27(2): 373–383. https://doi.org/10.1177/1073191117727346.

Rijnen, S. J., van der Linden, S. D., Emons, W. H., Sitskoorn, M. M., and Gehring, K. (2018). Repeated neuropsychological assessment using CNS Vital Signs. Prediction of cognitive outcome after surgery in patients with meningiomas and gliomas, 30(12): 49.

van der Linden, S. D., Rijnen, S. J. M., Emons, W. H. M., Sitskoorn, M. M. and Gehring, K. (2017). Test-retest reliability and practice effects of the computerized neuropsychological test battery CNS Vital Signs: Evaluation in a Dutch healthy sample. JINS. Journal of the International Neuropsychological Society, 23(supp. 2).

CHAPTER 29

Immediate Post-concussion Assessment and Cognitive Testing

*Christina Nuñez** and *Alexis Rosen*

The Immediate Post-concussion Assessment and Cognitive Testing (ImPACT) is a computerized battery of assessments used to help clinicians assess the impact of a concussion by assessing cognitive functioning following an injury. It was not designed to diagnose or determine treatment for concussion but rather to aid clinical determination. There are both adult and pediatric versions available. The FDA cleared ImPACT as a safe and effective medical device with support from over 250 peer-reviewed articles. Over half of the articles resulted from independent researchers. ImPACT was framed on the traditional neuropsychological testing standards outlined by the American Academy of Clinical Neuropsychology and the National Academy of Neuropsychology. ImPACT is comprised of baseline and post-concussion measures, which were designed to assess specific cognitive skills that are associated with concussions.

Normed Population

The ImPACT normative data is comprised of 17,013 individuals ages 10–59. The sample included 12,335 males and 4,678 females. The sample was drawn from high school and college students across the United States. Although not demographically sampled according to the US census, the sample was comprised of minorities based on the ratio present in the sampled school systems. There was no significant difference between the performance of minority athletes when compared to white athletes.

Nova Southeastern University, Fort Lauderdale, Florida, USA.
Email: ar3516@mynsu.nova.edu
* Corresponding author: cn584@mynsu.nova.edu

Athletes participated in one or more of the following sports: football, cheerleading, soccer, lacrosse, wrestling, baseball, softball, swimming, diving, rowing, volleyball, track and field, and cross country. The sample of older adults was selected from adult athletes, coaches, school administrators, and nurses.

Reliability

Internal Consistency

Very few studies evaluated the internal consistency of ImPACT. One study found the internal consistency to range from .88 to .94 in a sample of 2,304 high school and college students (Iverson et al. 2003). The four versions were found to be nonequivalent (Resch et al. 2013). Version one of verbal memory was nonequivalent to any of the other versions. In addition, Versions 2 and 4 of the verbal memory scale are nonequivalent. Versions 1 and 3 of the visual memory scale are nonequivalent. Versions 3 and 4 were nonequivalent for the reaction time and processing speed scales.

Test-Retest Reliability

Data provided by ImPACT showed moderate to high intraclass correlations with retests ranging from 30 days up to 2 years. The strongest intraclass correlation was seen for visual-motor speed with an average 30-day ICC of .86. The weakest intraclass correlation was seen for both visual memory and reaction time with an average 30-day ICC of .65. Subsequent studies have shown the intraclass correlation coefficient varies greatly study to study. The intraclass correlation coefficients varied from .37 to .76 across the four composite scores for a US-based sample. The most reliable measure was reaction time and visual-motor speed. Verbal and visual memory showed the greatest variability.

Validity

Construct Validity

ImPACT has been compared with a number of different assessments, including the Trails Making Test, Digit Symbol, Symbol Digit Modalities Test, and other sets of neuropsychological batteries. Trails Making Test A and B were correlated with ImPACT reaction time at $r = .61$ and $r = .44$, respectively (Schatz and Putz 2006). ImPACT processing speed was negatively correlated with the WAIS-R Digit Symbol Test at $r = -.51$ (Schatz and Putz 2006). ImPACT processing speed and reaction time were significantly correlated with the Symbol Digit Modalities Test at $r = .70$ and $r = -.60$, respectively (Iverson et al. 2005). When compared to the standard NFL neuropsychological battery, ImPACT was significantly correlated with small effects, with r-values ranging from .3 to .45 (Allen and Gfeller 2011). Marlander and colleagues (2010) found ImPACT to have "good convergent and discriminant validity" for memory and processing speed subtests.

Diagnostic Validity

ImPACT was able to differentiate individuals with concussions from individuals with other injuries. Those with concussions consistently had worse visual memory when compared to individuals with other injuries. Athletes who sought treatment for headaches prior to the baseline test performed significantly worse on visual memory when compared to those who did not seek treatment for headaches. Therefore, the visual memory subtest was found to be the most discriminate among those with concussions compared to other groups. Given the overlap concussion symptoms have with ADHD, it is critical to have background information on the test taker. The ImPACT system surveys the test taker for both a history of ADHD and learning disorders, as discrimination is difficult.

Test Procedures

ImPACT can be administered individually or in a group setting, requiring a sixth-grade reading level. The entire administration takes about 25 minutes to complete. The baseline assessment is FDA-cleared to be administered at the individual's home, while the post-concussion assessment is considered reliable only when administered by a qualified health professional. The qualified health professional may be present via telehealth services. The software guides the administration and is suggested to be conducted in a distraction-free, quiet environment. The individual is sat in front of a computer and asked to read instructions. A qualified health professional can ensure the testing environment is suitable and the individual understands the instructions. The software automatically guides the individual through a series of tests in the following order: Demographics, Symptom Scale, Word Memory, Design Memory, X's and O's, Symbol Match, Color Match, Three Letters, Word Memory Delayed Recall, and Design Memory Delayed Recall.

Scoring

The computer software automatically scores the administration. The software produces composite scores, a symptoms scale, a validity measure, an efficiency measure, and a reliable change index. The Verbal Memory composite score measures attention, learning, and memory of verbal stimuli. The Visual Memory Composite measures visual attention, scanning, learning, and memory of visual stimuli. Visual Motor Speed Composite measures visual processing, learning, memory, and visual-motor response speed. Reaction Time Composite measures average response time. Impulse Control Composite serves as a validity indicator and measures errors during testing. Additionally, the software automatically flags scores outside the Reliable Change Index.

Item Difficulty and Types of Errors

Items do not increase in difficulty as the test progresses, but the demands change as the individual moves from subtest to subtest. Each subtest is used to supply information to create the composite scores. The composite scores attempt to capture specific areas of functioning that are likely to be compromised due to a concussion. Common errors across subtests are the result of attention and speed. Individuals who attend poorly or are easily distracted may not view the exposures for the allotted time, limiting the information they can encode. The assessment largely depends on attention, as timed exposures are present in many of the subtests. Given the brevity of the assessment as a whole, attention becomes even more paramount.

How an individual chooses to prioritize speed could potentially lead to errors. Those prioritizing speed over accuracy may likely select an incorrect response to complete the assessment quickly. These individuals may score lower in Verbal Memory, Visual Memory, and Impulse Control Composite scores. An individual who chooses to prioritize accuracy over speed may compromise reaction time. These individuals may score lower in Visual-Motor Speed and Reaction Time Composite scores.

Task Demands and Strategies

The imPACT was designed to quickly assess various cognitive domains that are likely to be affected by a concussion. Word Memory measures attention and verbal recognition memory. During the subtest, the individual is presented with 12 target words over two series for 750 milliseconds of exposure. The individual is then presented with 24 words, 12 of which were the target words and 12 of which were distractor words from the same semantic category. The individual is then presented with a word and asked, "Was this one of the words displayed?" and responds, "yes" or "no." Design Memory measures attention and visual recognition memory. The designs were created in order to be difficult to encode verbally. During the subtest, the individual is presented with 12 target designs over two series for 750-millisecond of exposure. The individual is then presented with 24 designs, 12 of which were the target design and 12 of which were non-target designs. The non-target designs are rotated versions of the target designs. The individual is then presented with a design and asked, "Was this one of the designs displayed?" and responds, "yes" or "no." Both Word Memory and Design Memory have a delayed recall component, which is administered approximately 15–20 minutes later.

The X's and O's subtests measure visual motor and processing speed as well as visual working memory. During the subtest, a random assortment of Xs and Os is presented on the screen for 1.5 seconds. Three of the Xs or Os will be featured in yellow, and the individual is to remember the location of the three Xs or Os. When the exposure is complete, a distractor task is presented to interfere with memory rehearsal. The distractor task prompts the individual to press one key when an object appears and a different key when another object appears. The assortment reappears, and the individual is asked to identify which Xs and Os were previously yellow. The task is repeated for three trials. The Xs and Os serve as the memory test, and the distractor task measures reaction time and processing speed. Symbol Match measures memory, visual processing speed, and learning. Individuals are presented with a key in which a symbol is matched to a number. The individual is asked to select the number corresponding to a symbol as quickly as possible. After 27 trials, the key disappears, and the individual is asked to select the number corresponding to the symbol from memory.

Color Match measures impulse control and response inhibition. Similar to the Stroop color-word task, "Blue," "Green," and "Red" are displayed. The words are either displayed on a correct match; for example, "Blue" displayed in blue or an incorrect match, for example, "Blue" displayed in red. The individual is asked to click the box which presents a correct match as quickly as possible. Three letters measure working memory and visual-motor response speed. The individual is exposed to three consonants on the screen. Following the exposure, the individual is presented with a distractor task. During the task, the individual is asked to click numbers as quickly as possible backward from 25 to 1 on a five-by-five grid for 18 seconds. The individual is then asked to recall the three letters by typing the letters on the keyboard.

Clinical Applications in Research

Studies have shown ImPACT is sensitive to poor sleep. Ensure individuals are well rested the night before. Studies have shown athletes who sleep less than 7 hours the night before the baseline assessment performed significantly worse on verbal memory, visual memory, and reaction time when compared to athletes who slept more than 7 hours (McClure et al. 2014). An additional study found athletes with and without sleep difficulties performed similarly at baseline (Sufrinko et al. 2015). Following these same athletes, those with sleep difficulties performed worse on verbal memory and reaction when compared with those without sleep difficulties following an injury. Preinjury sleep difficulties may exacerbate concussion symptoms and neurocognitive impairment. Exercising before taking the ImPACT concussion test is generally discouraged because physical exertion has been shown to affect results. Physical exercise can increase heart rate, blood flow, and arousal levels, temporarily enhancing cognitive performance. Exercise-induced fatigue can also impair attention, memory, and reaction time.

Other concerns include sandbagging scores. Sandbagging is when an individual intentionally performs poorly on the baseline assessment, increasing their chances of returning to play following an injury. Although validity indicators are included in the baseline assessment, sandbagging may not be detected anywhere from 10.6% to 35%. Additional tests of effort and motivation may be useful to administer in conjunction with the baseline assessment to better detect sandbagging.

Studies have had mixed results when evaluating the performance of Black and White athletes. Some studies have shown significant differences between Black and White athletes in baseline symptom scores, visual-motor processing speed, and reaction time. White athletes, on average, had higher baseline visual-motor processing speed and reaction time. Black athletes, on average, had higher baseline symptom scores. Another study compared the baseline performance of Black and White athletes and found no differences across the scales (Kontos et al. 2013). Additional considerations should be considered when administering ImPACT on individuals who are racially or culturally diverse. The normative data may or may not be suitable for diverse athletes.

Research has also shown language affects all ImPACT scales. Various studies showed that Spanish-speaking athletes performed better on the English versions of ImPACT than the Spanish version. Additionally, Spanish-speaking athletes were found to perform poorer on ImPACT than compared to English-speaking athletes. These findings have implications for the congruency of test language for baseline and post-injury.

Cultural factors have been found to influence symptom reporting. A study examining 5,038 ImPACT baseline assessments of professional ice hockey players found that reporting concussion symptoms varied significantly by language of origin (Echemendia et al. 2020). ImPACT baselines were administered in English, French, Swedish, Russian, Czech, Finnish, and German were analyzed. The findings may suggest that some language groups may experience fewer symptoms than others, greater hesitancy to admit general or specific symptoms among some cultures or some symptoms may not be readily recognized by certain cultures.

Interpretation

ImPACT was specifically designed to serve as one tool for health providers to assess and monitor concussion post-injury. It was never intended to be the only tool used. Therefore, health professionals are encouraged to use multiple tools when assessing for concussions and determining if an athlete is safe to return to play.

1. The ImPACT software scores the responses and presents scores on a summary sheet. If the baseline is valid, the header of the summary sheet will read "Baseline." If the baseline is invalid, the header of the summary sheet will read "Baseline ++."
2. Post-injury scores will be compared to the individual's baseline score if available. If no baseline scores are available, the individual will be compared to the normative data. Scores of concerns are flagged in red on the summary score sheet. These scores suggest that the individual has not returned to baseline functioning as the values fall outside the expected range or deviate significantly from the individual's baseline scores. These red scores are designed to draw attention to potential areas of concern or impairment. In particular, the ImPACT software system flags scores in red when the individual's scores exceed the reliable change index score. The reliable change index score is used as a cut-off score to aid in determining marked changes from baseline to post-injury. It is recommended all values return within the reliable change score before an athlete can return to play. It is important to note that red scores alone do not provide a definitive diagnosis of a concussion. They serve as an indicator for further investigation and should be interpreted in conjunction with other clinical information, such as reported symptoms, medical history, and additional assessments.
3. In terms of concussion monitoring, the visual-motor speed composite score is the most reliable score on ImPACT (Dessy et al. 2017).
4. Deficits across visual-motor speed composite, visual memory composite, and reaction time composite have been associated with axonal damage to the oculomotor neurons (Tjarks et al. 2013).

5. Within 72 hours of a concussion, it is common to see a decline in both visual and verbal memory composite scores. Individuals also have lower performance on the reaction time composite and more symptom reporting (Iverson et al. 2003).
6. Deficits on the verbal memory composite and reaction time composite as well as higher total symptom scores, can persist 36 hours, 4 days, and even 7 days post-injury (Schatz et al. 2006).
7. Reading levels below that of sixth grade may present with difficulty understanding tasks as well as increased difficulty in both Word Memory and Word Memory Delayed Recall.
8. Poor sleep or individuals with sleep difficulties may perform lower verbal memory composite, visual memory composite, and reaction time composite scores.
9. Exercise prior to ImPACT can cause fatigue and impair attention, memory, and reaction time. Additionally, in terms of concussion monitoring, exercise should be introduced gradually back into the individual's routine as tolerated.
10. The testing environment should also be considered. Although ImPACT is approved to be administered from home, it is important to consider distractions in the environment. In many instances, ImPACT is done in a group setting. It is important to minimize distractions for the individual taking the assessment. Distractions can result in lower scores across scales, especially those related to reaction time.
11. consideration should be made for athletes with ADHD and/or learning disorders. These athletes may appear to be sandbagging on the baseline assessment when they are not. Athletes with ADHD, learning disorders, and those with comorbid a diagnosis of ADHD and learning disorders performed worse than normal on ImPACT. They may be more likely flagged for sandbagging when they are not.
12. Considerations should be made for athletes with other types of disorders and/or diagnoses. ImPACT may not be a fair measure depending on the individual's abilities. According to the developers, ImPACT should not be used with individuals with insomnia, PTSD, depression, memory impairments, dementia, delirium, those taking medications or some nutritional supplements, or those with any psychiatric or neurological disorder that impacts cognitive functioning.
13. Clients are more accurately classified when compared to their baseline versus the normative data (Schatz et al. 2006), suggesting an emphasis on testing at baseline.

References

Allen, B. J. and Gfeller, J. D. (2011). The Immediate Post-Concussion Assessment and Cognitive Testing battery and traditional neuropsychological measures: a construct and concurrent validity study. Brain injury, 25(2): 179–191. https://doi.org/10.3109/02699052.2010.541897.

Alsalaheen, B., Stockdale, K., Pechumer, D. and Broglio, S. P. (2016). Validity of the immediate post concussion assessment and cognitive testing (ImPACT). Sports Medicine, 46(10): 1487–1501. https://doi.org/10.1007/s40279-016-0532-y.

Asken, B. M., Clugston, J. R., Snyder, A. R. and Bauer, R. M. (2017). Baseline neurocognitive performance and clearance for athletes to return to contact. Journal of Athletic Training, 52(1): 51–57. https://doi.org/10.4085/1062-6050-51.12.27.

Brett, B. L. and Solomon, G. S. (2017). The influence of validity criteria on Immediate Post-Concussion Assessment and Cognitive Testing (ImPACT) test-retest reliability among high school athletes. Journal of Clinical and Experimental Neuropsychology, 39(3): 286–295. https://doi.org/10.1080/13803395.2016.1224322.

Broglio, S. P., Macciocchi, S. N., Ferrara, M. S., Collins, M., Maroon, J. C., Valadka, A. B. et al. (2007). Sensitivity of the concussion assessment battery. Neurosurgery, 60(6), 1050–1058. https://doi.org/10.1227/01.NEU.0000255479.90999.C0Tests in Sport-Related Concussion: Findings from the NCAA-DoD CARE Consortium. Sports Medicine (Auckland), 51(2): 351–365.

Caccese, J. B., DeWolf, R. M., Kaminski, T. W., Broglio, S. P., McAllister, T. W., McCrea, M. et al. (2019). Estimated age of first exposure to American football and neurocognitive performance amongst NCAA male student-sthletes: A cohort study. *Sports Medicine*, 49(3): 477–487. https://doi.org/10.1007/s40279-019-01069-x

Custer, A., Sufrinko, A., Elbin, R. J., Covassin, T., Collins, M. and Kontos, A. (2016). High baseline postconcussion symptom scores and concussion outcomes in athletes. Journal of Athletic Training, 51(2): 136–141. https://doi.org/10.4085/1062-6050-51.2.12.

Cottle, J. E., Hall, E. E., Patel, K., Barnes, K. P. and Ketcham, C. J. (2017). Concussion baseline testing: Preexisting factors, symptoms, and neurocognitive performance. Journal of Athletic Training, 52(2): 77–81. https://doi.org/10.4085/1062-6050-51.12.21.

Covassin, T., Swanik, C. B., Sachs, M., Kendrick, Z., Schatz, P., Zillmer, E. et al. (2006). Sex differences in baseline neuropsychological function and concussion symptoms of collegiate athletes. British Journal of Sports Medicine, 40: 923–927.

Czerniak, L. L., Liebel, S. W., Garcia, G.-G. P., Lavieri, M. S., McCrea, M. A., McAllister, T. W. et al. (2021). Sensitivity and specificity of computer-based neurocognitive tests in sport-related concussion: Findings from the NCAA-DoD CARE consortium. Sports Medicine, 51(2): 351–365. https://doi.org/10.1007/s40279-020-01393-7.

Dessy, A. M., Yuk, F. J., Maniya, A. Y., Gometz, A., Rasouli, J. J., Lovell, M. R. et al. (2017). Review of assessment scales for diagnosing and monitoring sports-related concussion. Cureus, 9(12): e1922–e1922. https://doi.org/10.7759/cureus.1922.

Dugan, S., Webbe, F. M. and LoGalbo, A. (2020). Convergent validity of baseline concussion measures: SCAT-5 and ImPACT. Archives of Clinical Neuropsychology, 35(5): 641–641. https://doi.org/10.1093/arclin/acaa036.45.

Echemendia, R. J., Thelen, J., Meeuwisse, W., Hutchison, M. G., Rizos, J., Comper, P. et al. (2020). Neuropsychological assessment of professional ice hockey players: A cross-cultural examination of baseline data across language groups. Archives of Clinical Neuropsychology, 35: 240–256. https://doi.org/10.1093/arclin/acz077.

Gaudet, C. E., Konin, J. and Faust, D. (2021). Immediate post-concussion and cognitive testing: Ceiling effects, reliability, and implications for interpretation. Archives of Clinical Neuropsychology, 36(4): 561–569. https://doi.org/10.1093/arclin/acaa074.

Glendon, K., Blenkinsop, G., Belli, A. and Pain, M. (2021). Prospective study with specific re-assessment time points to determine time to recovery following a sports-related concussion in university-aged student-athletes. Physical Therapy in Sport, 52: 287–296. https://doi.org/10.1016/j.ptsp.2021.10.008.

Hannah, T., Dreher, N., Li, A. Y., Shankar, D. S., Adams, R., Gometz, A. et al. (2020). Assessing the predictive value of primary evaluation with the immediate post-concussion assessment and cognitive test following head injury. Journal of Neurosurgery. Pediatrics, 26(2): 171–178. https://doi.org/10.3171/2020.2.PEDS19709.

Iverson, G. L., Lovell, M. R. and Collins, M. W. (2003). Interpreting change on ImPACT following sport concussion. The Clinical Neuropsychologist, 17(4): 460–467, doi:10.1076/clin.17.4.460.27934.

Kontos, A. P., Covassin, T., Elbin, R. J., and Parker, T. (2012). Depression and neurocognitive performance after concussion among male and female high school and collegiate athletes. Archives of Physical Medicine and Rehabilitation, 93(10): 1751–1756. https://doi.org/10.1016/j.apmr.2012.03.032.

Kontos, A. P., Elbin, R., Lau, B., Simensky, S., Freund, B., French, J. et al. (2013). Posttraumatic migraine as a predictor of recovery and cognitive impairment after sport-related concussion. The American Journal of Sports Medicine, 41(7): 1497–1504. https://doi.org/10.1177/0363546513488751.

Lempke, L. B., Lynall, R. C., Le, R. K., McCrea, M., McAllister, T. and Schmidt, J. D. (2021). The effects of on-field heat index and altitude on concussion assessments and recovery among NCAA athletes. Sports Medicine, 51(4): 825–835. https://doi.org/10.1007/s40279-020-01395-5.

Masterson, C. J., Tuttle, J. and Maerlender, A. (2019). Confirmatory factor analysis of two computerized neuropsychological test batteries: Immediate post-concussion assessment and cognitive test (ImPACT) and C3 logix. Journal of Clinical and Experimental Neuropsychology, 41(9): 925–932. https://doi.org/10.1080/13803395.2019.1641184.

McClure, D. J., Zuckerman, S. L., Kutscher, S. J., Gregory, A. J. and Solomon, G. S. (2014). Baseline neurocognitive testing in sports-related concussions: the importance of a prior night's sleep. The American Journal of Sports Medicine, 42(2): 472–478. https://doi.org/10.1177/0363546513510389.

Resch, J., Driscoll, A., McCaffrey, N., Brown, C., Ferrara, M. S., Macciocchi, S. et al. (2013). ImPact test-retest reliability: Reliably unreliable? Journal of Athletic Training, 48(4): 506–511. https://doi.org/10.4085/1062-6050-48.3.09.

Riberdy, C., Rindge, M., Daniel, M. and Pitkanen, E. (2018). Assessment - 4 retest reliability of the immediate post-concussion assessment and cognitive test using a two-factor theory with various interval schedules. Archives of Clinical Neuropsychology, 33(6): 692–702. https://doi.org/10.1093/arclin/acy060.09.

Riegler, K. E., Guty, E. T. and Arnett, P. A. (2019). Validity of the ImPACT post-concussion symptom scale (PCSS) affective symptom cluster as a screener for depression in collegiate athletes. Archives of Clinical Neuropsychology, 34(4): 563–574. https://doi.org/10.1093/arclin/acy081.

Schatz, P., Pardini, J. E., Lovell, M. R., Collins, M. W. and Podell, K. (2006). Sensitivity and specificity of the ImPACT Test Battery for concussion in athletes. Archives of Clinical Neuropsychology, 21(1): 91–99. https://doi.org/10.1016/j.acn.2005.08.001.

Servatius, R. J., Spiegler, K. M., Handy, J. D., Pang, K. C., Tsao, J. W. and Mazzola, C. A. (2018). Neurocognitive and fine motor deficits in asymptomatic adolescents during the subacute period after concussion. Journal of Neurotrauma, 35(8): 18–1014. https://doi.org/10.1089/neu.2017.5314.

Sufrinko, A., Pearce, K., Elbin, R. J., Covassin, T., Johnson, E., Collins, M. and Kontos, A. P. (2015). The effect of preinjury sleep difficulties on neurocognitive impairment and symptoms after sport-related concussion. The American Journal of Sports Medicine, 43(4): 830–838. https://doi.org/10.1177/0363546514566193.

Tjarks, B., Dorman, J. C., Valentine, V. D., Munce, T. A., Thompson, P. A., Kindt, S. L. et al. (2013). Comparison and utility of King-Devick and ImPACT® composite scores in adolescent concussion patients. Journal of the Neurological Sciences, 334(1): 148–153. https://doi.org/10.1016/j.jns.2013.08.015.

Tomczyk, C. P., Mormile, M., Wittenberg, M. S., Langdon, J. L. and Hunt, T. N. (2018). An examination of adolescent athletes and nonathletes on baseline neuropsychological test scores. Journal of Athletic Training, 53(4): 404–409. https://doi.org/10.4085/1062-6050-84-17.

Walton, S. R., Broshek, D. K., Freeman, J. R., Hertel, J., Meyer, J. P., Erdman, N. K. et al. (2020). Institutionally based ImPACT Test® normative values may differ from manufacturer-provided normative values. Archives of Clinical Neuropsychology, 35(3): 275–282. https://doi.org/10.1093/arclin/acz068.

Wallace, J., Moran, R., Beidler, E., McAllister Deitrick, J., Shina, J. and Covassin, T. (2020). Disparities on baseline performance using neurocognitive and oculomotor clinical measures of concussion. The American Journal of Sports Medicine, 48(11): 2774–2782. https://doi.org/10.1177/0363546520946753.

Wallace, J., Covassin, T., Moran, R. and Deitrick, J. M. (2017). Factors contributing to disparities in baseline neurocognitive performance and concussion symptom scores between black and white collegiate athletes. Journal of Racial and Ethnic Health Disparities, 5(4): 894–900. https://doi.org/10.1007/s40615-017-0437-y.

Weber, M. L., Dean, J.-H. L., Hoffman, N. L., Broglio, S. P., McCrea, M., McAllister, T. W. et al. (2018). Influences of mental illness, current psychological state, and concussion history on baseline concussion assessment performance. The American Journal of Sports Medicine, 46(7): 1742–1751. https://doi.org/10.1177/0363546518765145.

CHAPTER 30

NeuroTrax BrainCare

Aruna Ramrattan

NeuroTrax BrainCare (formerly known as Mindstreams) is a computerized neuropsychological battery. NeuroTrax was initially developed for research and clinical use, providing multiple predefined batteries (Hanna-Pladdy et al. 2010). It contains different sets of tests, initially to detect mild cognitive impairment (Dwolatzky et al. 2004). NeuroTrax consists of multiple scientifically validated tests that assess nine cognitive domains: memory, executive functioning, visual-spatial functioning, verbal functioning, attention, processing speed, motor skills, information processing speed, and problem-solving (Golan et al. 2020).

In 2014, NeuroTrax launched NeuroTrax BrainCare, expanding its purpose and clinical usage beyond mild cognitive impairment. NeuroTrax BrainCare is a computer-based neuropsychological battery that assists clinicians in establishing patient baselines, monitoring and measuring a patient's progress throughout treatment (based on test performance), and recommendations personalized for the patient's improvement and brain training. The cognitive domains assessed through NeuroTrax BrainCare include memory, executive function, attention, visual-spatial, verbal function, problem-solving, and working memory. The tests that measure these different cognitive domains include the Go-No-go Test, Verbal Memory, Non-Verbal Memory, Problem-Solving Test, Stroop Interference, Catch Game, Verbal Function, and Visual-Spatial Processing (Golan et al. 2020). NeuroTrax BrainCare also incorporates questionnaires to assess for psychosocial factors that may impact test performance.

Normed Population

NeuroTrax utilizes normative data that consists of test data from cognitively healthy participants compiled from more than ten research studies (Doniger 2014). The

Nova Southeastern University, Fort Lauderdale, Florida, USA.
Email: ar1734@mynsu.nova.edu

normative sample consisted of 1,569 participants with an expansive age range (< 18 yrs to > 80 yrs) and a variety of years of education (Doniger 2014). The normative sample is most heavily distributed between the 20–30-year age group and the 70–80-year age group; for education, the sample's mean is 14.4 years with a standard deviation of 3.2 years (Doniger 2014). Normative data in NeuroTrax accounts for the effects of age and education on cognitive performance (Doniger 2014). Outcome parameters calculated within the NeuroTrax system fit an Intelligence Quotient (IQ), like scale, with a mean of 100 and a standard deviation of 15 (Doniger 2014).

Test Procedures

NeuroTrax BrainCare may take anywhere between 30 to 60 minutes to complete. A participant is administered the battery on a computer and follows the on-screen instructions. Orientation to and skills in computer usage is not required; this test is user-friendly. A clinician is present during testing if the participant needs assistance. Once the assessment has been completed, the clinician generates a report including the participant's baseline scores along with progress scores if this test is a follow-up. The follow-up report consists of research-based guidance for clinicians to use in test result interpretation, recommendations, and treatment formulation.

Task Demands and Strategies

Each test domain is measured by a specific test. The Go-No-go Test presents participants with colored squares and instructs them to press a mouse button quickly for any color except red. The Verbal Memory Test asks participants to study and later recognize word pairs, in which they provide their response via the keyboard number pad. The Non-Verbal Memory Test requires participants to remember the orientation of eight patterns, which they must later match with the correct orientation from four options using the keyboard number pad. The Problem-Solving Test presents participants with incomplete patterns composed of geometric forms and prompts them to choose which of the six given forms best completes the pattern. Answers are selected with the keyboard number bad. The Stroop Interference test consists of three phases. In Level 1, participants must match the colored letters to squares. In Level 2, colored names must be matched to the squares. In Level 3, interference is introduced by presenting color names in conflicting ink colors. The Catch Game requires the participant to position a green horizontal bar on the screen to "catch" the white falling object as the game's speed increases over time. The Verbal Function Test asks participants to identify rhyming words with a previously shown picture and a separate section where participants match words to pictures. The Visual-Spatial Processing Test contains a computer-generated scene containing a red pillar. Participants are instructed to imagine viewing the scene from the vantage point of the red pillar. Four alternate views of the scene are shown as choices for the participant to choose from (Bar-Hen et al. 2015).

Scoring

Depending on the age and cognitive functioning, NeuroTrax BrainCare may take anywhere between 30 to 60 minutes to complete, and an objective cognitive functioning profile is provided to patients (Golan et al. 2020). This profile includes scores of the seven listed domains and a global cognitive score (GCS). The GCS is the average of all seven domain scores (Golan et al. 2020). Scores are automatically computed in a generated NeuroTrax BrainCare report, which includes raw scores and age/education-adjusted normalized scores (with a mean of 100 and standard deviation of 15), similar to an IQ scale (Doniger 2014). Lower scores indicate cognitive impairment (Doniger 2014).

Reliability

Normally, this test is administered prior to treatment to assess a patient's cognitive baseline score, which can then be readministered annually to track cognitive changes throughout treatment. Different versions of NeuroTrax BrainCare are administered throughout a person's treatment to minimize learning effects during repeated administration (Doniger 2014). Test-retest reliability coefficients for NeuroTrax BrainCare versions ranged from .64 to .84 (Bar-Hen et al. 2015). Each cognitive domain in the NeuroTrax BrainCare battery has three to five variations, which lends to good test-retest validity during re-administration in instances where a pre-test, mid-test, or post-test is desired (Bar-Hen et al. 2015).

Validity

Construct and Discriminant Validity

Schweiger and colleagues (2007) conducted a clinical construct and discriminant validity study of NeuroTrax tests for the diagnosis of Attention-Deficit/ Hyperactivity Disorder (ADHD) in young adults. While neuropsychological tests, such as continuous performance tests, may provide information on cognitive functioning, they are not extensive or specific for those diagnosed with ADHD (Schweiger et al. 2007). Additionally, while there is a plethora of research supporting the diagnostic processes of ADHD in children, this is quite limited in the adult population due to reasons such as high comorbidity rates, difficulty in recollecting childhood events, and locating reliable informants (Schweiger et al. 2007).

NeuroTrax tests assess multiple domains, which the authors of this study used to assess 29 young male ADHD adults. In addition to the NeuroTrax battery, the subjects were administered an expanded Go-No-go Test and Connor's CPT-II. Also, note that discriminant validity was examined by comparing healthy controls of similar age and education. Results of this study showed that the expanded Go-No-go Test and Connor's CPT-II results were significantly correlated in the participants with an ADHD diagnosis, demonstrating poor performance in comparison to the cognitively healthy controls. Within the NeuroTrax battery, the ADHD subjects were also found to perform more poorly on the Stroop Interference and Staged Information Processing Speed tests (Schweiger et al. 2007).

Research has indicated that adults diagnosed with ADHD have impairments in executive and attentional functions similar to children (Schweiger et al. 2007). Neuropsychological functioning in non-verbal working memory tasks also appears to be impaired in adult and child populations (Schweiger et al. 2007). On the Stroop Interference test in the NeuroTrax battery, which measures response inhibition, adult ADHD subjects appeared to perform poorly (Schweiger et al. 2007). The Stroop Interference test also differentiates adults with ADHD from depressed adults and is noted by Schweiger and colleagues (2007) as an indication of good discriminant validity. Children and adults with ADHD also displayed poor performance on arithmetic tasks and psychomotor performance speed tasks (Schweiger et al. 2007). Studies have also displayed adults with ADHD performing poorly on continuous performance tests and measures of reaction time, along with the number of commission errors attained (Schweiger et al. 2007). While continuous performance tests are frequently used in the diagnosis of ADHD, again, they cannot differentiate ADHD from other cognitive disorders (Schweiger et al. 2007). While Conner's CPT-II can detect attentional deficits, attentional deficits are diagnostic criteria for many disorders. Schweiger and colleagues (2007) conducted this study to determine the validity of NeuroTrax tests in detecting attentional deficits by examining the different cognitive aspects NeuroTrax measures.

Utilizing NeuroTrax tests in detecting attentional deficits differs from the widespread use of test batteries that consist of a variety of tests needed to assess underlying skills (Schweiger et al. 2007). This approach may increase large variability due to the unstandardized nature of combining different tests, whereas NeuroTrax utilizes a single standardized scale through age and education, which may decrease variability in results (Schweiger et al. 2007). Additionally, while current neuropsychological batteries for ADHD consist of multiple tests, this also means that extensive testing time is required (Schweiger et al. 2007). The NeuroTrax battery is time-friendly while still containing the ability to assess multiple cognitive functioning domains of adults with ADHD.

Participants in this study diagnosed with ADHD, along with the healthy controls, all completed the NeuroTrax battery, which was initially designed to detect mild cognitive impairment. Results of Schweiger and colleagues' (2007) study indicated that NeuroTrax tests can diagnose attentional deficits. Correspondence of results was shown between the NeuroTrax expanded Go-No-go variables and Connor's CPT-II variables (Schweiger et al. 2007). The NeuroTrax Go-No-go test was able to identify attentional and impulsive deficits that differentiated the ADHD and the healthy group from one another (Schweiger et al. 2007). For example, commission errors increased, a slower reaction time, a greater variability in reaction time, and reduced accuracy in responses were displayed (Schweiger et al. 2007). While continuous performance tests can indicate the same between ADHD and healthy controls, those with other disorders can also have a low performance on continuous performance tests, which indicates no unique distinction between disorders—traumatic brain injury, frontal lobe disorders, or other psychopathologies (Schweiger et al. 2007).

Overall, this study demonstrated that using the NeuroTrax battery identifies participants with ADHD as performing more poorly on the Stroop Interference test and Staged Information Processing Speed tests, which is consistent with research that indicates the Stroop Interference Test efficiency in identifying executive function deficits (Schweiger et al. 2007). This study also found that the ADHD group performed well in Verbal Function Rhyming and Finger-Tapping tests, which indicates that the ADHD group is not suffering from general cognitive or motor declines that may be impacting executive functioning and attention (Schweiger et al. 2007). While this study displayed the validity of NeuroTrax tests for assessing ADHD in adults, the battery singlehandedly cannot necessarily diagnose ADHD and does not display a profile unique from other pathologies (Schweiger et al. 2007). Regardless, the construct validity of NeuroTrax tests has been demonstrated by Schweiger and colleagues (2007).

Concurrent Validity

Hanna-Pladdy and colleagues (2010) conducted a study to determine the utility of the NeuroTrax battery as a cognitive screening battery for Parkinson's disease. The cognitive performance of 50 Parkinson's disease patients was compared on NeuroTrax, the Mini-Mental State Examination (MMSE), and the Montreal Cognitive Assessment (MOCA). The MMSE is a common cognitive screening instrument but has not been validated specifically for use in the Parkinson's disease population and may also be less sensitive to milder forms of Parkinson's disease deficits (Hanna-Pladdy et al. 2010). The MOCA, on the other hand, demonstrates increased sensitivity in detecting mild cognitive impairments in the elderly population and with the Alzheimer's disease population (Hanna-Pladdy et al. 2010). The MOCA's sensitivity is partly due to its memory testing that consists of more words, fewer learning trials in the test, and longer delay times compared to the MMSE (Hanna-Pladdy et al. 2010). Nevertheless, the MOCA has been shown to be a good screening measure, although further investigation is needed to indicate the MOCA as a good diagnostic tool for those with Parkinson's disease (Hanna-Pladdy et al. 2010).

Hanna-Pladdy and colleagues (2010) aimed to study NeuroTrax tests, which provided a predefined computerized battery, to assess its ability to provide a cognitive profile for Parkinson's disease patients in comparison to impairment displayed on MMSE and MOCA results (Hanna-Pladdy et al. 2010). As the NeuroTrax battery was initially designed to detect mild cognitive impairments, it has not been solely validated for the Parkinson's disease population. Though it has been validated to assess the neuropsychological age-related cognitive decline of patients, it is diagnostic utility for Parkinson's disease is yet to be examined (Hanna-Pladdy et al. 2010).

This study identified correlations for impairment in the NeuroTrax battery and the MMSE (Hanna-Pladdy et al. 2010). Also, there was a slight correlation between the NeuroTrax battery and the MOCA (Hanna-Pladdy et al. 2010). NeuroTrax identified 8% of participants as impaired, the MOCA identified 54% of the sample as impaired, and the MMSE identified 14% of the participants as impaired (Hanna-Pladdy et al. 2010). Hanna-Pladdy and colleagues (2010) conducted several stepwise regressions which indicated executive functioning and verbal functioning as the best predictors for cognitive functioning on the NeuroTrax battery and memory recall, serial sevens, naming, and abstraction as the best predictors in the MOCA (Hanna-Pladdy et al. 2010). This suggests that NeuroTrax tests may consist of the ability to identify executive cognitive deficits in Parkinson's disease (Hanna-Pladdy et al. 2010). The MOCA identifies deficits through different cognitive domains and appears to be more sensitive and stringent in classifying impairments (Hanna-Pladdy et al. 2010).

Compared to the MOCA and MMSE, the NeuroTrax battery was able to identify mild cognitive deficits in Parkinson's disease patients better, with 40% falling in the below-average to borderline range (Hanna-Pladdy et al. 2010). The MMSE did not identify any subjects as borderline, and the MOCA identified 8% as borderline (Hanna-Pladdy et al. 2010). Conclusively, the NeuroTrax battery and MOCA appear to be more sensitive than the MMSE in identifying early cognitive impairment in Parkinson's disease, although it is not specifically identified whether a mild cognitive impairment or dementia is being identified in the NeuroTrax battery or the MOCA (Hanna-Pladdy et al. 2010). It is also important to note that the MOCA was developed with a mild cognitive impairment and Alzheimer's disease population, meaning that normative data from the MOCA may not necessarily translate accurately to the Parkinson's disease population (Hanna-Pladdy et al. 2010). In other words, the recommended cutoff score on the MOCA, 26, may not be appropriate or applicable to the Parkinson's disease population (Hanna-Pladdy et al. 2010). This may affect the correlations found between the MOCA and NeuroTrax tests.

It is also important to consider that the NeuroTrax battery is a computerized assessment that has the ability to minimize floor and ceiling effects, provide accuracy in the speed of responses, and may also be able to provide information regarding speed of response that is relevant to bradykinesia and other executive deficits that are evident in Parkinson's disease (Hanna-Pladdy et al. 2010). Although a computerized system of cognitive assessments is beneficial for the elderly population, its utility in the Parkinson's disease population has not been clarified yet (Hanna-Pladdy et al. 2010). Considerations for this include Parkinson's disease participants utilizing motor responses to complete computerized tasks (Hanna-Pladdy et al. 2010). Considering the motor deficits accompanying Parkinson's disease, accurate assessment of cognitive functioning may be affected (Hanna-Pladdy et al. 2010). While Hanna-Pladdy and colleagues (2010) were interested in examining the utility of the NeuroTrax computerized battery for cognitive screening and Parkinson's disease, they were able to identify how this computerized cognitive battery may affect accurate assessment of those with Parkinson's disease or those who display early deficit. Regarding pathologies that include motor impairments, NeuroTrax tests may display limited efficacy. Nevertheless, it is a useful screening tool to identify mild cognitive impairment where motor deficits are not of concern.

Performance Validity

It would be pertinent to discuss performance validity when examining neuropsychological assessments as the cooperation of an examinee influences test performance (Bar-Hen et al. 2015). Normally, it is a concern whether neuropsychological assessments have an embedded measure of performance validity or if tests can detect negative response biases (NRB) as these greatly threat validity (Bar-Hen et al. 2015). Bar-Hen and colleagues (2015) developed an empirically supported algorithm to measure negative response bias within the NeuroTrax computerized neuropsychological battery. Archived medical data of 75 outpatients with mild to moderate head injuries were utilized in this study. All were in litigation, and they were classified as either having a low probability for negative response bias or a high probability for negative response bias measured by the Test of Memory Malingering (TOMM). The authors of this study utilized logistic regression analysis to determine whether certain variables were prone to exaggeration, which would appear as large differences between the group scores (Bar-Hen et al. 2015). The developed algorithm displayed high specificity at 98% and sensitivity at 87.5%, correctly identifying 94% of the negative response bias cases. This study aimed to examine and provide an approach that can automatically compute threats to validity while assessing cognitive skills (Bar-Hen et al. 2015).

The researchers of this study generally found that malingerers performed more poorly than patients with low negative response biases on memory recognition (Bar-Hen et al. 2015). Additionally, the high negative response bias group displayed no improvement in their scores for repeated exposure tasks where the material was expected to be learned and reflect a normal learning pattern (Bar-Hen et al. 2015). In fact, the high negative response bias group displayed a decline in their scores over time (Bar-Hen et al. 2015). Thirdly, the high negative response group did not exhibit the Stroop effect during the administration of the Stroop test (Bar-Hen et al. 2015). Overall, the high negative response bias group did not follow the typical learning curve expected in normal participants and low negative response bias patients and additionally exhibited poor performance (Bar-Hen et al. 2015).

Clinical Applications in Research

In a study conducted by Gudesblatt and colleagues (2018), the NeuroTrax battery was administered to multiple sclerosis (MS) patients before and during Natalizumab treatment to track the progression of treatment and to monitor cognitive change over time. Natalizumab is a drug that reduces disease activity (Gudesblatt et al. 2018). This study measured changes from baseline in GCS and the participant domain scores after 24 infusions of the drug. After the annual administration of NeuroTrax, improvement and stabilization in cognition were identified during treatment with Natalizumab (Gudesblatt et al. 2018). Participant domain scores for all patients indicated significant improvement across all domains from Year 1 baseline scores to Year 2, except in one domain – Visual-Spatial Processing (Gudesblatt et al. 2018). A total of three versions of NeuroTrax were administered to all patients – a baseline of administration, a second administration at one year, and a third administration at two years during Natalizumab treatment (Gudesblatt et al. 2018). Besides the general improvement of cognitive functioning as indicated by the global cognitive score of patients, NeuroTrax was utilized to assess Natalizumab treatment efficacy for participants with remitting multiple sclerosis over two years (Gudesblatt et al. 2018).

Tal and colleagues (2017) conducted a study assessing the neurotherapeutic effect of hyperbaric oxygen therapy (HBOT) on prolonged post-concussion syndrome (PCS) as a result of traumatic brain injury (TBI). NeuroTrax was utilized to evaluate the cognitive functioning of the participants. The participant's cognitive index scores were gathered from the executive functioning, memory, attention, speed of information processing, visual-spatial, verbal function, and motor skills domains (Tal et al. 2017). In this study, the researchers chose to exclude the verbal domain score as only eight patients' scores had been reliably calculated (53% of the research group) (Tal et al. 2017). Researchers then calculated the GCS—the average of all index scores (Tal et al. 2017). The results for the neurocognitive function of patients indicated that there was an improvement in global cognitive scores (Tal et al. 2017). The domains that displayed the greatest improvements from hyperbaric oxygen therapy were memory, executive function, and information processing speed (Tal et al. 2017). Within this study, the improvement in functional cognition shown in NeuroTrax results correlated with the increased integrity of brain fibers, demonstrated through highly sensitive perfusion magnetic resonance imaging (MRI) and diffusion tensor imaging (DTI) (Tal et al. 2017). As for regional changes in brain microstructure integrity, which also correlates with the NeuroTrax findings, statistically significant increases were found in regions related to motor function; there were increases in cerebral blood flow (CBF) in frontal white matter, association fibers, motor function related structures, and structures related to memory functioning (Tal et al. 2017). There were also increases in cerebral blood volume (CBV) in regions related to sensory motor function and executive functioning, along with regions related to memory functioning (Tal et al. 2017). As demonstrated in this study, NeuroTrax can be utilized to track cognitive changes, whether improvements or declines and can serve as a supplemental aid in experiments to help expand on test interpretation and case conceptualization.

Interpretation

After completing NeuroTrax BrainCare, clinicians may examine scores to extract additional information regarding the participant's performance. Each test can be interpreted separately to identify strengths and weaknesses in the cognitive profile.

The Go-No-go Response Inhibition Test gauges an individual's executive function and attentional capacities (Doniger 2014). Several critical performance metrics can be analyzed.

1. Accuracy: Assessing for accuracy quantifies the frequency with which the participant achieves correct responses when required and refrains from responding when instructed not to. This serves as an indicator of the participant's capacity for accurate decision-making.
2. Response Time: This metric measures the speed with which the participant initiates a response when given a stimulus during the test. Response times, which are faster, often correlate with greater attentional and decision-making abilities.

3. Response Time Standard Deviation: This measure evaluates the consistency of an individual's response times. The higher the standard deviation, the greater the variability in reaction times, which may be indicative of issues in sustained attention and decision-making consistency.
4. Errors of Commission: Commission errors occur when the participant responds incorrectly to a stimulus that requires no response. This may reflect impulsivity or difficulties with inhibition.
5. Errors of Omission: Omission errors occur when the participant fails to respond where a response is expected. Such errors may signify issues with sustained attention or challenges in initiating actions when necessary.
6. Response Time for Errors of Commission: This metric assesses the speed at which the participant corrects their mistake after responding incorrectly. This provides insight into the participant's ability to identify and correct their errors promptly.

The Go-No-go Response Inhibition Test captures critical aspects of a participant's cognitive performance, including the parameters discussed above. These offer insights into executive function and attentional performance.

The Non-Verbal and Verbal Memory Tests evaluate a participant's memory function by focusing on the participant's capacity to retain and recall non-verbal and verbal information (Doniger 2014). Within these tests, there are multiple parameters that can be examined.

1. Immediate Recognition (4 Trails): For these segments, the participant needs to immediately recognize and recall the non-verbal or verbal information presented over four trials to assess their ability to remember and accurately recognize presented information. Accuracy is the key metric in these segments, measuring participant's success in accurately detecting previously encountered items.
2. Final Immediate Recognition Task (Combining All Four Trials): The last immediate recognition task consolidates the information across all four trials. This trial assesses the participant's ability to accurately recognize and recall the non-verbal or verbal material presented in the test.
3. Delayed Recognition: This metric occurs after a brief delay period. When this task is presented, the participant is asked to recognize and recall the previously displayed non-verbal or verbal material. The primary focus is to assess the participant's accuracy to determine how effectively they can retain and recognize information over time and with delayed recall.

In sum, the Non-verbal and Verbal Memory Tests help to assess a participant's memory capability with non-verbal and verbal material. It measures abilities in immediate recognition across multiple repetitions, immediate recognition with a culmination of all material, and lastly, delayed recognition presented after a specified amount of time. This test provides valuable insight into a participant's memory functioning.

The Problem-Solving Test (Non-Verbal IQ) assesses executive functioning by primarily focusing on a participant's ability to solve complex problems accurately (Doniger 2014). Participants are presented with a series of geometric puzzles, which become more complex as the test progresses (Doniger 2014). The test continues until the participant's performance declines to a certain level of accuracy (Doniger 2014).

1. Geometric Puzzles: These puzzles begin at a relatively simple level and become progressively more intricate as the test advances. This progression in complexity challenges the participant's problem-solving skills. More accuracy in answering correctly may give insight into the participant's executive functioning skills.
2. Termination Criteria: This test terminates once the participant's performance begins to decline. This indicates the participant's ability to maintain effective problem-solving skills under increasing difficulty.
3. Accuracy: The total accuracy score for this test is the outcome parameter. This score reflects the participant's performance across the varying difficulty levels and provides an overall assessment of the participant's problem-solving abilities and accuracy during different levels of complexity.

Overall, the Problem-Solving Test assesses a participant's executive function by measuring their ability to solve geometric puzzles of increasing difficulty. This test offers valuable insight into a participant's problem-solving capabilities.

The Stroop Interference test evaluates executive function and attentional capabilities by analyzing a participant's performance in accuracy, average response time, and response time standard deviation (Doniger 2014).

1. Accuracy: Accuracy is crucial in the Stroop Interference test as it assesses a participant's ability to provide the correct response while inhibiting the interference caused by conflicting information. Accuracy indicates a participant's proficiency in managing executive function and attention when there are conflicting stimuli.
2. Average Response Time: This metric quantifies the average time it takes for the participant to respond to each stimulus during the test. Shorter average response times may indicate quicker and more efficient executive function and attentional control when presented with interference.
3. Response Time Standard Deviation: Standard deviations in response time assess the consistency of the participant's reaction times. Lower standard deviations may indicate more consistent response times. This would also indicate better-sustained attention and steady executive function, even in the presence of interference.

In sum, the Stroop Interference Test assesses executive function and attention by analyzing accuracy, average response time, and response time standard deviation. This test can provide valuable insight into an individual's capabilities in managing conflicting stimuli and maintaining focus under challenging conditions.

The Catch Game Test is unique in that it assesses a participant's executive function and motor skills (Doniger 2014). This includes motor-related response time, motor learning, motor planning, and performance speed (Doniger 2014).

1. Response Time and Associated Variance for the First Move: The first move in this test indicates a few important insights. The time to take and initiate the first move and any variance associated with this first move can be analyzed. Quicker

and more consistent response times indicate better executive function and motor skills, especially when under time constraints.
2. Number of Direction Changes Per Trial: As the white object falls to the bottom of the screen, the participant must maneuver the green horizontal paddle at the bottom of the screen to "catch" the white object. The number of direction changes made during each trial indicates the participant's capacity to adapt and switch motor responses swiftly. A higher number of changes may indicate better motor flexibility.
3. Error of Missed Catches: When a participant fails to catch the white object, it is considered an error. Errors are recorded and indicate the participant's ability to maintain precision and control in their motor responses. The fewer the errors, the more accurate motor skills and executive function.
4. Total Performance Score: The total performance score assesses the participant's ability to combine executive function and motor skills with increasing difficulty.

By analyzing response times, direction changes, errors, and total performance scores, the Catch Game offers insight into an individual's executive and motor skills, particularly their ability to adapt and respond accurately under time constraints with increasing difficulty.

In the Verbal Function Test, accuracy is the primary parameter (Doniger 2014). Accuracy is assessed in both sections of this test, Rhyming and Picture Identification.

1. Rhyming: This section assesses higher-order skills. Accuracy is measured by the participant's ability to correctly identify and select the word that rhymes with the preceding picture, reflecting a higher level of verbal proficiency.
2. Picture Identification: This section focuses on basic verbal skills. Accuracy is measured by the individual's ability to identify and match the correct word with the preceding picture, assessing their fundamental verbal skills.

The Verbal Function Test assesses a participant's verbal proficiency across different verbal tasks.

In the Visual Spatial Processing Test, accuracy is the primary parameter as well. In this test, accuracy measures a participant's abstract spatial ability capacities (Doniger 2014).

1. Total Accuracy Score: The total accuracy score is derived from assessing the participant's performance across multiple trials and perspectives. It assesses how accurately they can match the presented perspectives with the imagined perspective from the red pillar's location.

The Visual-Spatial Processing Test is designed to provide insights into a participant's proficiency and accuracy in visual-spatial skills and their ability to manipulate spatial information.

NeuroTrax BrainCare generates interpretive and patient reports after completion of the assessment battery. NeuroTrax BrainCare reports typically indicate the participant's domain scores and the GCS score, along with comments on strengths and weaknesses identified in the patient.

Additionally, for each successive re-administration of a NeuroTrax BrainCare version, reports will include previous scores, such as pre-test scores. Reports also include a graph of scores along with readministered versions. From this, clinicians can see a visual representation that indicates whether there were specific improvements in certain domains, whether a steady cognitive level had been maintained in a domain, or whether there has been cognitive decline.

Suggestions for strengths and weaknesses are provided after scores are generated (Doniger 2014). Comparisons baseline scores for each successive administration are compared side by side in graphs to show whether there has been a decline or improvement in the areas of cognitive functioning, which can help indicate target areas for cognitive training (Doniger 2014). NeuroTrax BrainCare reports also note changes from a patient's previous visit (Doniger 2014). Of note, it is essential to remember that this test does not replace a full comprehensive neuropsychological battery or suggests a diagnosis or determine the course of treatment. NeuroTrax BrainCare is beneficial for tracking cognitive improvement and decline to help monitor the progression of treatment or one's cognitive functioning.

References

Bar-Hen, M., Doniger, G. M., Golzad, M., Geva, N. and Schweiger, A. (2015). Empirically derived algorithm for performance validity assessment embedded in a widely used neuropsychological battery: Validation among TBI patients in litigation. Journal of Clinical and Experimental Neuropsychology, 37(10): 1086–1097. doi:https://doi.org/10.1080/13803395.2015.1078294.

Doniger, G. M. (2014). Guide to Normative Data. NeuroTrax Corporation.

Doniger, G. M. (2014). NeuroTrax™ Computerized Cognitive tests: Test Descriptions. NeuroTrax Corporation.

Doniger, G. M., Simon, E. S. and Zivotofsky, A. Z. (2006). Comprehensive computerized assessment of cognitive sequelae of a complete 12-16 hour fast. Behavioral Neuroscience, 120(4): 804–816.

Dwolatzky, T., Whitehead, V., Doniger, G. M., Simon, E. S., Scheiger, A., Jaffe, D. et al. (2004). Validity of the Mindstreams computerized cognitive battery for mild cognitive impairment. Journal of Molecular Neuroscience, 24(1): 33–44.

Golan, D., Doniger, G. M., Srinivasan, J., Sima, D. M., Zarif, M., Bumstead, B. et al. (2020). The association between MRI brain volumes and computerized cognitive scores of people with multiple sclerosis. Brain and Cognition, 145: 8. doi:https://doi.org/10.1016/j.bandc.2020.105614.

Gudesblatt, M., Wissemann, K., Zarif, M., Bumstead, B., Fafard, L., Wilken, J. et al. (2018). Correction to: Improvement in cognitive function as measured by NeuroTrax in patients with relapsing multiple sclerosis treated with natalizumab: A 2-year retrospective analysis. CNS Drugs, 32(12): 1183. doi:https://doi.org/10.1007/s40263-018-0574-9.

Hanna-Pladdy, B., Enslein, A., Fray, M., Gajewski, B. J., Pahwa, R. and Lyons, K. E. (2010). Utility of the NeuroTrax computerized battery for cognitive screening in parkinson's disease: Comparison with the MMSE and the MoCA. International Journal of Neuroscience, 120(8): 538–543. doi:https://doi.org/10.3109/00207454.2010.496539.

Schweiger, A., Abramovitch, A., Doniger, G. M. and Simon, E. S. (2007). A clinical construct validity study of a novel computerized battery for the diagnosis of ADHD in young adults. Journal of Clinical and Experimental Neuropsychology, 29: 100–111. doi: 10.1080/13803390500519738.

Tal, S., Hadanny, A., Sasson, E., Suzin, G. and Efrati, S. (2017). Hyperbaric oxygen therapy can induce angiogenesis and regeneration of nerve fibers in traumatic brain injury patients. Frontiers in Human Neuroscience, 11, 12. doi:https://doi.org/10.3389/fnhum.2017.00508.

CHAPTER 31

Cambridge Automated Neuropsychological Test Automated Battery (CANTAB)

Etiane Navarro

The Cambridge Automated Neuropsychological Test Battery (CANTAB) is a computerized software composed of 25 cognitive assessments (*Cognitive tests*. Cambridge n.d; Lenehan et al. 2016). It was written and developed by Barbara Sahakian, Trevor Robbins, and colleagues in the 1980s at Cambridge University in London (Roque et al. 2011; Smith et al. 2013). The administration software is compatible with a desktop computer or an iPad. CANTAB developers argue that the computerized software is encoded to gauge the sensitivity to many neurological and psychiatric disorders (*Cognitive tests*. Cambridge n.d). The computerized battery has also been validated in pharmacological research (Cambridge Cognition Ltd. 2006; Wild and Musser 2014). The tests are independent of language comprehension and speech. The developers argue that CANTAB is effective cross-culturally and the battery is translated into 45 languages. CANTAB is widely used in 50 countries throughout clinical settings and research (Cambridge Cognition Ltd. 2006).

Trained assistants can administer the battery without reliance on verbal instruction. CANTAB allows for an array of battery selections that include different subtests tailored to the patient's needs (*Cognitive tests*. Cambridge n.d). The batteries can measure neuropsychological performance in cognitive domains such as working memory, learning and executive function; visual, verbal, and episodic memory; attention information processing and reaction time; social and emotion

Nova Southeastern University.

recognition, decision making, and response control (Cambridge Cognition Ltd. 2006; *Cognitive tests*. Cambridge n.d; Roque et al. 2011).

The software does not require pre-baseline participant training since it is self-adjusted in the program according to the individual's performance. Instead, each section begins with a built-in effortless motor screening practice phase at the start of the battery, allowing participants to familiarize themselves with the task and ensure they can navigate with the computer mouse or touch screen accurately (Cambridge Cognition Ltd. 2006).

Normed Population

The developers' primary objective with the computerized software that measured cognition, consisted of having a more extensive global and diverse population outreach that was not limited to the field of neuropsychology. Although the CANTAB has been used in 50 countries and translated into 45 languages, some aspects of the application of the computerized tests are questionable and could result in over-pathologizing individuals from different cultural groups. The literature expressed a significant concern, particularly with very young individuals and older adults (Luciana 2003; Vermeulen et al. 2018; Wild and Musser 2014). Researchers suggest that CANTAB's computerized software has greater utility for individuals with a better understanding of operating mechanisms in a computer test. Older adults and young children may lack training and knowledge in computer use and understanding of computerized software to such a degree that the assessment results may be compromised (Vermeulen et al. 2018).

CANTAB's developers argue that the battery is language and culture-independent, meaning that an individual's culture should not influence task performance (Roque et al. 2011). They exclude subtests such as VMR and AGN as they contain language-dependent stimuli. Whereas Toornstra et al. (2020) argue in research performed on pediatric a sample from Ukraine that the culture impacts thinking processes, knowledge, values, and beliefs based on social experiences. Cultural variances are linked to CANTAB's norms, which are established in western societies. In neuropsychology, the interpretation and analysis of test scores of non-western groups may contribute to a misinterpretation in cognitive frameworks that distinguish typical and atypical development (Green et al. 2019; Toornstra et al. 2020).

Test Procedures

Attention Processing & Psychomotor Speed Subtests

Motor Screening Test (MOT)

The Motor Screening Test is a task (*Cognitive tests*. Cambridge n.d), used to familiarize individuals with the touch screen and computer and provides a simple reaction time measure (Cambridge Cognition Ltd. 2006). The primary goal is not to assess cognition but to provide a general baseline for sensory psychomotor function and comprehension to proceed with the battery (Roque et al. 2011). The test allows researchers to identify vision, movement, and language comprehension deficits. The creators of the software recommend that MOT is administered before any other subtests that are included in the battery. The psychomotor speed task takes approximately one minute to complete. The procedure consists of a series of crosses shown in different locations on the screen. The individual is asked to touch or click on each cross using the index finger of the dominant hand.

Attention Switching Task (AST)

The Attention Switching Task measures a function in executive function of the ability to switch attention processed by the frontal lobe. The patient needs to determine the side or direction of the arrow that is being presented on the screen (Karlsen et al. 2022). The arrow varies in position (right or left) and direction (right or left). The first outcome measure consists of the congruent and incongruent trials. The second outcome measure include the difference in mean response time between task switching.

Reaction Time Test (RTI)

The Reaction Time Test (*Cognitive tests*. Cambridge n.d) measures mental processes involving motor and speeds. The subtest assesses the individual's movement time, reaction time, response accuracy, and impulsivity. The administration time is approximately three minutes. The individual must select and hold a button at the screen's bottom. Circles are presented at the top of the screen. In each trial, a yellow dot will appear in one of the circles. The individual must respond quickly, clicking the button at the bottom of the screen and selecting the circle in which the dot appeared. The assessment's outcome measures include reaction time and speed.

Rapid Visual Information Processing (RVP)

The Rapid Visual Information Processing task (*Cognitive tests*. Cambridge n.d) measures sustained attention. The administration of this task takes approximately seven minutes. The individual is presented with a white box in the center of the screen. Digits from two to nine appear in the box in random order, at 100 digits per minute. Individuals must detect target sequences of digits, such as 2-4-6, 3-5-7, 4-6-8. When the individual sees the target sequence, they must respond quickly and select the button in the center of the screen.

Match to Sample Visual Search (MTS)

The Match to Sample Visual Search task (*Cognitive tests*. Cambridge n.d) measures attention and visual searching with a speed-accuracy trade-off. The task administration is approximately seven minutes. The subtest consists of a complex visual pattern displayed in the middle of the screen. After a brief delay, several similar patterns appear in a circle of boxes around the edge of the screen. Only one of these patterns corresponds to the pattern in the center of the screen. The individual must indicate which is the correct one by selecting it. The outcome of this task includes the accuracy and reaction.

Adaptive Tracking Tasks (ATT)

The Adaptive Tracking Tasks (*Cognitive tests*. Cambridge n.d) measures visuomotor coordination and vigilance. The task administration is approximately seven minutes. In this test, a small circle (target) will continuously move across the screen in a semi-randomized fashion to minimize the individual's ability to predict the target's trajectory. The instructions include following the target shown on the screen with a finger or mouse and consistency in the center of the moving target. During the assessment, the circle's speed adjusts to the individual's capacity to keep the dot in the circle. The task is sensitive to the individual's performance by adapting accordingly. The outcome measures consist of accuracy and adaptation to the speed adjustment.

Executive Function Subtests

Cambridge Gambling Task (CGT)

The Cambridge Gambling Task (*Cognitive tests*. Cambridge n.d) measures decision-making and risk-taking behaviors outside a learning context. The task administration is approximately eighteen minutes. The task consists of ten boxes across the top of the screen: some are red, and some are blue. The ratio of red and blue boxes will vary between stages, but there will always be one box that contains a yellow token. The 'Red' and 'Blue' buttons at the bottom of the screen need to be used to choose the box color in which the individual thinks the token is hidden. The individual starts with 100 points and selects a proportion of these points to bet on their decision, increasing or decreasing the original bet. Individuals press a button when it shows the proportion of their score they would like to bet. Depending on their decision and where the token is hidden, these points will either be added or taken away from their total score. The outcome measures consist of risk-taking, decision-making, decision time, risk adjustment, delay aversion, and impulsivity.

Intra-Extra-Dimensional Set Shift (IED)

The intra-Extra Dimensional Set Shift (*Cognitive tests*. Cambridge n.d) is a rule acquisition and reversal test. The task involves visual discrimination and attentional set formation maintenance, shifting, and flexibility of attention. This subtest is sensitive to changes in the frontostriatal areas of the brain and is analogous to the Wisconsin Card Sorting Test. The task administration is approximately seven minutes. The test uses two artificial dimensions: pink shapes and white lines. Individuals must use feedback to work out a rule that determines which stimulus is correct. After six correct responses, the stimuli and/or rule change. Initially, the task will involve made-up stimuli of just one of the dimensions. Later in the task, combination stimuli are used. The shifts in a rule are initially intra-dimensional and later become extra-dimensional. The outcome measures include discriminating the number of errors made, the number of trials and stages completed, and latency.

Multitasking Test (MTT)

The Multitask Test (*Cognitive tests*. Cambridge n.d) measures the individual's ability to manage conflicting information provided by the direction of an arrow and its location on the screen and ignore task-irrelevant information. The task administration is approximately eight minutes. The test displays an arrow on either side of the screen and can point in either direction. The top of the screen displays a cue indicating that a right or left selection must be made dependent on the location of the arrow. The task would switch, changing the strategy to which the individual must adapt. By switching tasks, there is a higher demand for cognitive skills that include flexibility. The stimuli presented may be congruent or incongruent. The outcome measures consist of response latencies and error scores demonstrating the individual's ability to manage multitasking and the interference of incongruent task-irrelevant information on task performance.

One Touch Stockings of Cambridge (OTS)

The One Touch Stockings of Cambridge (*Cognitive tests*. Cambridge n.d) is an executive function subtest based upon the Tower of Hanoi. The test assesses spatial planning and working memory. The length of the administration is approximately ten minutes—it consists of a divided screen containing three colored balls. They appear to be stacked suspended from a beam. The instructions for the task are verbal. There is a row of numbered boxes along the bottom of the screen. The trial item teaches the individual how to move the balls to copy the pattern in the upper display. Next, the system would prompt three different moves to complete a problem, concluding the teaching block. The individual commences the task with previously learned strategies. The task outcome measures contain the number of problems solved on the first choice, the mean choices to correct responses, the mean latency to the first choice, and the mean latency to correct responses—each measure calculates all problems or problems with a specified number of moves.

Stocking of Cambridge (SOC)

The Stocking of Cambridge (*Cognitive tests*. Cambridge n.d) is a spatial planning task requiring individuals to problem-solve strategies to match two sets of stimuli. The task administration is approximately ten minutes—three stockings containing three colored balls are suspended from a beam for this task. The two sections appear at the top and bottom of the screen—the arranged balls are in different patterns in each display. The individual must move the balls in the bottom section to copy the pattern in the top section. The balls are moved one at a time by selecting the required ball, then selecting the position in which it should remain. The participant is instructed to make as few moves as possible to match the two patterns. Phases account for movement time in which participants copy moves made by the computer. The moves result from previous moves made by the individual recorded by the system.

Spatial Working Memory (SWM)

The Spatial Working Memory task (*Cognitive tests*. Cambridge n.d) measures the retention and manipulation of visuospatial information. It is an executive function test that measures strategy and working memory errors. The task administration is approximately four minutes. The task begins with several colored squares on the screen. The color and position of the boxes used are changed from trial to trial to discourage the use of stereotyped search strategies.

Stop Signal Task (SST)

The Stop Signal Task (*Cognitive tests*. Cambridge n.d) is a classical approach to measuring response inhibition. The task administration is approximately fourteen minutes. The participant must respond to an arrow stimulus by selecting one of two options, depending on the direction in which the arrow points. The individual must withhold making that response if an auditory tone is present. The task is designed to adapt to the individual's performance. The outcome measures include the direction of errors, proportion of successful stops, reaction time on Go trials, and stop signal reaction time.

CognitionKit Digit Symbol Substitution Task (DSST)

The CognitionKit task (*Cognitive tests*. Cambridge n.d) is a global measure of cognitive ability. The task administration is approximately ninety seconds. The task presents individuals with an array of abstract symbols associated with numbers. When a particular number is highlighted on the screen, the individual must draw the corresponding abstract shape using their index finger on the smartphone image presented on the computer or iPad screen. The individual must try to complete as many symbol-to-number matches within the allocated timeframe. The outcome measures consist of the total correct errors made by the individual and latency.

Memory Subtests

Delayed Match to Sample (DMS)

The Delayed Matching to Sample task (*Cognitive tests*. Cambridge n.d) simultaneously measures visual matching ability and short-term visual recognition memory for items with non-verbalizable patterns. The task administration is approximately seven minutes. In the subtest, the individual discriminates between presented visual patterns that are abstract and non-verbal. The pattern that matches the sample must be selected in which several case patterns are shown simultaneously. Whereas in other trials, there is a delay in between patterns. The outcome measures include latency, the number of correct patterns selected, and statistical measures providing the probability of an error after a correct or incorrect response.

Digit Span (DGS)

The Digit Span task (*Cognitive tests*. Cambridge n.d) measures verbal short-term and working memory. The task is verbal with auditorily presented stimuli. The individual speaks responses and is scored automatically by the software. Two modalities are presented, forward digit span and reverse digit span. The individual is provided a series of random numbers and is asked to repeat them in the order presented or backward. The task measures cognitive skills to activate verbal working memory, attention, cognitive control, and executive function. The task administration is approximately one to three minutes, dependent on the individual's performance. The outcome measures consist of the direction of the task, the longest sequence successfully remembered, and the total number of attempts.

Paired Associates Learning (PAL)

The Paired Associates Learning task (*Cognitive tests.* Cambridge n.d; Vermeulen et al. 2018) is a measure of visual memory and processes related to acquiring new knowledge. The subtest is also available in a simplified version consisting of 8 stages. The task administration time consists of approximately eight minutes. Boxes are displayed on the screen and are "opened" in a randomized order. One or more of them will contain a pattern. The patterns are then displayed in the middle of the screen, one at a time, and the individual must select the box in which the pattern was initially located. If the individual makes an error, the system will demonstrate the correct pattern to remind the individual of the correct method.

Pattern Recognition Memory (PRM)

The Pattern Recognition Memory task (*Cognitive tests*. Cambridge n.d; Vermeulen et al. 2018) measures visual pattern recognition memory in a two-choice discrimination paradigm. The task administration time is approximately four minutes which includes immediate and delayed recall of memory items. The task consists of two phases that measure immediate and delayed recall. The participant is presented with a series of visual patterns, one at a time, in the center of the screen. These patterns are designed to avoid the ability to provide verbal labels. In the recognition phase, the participant must choose between a pattern they have already seen and a novel one. In this phase, the test patterns are presented in reverse order to the original order of presentation. The process is repeated with new patterns. The second phase is administered to the individual after a delay, typically 10–20 minutes from the first phase. The outcome measures include the number and percentage of correct trials and latency.

Verbal Recognition Memory (VRM)

The Verbal Recognition task (*Cognitive tests*. Cambridge n.d; Vermeulen et al. 2018) measures verbal memory and new learning. The subtest evaluates the ability to encode and retrieve verbal information, with recall tapping into frontotemporal networks and recognition assessing hippocampal areas. The task administration is approximately 6 minutes (including immediate and delayed recall assessment). A sequence of words is shown on the screen one by one. The individual is tasked with recalling the words, while a rater marks which ones they remembered. In the second phase, there are two words, one from the original list and one distractor, and the individual chooses which one they have seen earlier in a 2-force choice paradigm. The latest recognition phase is repeated after a delay. The outcome measures include the number of different words for the free-recall phase and the number of correct and incorrect responses for the immediate and delayed recognition parts of the test.

Spatial Span (SSP)

The Spatial Span task (*Cognitive tests*. Cambridge n.d; Vermeulen et al. 2018) measures visuospatial working memory. The task administration is approximately five minutes. White squares appear on the screen, some of which briefly change color in a variable sequence. The individual is asked to select the boxes which change color in the same order displayed by the computer or reverse order. The number of boxes gradually increases as the sequence progresses, and the color varies throughout the task. The outcome measures include span length, the ability to recall, the errors, the number of attempts, and latency.

Verbal Paired Associates (VPA)

The Verbal Paired Associate Task (*Cognitive tests*. Cambridge n.d; Vermeulen et al. 2018) measures associative and episodic memory in which the task is to remember a set of word pairs. The software presents a verbal task with auditory stimuli to the individual and verbalizes responses. The responses are scored automatically. The levels are calibrated to parallel forms of the task for future re-testing. The administration is dependent on the individual's performance ranging approximately between one and four minutes and an additional thirty seconds for recall.

The individual listens to a spoken set of eight pairs of words. They are asked to remember the target word that appeared paired with a prompt word. If the individual does not correctly recall all eight pairs, two further attempts are provided. The software allows for a delayed recall variant of the task, which is given after another intervening task. This would allow the assessment of the ability to recall learned word pairs without hearing stimuli.

CognitionKit N-Back (NBX)

The CognitionKit N-Back task (*Cognitive tests*. Cambridge n.d; Vermeulen et al. 2018) measures attention and working memory. The administration is approximately two minutes. The task consists of the individual viewing a stream of abstract shapes. In the 1-Back variant, the individual discriminates between the stimulus presented and determines if a response is necessary. The 2-Back version is similar, but the individual is asked to compare the current stimulus based on their recall of the initial stimulus. The task outcome measures include the overall score, accuracy, and target sensitivity.

Social & Emotional Cognition Subtests

Emotional Bias Task (EBT)

The Emotional Bias Task (*Cognitive tests*. Cambridge n.d; Vermeulen et al. 2018) measures perceptual bias in facial emotion perception. The task administration is approximately four minutes. The task consists of presenting images of faces that are morphed between two emotions of varying intensities. The variants include happy to sad, happy to angry, or happy to disgusted. Each face is displayed for 150 ms, and the individual must select an emotion. The outcome measures consist of the bias point, the number of trials selected as happy compared to the alternative emotion. A scale is adjusted from 0 to 15 to determine the extent and direction of bias. Additionally, latency and the number of times each emotion was selected.

Emotion Recognition Task (ERT)

The Emotion Recognition Task (*Cognitive tests*. Cambridge n.d; Vermeulen et al. 2018) measures the ability to identify the six basic emotions in facial expressions along a continuum of expression magnitude. The task administration ranges approximately between six and ten minutes. Computer-morphed images derived from the facial features of real individuals, each showing a specific emotion, are displayed on the screen, one at a time. Each face is displayed for 200 ms and then immediately covered up to prevent residual image processing. The participant must select which emotion the face displayed from the six options (sadness, happiness, fear, anger, disgust, or surprise). The outcome measures consist of the number of correct or incorrect and overall response latencies, which can be looked at either across individual emotions or across all emotions at once.

Scoring

The use of a computerized system facilitates standardized scoring related to the feedback recorded by the software. The scores are computed from a large pool of normative data, which is then compared to the patient's scores (Fray et al. 1996). The subtests' scoring must be adjusted according to their scoring form. On some subtests, the total score derives from errors and/or trials. The subtests also differentiate in scoring interpretation, where a higher score indicates the worst performance, as seen in RTI, SST, and SWM. In other subtests such as AST, DMS, IED, MTS, PRM, RVP, SOC, SRM, and SSP, the scoring is interpreted as a higher score being indicative of better performance (Green et al. 2019; Karlsen et al. 2022). There should be a conservative interpretation of the CANTAB since some scores must be reversed to avoid misinterpretation. The CANTAB automated scoring system only provides normalized scores for a subset of available tests and outcome measures.

Item Difficulty and Types of Errors

Most batteries in CANTAB are progressive in difficulty creating a ceiling based on the individual's performance (Cambridge Cognition Ltd. 2006). Most CANTAB subtests rely on the difficulty level to determine the individual's highest level of cognitive processing performance (Cambridge Cognition Ltd. 2006). This method has consistently demonstrated sensitivity to impaired individuals. The CANTAB batteries vary in test-retest reliability that may be guarded against learning effects over repeated testing sessions (*Cognitive tests*. Cambridge n.d). The design and configuration of the CANTAB tests help minimize test-taking and computer-use anxiety and errors (Wild and Musser 2014). The computerized program consists of pre-arranged sets of subtests categorized according to the patient's needs based on clinical symptomatology, ranging from psychopathology, neurological, or behavioral manifestations (*Cognitive tests*. Cambridge n.d).

Attention Processing & Psychomotor Speed Subtests

The assessment of attention processing and psychomotor speed accounts for the individual's ability to selectively attend to or ignore relevant or irrelevant information (*Cognitive tests*. Cambridge n.d). This category primarily measures sustained attention and the relationships between cognitive functions and physical activities. Measures of psychomotor speed are evaluated based on the individual's response to rapid changes in the environment allowing for the assessment and quantification of reaction time, movement time, and vigilance (Cambridge Cognition Ltd 2006). The attention and psychomotor speed subtests in CANTAB include Motor Screening Test (MOT), Reaction Time Test (RTI), Rapid Visual Information Processing (RVP), Match to Sample Visual Search (MTS), and Adaptive Tracking Tasks (ATT) (*Cognitive tests*. Cambridge n.d). RVP's level of difficulty varies with either one- or three-target sequences that the individual must watch concurrently.

Executive Function Subtests

The executive function subtests involve assessing high-order thinking and decision-making (*Cognitive tests*. Cambridge n.d). The domain is subdivided into mental flexibility, planning, the ability to implement strategic thinking for problem-solving, and response inhibition. The subtests in this domain consist of the Cambridge Gambling Task (CGT), Intra-Extra Dimensional Set Shift (IED), Multitasking Test (MTT), OneTouch Stockings of Cambridge (OTS), Spatial Working Memory (SWM), Stockings of Cambridge (SOC), Stop Signal Task (SST), and CognitionKit Digit Symbol Substitution Task (DSST). The outcome measures for Stockings of Cambridge consists of reached difficulty level, the mean of moves used and thinking time. Spatial working memory test aims for the individual to apply a process of elimination; as the individual demonstrates the ability to solve the presented task, the level of difficulty increases. The outcome measures include errors made and strategy.

Memory Subtests

CANTAB defines memory as the ability to store information in long or short-term memory (Cognitive tests. Cambridge n.d). Memory domains are subdivided into episodic memory, recognition memory, and working memory. The subtests included in this domain consist of Delayed Match to Sample (DMS), Digit Span (DGS), Paired Associates Learning (PAL), Pattern Recognition Memory (PRM), Spatial Span (SSP), Verbal Paired Associates (VPA), Verbal Recognition Memory (VRM), and CognitionKit N-Back (NBX). The paired associates learning subtest involves a higher level of difficulty measures that increase with the progression of the subtest to assess the individual's high-functioning. The outcome measures include the errors made by the individual. It records the number of trials required to locate the patterns correctly, memory scores, and completed stages. Verbal pair associates outcome measures consist of the errors made by the individual during each attempt, the number of attempts, and a score that considers the difficulty level of the items learned or missed.

Social & Emotional Cognition Subtests

The Social and Emotional Cognition subtests (*Cognitive tests*. Cambridge n.d; Vermeulen et al. 2018) assess affective information processing by exploring the individual's response to emotion-laden stimuli. The social cognition subtests are subdivided into two domains: emotion recognition and emotional bias. The subtests included in this domain consist of Emotional Bias Task (EBT), and Emotion Recognition Task (ERT).

Reliability

In theory, reliability coefficients indicate the degree to which a test outcome is consistent when the measurement is repeated and demonstrated to be free of error (Karlsen et al. 2022; Syväoja et al. 2015). Test-retest reliability consists of the stability of test scores over time. Although some measures in CANTAB may assess cognitive processes, they have very low reliability for test-retest (Cacciamani et al. 2018). CANTAB's developers suggest that different subtests may be previously arranged into batteries that would prevent familiarity and learning effects (*Cognitive tests*. Cambridge n.d). Measures of reliability provided in the technical manual (Cambridge Cognition Ltd. 2006) suggest that the overall reliability for test-retest varies between subtests. Reliability coefficients for test-retest 4-week period were calculated in healthy volunteers and patients in delayed matching to sample (DMS) number correct $r = 0.56$, paired associates learning (PAL) first trial memory score $r = 0.68$, average trials to success $r = 0.86$, and spatial working memory (SWM) total errors $r = 0.68$. The assessed test- retest reliability over 1 and 2 years in healthy patients and patients diagnosed with schizophrenia. Spatial working memory (SWM) between errors: healthy volunteer 56-week r = 0.52, 66-week r = 0.65; schizophrenia 74-week r = 0.62, 100-week r = 0.62; strategy: healthy volunteer 56-week r = 0.54, 66-week r = 0.60; schizophrenia 74-week r = 0.40, 100-week r = 0.57.

Cacciamani et al. (2018) argue that CANTAB's batteries are structured where practice effect is associated with learning strategies that fail to assess individuals at later times, raising concern about the interpretation of results in longitudinal studies using specifically SWM and PAL. Researchers studied Italian patients diagnosed with mild cognitive impairment and created a baseline followed up at six and twelve months (Cacciamani et al. 2018). To effectively discriminate between patients with Alzheimer's Disease (AD) and mild cognitive impairment, individuals underwent cerebrospinal fluid (CSF) analysis to measure AD biomarkers during their baseline visit. Their results were consistent with practice effects in performance and noticed an improvement in testing scores leading to an overestimation of treatment and underestimation of disease progression. The learning effect is applied across the literature in subtests such as SRM, SSP, IED, SOC, PRM, PAL, DMS, and SWM (Cacciamani et al. 2018; Karlsen et al. 2022; O'Connell et al. 2004; Syväoja et al. 2015). The strategic task observed in these patients involves memory processes that are a result of top-down modulation by the prefrontal cortex.

The training phase could mask the current severity of the cognitive decline. CANTAB's approach to using subtests on multiple occasions with the same patient is unsuitable for clinical practice aimed at monitoring disease progression over time (Cacciamani et al. 2018). Low test-retest is common in neuropsychological assessment. CANTAB reliability coefficients are like those obtained in traditional neuropsychological test batteries (Karlsen et al. 2022). Measurement error surrounding test-retest scores is significant in CANTAB; therefore, clinicians must proceed with caution when interpreting the scores obtained. The stability of CANTAB subtests needs to be confirmed in various target populations to ensure the validity and reliability of the battery (Syväoja et al. 2015).

According to the literature, computer technology has increased the efficiency and standardization of test administration. Electronic data is recorded and scored, minimizing potential human error, and increasing the accuracy of timing and response latencies (Syväoja et al. 2015). The research suggests that computer-based test batteries may not displace psychometric characteristics of traditional neuropsychological assessments due to low reliability and validity. Patients can become familiar with a test, but clinicians must caution when the novelty of the measure is diminished by the patient (Henry and Bettenay 2010).

Validity

The literature is scarce on research data that contributes to the assessment of the CANTAB's reliability and validity (Lenehan et al. 2016; Rodriguez-Toscano et al. 2020; Syväoja et al. 2015). Although the developers argue that sensitivity across various measures of cognitive domains, such as the PAL and story recall provides a modest correlation (–.19 immediate; –.21 delayed recall), research in diverse populations appears otherwise. CANTAB's interpretations in research highly rely on the results provided based upon the researchers' interpretation, and they were not due to any Pet Scan or MRI imaging to determine the results. There is a lack of consensus on the applicability of the battery that would create a reliable and valid measure of cognitive assessment.

The CANTAB batteries have been applied in the assessment of cognitive function. The battery was developed to extend paradigms to test monkeys' neurobiological and neurochemical processes impacting behavior (Robbins et al. 1994). The battery became a cognitive functional assessment tool for patients diagnosed with Alzheimer's Disease (AD). Researchers have investigated and focused on CANTAB's sensitivity and utility (Luciana 2003; Luciana and Nelson 2002; Robbins et al. 1994). The subtests demonstrate sensitivity to differentiate between general ability across various age groups. As a result, researchers continue to explore the convergent validity of CANTAB across various clinical populations (Smith et al. 2013).

Although CANTAB has been demonstrated to produce differences between groups measuring cognitive functions, it is difficult to infer that CANTAB is a battery that could replace traditional neuropsychological assessment. In an elderly study by Robbins et al. (1994), only two cognitive domains correlated with a significant assessment of cognitive function and age. The researchers argued that not all subtests, such as Intelligence Quotient (IQ), were consistent when comparing the CANTAB to traditional neuropsychological tests. Robbins et al. (1994) theoretical speculations argue that CANTAB does not appear to be sensitive to an individual's strategies to perform a task as noticed in traditional tests leading to a different outcome in results. Furthermore, the study included a crossover in age groups in which younger individuals performed better than older adults. The outcome may suggest that older adults are at a disadvantage when using CANTAB due to their lack of familiarity with the software, a computer or iPad use (Luciana 2003; Robbins et al. 1994).

The validity of CANTAB is jeopardized in the very young children and older adult populations (Luciana and Nelson 2002; Robbins et al. 1994). Studies speak heavily to how speed may be a contributing factor in observed differences in younger populations versus older populations. A theoretical explanation consists of the older adult being slow at performing the tasks due to confusion involving the computerized software. *Speed* is an essential function assessed in categories such as attention processing and psychomotor speed. Younger individuals could make fewer errors due to the readily available exposure to technology versus older adults. The processing time is also vital in computerized tests. Individuals could be delayed due to confusion in understanding a computerized task or its instructions, leading to inaccuracy and low validity of the battery (Robbins et al. 1994; Rodriguez-Toscano et al. 2020).

The construct validity of CANTAB largely relies on the ability of test measures to discriminate between various clinical populations (Lenehan et al. 2016). A computerized test does not measure components sensitive to standard neuropsychological batteries corresponding to cognitive domains. Smith et al. (2013) conducted a correlational analysis exploring the principal components previously established from traditional neuropsychological batteries. He suggested that CANTAB's validity is weak and measures "general" cognition versus distinct cognitive domains. Research is consistent in demonstrating inconsistent patterns of association with domain-specific composites derived from traditional neuropsychological batteries (Lenehan et al. 2016; Smith et al. 2013; Toornstra et al. 2020; Syväoja et al. 2015).

Task Demands and Strategies

The CANTAB software has been adaptable to various clinical and research populations. The task demands vary between subtests based on the progression of the individual's ability in each subtest. The computerized battery cannot provide information regarding the individual's observable behaviors to determine noticeable strategies as they navigate through the subtest (Militello et al. 2010). In CANTAB paired associates learning test, the patterns are designed to increasingly become challenging to verbalize information and prevent verbal rehearsal as a strategy. Another strategy found in spatial working memory is the assessment of problems with six or more boxes, the number of different boxes used by the individual to begin a new search for a token within the same trial (Cambridge Cognition Ltd 2006). The developers suggest that individuals diagnosed with schizophrenia could not develop a systematic strategy to complete the task (Cambridge Cognition Ltd 2006).

The performance in CANTAB batteries improves over time due to learning effects and strategies adopted by an individual. Changes in performance due to learned strategies are noticed across various populations, making it challenging to differentiate between practice and recovery (Cambridge Cognition Ltd 2006). An exploratory study suggested that individuals reported strategies in the delayed matching sample task (Militello et al. 2010). Individuals reported memorization of all colors, note 1–2 memorable shapes, and recalling the contents of boxes in two specific locations. In CANTAB's cambridge gambling task, the strategies included always betting on the color with a larger number of squares and finding a pattern (Militello et al. 2010). Individuals can articulate strategies for recurrent themes and reveal interesting, idiosyncratic approaches.

Clinical Applications in Research

The computerized batteries have been applied to investigate cognitive functionality in populations diagnosed with a neurodegenerative disease. Sahakian and Owen (1992) assessed patients with Alzheimer's and Parkinson's Disease and individuals with neurosurgical procedures with localized excisions to the frontal and temporal lobes. They wanted to adapt the test previously demonstrated to assess executive function in animals and apply the theoretical rationale by exploring cognitive function in these patients. The study compared the CANTAB to Wisconsin Card Sort Test (WSCT), which is known to be sensitive to frontal lobe dysfunction (Sahakian and Owen 1992). Researchers noted that the CANTAB battery assessed different cognitive function compared to WSCT in patients (Robbins et al. 1998; Sahakian and Owen 1992).

Gonçalves et al. (2016) argue about the generalizability of CANTAB in clinical settings in patients diagnosed with dementia. An older adult with a dementia diagnosis is strongly associated with entering institutional care. Researchers argue that neuropsychological assessments for older individuals living in retirement homes are required to ensure adequate detection and monitoring of cognitive deficits that are a part of neurodegenerative disorders (Gonçalves et al. 2016). There are many technological advancements, and Gonçalves et al. (2016) proposed that older adults are fastly adopting technology in various aspects of life. It was suggested that computerized tests could replace traditional neuropsychological assessments. CANTAB is primarily a measure of cognitive performance rather than a structural domain-specific functional assessment (Gonçalves et al. 2016; Toornstra et al. 2020).

CANTAB has been applied in the assessment of cognitive function in schizophrenia patients. Researchers have examined the nature of the impairment and the association with focal brain regions (Levaux et al. 2007). The research in this group comparing traditional neuropsychological assessment and CANTAB tests is in its infancy stages. The study of schizophrenia raises practical and methodological concerns. The application of CANTAB in schizophrenia patients cannot replace traditional neuropsychological batteries that have demonstrated to be effective across the literature (Levaux et al. 2007). According to the literature, the overall application of CANTAB must be proceeded with caution and must draw prudent interpretations in the assessment of cognitive deficits in schizophrenia since only a subtest of visuospatial ability has been tested to be effective and sensitive in individuals (Levaux et al. 2007). Traditional neuropsychological assessment continues to be the gold standard in patients that have been diagnosed with schizophrenia.

The computerized batteries widely examine various age groups. CANTAB was utilized to determine if ADHD could be predicted by the software (Fried et al. 2020). The results failed to demonstrate any diagnostic utility for the CANTAB, even when utilizing the most vigorous tests such as AGN and RTI. The research suggests that the outcome may be due to the practice effect noticed across various subtests within CANTAB, where normal individuals were compared to individuals diagnosed with the disorder (Fried et al. 2020).

Luciana and Nelson (2002) argue that one of the challenges in assessing children while using CANTAB is the lack of touch sensitivity that is not detected by the computer software. Additionally, young children tend to be fatigued and lack the motivation to perform tasks that would negatively impact their task performance. CANTAB seems to be lacking sensitivity of measure for specific abilities, such as memory capacity, working memory for spatial locations, and effective planning, that are not reached until 12 years of age (Luciana and Nelson 2002). It is then that clinicians must be cautious when administering a computerized test that lacks sensitivity in function or development, that may lead to over-pathologizing children (Luciana 2003; Luciana and Nelson 2002).

Although the CANTAB has been used in 50 countries and translated into 45 languages, some aspects of the application of the computerized tests are questionable and could result in over-pathologizing individuals from different cultural groups. The literature expressed a significant concern, particularly with very young individuals and older adults (Luciana 2003; Vermeulen et al. 2018; Wild and Musser 2014). Researchers suggest that CANTAB's computerized software has greater utility for individuals with a better understanding of operating mechanisms in a computer test. Older adults and young children may lack training and knowledge in computer use and understanding of computerized software to such a degree that the assessment results may be compromised (Vermeulen et al. 2018).

CANTAB's developers argue that the battery is language and culture-independent, meaning that an individual's culture should not influence task performance (Roque et al. 2011). They exclude subtests such as VMR and AGN as they contain language-dependent stimuli. Whereas Toornstra et al. (2020) argue in research performed on pediatric a sample from Ukraine that the culture impacts thinking processes, knowledge, values, and beliefs based on social experiences. Cultural variances are linked to CANTAB's norms, which are established in western societies. In neuropsychology, the interpretation and analysis of test scores of non-western groups may contribute to a misinterpretation in cognitive frameworks that distinguish typical and atypical development (Green et al. 2019; Toornstra et al. 2020).

Interpretation

The ability to receive, process, and respond to incoming stimuli from the environment efficiently is vital for functioning in daily life activities (Cambridge Cognition Ltd. 2006). Computerized tests have been incorporated into neuropsychology assessment for decades in assessing complex cognitive functions (Sahakian and Owen 1992). CANTAB developers argue that the computerized battery provides a sound understanding of the complexities of cognitive structural function (Cambridge Cognition Ltd. 2006). Researchers have examined the CANTAB tests for neuropsychological assessment of neurodegenerative diseases, children, schizophrenia, and ADHD. Overall, the effectiveness of the tests has been inconsistent across the literature. The subtests are not measuring what they are supposed to measure, leading to low applicability and utility (Luciana and Nelson 2002). These may be due to CANATAB's computer-based interpretations that do not account for clinical behavioral observations leading to false positives. Computerized interpretations tend to have shortcuts precluding the overall neuropsychological assessment.

References

Cacciamani, F., Salvadori, N., Eusebi, P., Lisetti, V., Luchetti, E., Calabresi, P. and Parnetti, L. (2018). Evidence of practice effect in CANTAB spatial working memory test in a cohort of patients with mild cognitive impairment. Applied Neuropsychology. Adult, 25(3): 237–248. https://doi.org/10.1080/23279095.2017.1286346.

Cambridge Cognition Ltd. (2006). CANTABeclipsetm: Software User Guide. Manual version 3. Cambridge: Cambridge Cognition Ltd.

Cognitive tests. Cambridge Cognition. (n.d.). Retrieved June 6, 2022, from https://www.cambridgecognition.com/cantab/cognitive-tests/.

Fray, P. J., Robbins, T. W. and Sahakian, B. J. (1996). Neuorpsychiatyric applications of CANTAB. International Journal of Geriatric Psychiatry, 11(4): 329–336. https://doi.org/10.1002/(SICI)1099-1166(199604)11:4<329::AID-GPS453>3.0.CO;2-6.

Fried, R., DiSalvo, M., Kelberman, C. and Biederman, J. (2021). Can the CANTAB identify adults with attention-deficit/hyperactivity disorder? A controlled study. Applied Neuropsychology: Adult, 28(3): 318–327. https://doi.org/10.1080/23279095.2019.1633328.

Gonçalves, M. M., Pinho, M. S. and Simões, M. R. (2016). Test–retest reliability analysis of the cambridge neuropsychological automated tests for the assessment of dementia in older people living in retirement homes. Applied Neuropsychology: Adult, 23(4): 251–263. https://doi.org/10.1080/23279095.2015.1053889.

Green, R., Till, C., Al-Hakeem, H., Cribbie, R., Téllez-Rojo, M. M., Osorio, E., Hu, H. and Schnaas, L. (2019). Assessment of neuropsychological performance in Mexico City youth using the Cambridge Neuropsychological Test Automated Battery (CANTAB). Journal of Clinical and Experimental Neuropsychology, 41(3): 246–256. https://doi-org/10.1080/13803395.2018.1529229.

Henry, L. A. and Bettenay, C. (2010). The assessment of executive functioning in children. Child and Adolescent Mental Health, 15(2): 110–119. https://doi.org./10.1111/j.1475-3588.2010.00557.x.

Karlsen, R. H., Karr, J. E., Saksvik, S. B., Lundervold, A. J., Hjemdal, O., Olsen, A., Iverson, G. L. and Skandsen, T. (2022). Examining 3-month test-retest reliability and reliable change using the Cambridge Neuropsychological Test Automated Battery. Applied Neuropsychology. Adult, 29(2): 146–154.

Lenehan, M. E., Summers, M. J., Saunders, N. L., Summers, J. J. and Vickers, J. C. (2016). Does the cambridge automated neuropsychological test battery (CANTAB) distinguish between cognitive domains in healthy older adults? Assessment, 23(2): 163–172. https://doi.org/10.1177/1073191115581474.

Levaux, M., Potvin, S., Sepehry, A. A., Sablier, J., Mendrek, A. and Stip, E. (2007). Computerized assessment of cognition in schizophrenia: Promises and pitfalls of CANTAB. European Psychiatry: The Journal of the Association of European Psychiatrists, 22(2): 104–115. https://doi.org/70198217/se-2.

Luciana, M. (2003). Practitioner review: Computerized assessment of neuropsychological function in children: Clinical and research applications of the cambridge neuropsychological testing automated battery (CANTAB). Journal of Child Psychology and Psychiatry, 44(5): 649–663. https://doi.org/10.1111/1469-7610.00152.

Luciana, M. and Nelson, C. A. (2002). Assessment of neuropsychological function through use of the cambridge neuropsychological testing automated battery: Performance in 4- to 12-year-old children. Developmental Neuropsychology, 22(3): 595–624. https://doi.org/10.1207/S15326942DN2203_3.

Militello, L. G., Nemeth, K., Arbuckle, N. B. and Quill, 'Laurie L. (2010). Self-Report Methods for Cambridge Neurological Test Battery (CANTAB) strategies. Proceedings of the Human Factors and Ergonomics Society Annual Meeting, 54(26): 2211–2215. https://doi-org.ezproxylocal.library.nova.edu/10.1177/154193121005402606.

O'Connell, H., Coen, R., Kidd, N., Warsi, M., Chin, A. and Lawlor, B. A. (2004). Early detection of alzheimer's disease (AD) using the CANTAB paired associates learning test. International Journal of Geriatric Psychiatry, 19(12): 1207–1208. https://doi.org /10.1002/gps.1180.

Robbins, T. W., James, M., Owen, A. M., Sahakian, B. J., Lawrence, A. D., McInnes, L. et al. (1998). A study of performance on tests from the CANTAB battery sensitive to frontal lobe dysfunction in a large sample of normal volunteers: Implications for theories of executive functioning and cognitive aging. Journal of the International Neuropsychological Society, 4(5): 474–490. https://doi.org/10.1017/S1355617798455073.

Robbins, T. W., James, M., Owen, A. M., Sahakian, B. J., McInnes, L. and Rabbitt, P. (1994). Cambridge neuropsychological test automated battery (CANTAB): A factor analytic study of a large sample of normal elderly volunteers. Dementia, 5(5): 266–281. https://doi.org /618602363/se-2?accountid=6579.

Rodriguez-Toscano, E., López, G., Mayoral, M., Lewis, S., Lees, J., Drake, R., Arango, C. and Rapado-Castro, M. (2020). A longitudinal comparison of two neurocognitive test batteries in patients with schizophrenia and healthy volunteers: Time effects on neuropsychological performance and their relation to functional outcome. Schizophrenia Research, 216: 347–356. https://doi-org/10.1016/j.schres.2019.11.018.

Roque, D. T., Teixeira, R. A. A., Zachi, E. C. and Ventura, D. F. (2011). The use of the cambridge neuropsychological test automated battery (CANTAB) in neuropsychological assessment: Application in brazilian research with control children and adults with neurological disorders. Psychology & Neuroscience, 4(2): 255–265. https://doi.org. /10.3922/j.psns.2011.2.011.

Sahakian, B. J. and Owen, A. M. (1992). Computerized assessment in neuropsychiatry using CANTAB: discussion paper. Journal of the Royal Society of Medicine, 85(7): 399–402.

Smith, P. J., Need, A. C., Cirulli, E. T., Chiba-Falek, O. and Attix, D. K. (2013). A comparison of the cambridge automated neuropsychological test battery (CANTAB) with "traditional" neuropsychological testing instruments. Journal of Clinical and Experimental Neuropsychology, 35(3): 319–328. https://doi.org/10.1080/13803395.2013.771618.

Syväoja, H. J., Tammelin, T. H., Ahonen, T., Räsänen, P., Tolvanen, A., Kankaanpää, A. and Kantomaa, M. T. (2015). Internal Consistency and Stability of the CANTAB Neuropsychological Test Battery in Children. Psychological Assessment, 27(2): 698–709. https://doi-org/10.1037/a0038485.

Toornstra, A., Hurks, P. P. M., Van der Elst, W., Kok, G. and Curfs, L. M. G. (2020). Measuring visual matching and short-term recognition memory with the CANTAB® delayed matching to sample task in schoolchildren: Effects of demographic influences, multiple outcome measures and regression-based normative data. Child Neuropsychology, 26(2): 189–218. https://doi.org/10.1080/09297049.2019.1642316.

Vermeulen, K., Staal, W. G., Janzing, J. G. E., van de Ven, F., Oomens, W., van Dongen, L. C. M., van Bokhoven, H., Kleefstra, T. and Egger, J. I. M. (2018). Computerized neurocognitive assessment in rare genetic disorders with moderate to profound intellectual disabilities: A proof of principle study. Clinical Neuropsychiatry: Journal of Treatment Evaluation, 15(6): 325–332. https://doi.org/2174054433/se-2?accountid=6579.

Wild, K. V. and Musser, E. D. (2014). The cambridge neuropsychological test automated battery in the assessment of executive functioning. pp. 171–190. *In*: Goldstein, S. and J. A. Naglieri (Eds.). Handbook of Executive Functioning; Handbook of Executive Functioning (Chapter xix, 567 Pages) Springer Science + Business Media, New York, NY. https://doi.org/10.1007/978-1-4614-8106-5_11/1619503857/se-2?accountid=6579.

Index

A

B

C

D

E

F

G

H

I

L

M

N

O

P

Q

R

S

9781032314099